# MY Love STORY!!

**9**

Story
KAZUNE KAWAHARA

Art
ARUKO

# MY love STORY!!

## 9

CONTENTS

## STORY Thus Far...

Takeo Goda, a first-year high school student, is a hot-blooded guy who is 6'6" tall and weighs 265 pounds. Boys look up to him, but the girls he falls in love with all end up liking his handsome best friend, Makoto Sunakawa! But that all changes when Takeo saves Rinko Yamato from a groper on the train, and she becomes his girlfriend.

When Takeo meets Yamato's parents for the first time at their home, nervousness makes him awkward—and it doesn't help that her dog bites him! But in the end, he and her family make good impressions on each other.

Meanwhile, Makoto's sister Ai has been consistently rebuffing Oda's romantic advances. Lately, though, she's begun to realize that she's more drawn to him than before, and their relationship gets a little better.

Now that it's summer, Yamato starts working at a pastry shop, where she's surrounded by people doing work she's always dreamed of. Takeo quietly keeps an eye on her, and he discovers that a handsome pastry chef named Ichinose is taking an interest in Yamato—and being overly familiar by calling her by her first name!

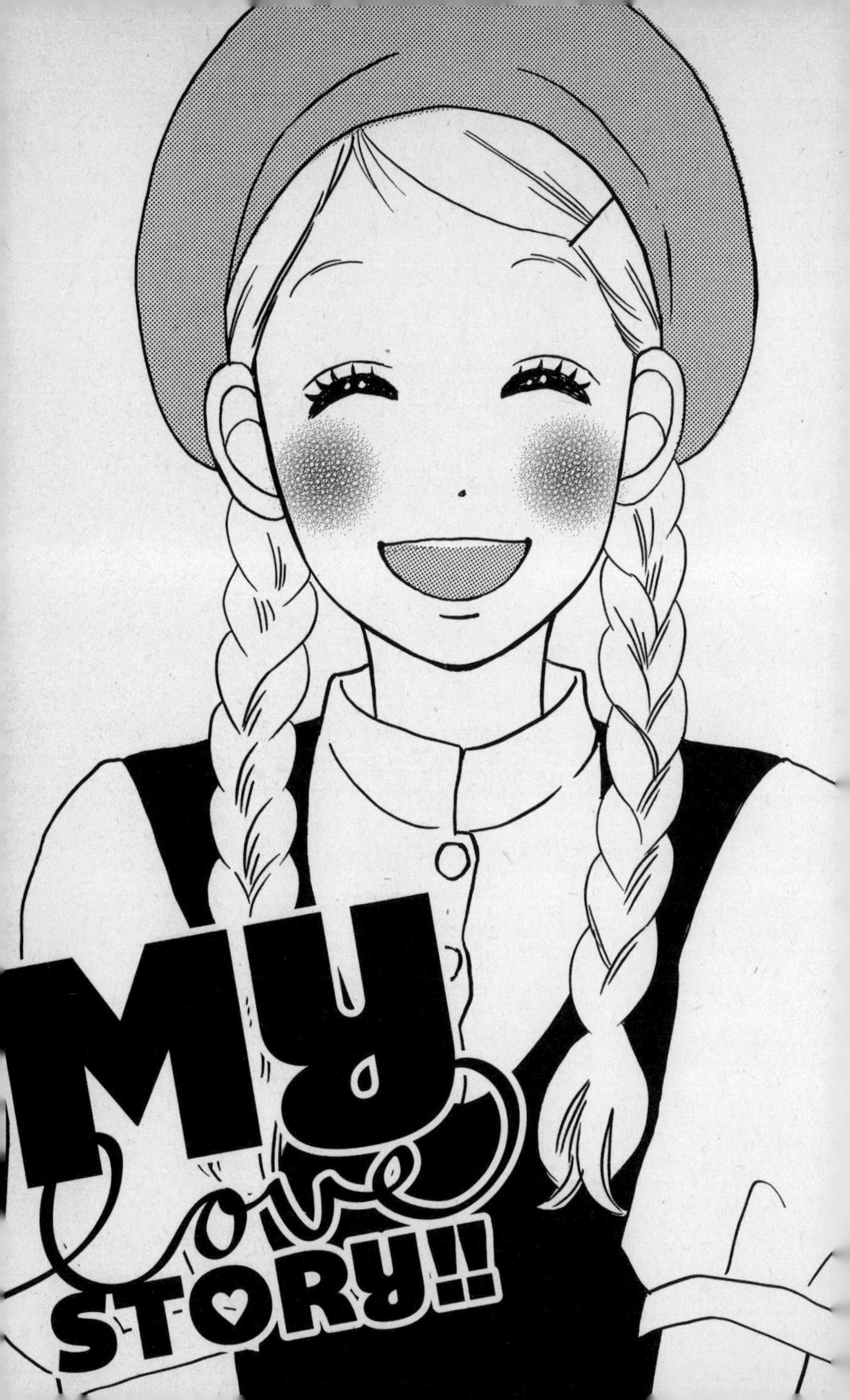
My Love STORY!!

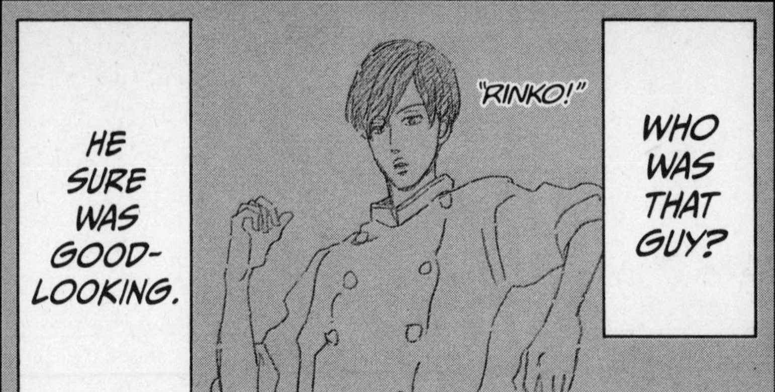
WHO WAS THAT GUY?
"RINKO!"
HE SURE WAS GOOD-LOOKING.
SHWAAA...

# MY love STORY!!

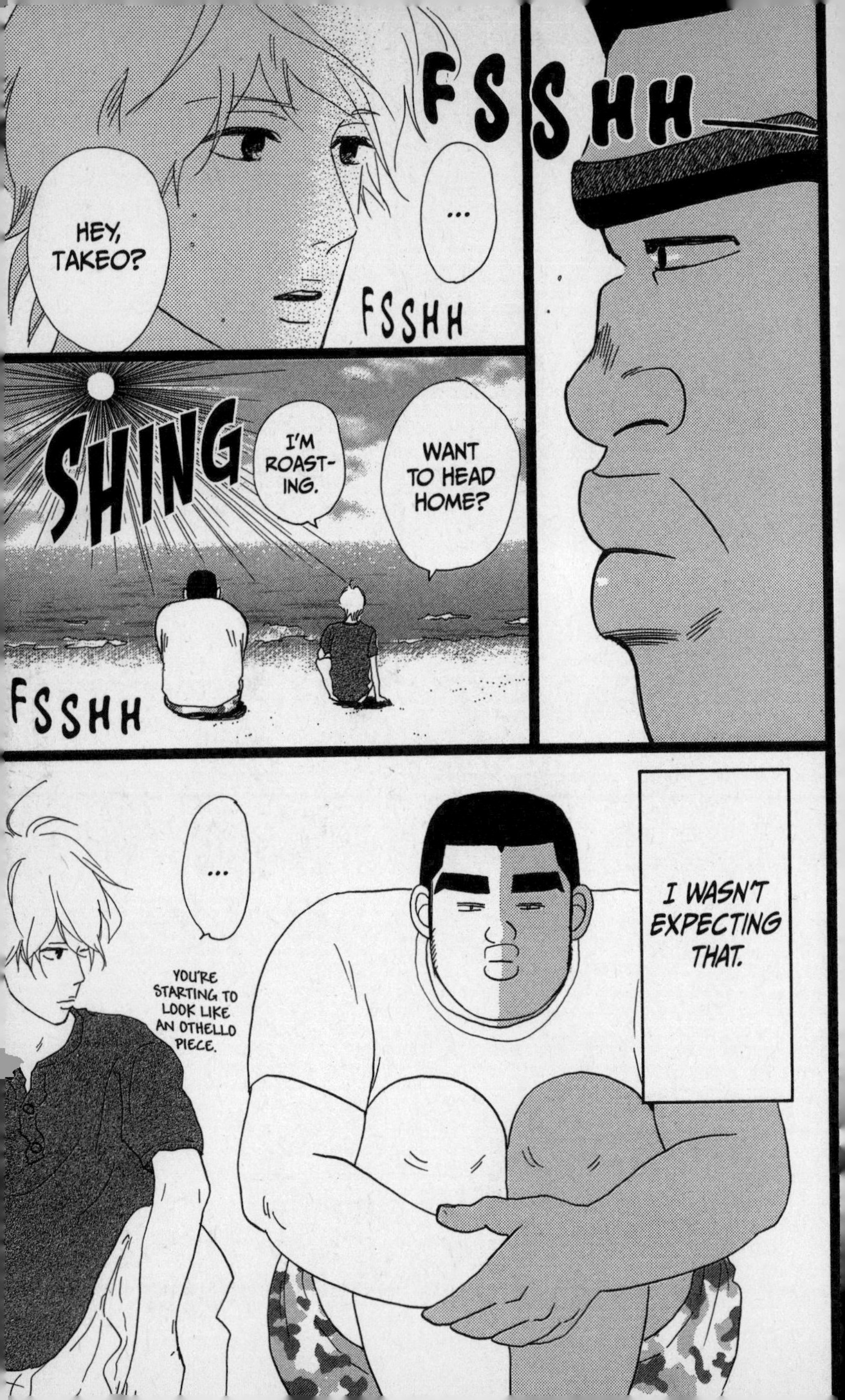

FSSHH
...
HEY, TAKEO?
FSSHH
WANT TO HEAD HOME?
I'M ROAST-ING.
SHING
FSSHH
I WASN'T EXPECTING THAT.
...
YOU'RE STARTING TO LOOK LIKE AN OTHELLO PIECE.

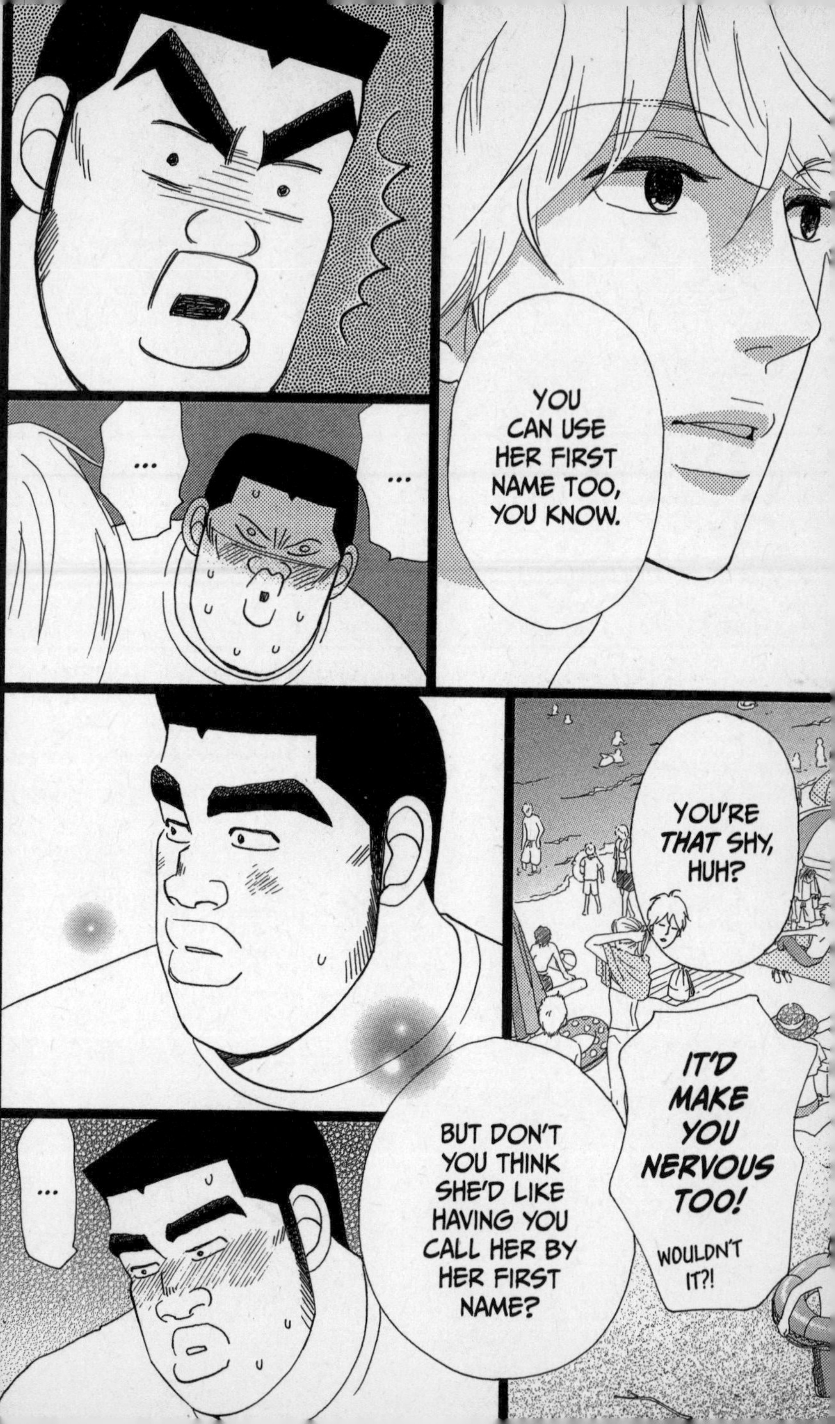
YOU CAN USE HER FIRST NAME TOO, YOU KNOW.
...
...
YOU'RE *THAT* SHY, HUH?
IT'D MAKE YOU NERVOUS TOO!
WOULDN'T IT?!
BUT DON'T YOU THINK SHE'D LIKE HAVING YOU CALL HER BY HER FIRST NAME?
...

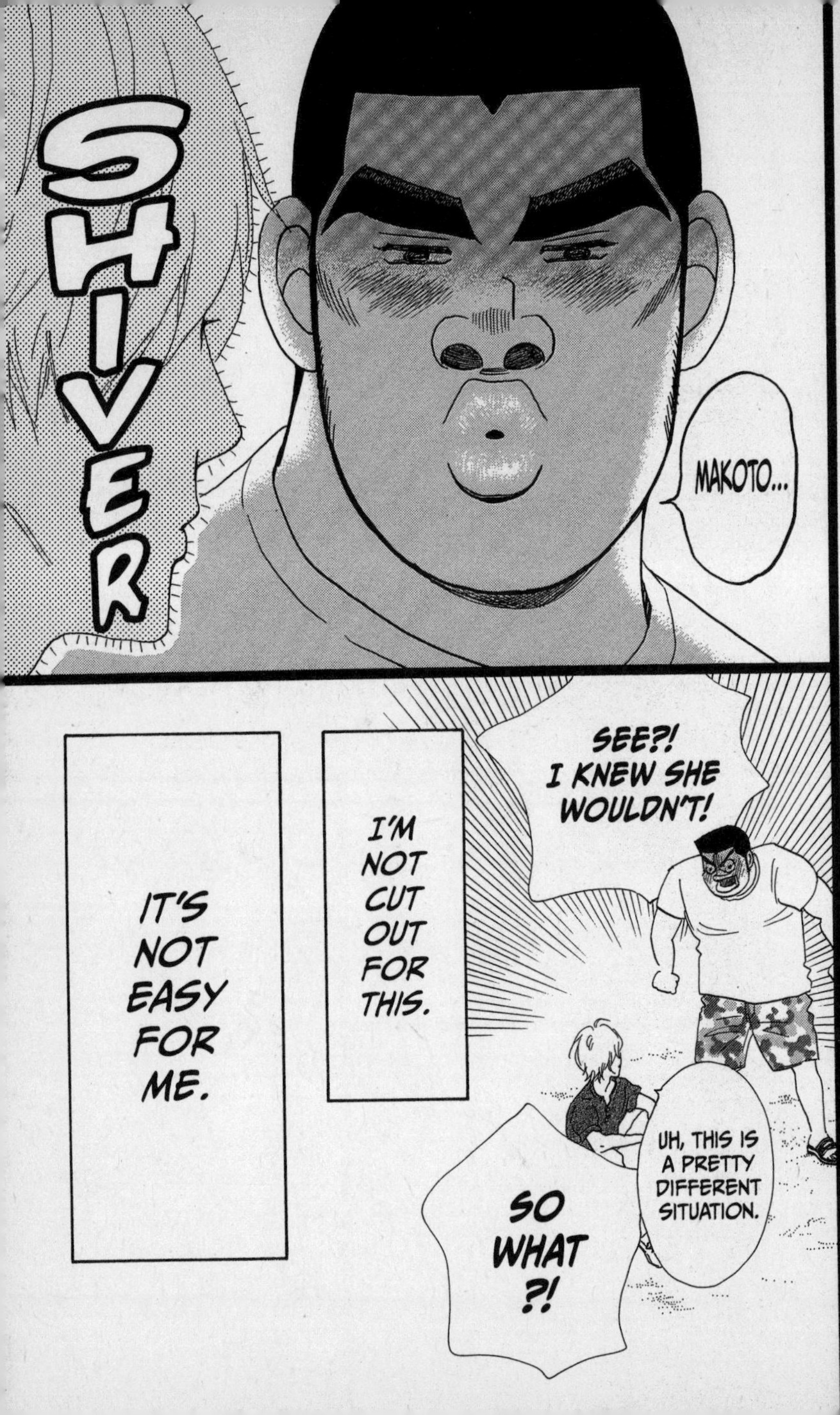
MAKOTO...
SHIVER
SEE?! I KNEW SHE WOULDN'T!
UH, THIS IS A PRETTY DIFFERENT SITUATION.
SO WHAT?!
I'M NOT CUT OUT FOR THIS.
IT'S NOT EASY FOR ME.

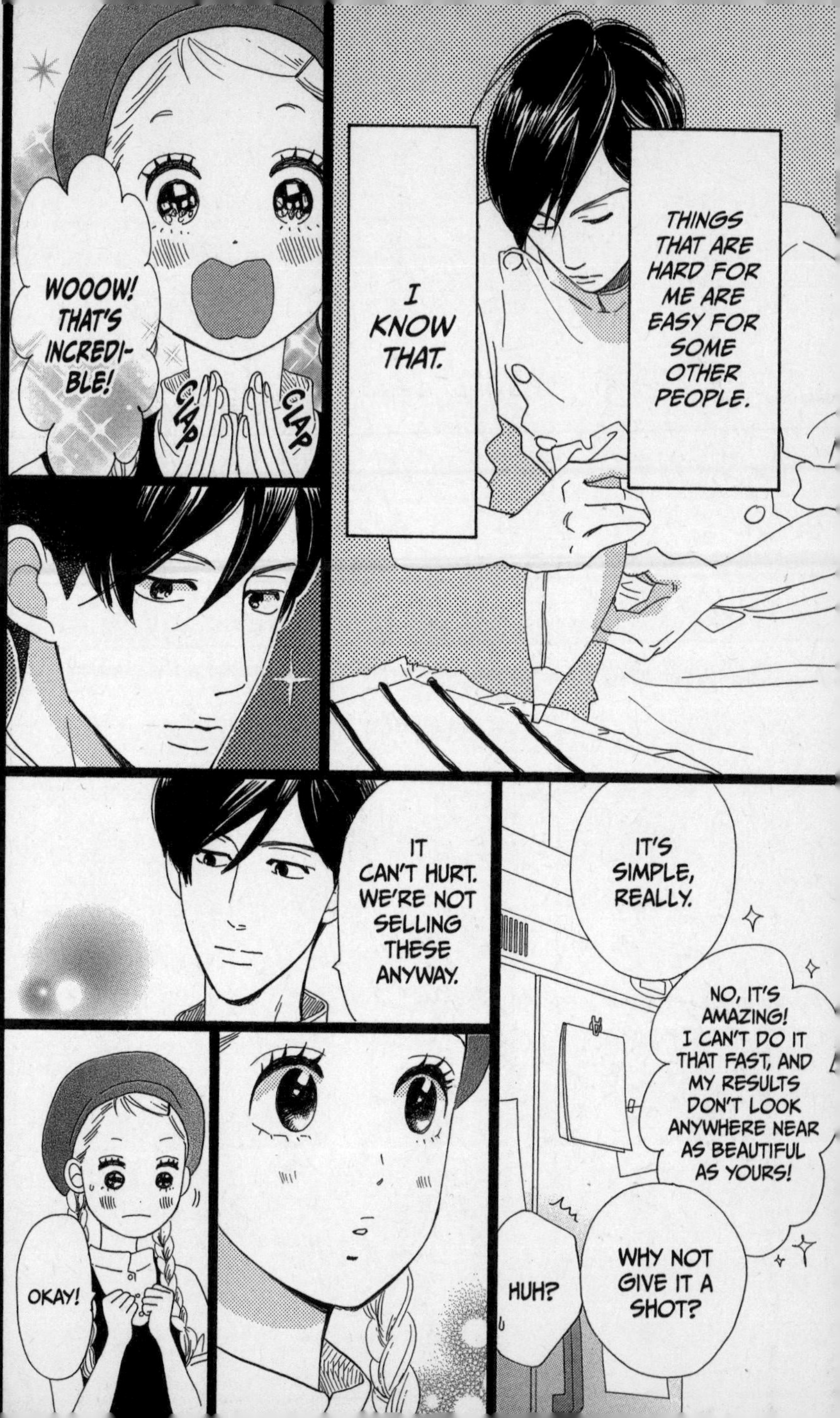
THINGS THAT ARE HARD FOR ME ARE EASY FOR SOME OTHER PEOPLE.
I KNOW THAT.
WOOOW! THAT'S INCREDI-BLE!
CLAP
CLAP
IT'S SIMPLE, REALLY.
NO, IT'S AMAZING! I CAN'T DO IT THAT FAST, AND MY RESULTS DON'T LOOK ANYWHERE NEAR AS BEAUTIFUL AS YOURS!
WHY NOT GIVE IT A SHOT?
HUH?
IT CAN'T HURT. WE'RE NOT SELLING THESE ANYWAY.
OKAY!

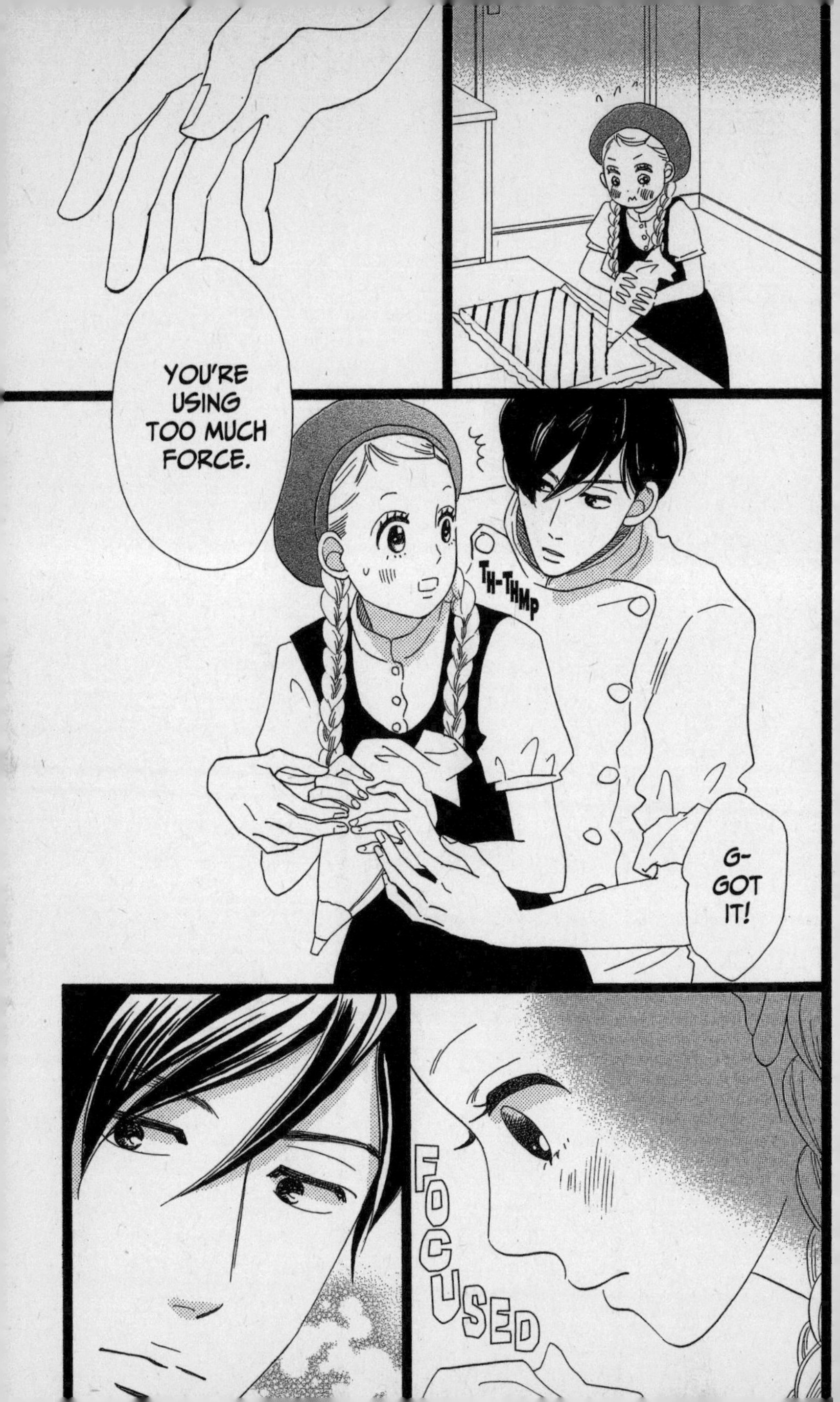
YOU'RE USING TOO MUCH FORCE.
TH-THMP
G-GOT IT!
FOCUSED

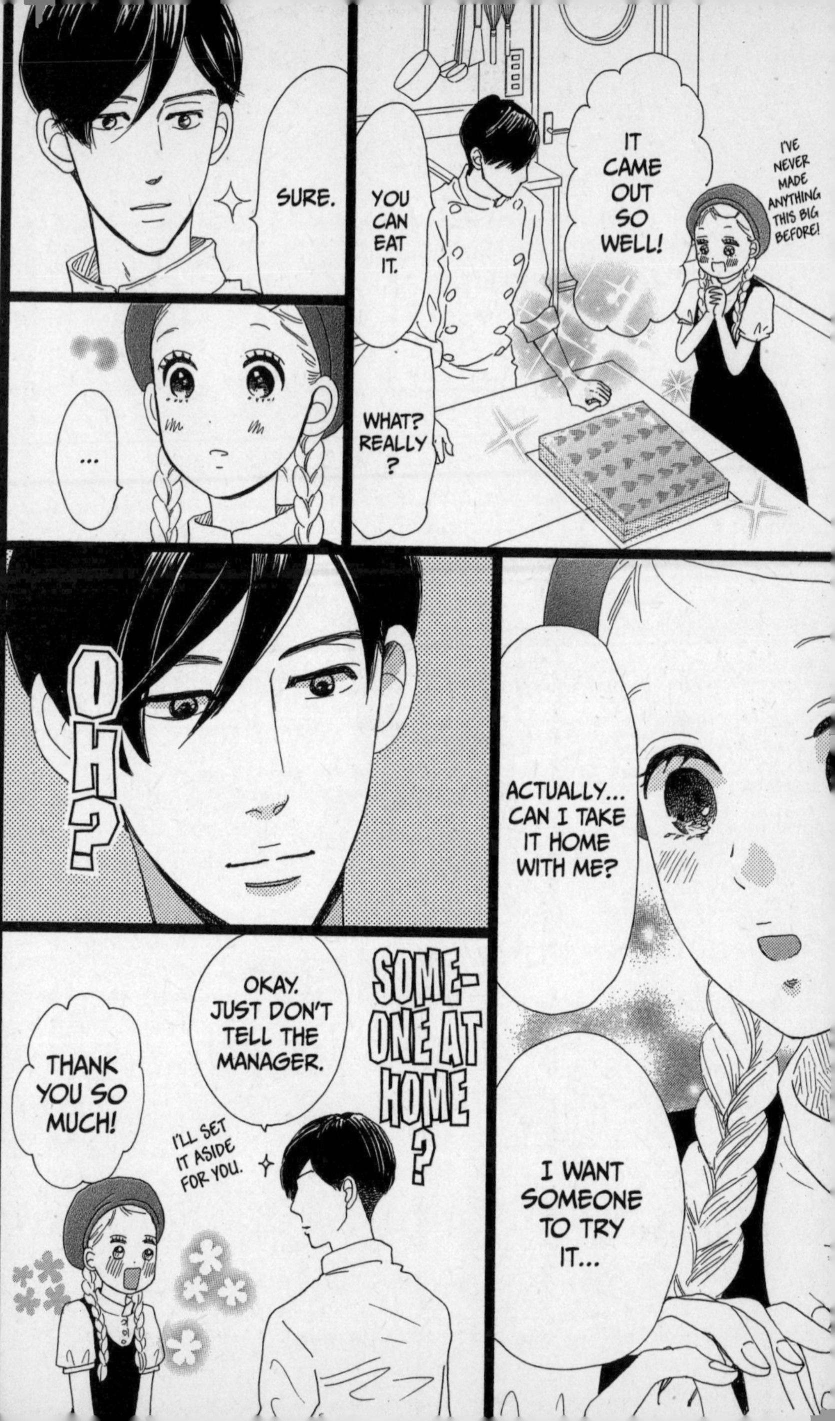
IT CAME OUT SO WELL!
I'VE NEVER MADE ANYTHING THIS BIG BEFORE!
YOU CAN EAT IT.
WHAT? REALLY?
SURE.
...
ACTUALLY... CAN I TAKE IT HOME WITH ME?
I WANT SOMEONE TO TRY IT...
OH?
SOME-ONE AT HOME?
OKAY. JUST DON'T TELL THE MANAGER.
I'LL SET IT ASIDE FOR YOU.
THANK YOU SO MUCH!

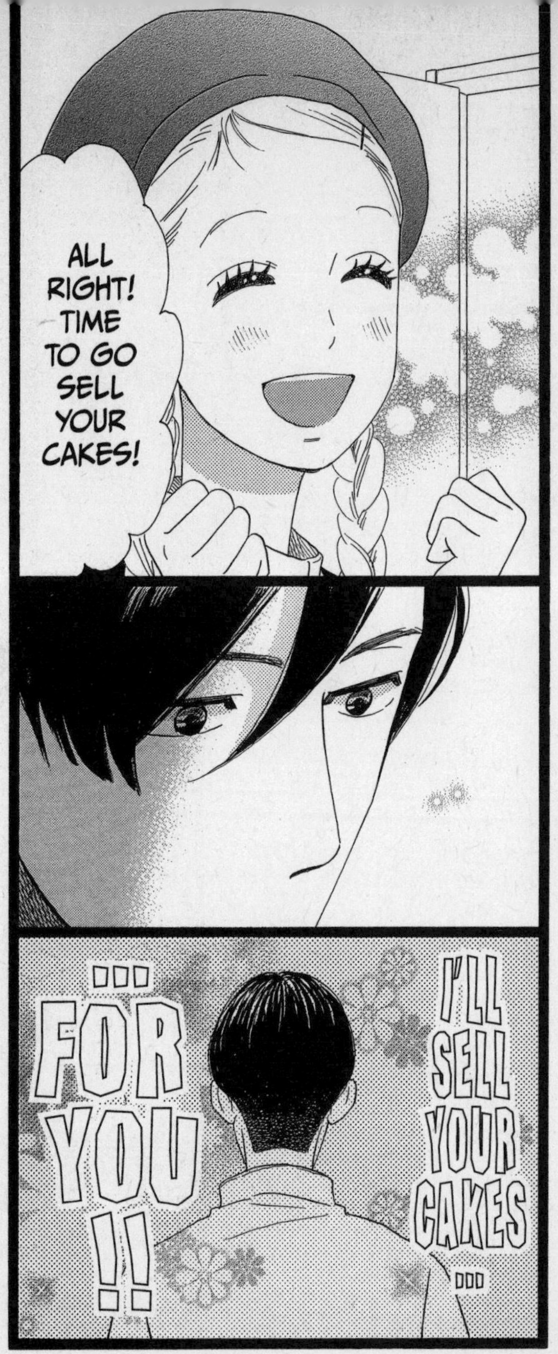
ALL RIGHT! TIME TO GO SELL YOUR CAKES!
I'LL SELL YOUR CAKES...
...FOR YOU!!

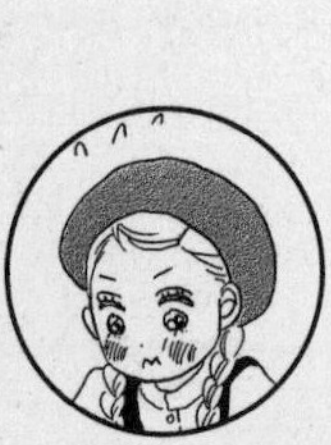

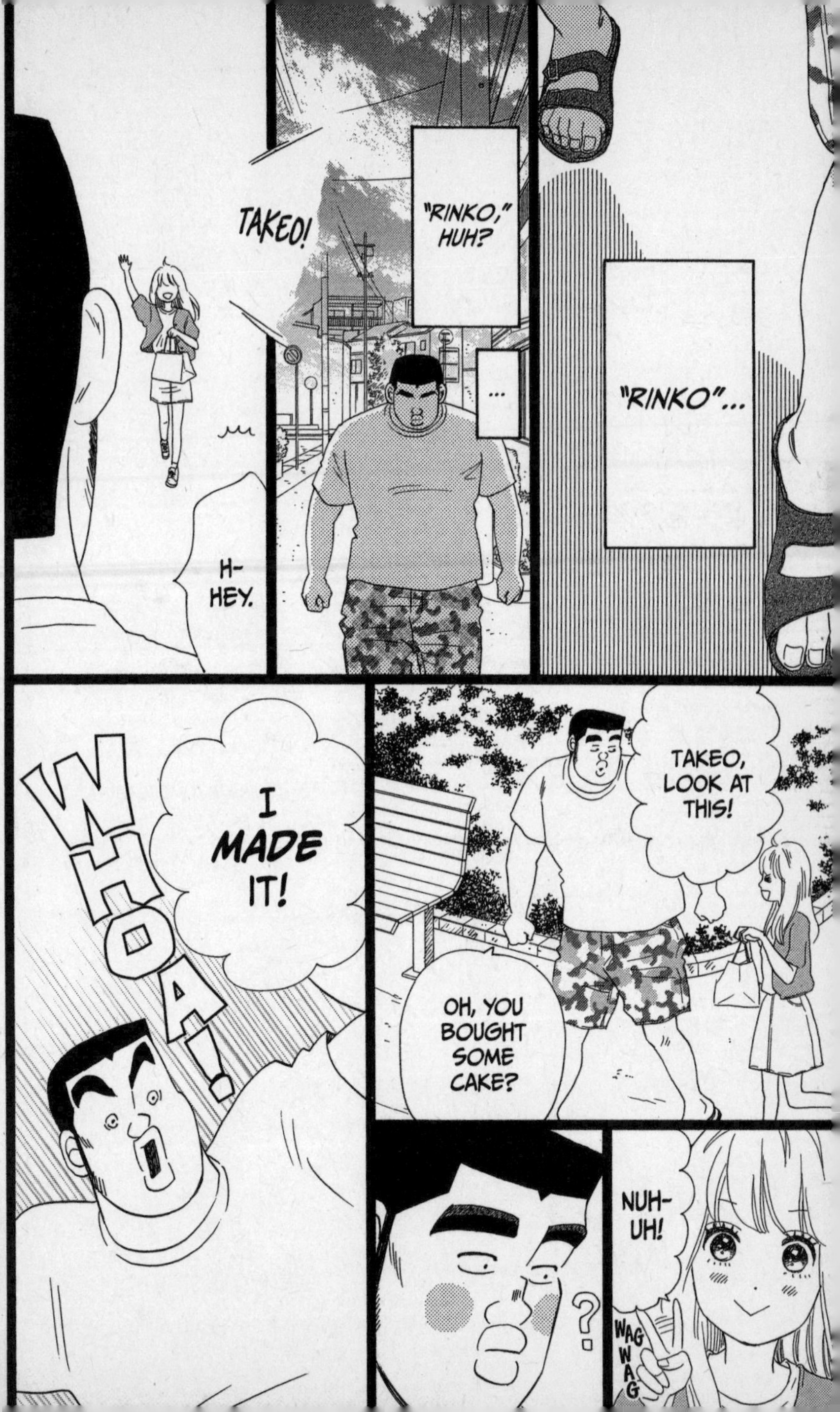
"RINKO"...
"RINKO," HUH?
...
TAKEO!
H-HEY.
TAKEO, LOOK AT THIS!
OH, YOU BOUGHT SOME CAKE?
NUH-UH!
WAG WAG
?
I MADE IT!
WHOA!

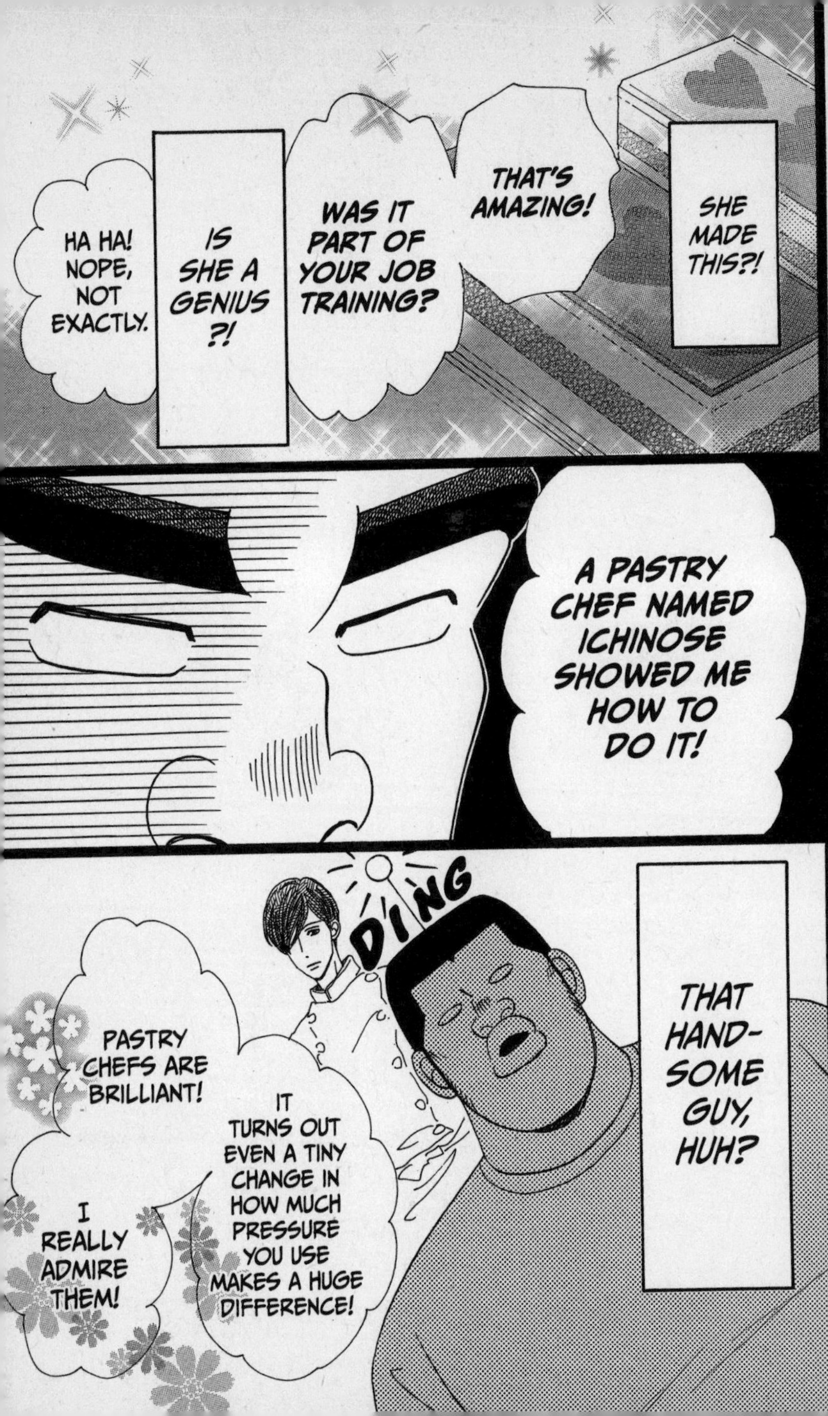
SHE MADE THIS?!
THAT'S AMAZING!
WAS IT PART OF YOUR JOB TRAINING?
IS SHE A GENIUS ?!
HA HA! NOPE, NOT EXACTLY.
A PASTRY CHEF NAMED ICHINOSE SHOWED ME HOW TO DO IT!
THAT HANDSOME GUY, HUH?
DING
IT TURNS OUT EVEN A TINY CHANGE IN HOW MUCH PRESSURE YOU USE MAKES A HUGE DIFFERENCE!
PASTRY CHEFS ARE BRILLIANT!
I REALLY ADMIRE THEM!

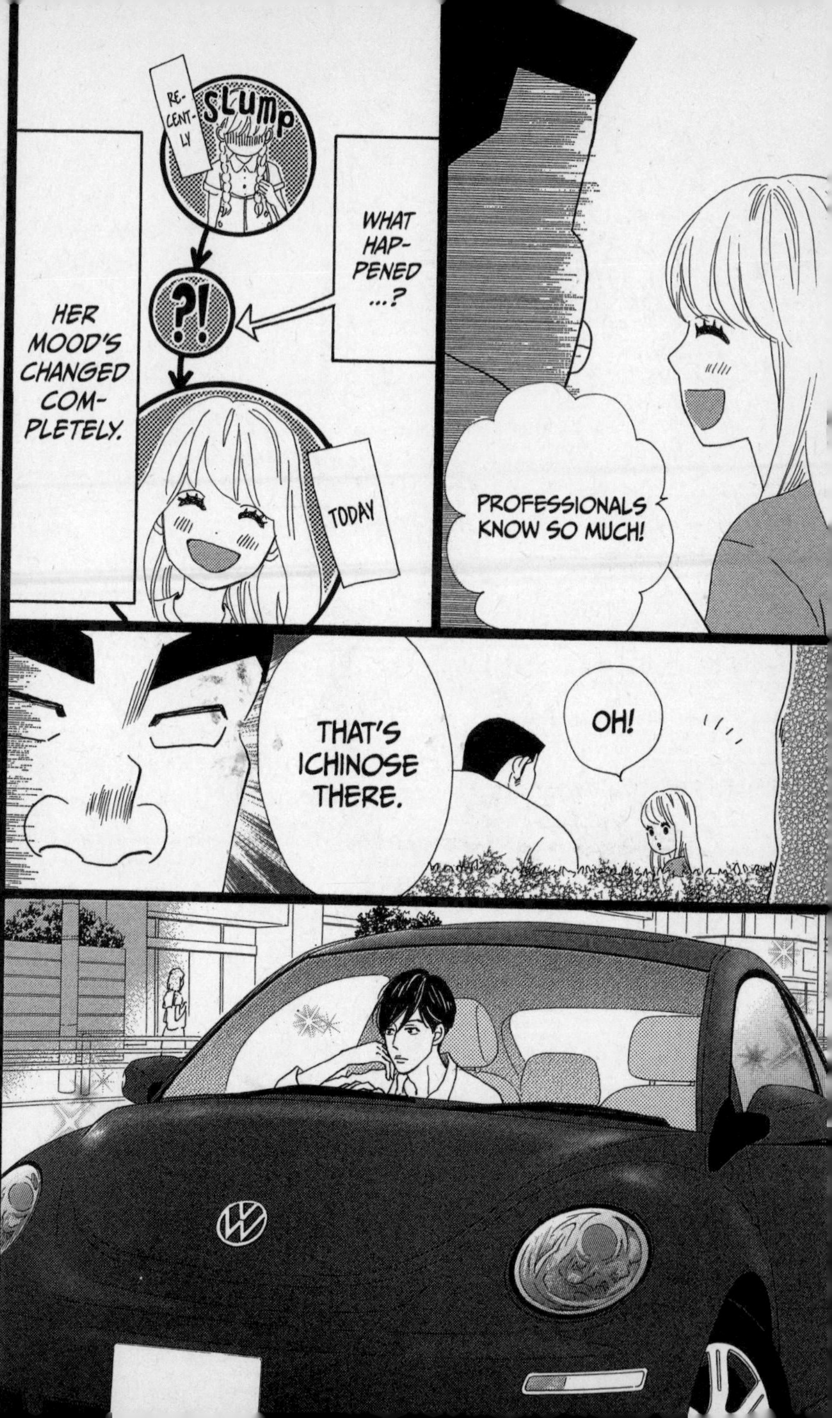
PROFESSIONALS KNOW SO MUCH!
RE-CENT-LY
SLUMP
WHAT HAP-PENED ...?
?!
TODAY
HER MOOD'S CHANGED COM-PLETELY.
OH!
THAT'S ICHINOSE THERE.

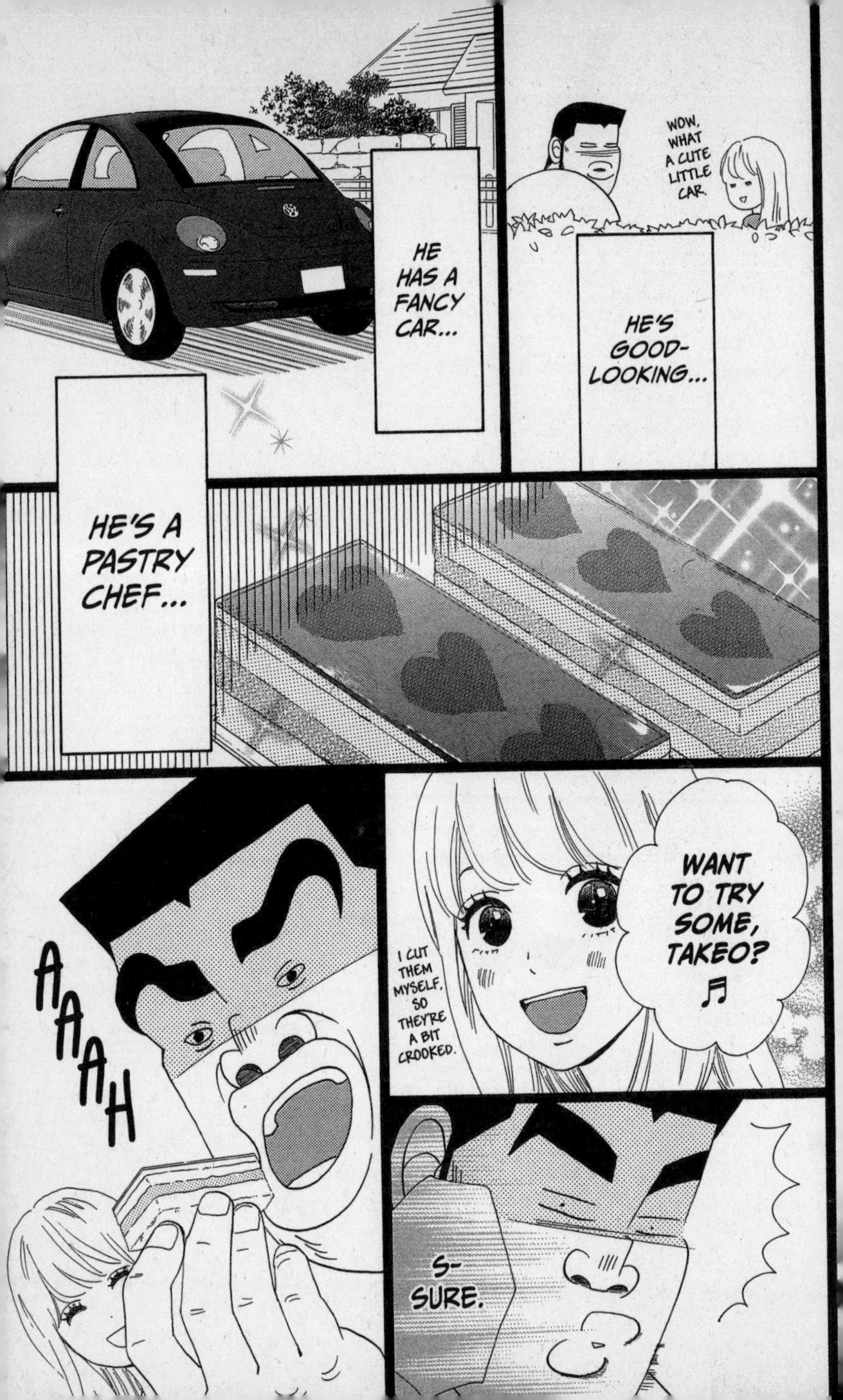
WOW, WHAT A CUTE LITTLE CAR.
HE'S GOOD-LOOKING...
HE HAS A FANCY CAR...
HE'S A PASTRY CHEF...
WANT TO TRY SOME, TAKEO? ♬
I CUT THEM MYSELF, SO THEY'RE A BIT CROOKED.
S-SURE.
AAAH

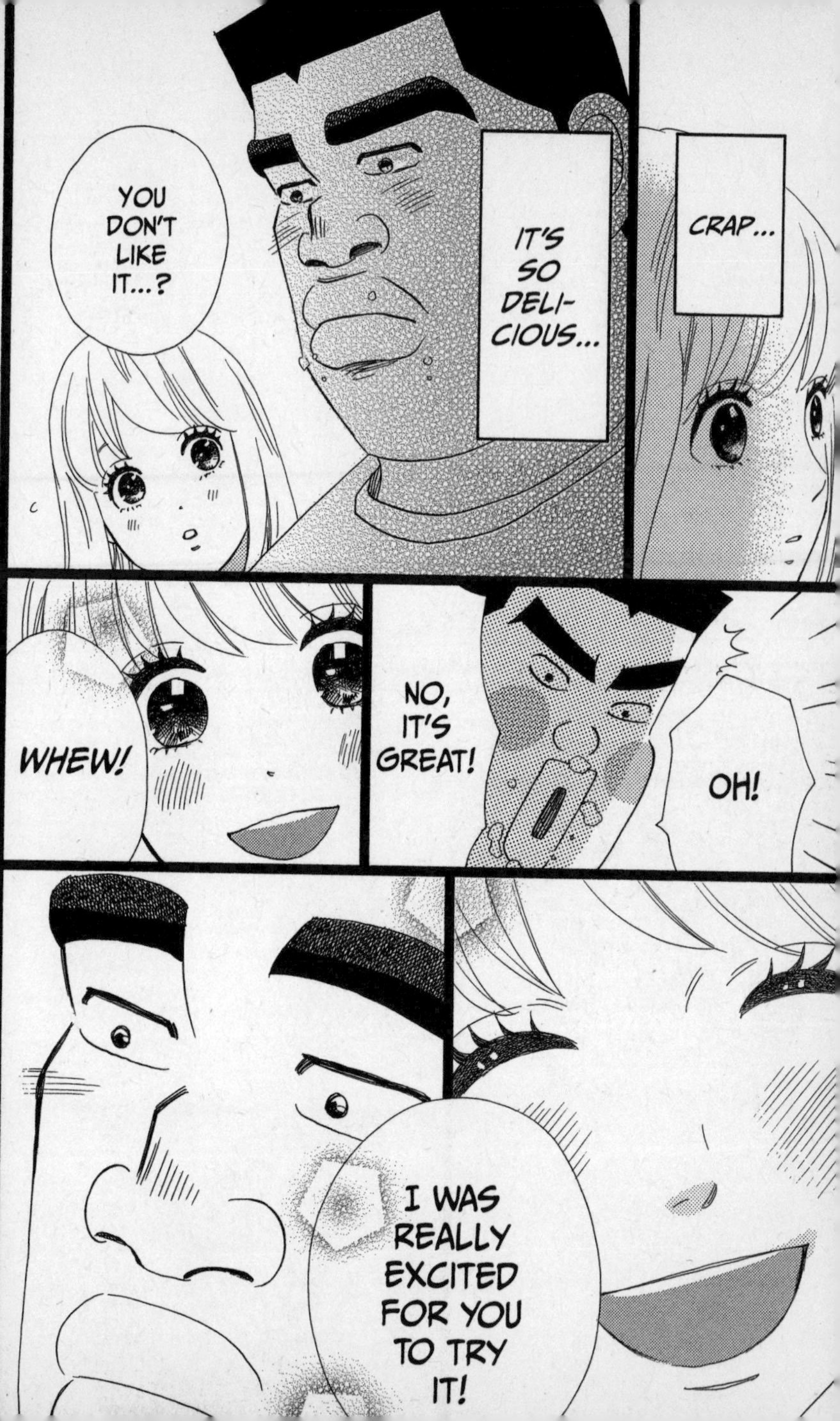
CRAP...
IT'S SO DELICIOUS...
YOU DON'T LIKE IT...?
OH!
NO, IT'S GREAT!
WHEW!
I WAS REALLY EXCITED FOR YOU TO TRY IT!

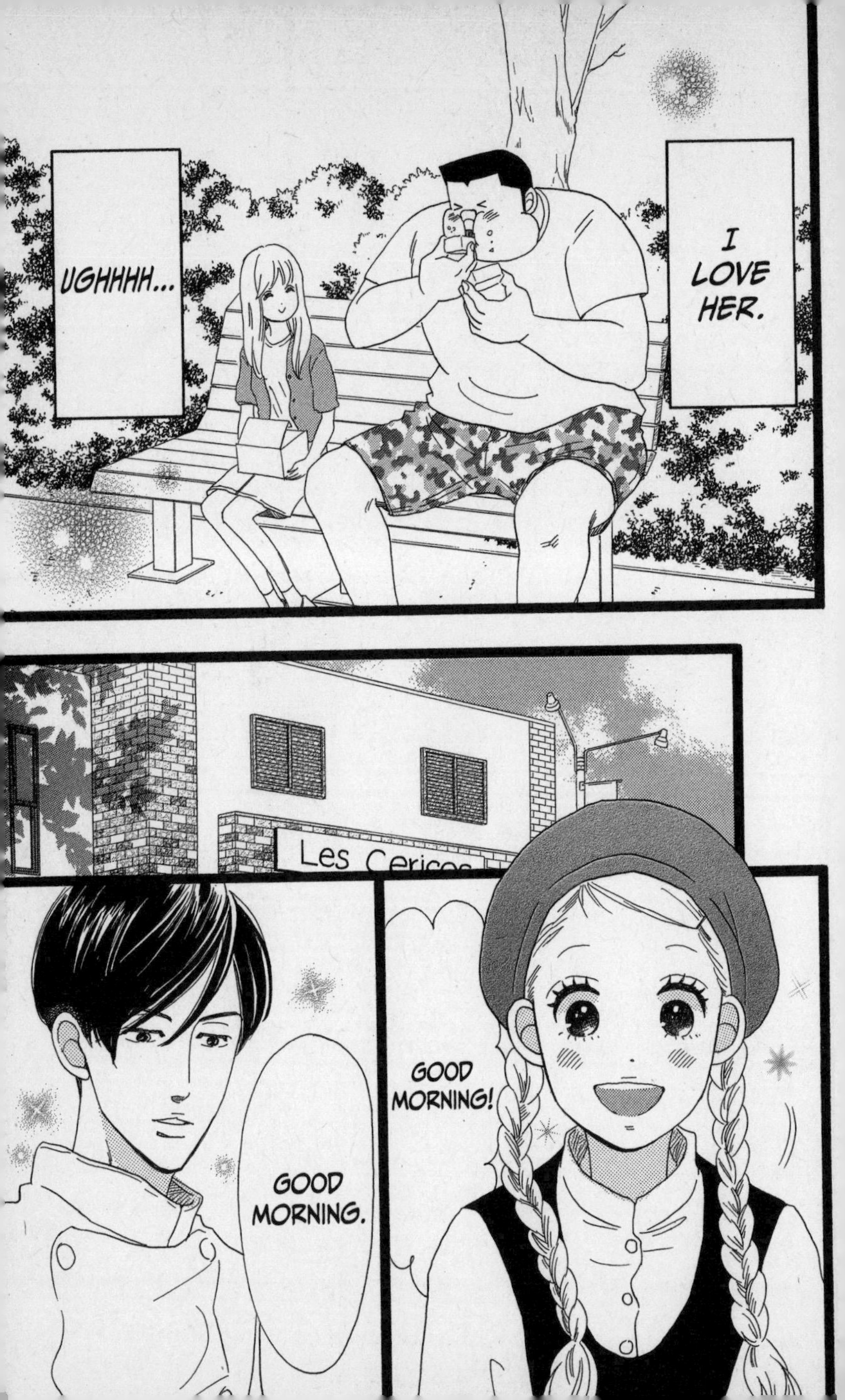
I LOVE HER.
UGHHHH...
Les Cericos
GOOD MORNING!
GOOD MORNING.

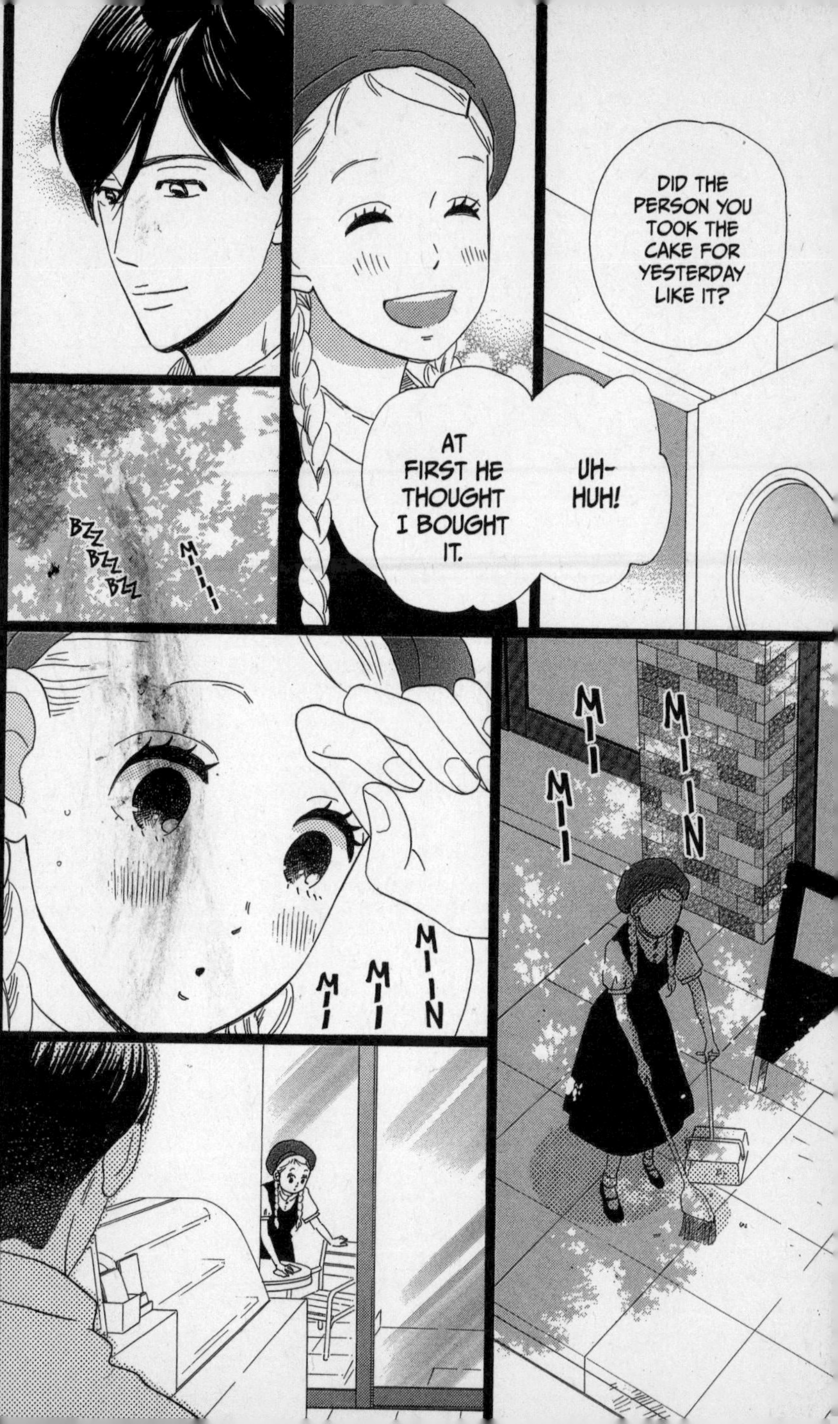

DID THE PERSON YOU TOOK THE CAKE FOR YESTERDAY LIKE IT?
UH-HUH!
AT FIRST HE THOUGHT I BOUGHT IT.
BZZ BZZ BZZ
MIIII
MIIIN
MII
MII
MIIIN
MII
MII

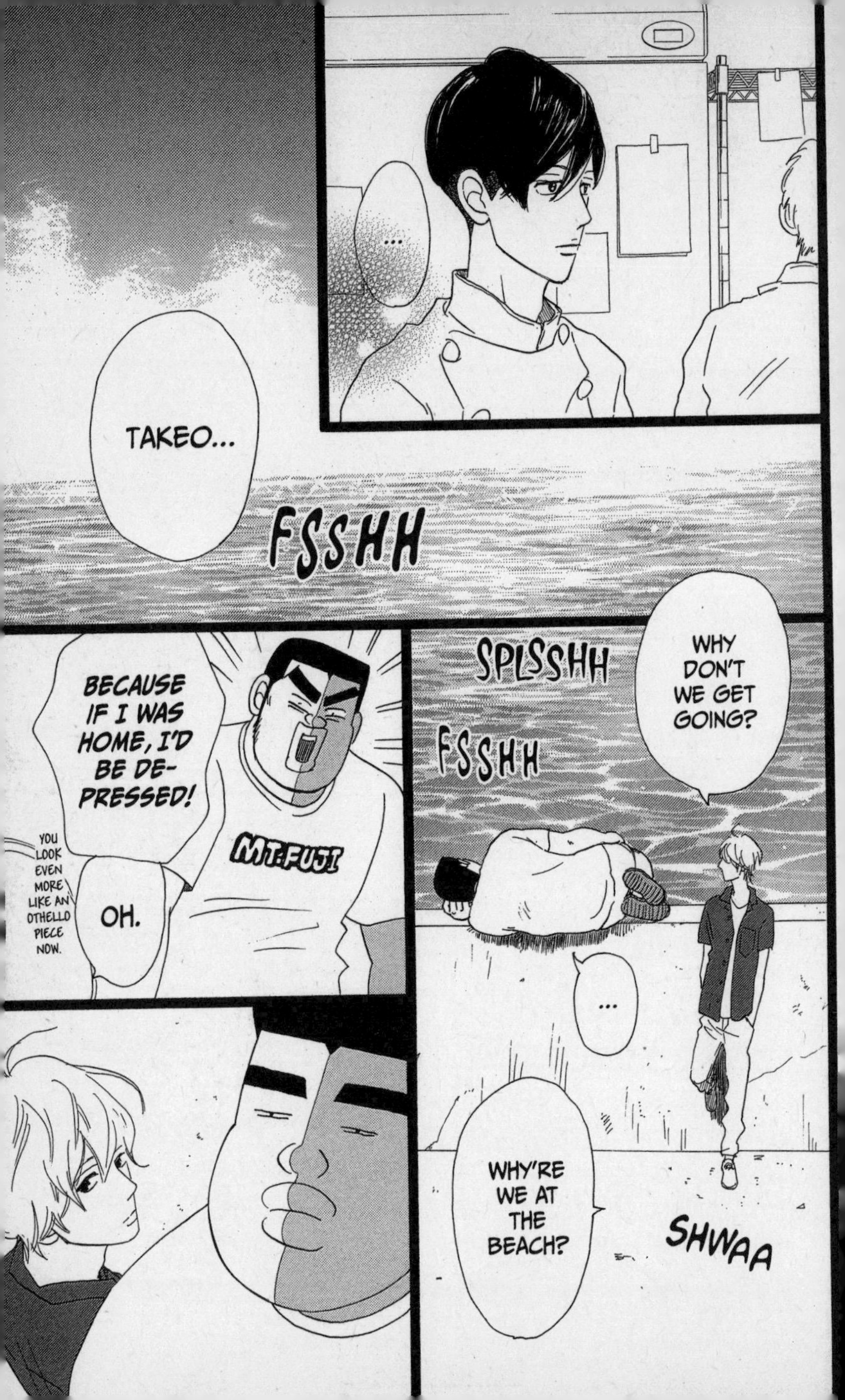
...
TAKEO...
FSSHH
WHY DON'T WE GET GOING?
SPLSSHH
FSSHH
...
SHWAA
WHY'RE WE AT THE BEACH?
BECAUSE IF I WAS HOME, I'D BE DE-PRESSED!
MT.FUJI
OH.
YOU LOOK EVEN MORE LIKE AN OTHELLO PIECE NOW.

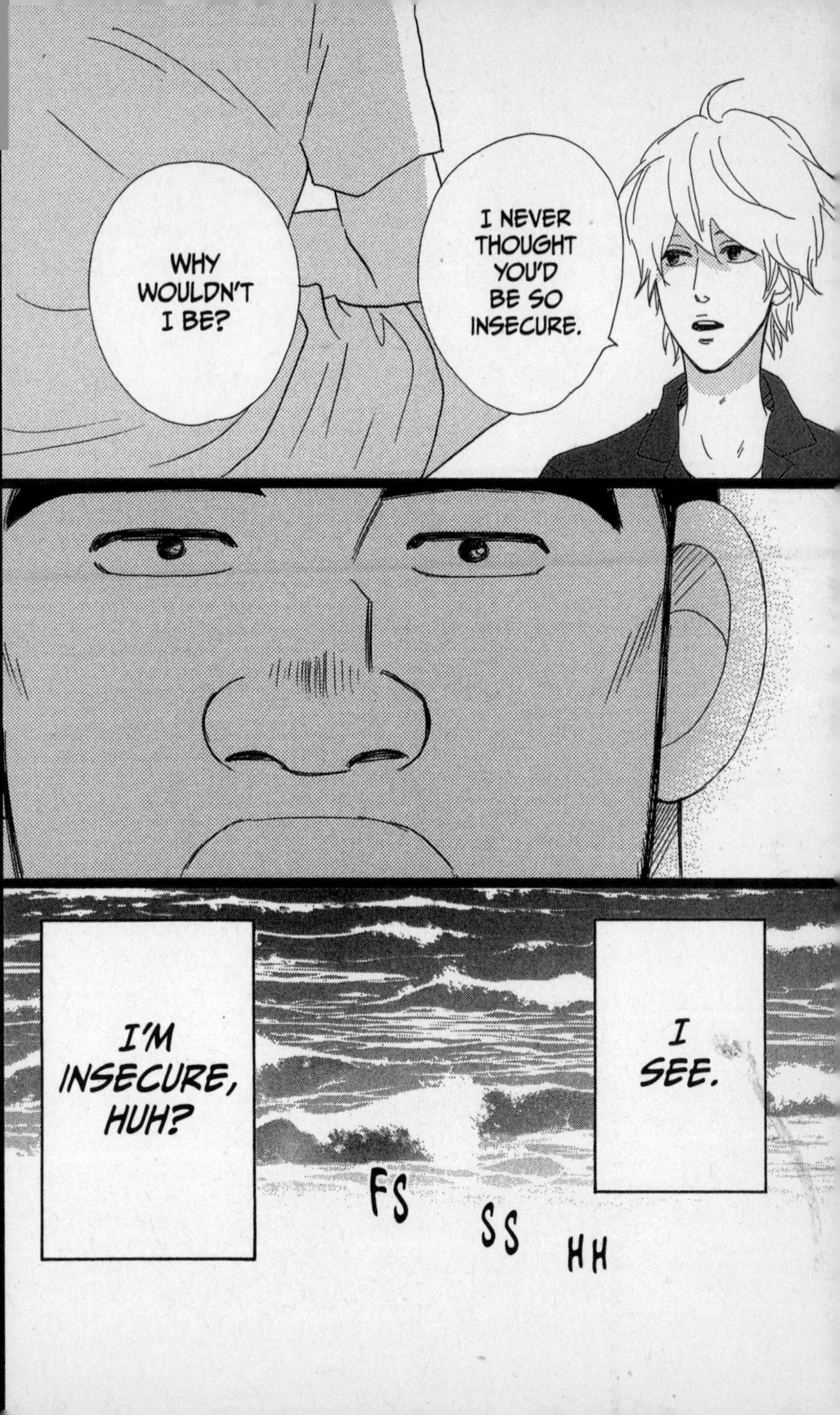
I NEVER THOUGHT YOU'D BE SO INSECURE.
WHY WOULDN'T I BE?
I SEE.
I'M INSECURE, HUH?
FS SS HH

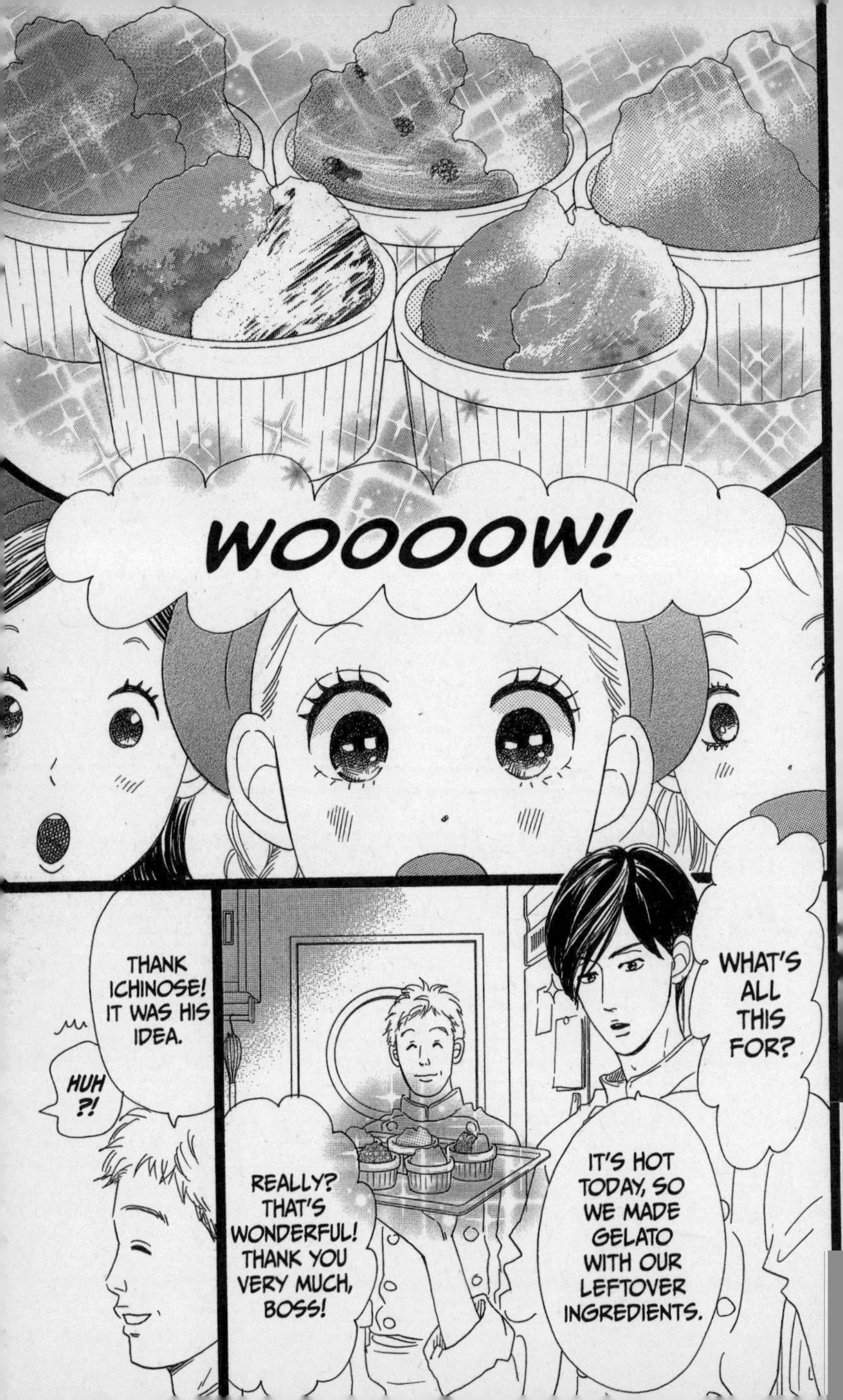
WOOOOW!
WHAT'S ALL THIS FOR?
IT'S HOT TODAY, SO WE MADE GELATO WITH OUR LEFTOVER INGREDIENTS.
REALLY? THAT'S WONDERFUL! THANK YOU VERY MUCH, BOSS!
THANK ICHINOSE! IT WAS HIS IDEA.
HUH?!

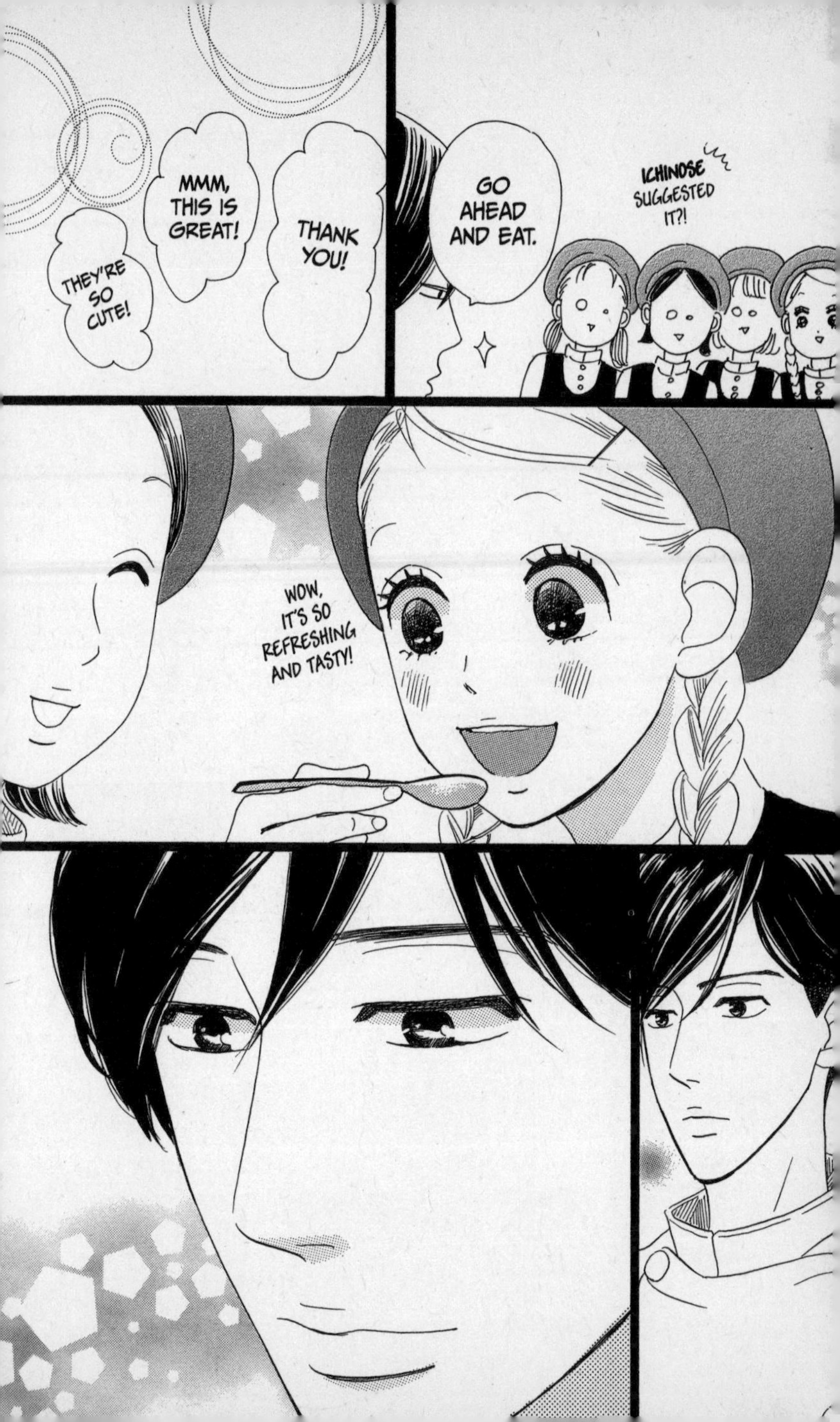
GO AHEAD AND EAT.
ICHINOSE SUGGESTED IT?!
THANK YOU!
MMM, THIS IS GREAT!
THEY'RE SO CUTE!
WOW, IT'S SO REFRESHING AND TASTY!

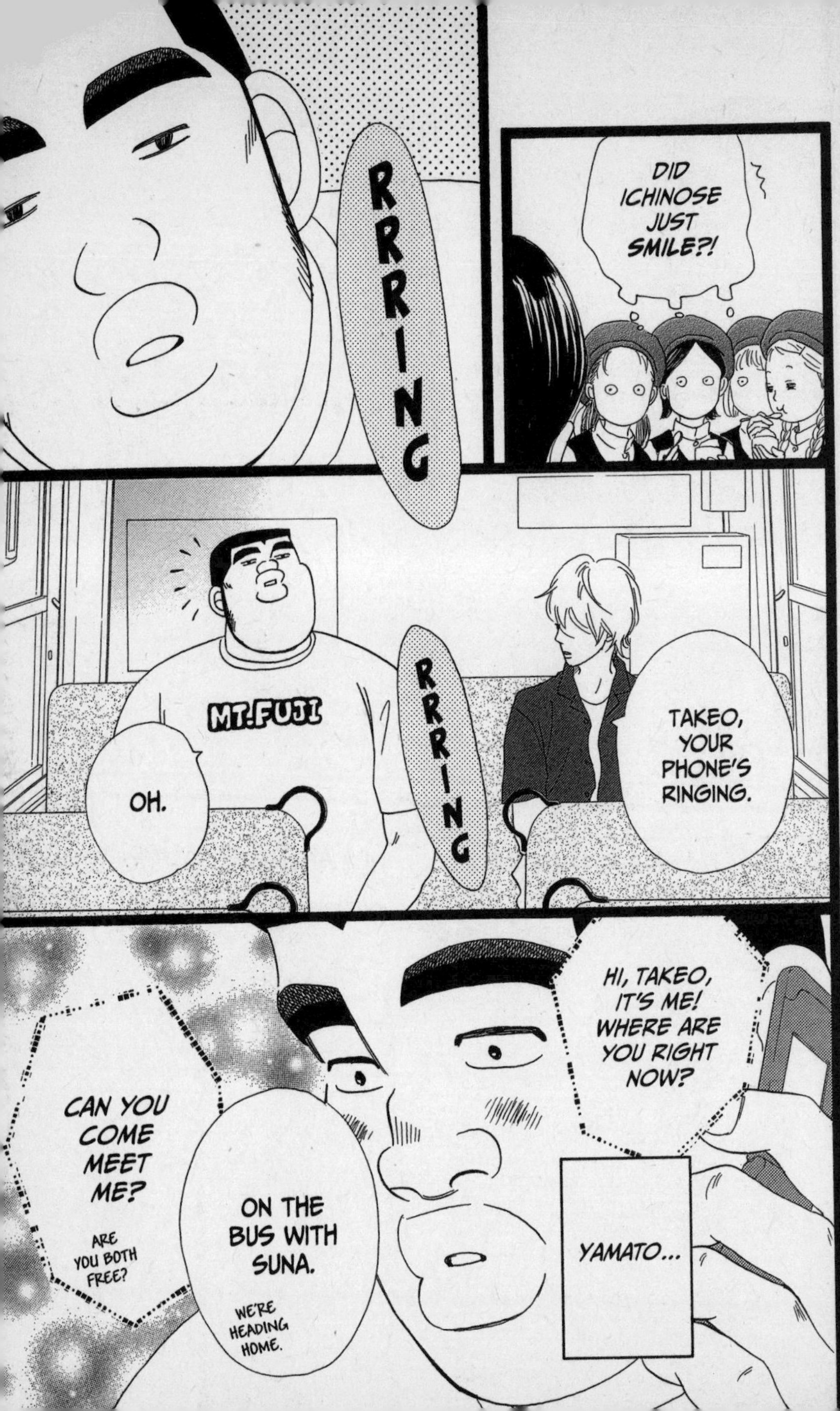
DID ICHINOSE JUST SMILE?!
RRRING
TAKEO, YOUR PHONE'S RINGING.
RRRING
OH.
HI, TAKEO, IT'S ME! WHERE ARE YOU RIGHT NOW?
YAMATO...
ON THE BUS WITH SUNA.
WE'RE HEADING HOME.
CAN YOU COME MEET ME?
ARE YOU BOTH FREE?

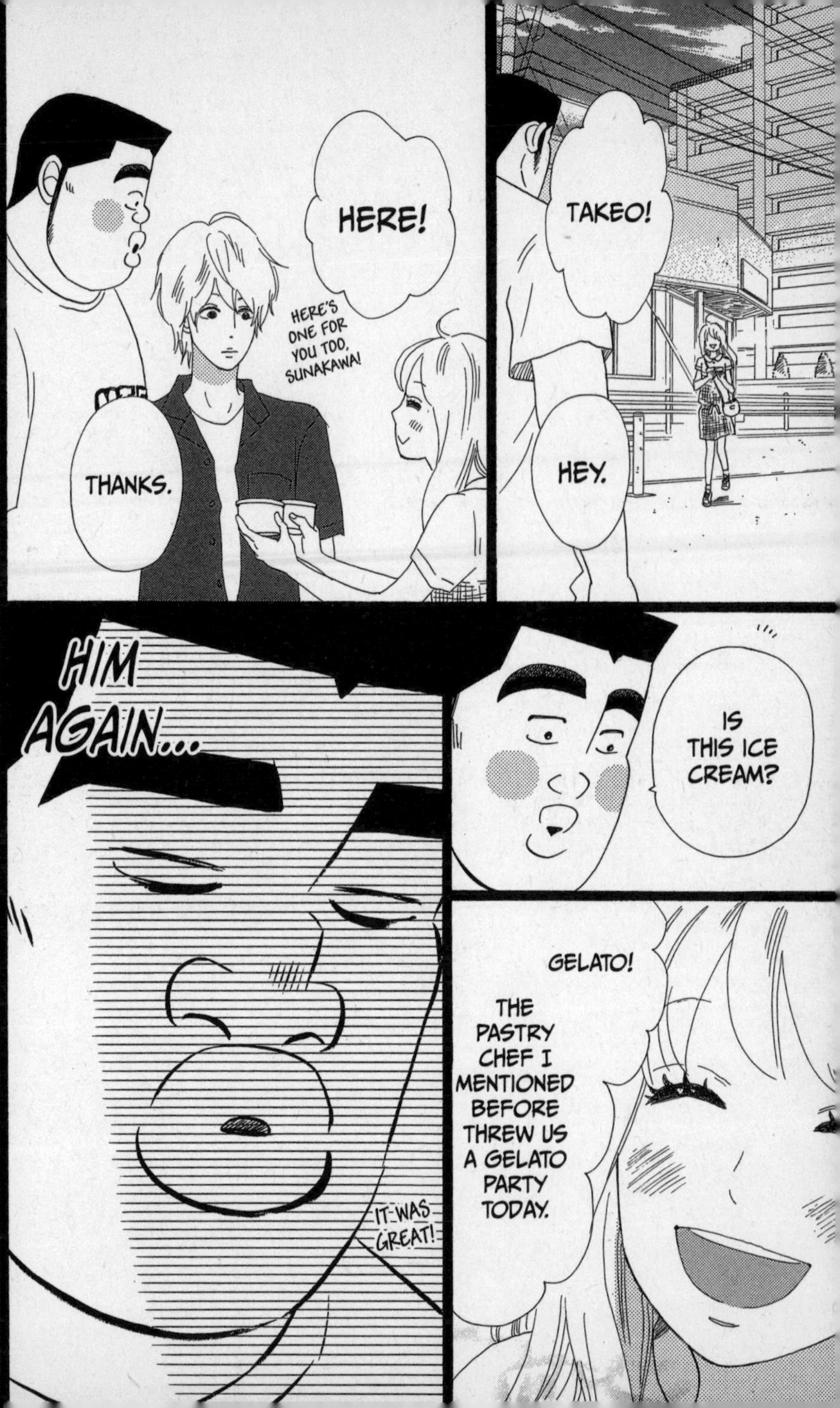
TAKEO!
HEY.
HERE!
HERE'S ONE FOR YOU TOO, SUNAKAWA!
THANKS.
IS THIS ICE CREAM?
GELATO!
THE PASTRY CHEF I MENTIONED BEFORE THREW US A GELATO PARTY TODAY.
HIM AGAIN...
IT WAS GREAT!

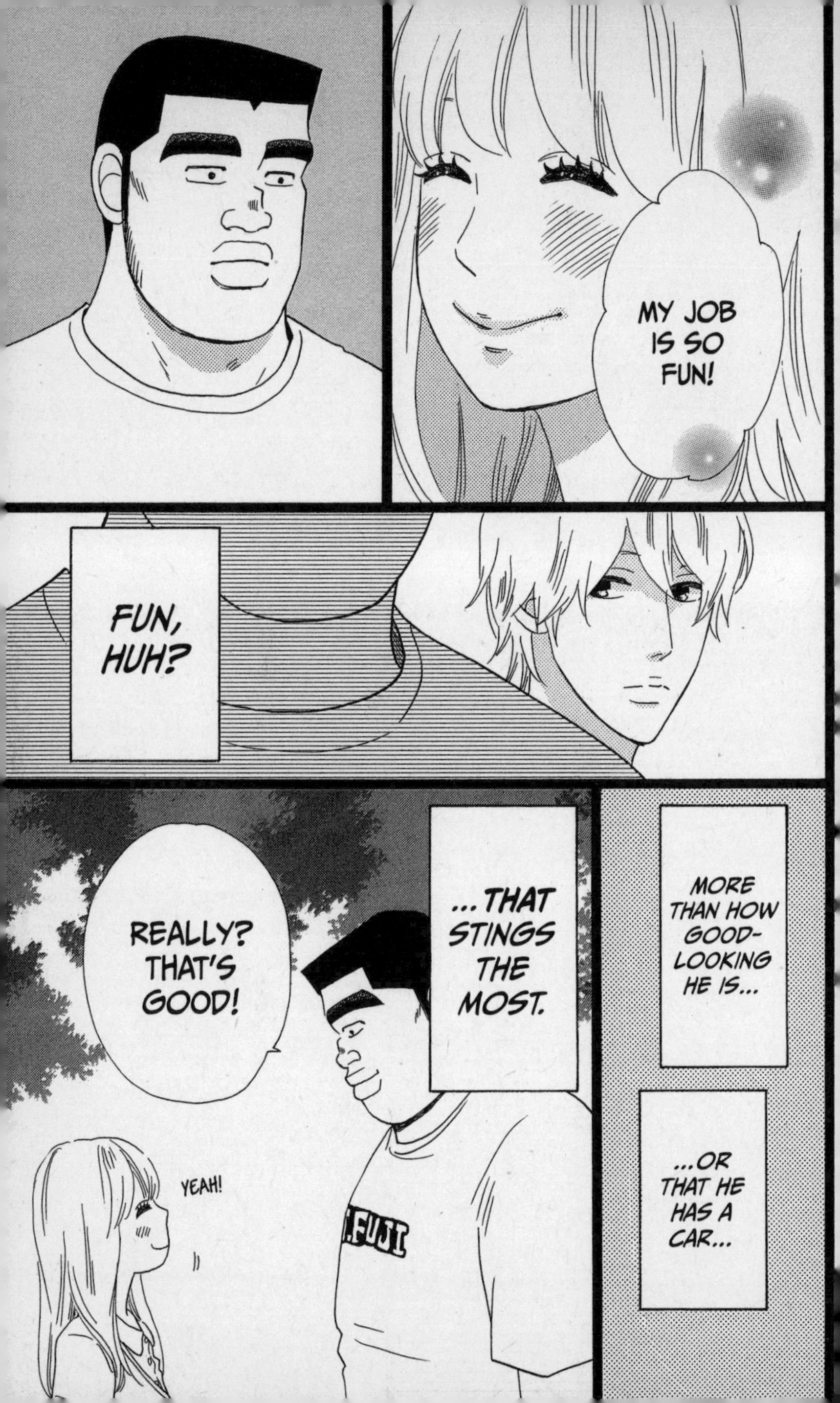
MY JOB IS SO FUN!
FUN, HUH?
MORE THAN HOW GOOD-LOOKING HE IS...
...OR THAT HE HAS A CAR...
...THAT STINGS THE MOST.
REALLY? THAT'S GOOD!
YEAH!
FUJI

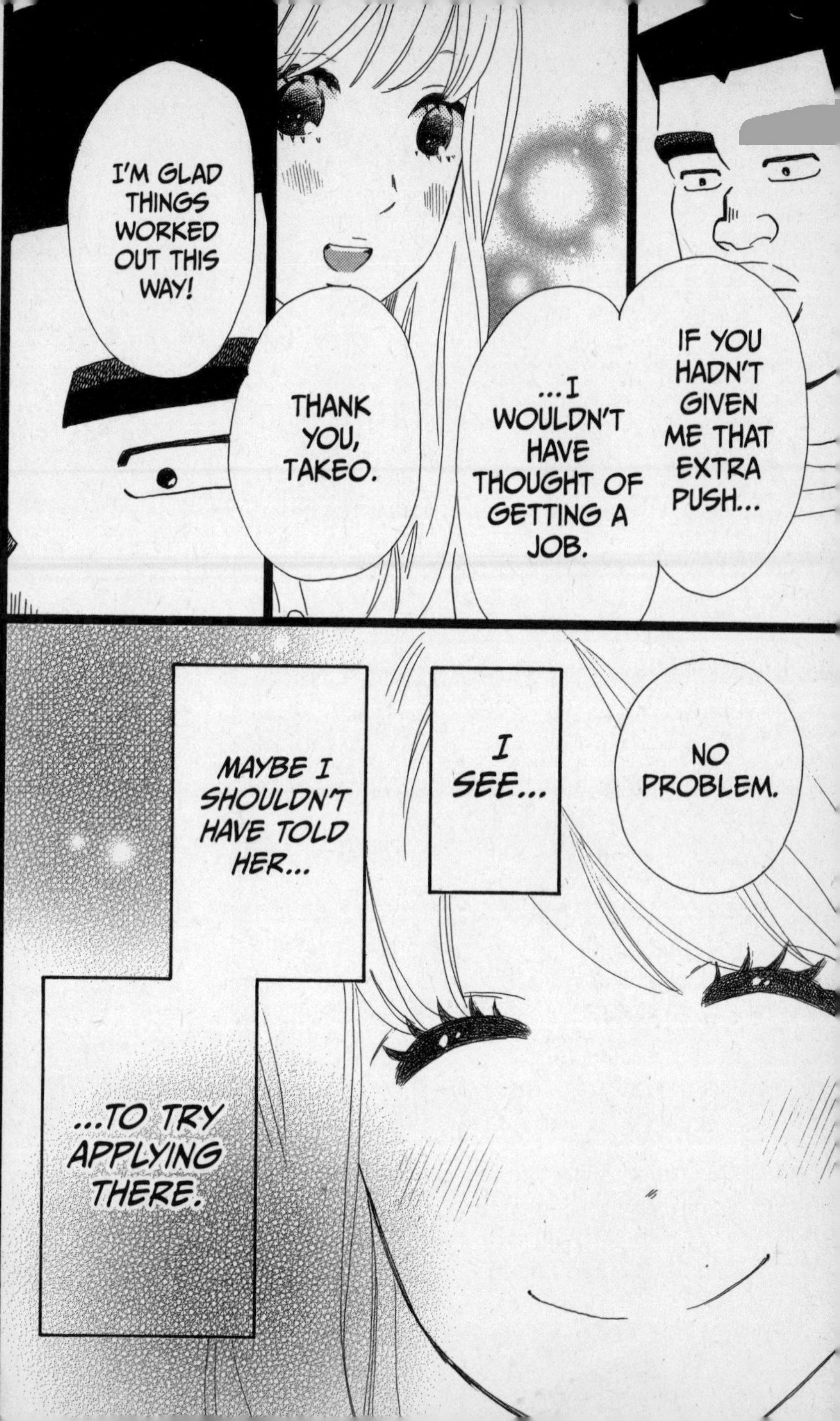
IF YOU HADN'T GIVEN ME THAT EXTRA PUSH...
...I WOULDN'T HAVE THOUGHT OF GETTING A JOB.
THANK YOU, TAKEO.
I'M GLAD THINGS WORKED OUT THIS WAY!
NO PROBLEM.
I SEE...
MAYBE I SHOULDN'T HAVE TOLD HER...
...TO TRY APPLYING THERE.

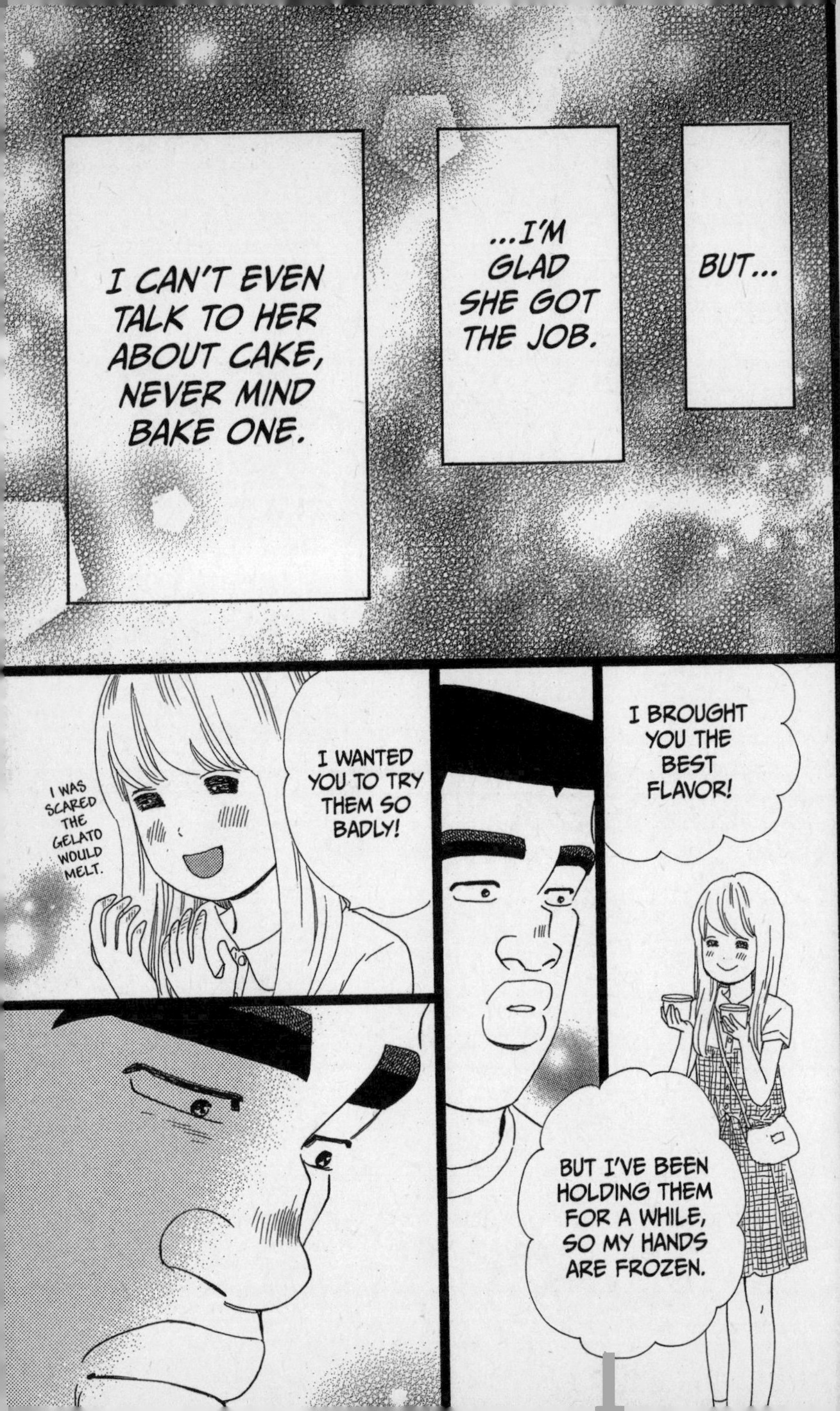
BUT...
...I'M GLAD SHE GOT THE JOB.
I CAN'T EVEN TALK TO HER ABOUT CAKE, NEVER MIND BAKE ONE.
I BROUGHT YOU THE BEST FLAVOR!
BUT I'VE BEEN HOLDING THEM FOR A WHILE, SO MY HANDS ARE FROZEN.
I WANTED YOU TO TRY THEM SO BADLY!
I WAS SCARED THE GELATO WOULD MELT.

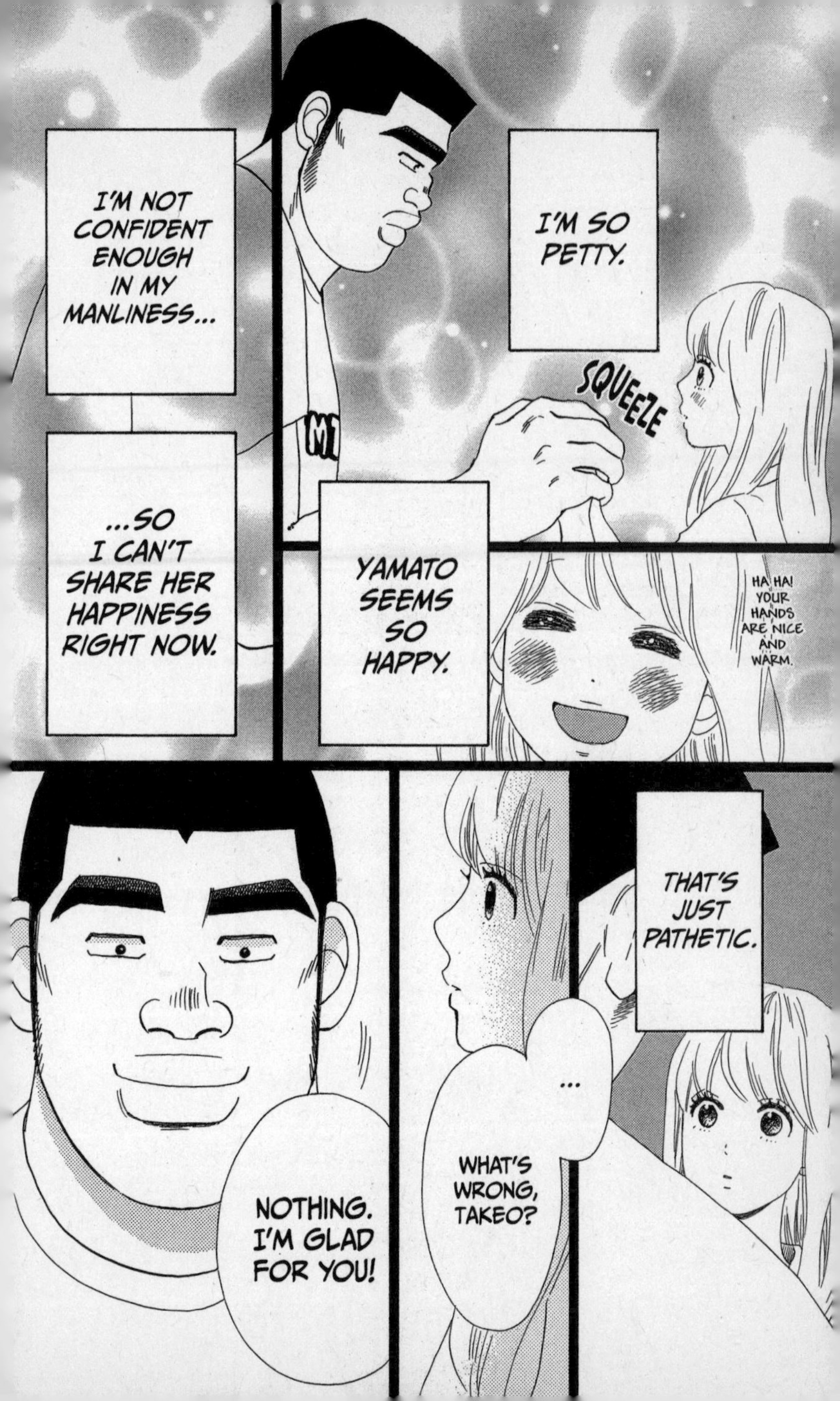
I'M SO PETTY.
SQUEEZE
YAMATO SEEMS SO HAPPY.
HA HA! YOUR HANDS ARE NICE AND WARM.
I'M NOT CONFIDENT ENOUGH IN MY MANLINESS...
...SO I CAN'T SHARE HER HAPPINESS RIGHT NOW.
THAT'S JUST PATHETIC.
...
WHAT'S WRONG, TAKEO?
NOTHING. I'M GLAD FOR YOU!

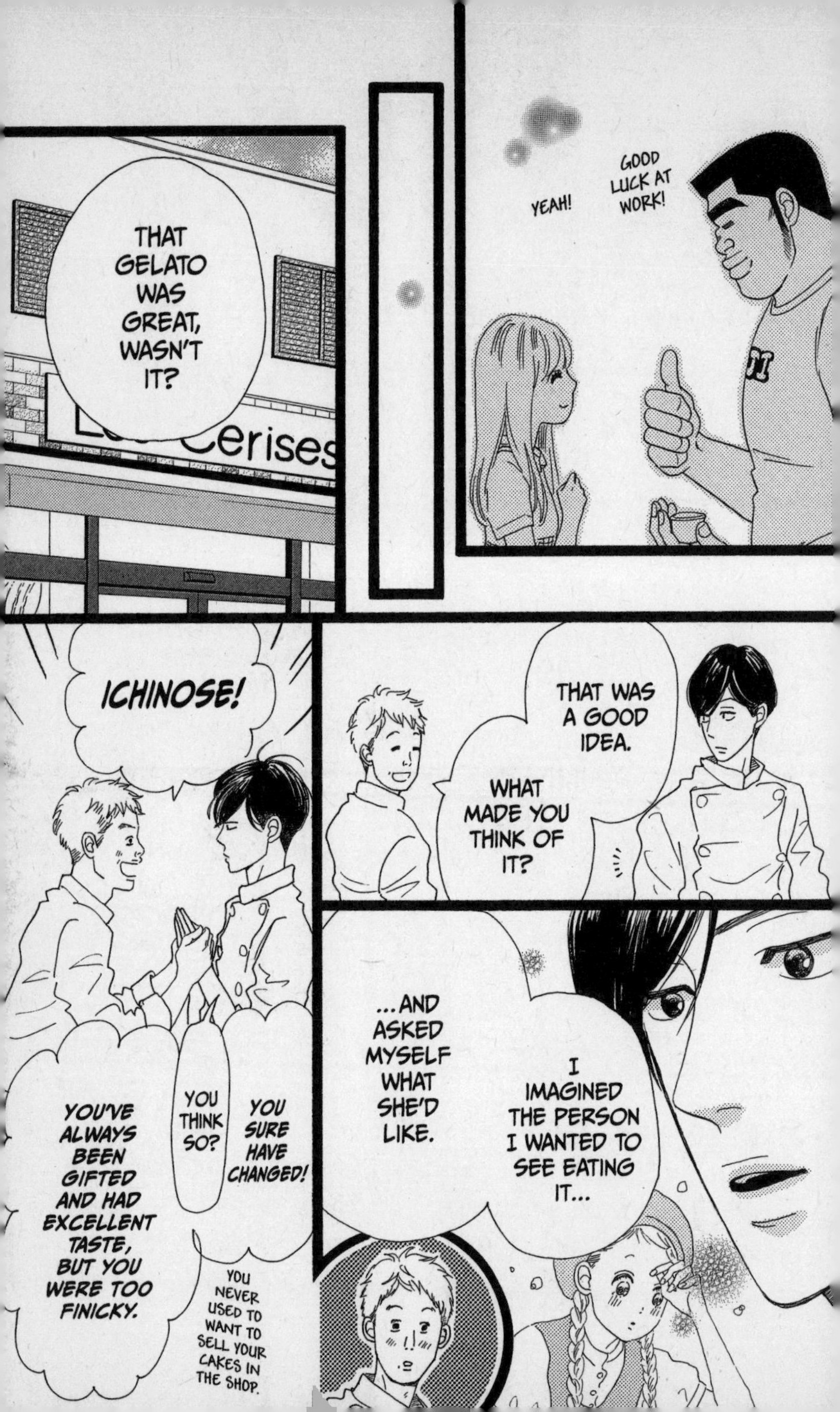

GOOD LUCK AT WORK!
YEAH!
THAT GELATO WAS GREAT, WASN'T IT?
Cerises
THAT WAS A GOOD IDEA.
WHAT MADE YOU THINK OF IT?
I IMAGINED THE PERSON I WANTED TO SEE EATING IT...
...AND ASKED MYSELF WHAT SHE'D LIKE.
ICHINOSE!
YOU SURE HAVE CHANGED!
YOU THINK SO?
YOU'VE ALWAYS BEEN GIFTED AND HAD EXCELLENT TASTE, BUT YOU WERE TOO FINICKY.
YOU NEVER USED TO WANT TO SELL YOUR CAKES IN THE SHOP.

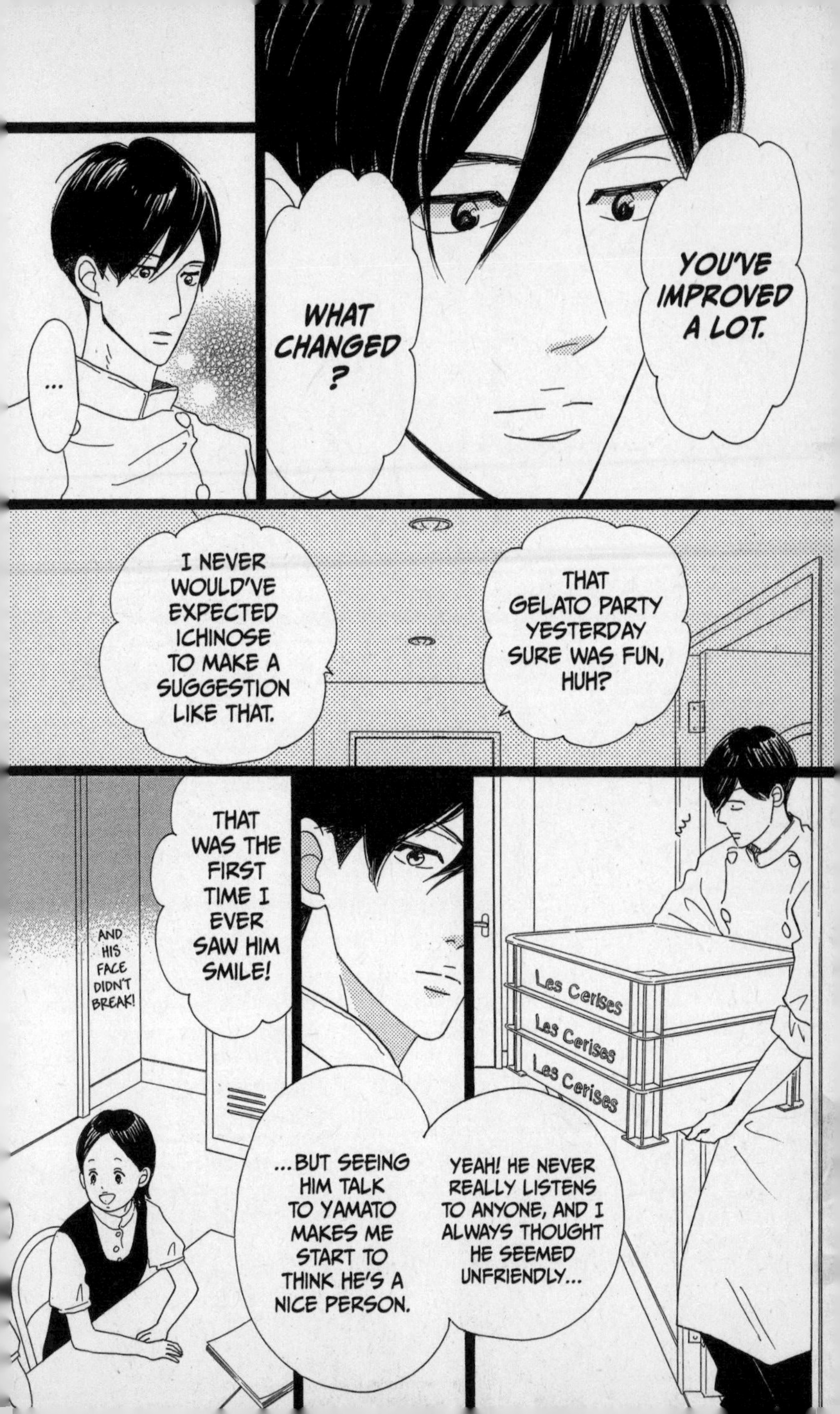

YOU'VE IMPROVED A LOT.
WHAT CHANGED?
...
THAT GELATO PARTY YESTERDAY SURE WAS FUN, HUH?
I NEVER WOULD'VE EXPECTED ICHINOSE TO MAKE A SUGGESTION LIKE THAT.
Les Cerises
Les Cerises
Les Cerises
THAT WAS THE FIRST TIME I EVER SAW HIM SMILE!
AND HIS FACE DIDN'T BREAK!
YEAH! HE NEVER REALLY LISTENS TO ANYONE, AND I ALWAYS THOUGHT HE SEEMED UNFRIENDLY...
...BUT SEEING HIM TALK TO YAMATO MAKES ME START TO THINK HE'S A NICE PERSON.

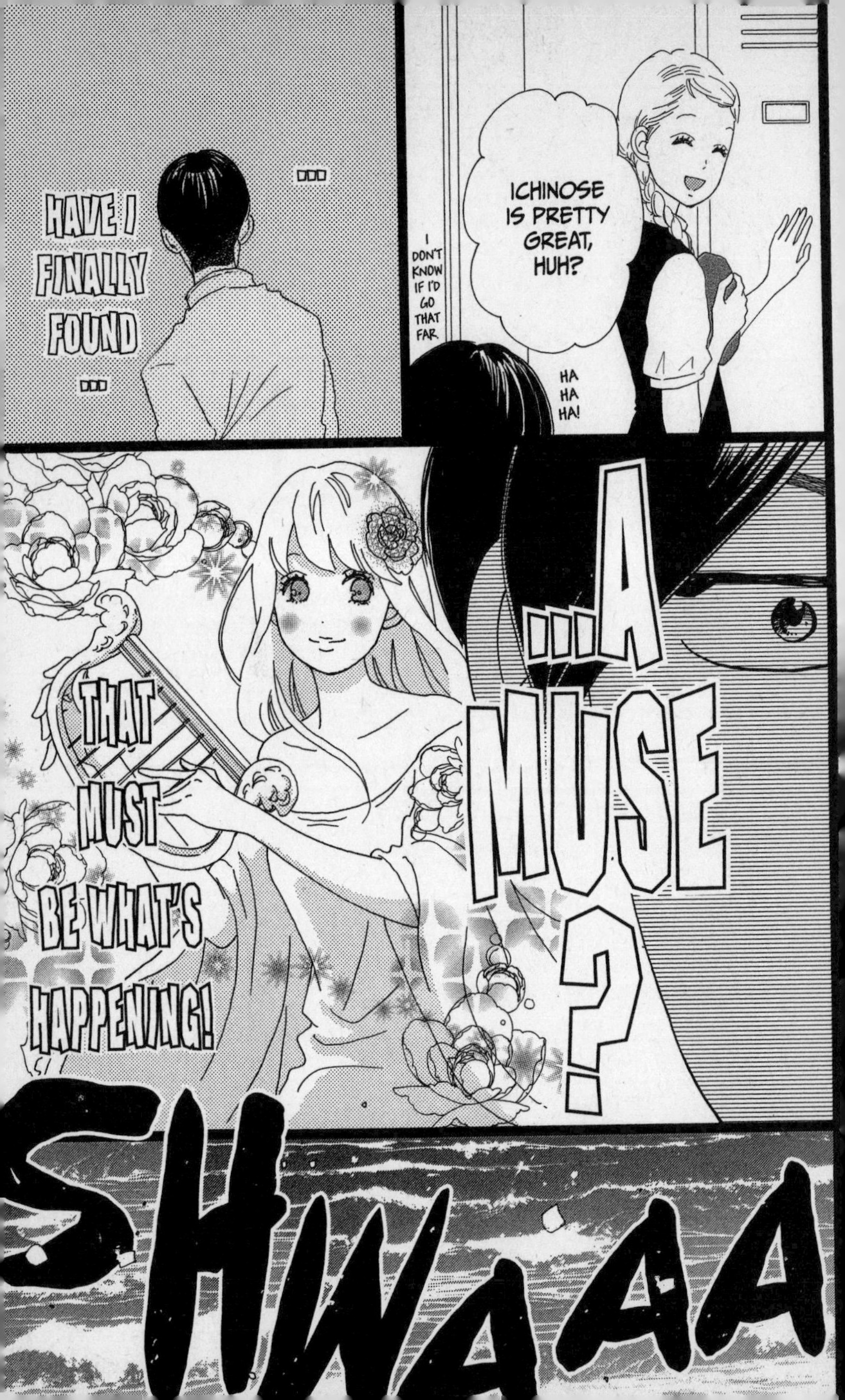
ICHINOSE IS PRETTY GREAT, HUH?
I DON'T KNOW IF I'D GO THAT FAR
HA HA HA!
...
HAVE I FINALLY FOUND ...
...A MUSE?
THAT MUST BE WHAT'S HAPPENING!
SHWAAA

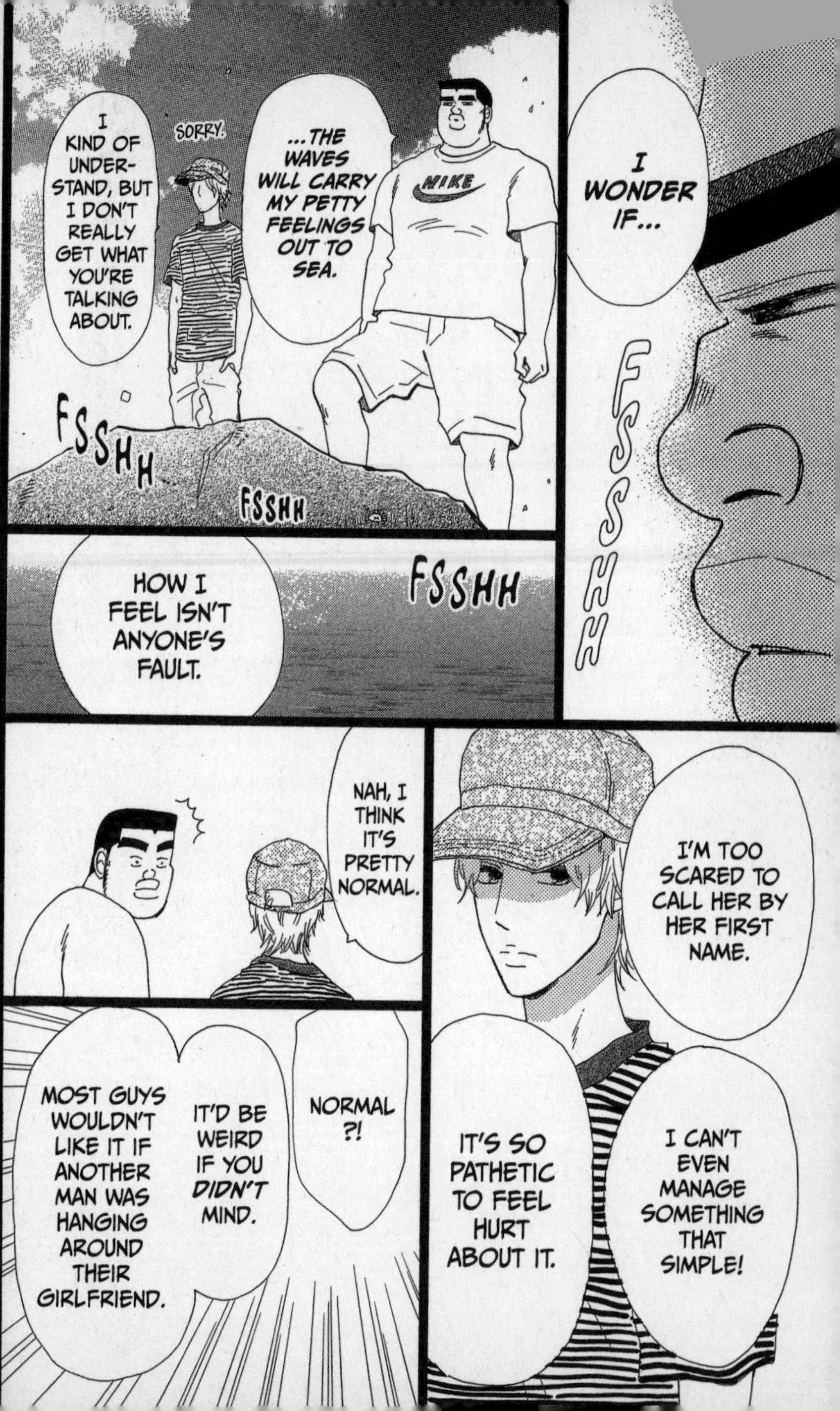
I WONDER IF...
FSSSHHH
...THE WAVES WILL CARRY MY PETTY FEELINGS OUT TO SEA.
SORRY.
I KIND OF UNDERSTAND, BUT I DON'T REALLY GET WHAT YOU'RE TALKING ABOUT.
FSSHH
FSSHH
FSSHH
HOW I FEEL ISN'T ANYONE'S FAULT.
I'M TOO SCARED TO CALL HER BY HER FIRST NAME.
I CAN'T EVEN MANAGE SOMETHING THAT SIMPLE!
IT'S SO PATHETIC TO FEEL HURT ABOUT IT.
NAH, I THINK IT'S PRETTY NORMAL.
NORMAL?!
IT'D BE WEIRD IF YOU *DIDN'T* MIND.
MOST GUYS WOULDN'T LIKE IT IF ANOTHER MAN WAS HANGING AROUND THEIR GIRLFRIEND.

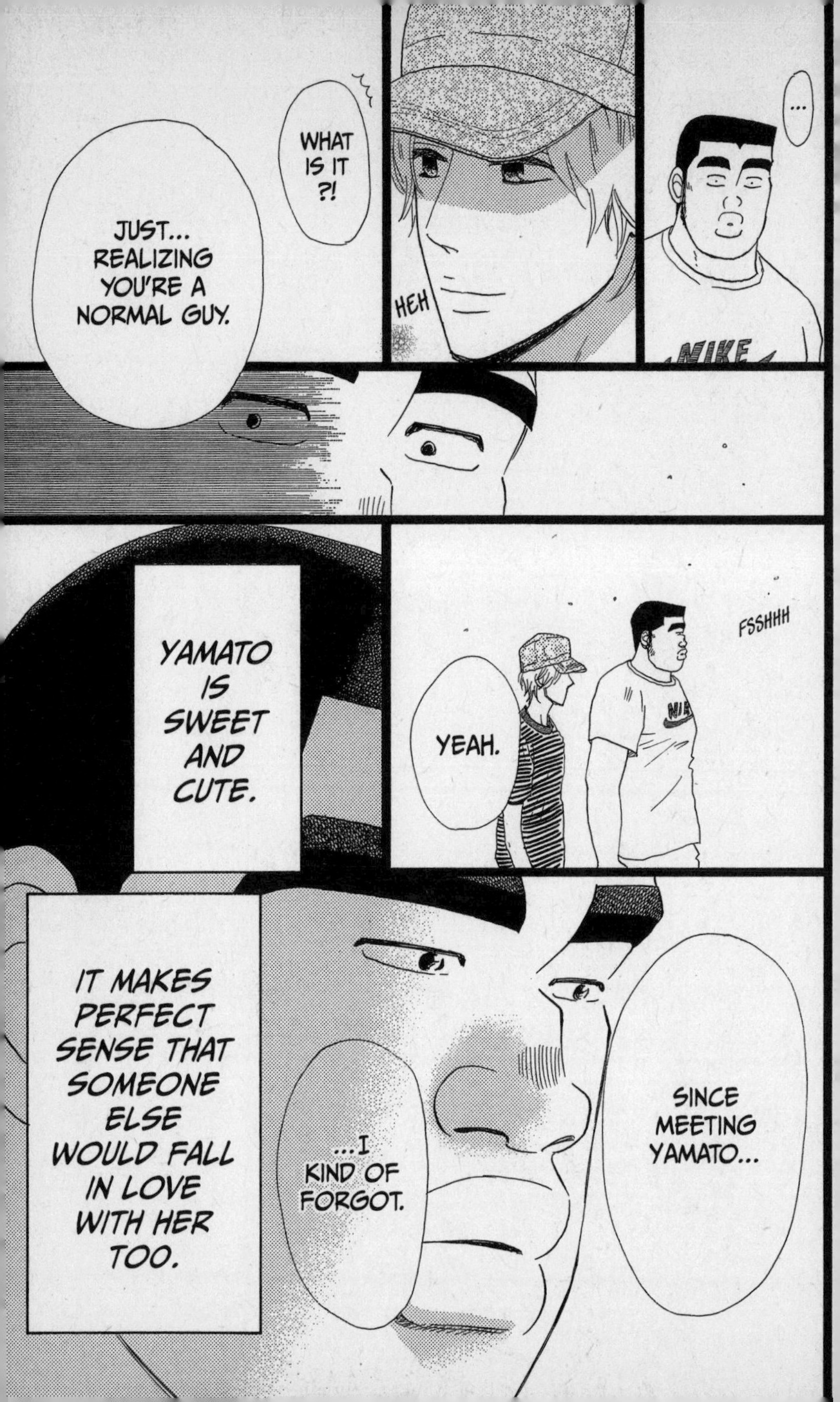
...
WHAT IS IT ?!
HEH
JUST... REALIZING YOU'RE A NORMAL GUY.
FSSHHH
YEAH.
YAMATO IS SWEET AND CUTE.
SINCE MEETING YAMATO...
...I KIND OF FORGOT.
IT MAKES PERFECT SENSE THAT SOMEONE ELSE WOULD FALL IN LOVE WITH HER TOO.

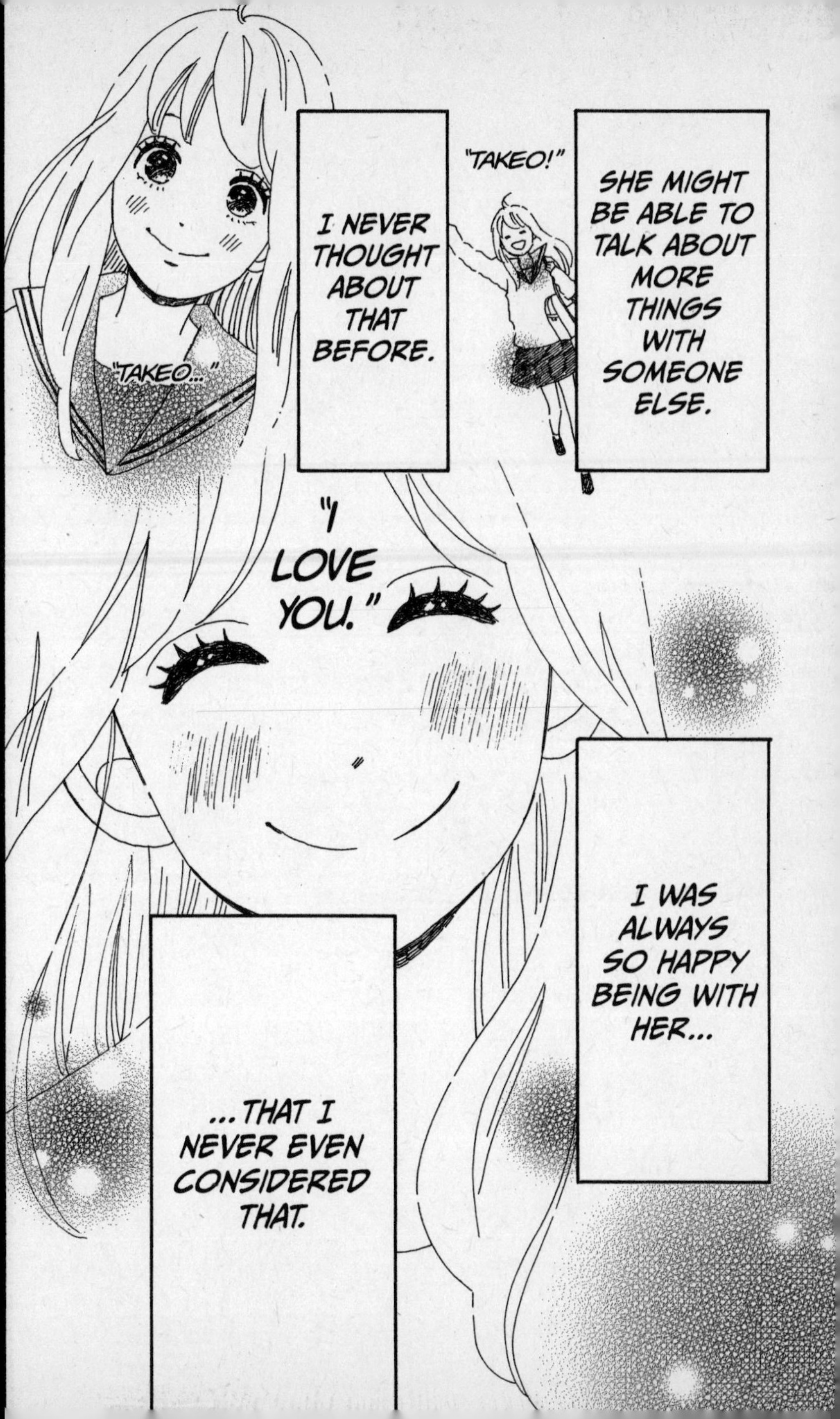
SHE MIGHT BE ABLE TO TALK ABOUT MORE THINGS WITH SOMEONE ELSE.
"TAKEO!"
I NEVER THOUGHT ABOUT THAT BEFORE.
"TAKEO..."
"I LOVE YOU."
I WAS ALWAYS SO HAPPY BEING WITH HER...
...THAT I NEVER EVEN CONSIDERED THAT.

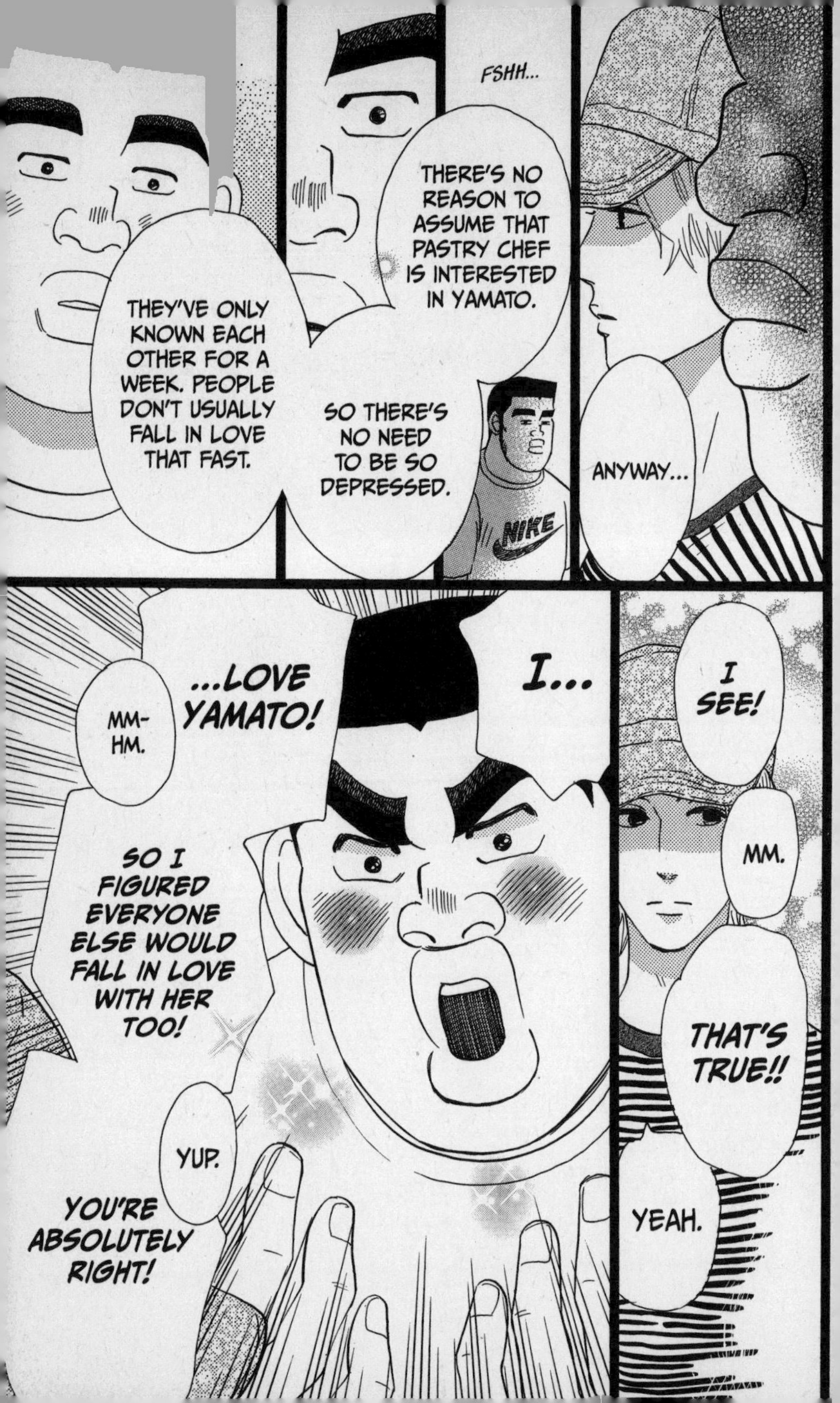
ANYWAY...
FSHH...
THERE'S NO REASON TO ASSUME THAT PASTRY CHEF IS INTERESTED IN YAMATO.
SO THERE'S NO NEED TO BE SO DEPRESSED.
NIKE
THEY'VE ONLY KNOWN EACH OTHER FOR A WEEK. PEOPLE DON'T USUALLY FALL IN LOVE THAT FAST.
I SEE!
MM.
THAT'S TRUE!!
YEAH.
I...
...LOVE YAMATO!
MM-HM.
SO I FIGURED EVERYONE ELSE WOULD FALL IN LOVE WITH HER TOO!
YUP.
YOU'RE ABSOLUTELY RIGHT!

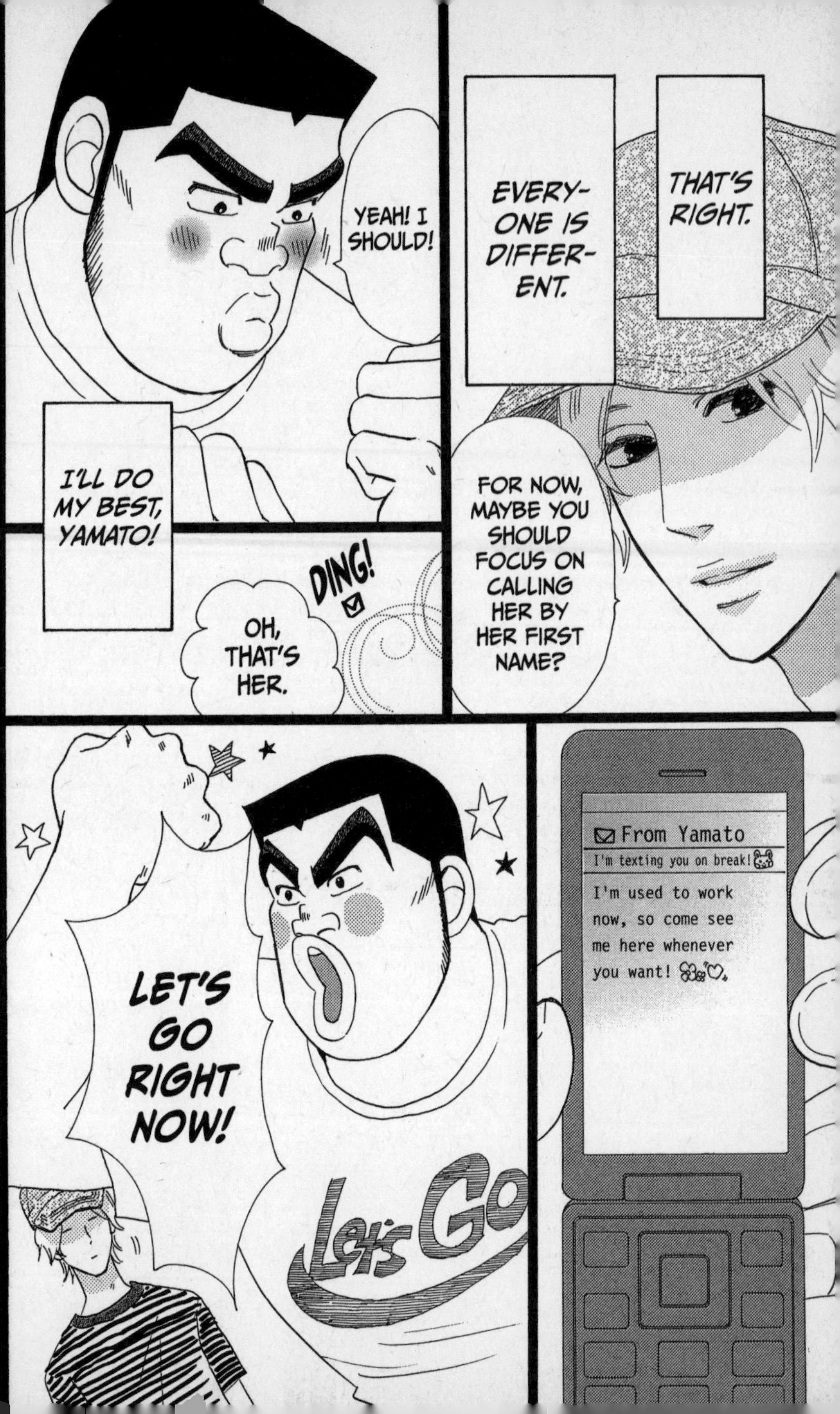
THAT'S RIGHT.
EVERY-ONE IS DIFFER-ENT.
FOR NOW, MAYBE YOU SHOULD FOCUS ON CALLING HER BY HER FIRST NAME?
YEAH! I SHOULD!
I'LL DO MY BEST, YAMATO!
DING!
OH, THAT'S HER.
From Yamato
I'm texting you on break!
I'm used to work now, so come see me here whenever you want!
LET'S GO RIGHT NOW!
Let's Go

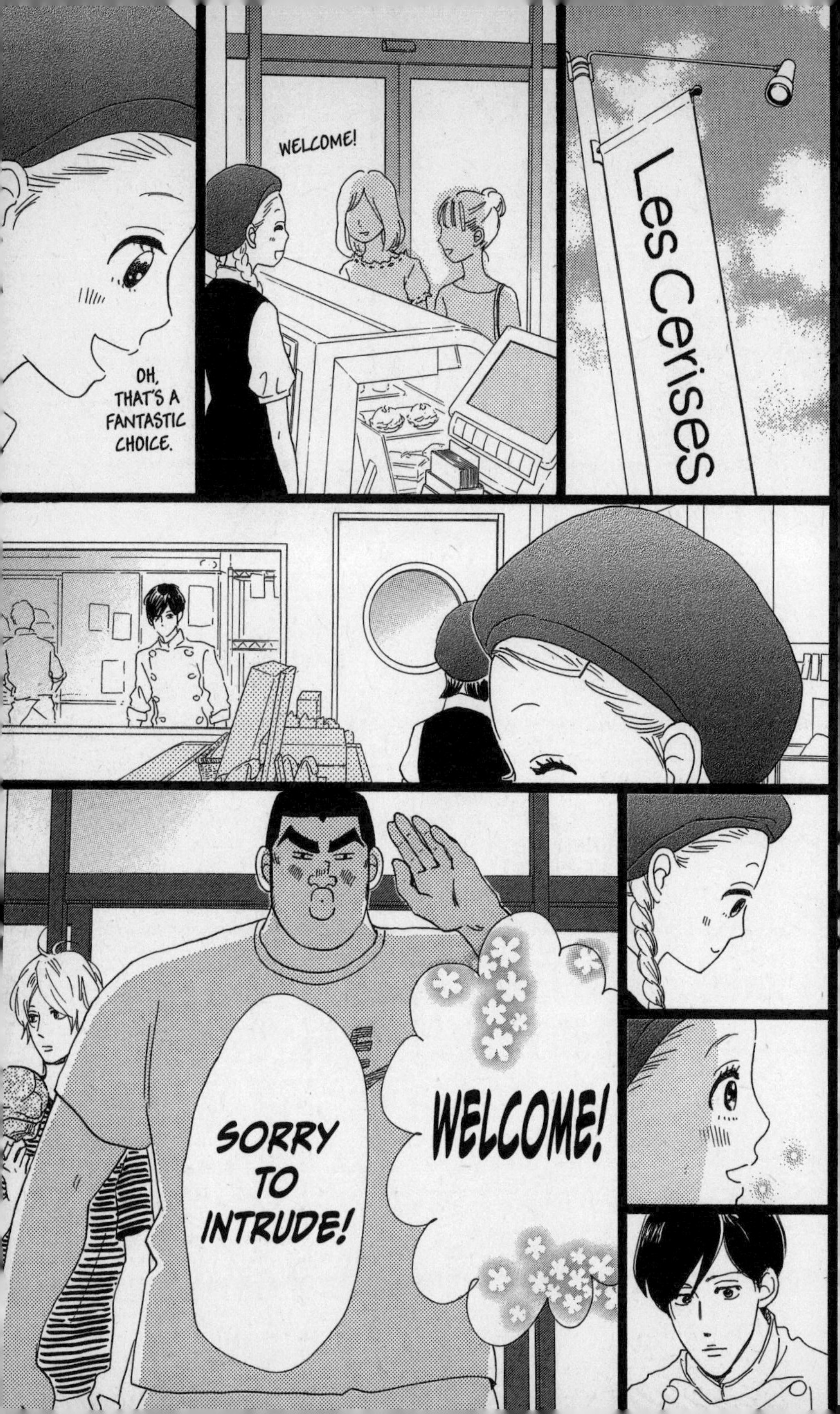
Les Cerises
WELCOME!
OH, THAT'S A FANTASTIC CHOICE.
WELCOME!
SORRY TO INTRUDE!

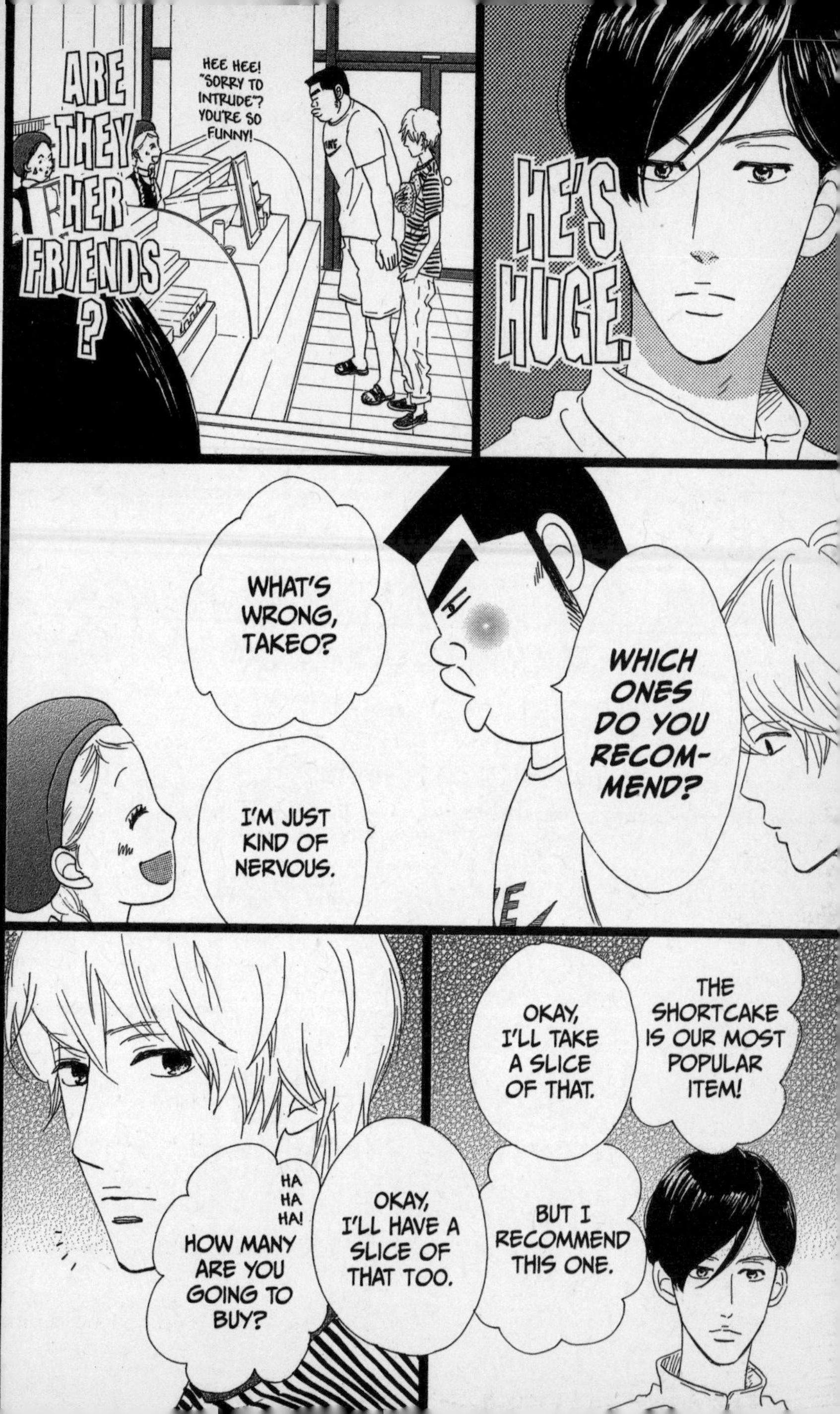
HE'S HUGE.
HEE HEE! "SORRY TO INTRUDE"? YOU'RE SO FUNNY!
ARE THEY HER FRIENDS?
WHICH ONES DO YOU RECOMMEND?
WHAT'S WRONG, TAKEO?
I'M JUST KIND OF NERVOUS.
THE SHORTCAKE IS OUR MOST POPULAR ITEM!
OKAY, I'LL TAKE A SLICE OF THAT.
BUT I RECOMMEND THIS ONE.
OKAY, I'LL HAVE A SLICE OF THAT TOO.
HA HA HA!
HOW MANY ARE YOU GOING TO BUY?

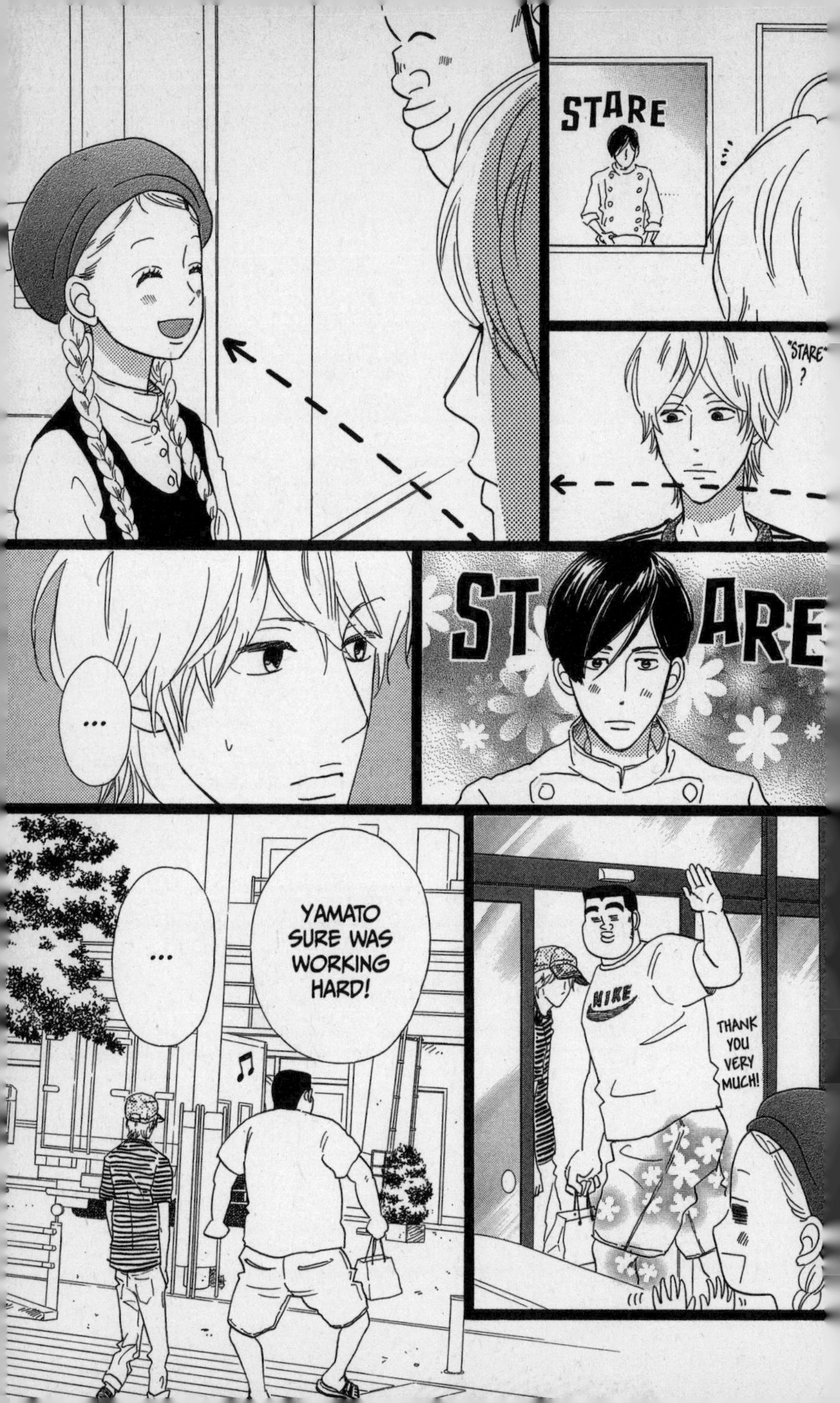
STARE
"STARE"?
STARE
...
THANK YOU VERY MUCH!
YAMATO SURE WAS WORKING HARD!
...

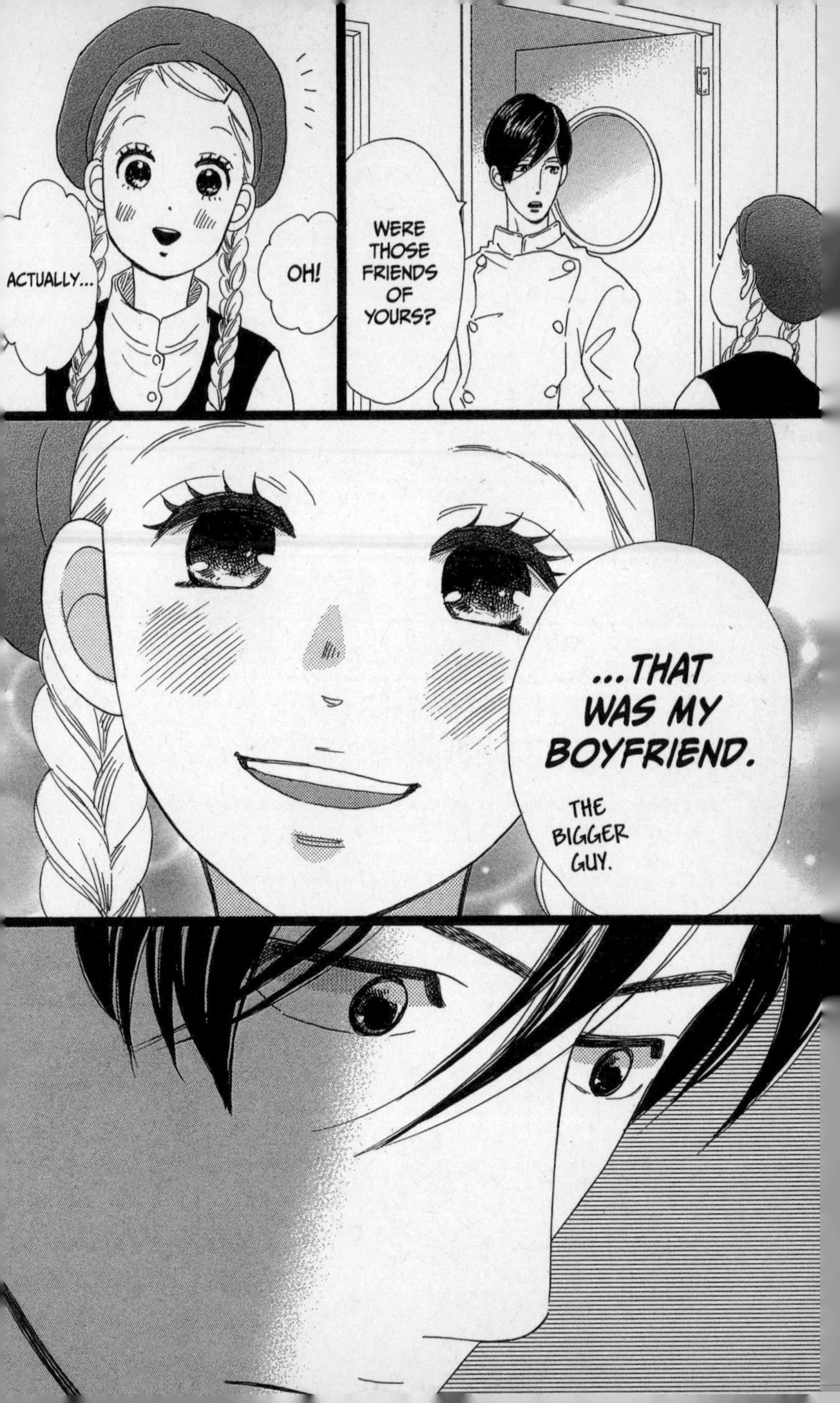
WERE THOSE FRIENDS OF YOURS?
OH!
ACTUALLY...
...THAT WAS MY BOYFRIEND.
THE BIGGER GUY.

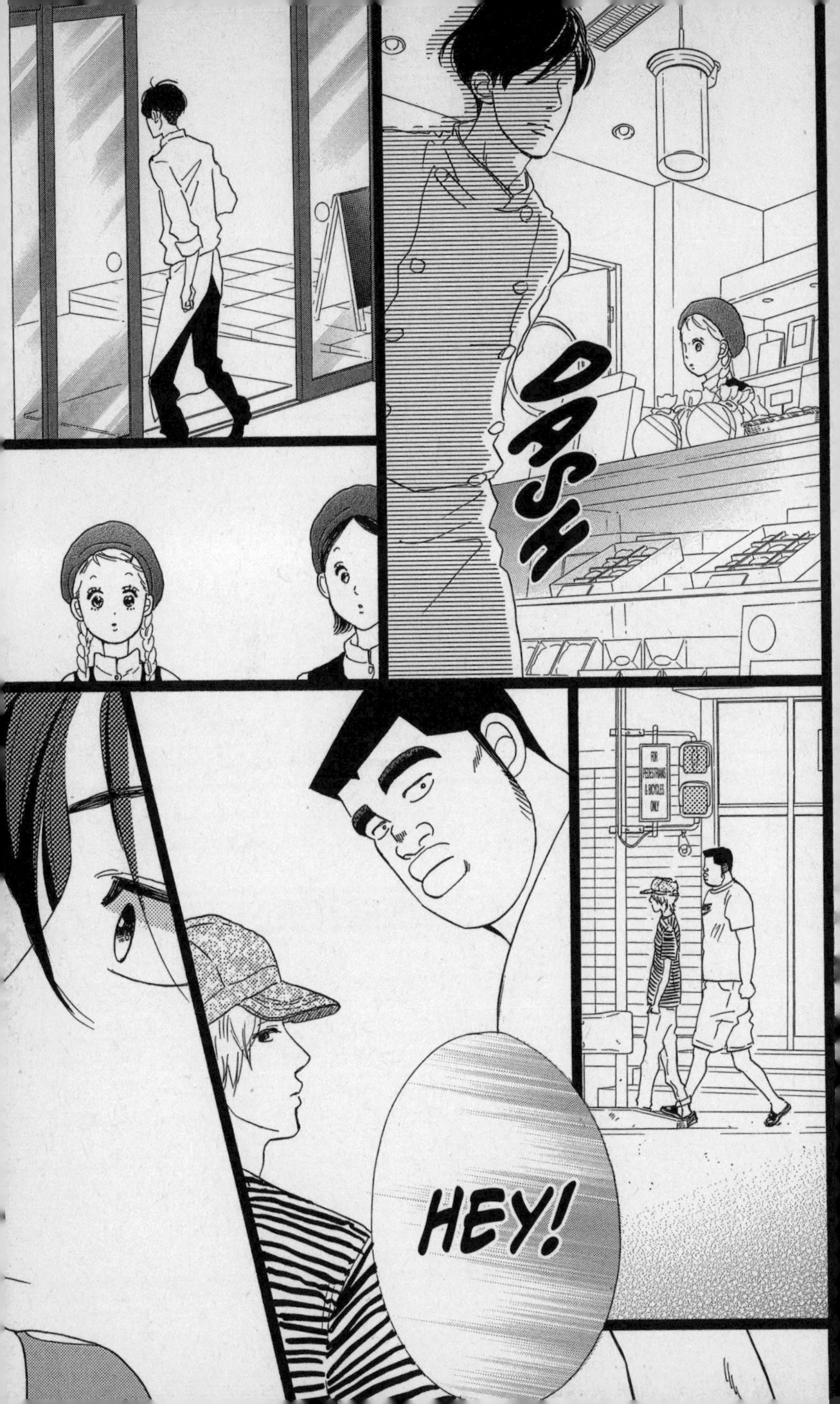
DASH
FOR PEDESTRIANS & BICYCLES ONLY
HEY!

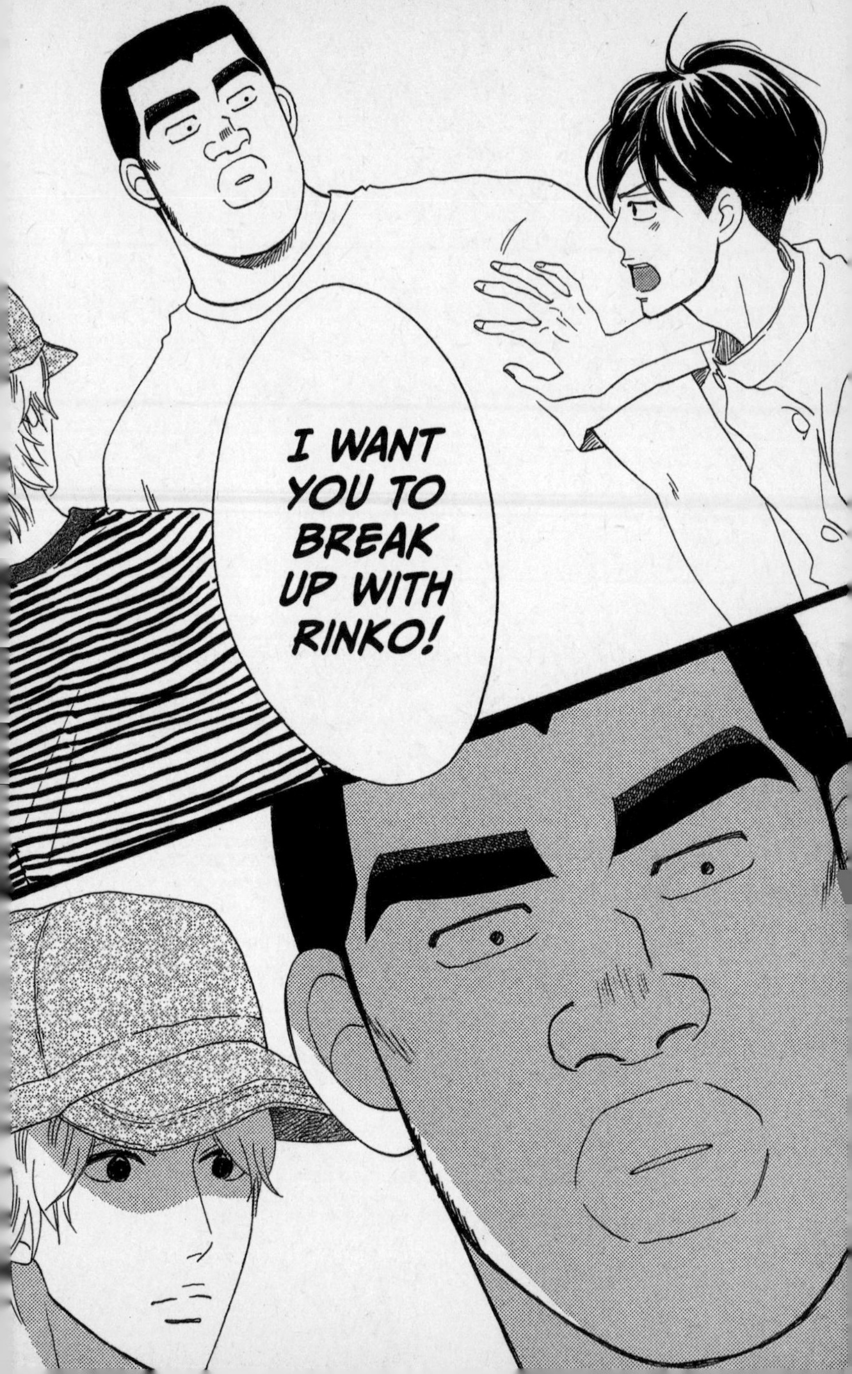
I WANT YOU TO BREAK UP WITH RINKO!

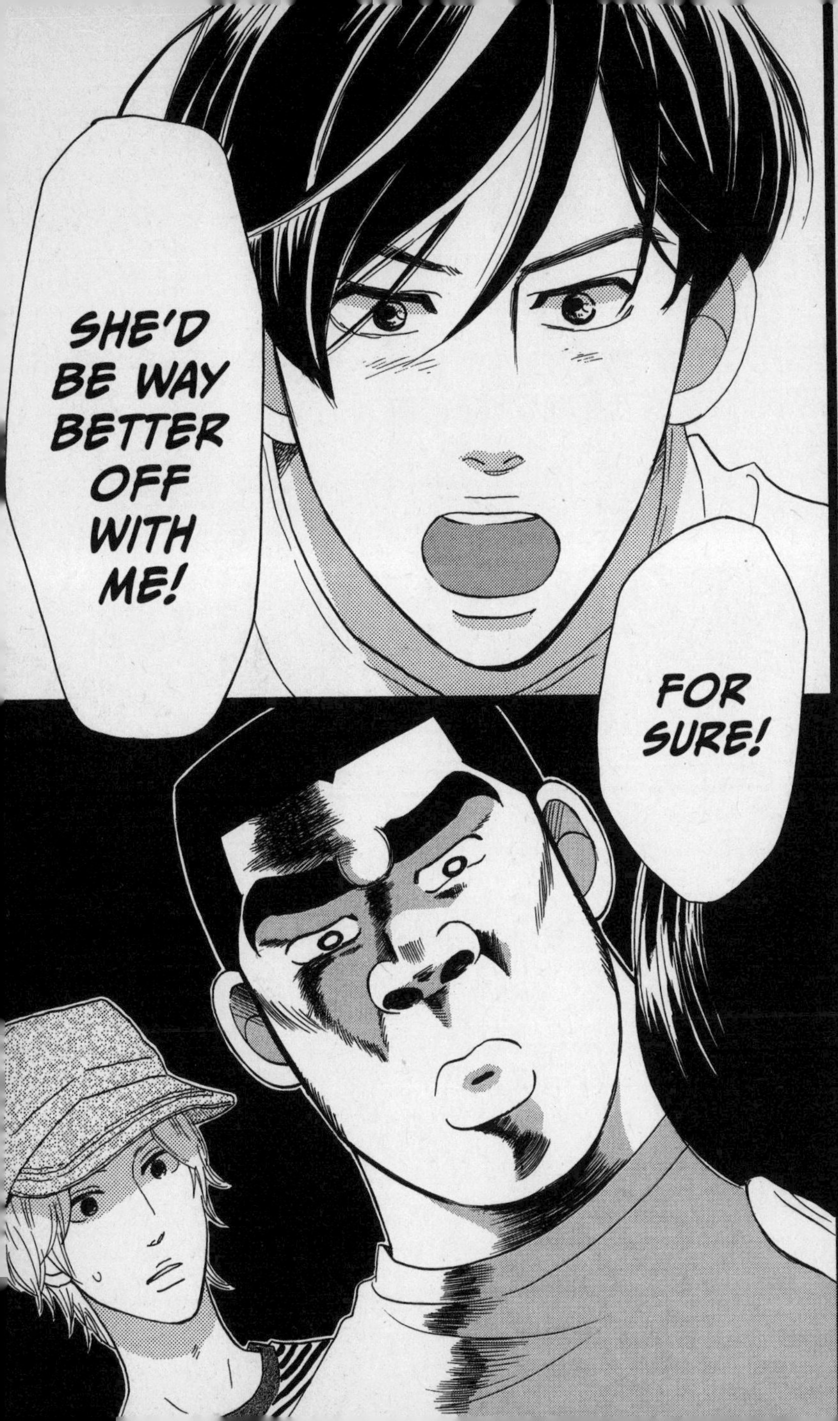
SHE'D BE WAY BETTER OFF WITH ME!
FOR SURE!

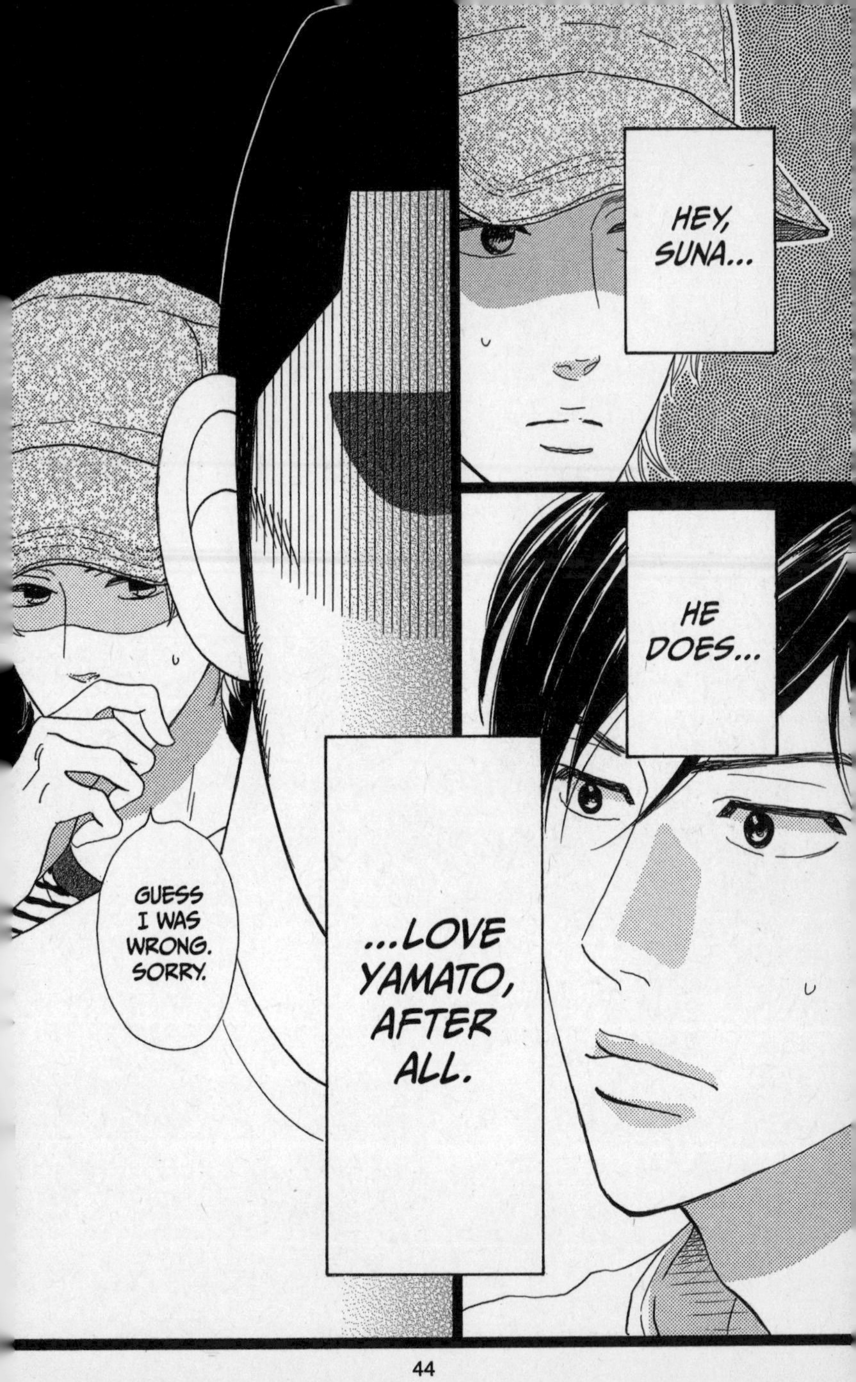
HEY, SUNA...
HE DOES...
...LOVE YAMATO, AFTER ALL.
GUESS I WAS WRONG. SORRY.

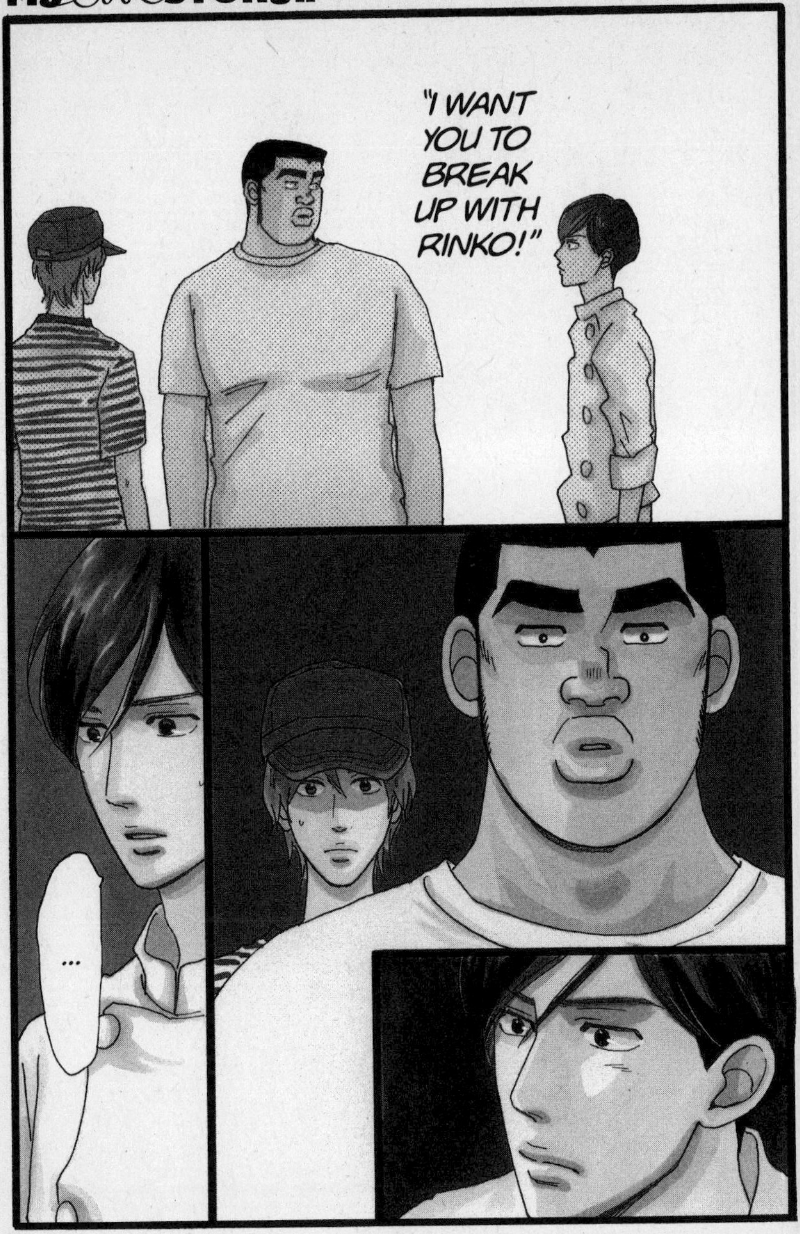
"I WANT YOU TO BREAK UP WITH RINKO!"
...

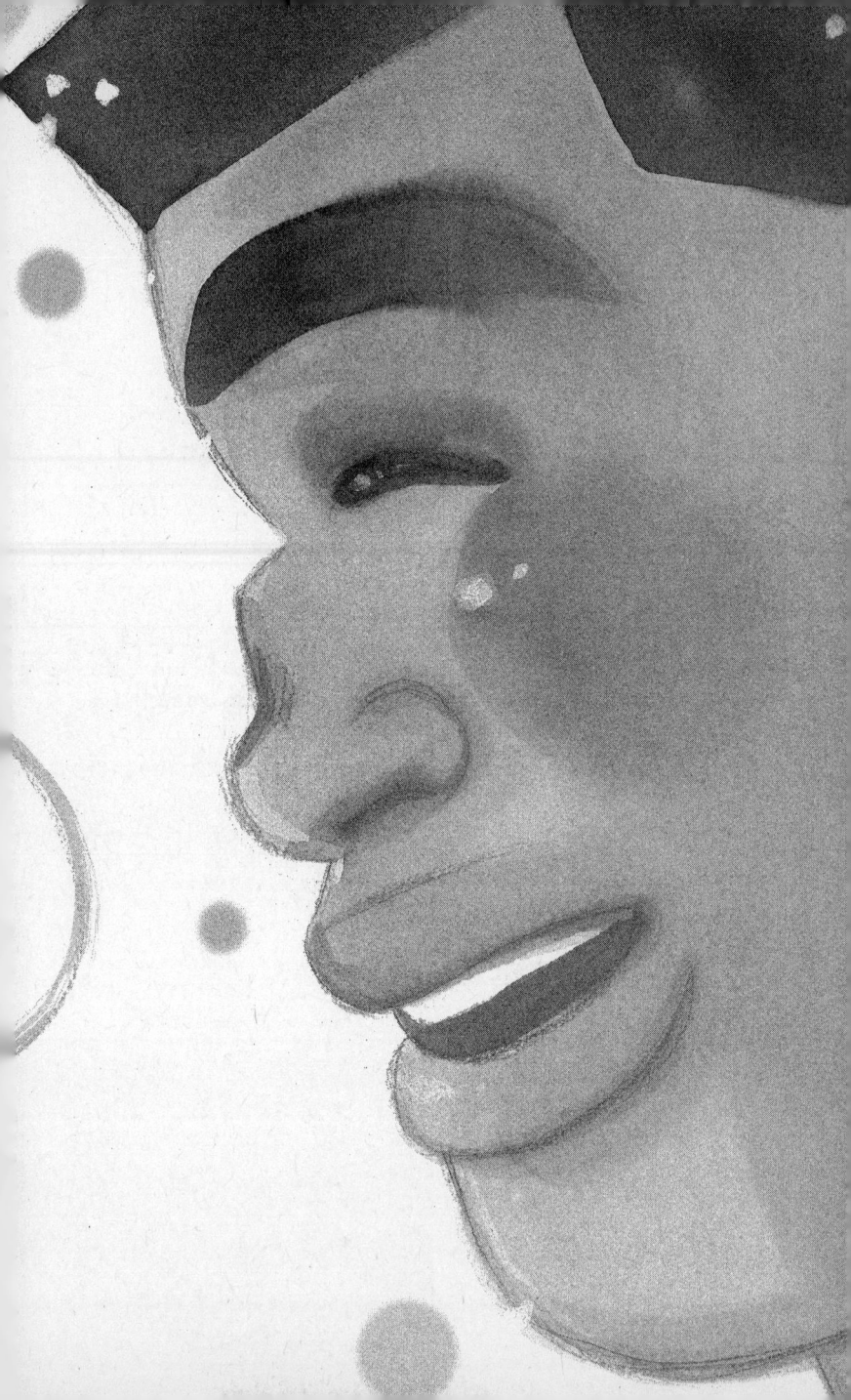

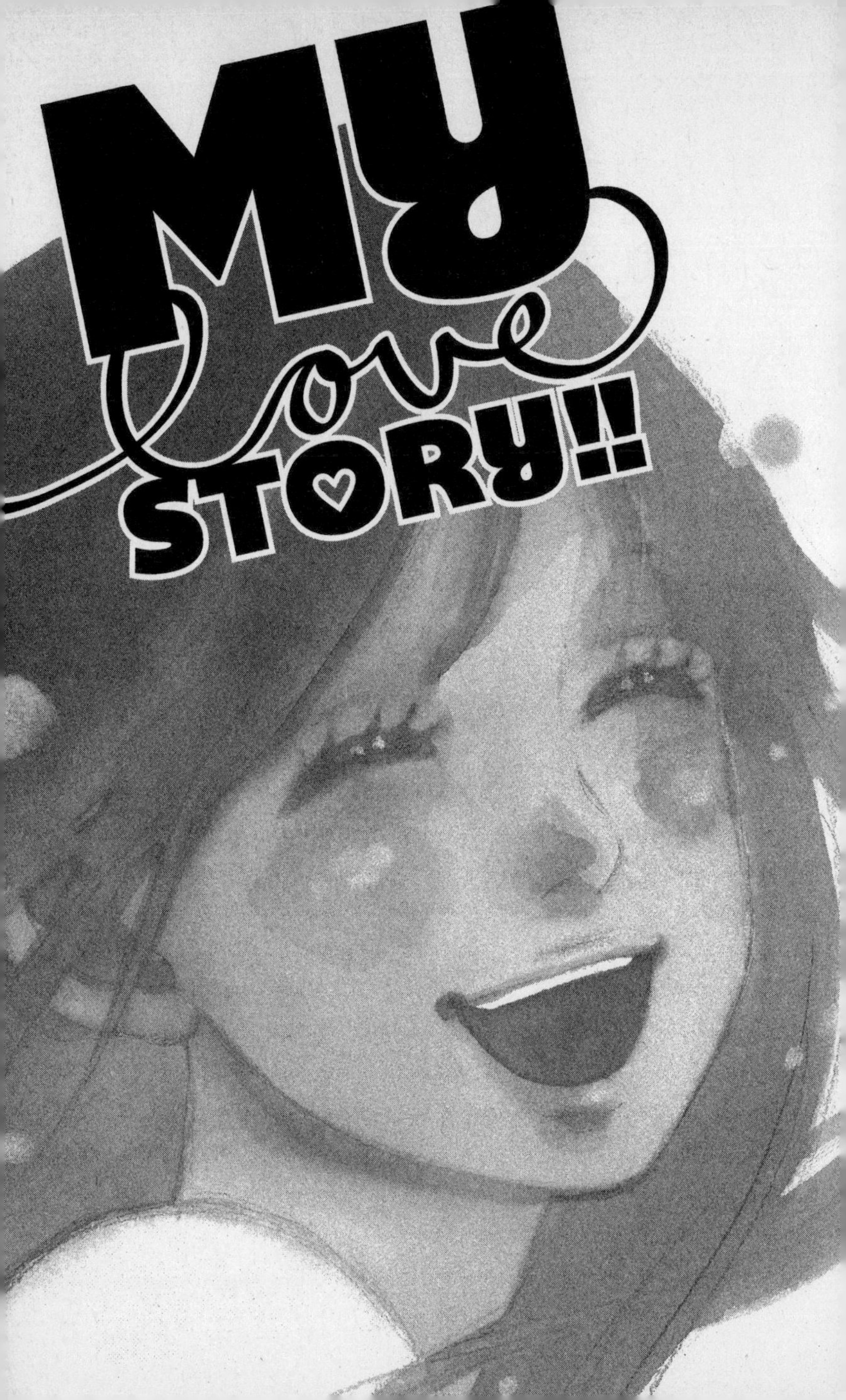
MY Love STORY!!

# IT'S VOLUME 9!!

## THANK YOU SO MUCH!!

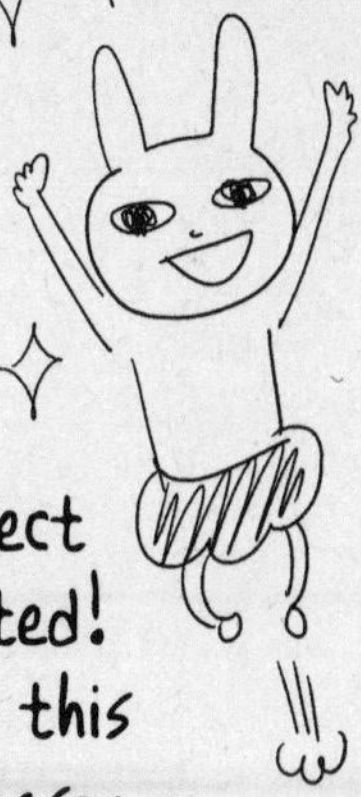

I never know what to write in these spaces. I always get the perfect idea after the book has been printed! But this time, I'm thrilled because this series is getting a movie! It's a reason to celebrate! I celebrated when it got an anime too. That's a lot of celebration for *My Love Story!!* The second I was told who'd be in the movie, I sent Kawahara Sensei (←she was really busy at the time) an excited text message and gushed at her. I felt bad for bothering her, but she was glad to hear about it, so we got to be excited together. It's a time to be excited and happy! I'm really looking forward to the movie, and I hope tons of people enjoy it. That's my biggest dream for it. Please keep following the anime and the manga. The anime's great, isn't it?! Well, see you again in volume 10!

May 2015
Aruko

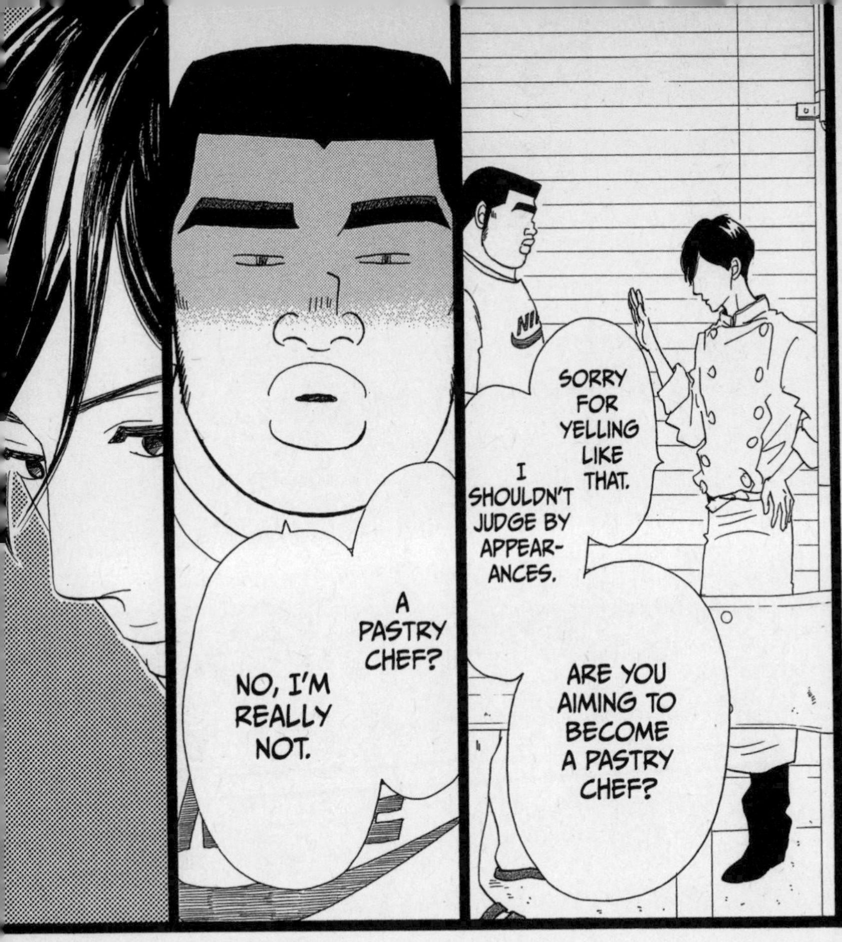
SORRY FOR YELLING LIKE THAT.
I SHOULDN'T JUDGE BY APPEAR-ANCES.
ARE YOU AIMING TO BECOME A PASTRY CHEF?
A PASTRY CHEF?
NO, I'M REALLY NOT.

MY love STORY!!

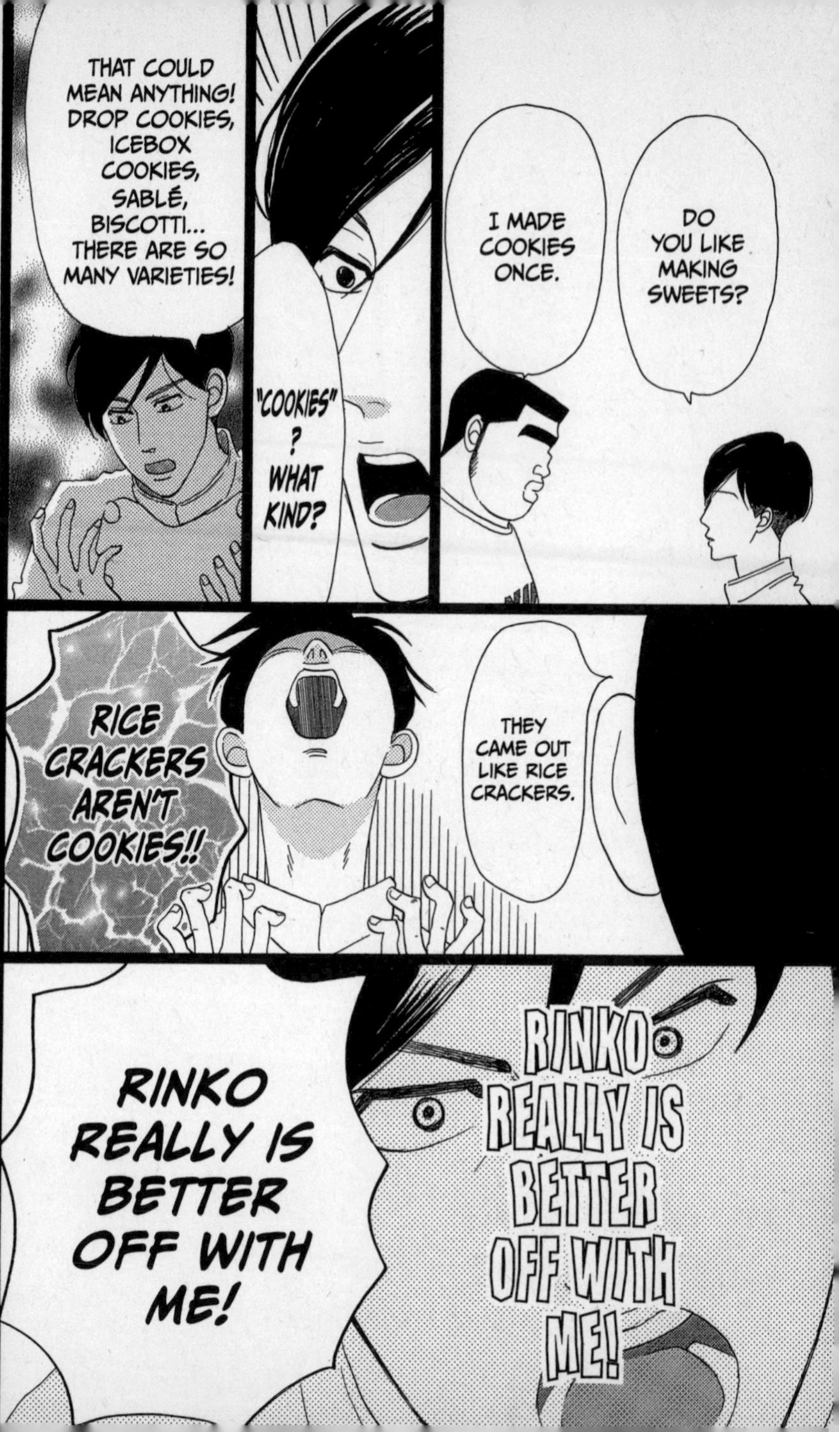
DO YOU LIKE MAKING SWEETS?
I MADE COOKIES ONCE.
"COOKIES"? WHAT KIND?
THAT COULD MEAN ANYTHING! DROP COOKIES, ICEBOX COOKIES, SABLÉ, BISCOTTI... THERE ARE SO MANY VARIETIES!
THEY CAME OUT LIKE RICE CRACKERS.
RICE CRACKERS AREN'T COOKIES!!
RINKO REALLY IS BETTER OFF WITH ME!
RINKO REALLY IS BETTER OFF WITH ME!

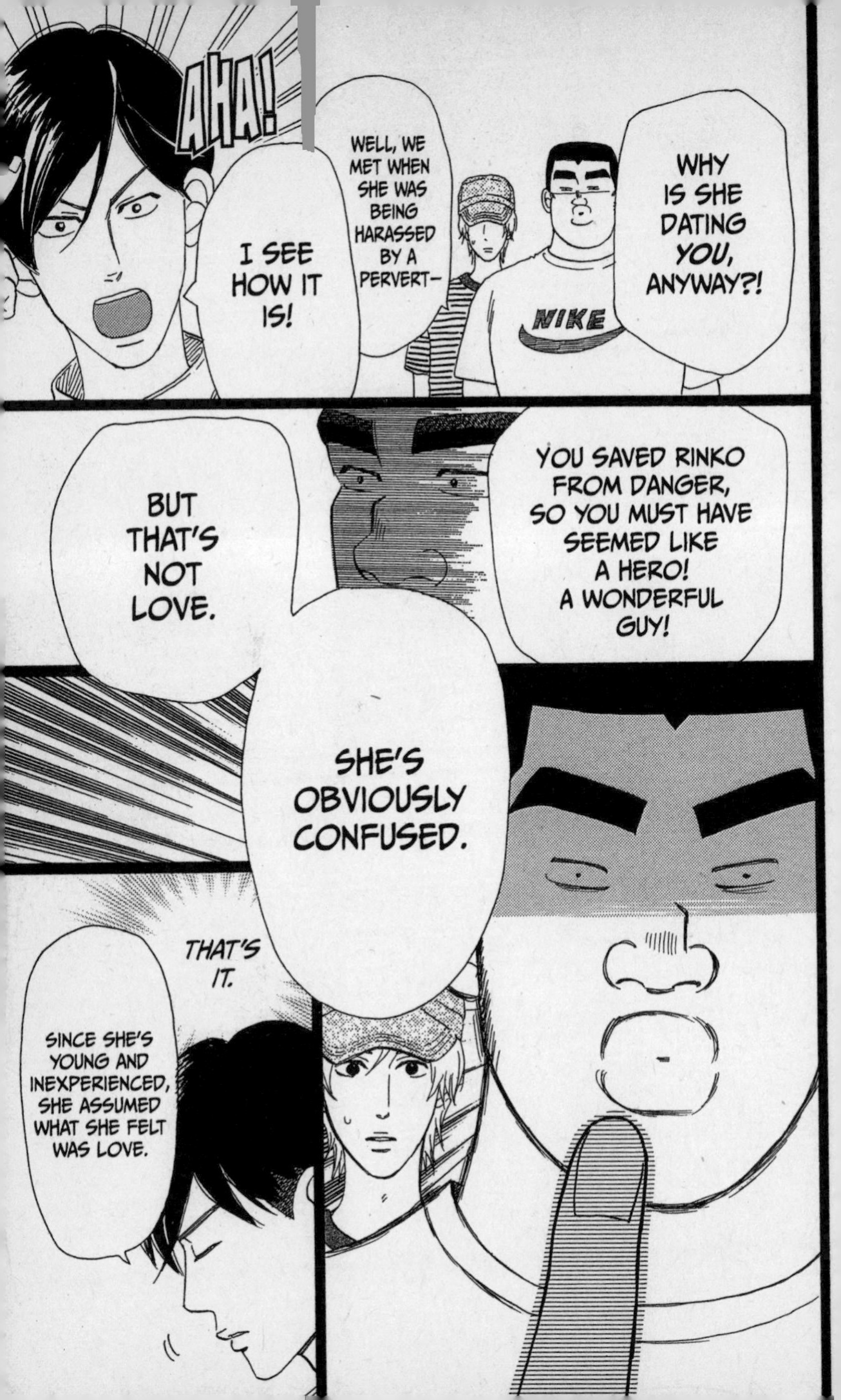
WHY IS SHE DATING *YOU*, ANYWAY?!
WELL, WE MET WHEN SHE WAS BEING HARASSED BY A PERVERT–
AHA!
I SEE HOW IT IS!
YOU SAVED RINKO FROM DANGER, SO YOU MUST HAVE SEEMED LIKE A HERO! A WONDERFUL GUY!
BUT THAT'S NOT LOVE.
SHE'S OBVIOUSLY CONFUSED.
THAT'S IT.
SINCE SHE'S YOUNG AND INEXPERIENCED, SHE ASSUMED WHAT SHE FELT WAS LOVE.

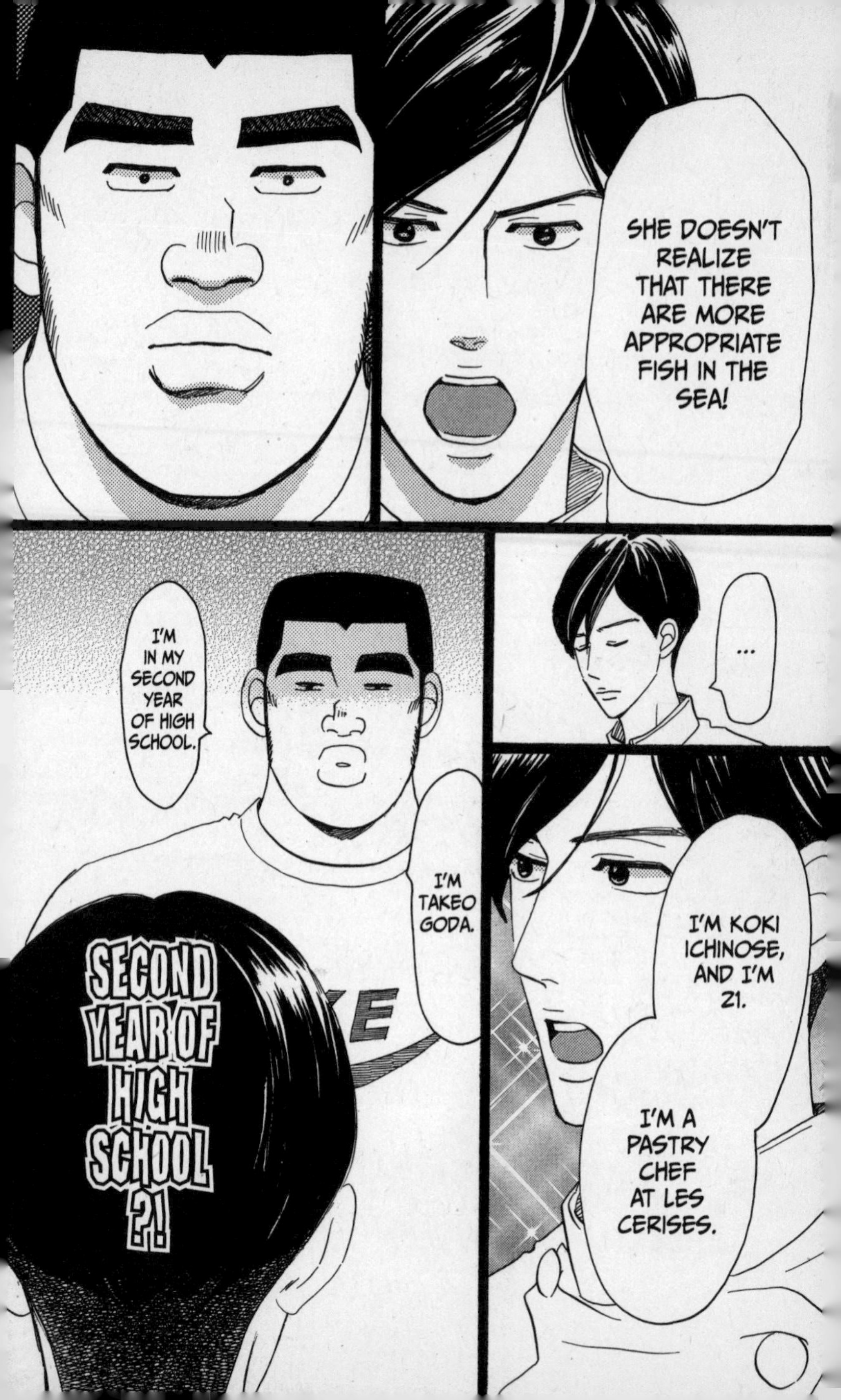
SHE DOESN'T REALIZE THAT THERE ARE MORE APPROPRIATE FISH IN THE SEA!
...
I'M KOKI ICHINOSE, AND I'M 21.
I'M A PASTRY CHEF AT LES CERISES.
I'M TAKEO GODA.
I'M IN MY SECOND YEAR OF HIGH SCHOOL.
SECOND YEAR OF HIGH SCHOOL?!

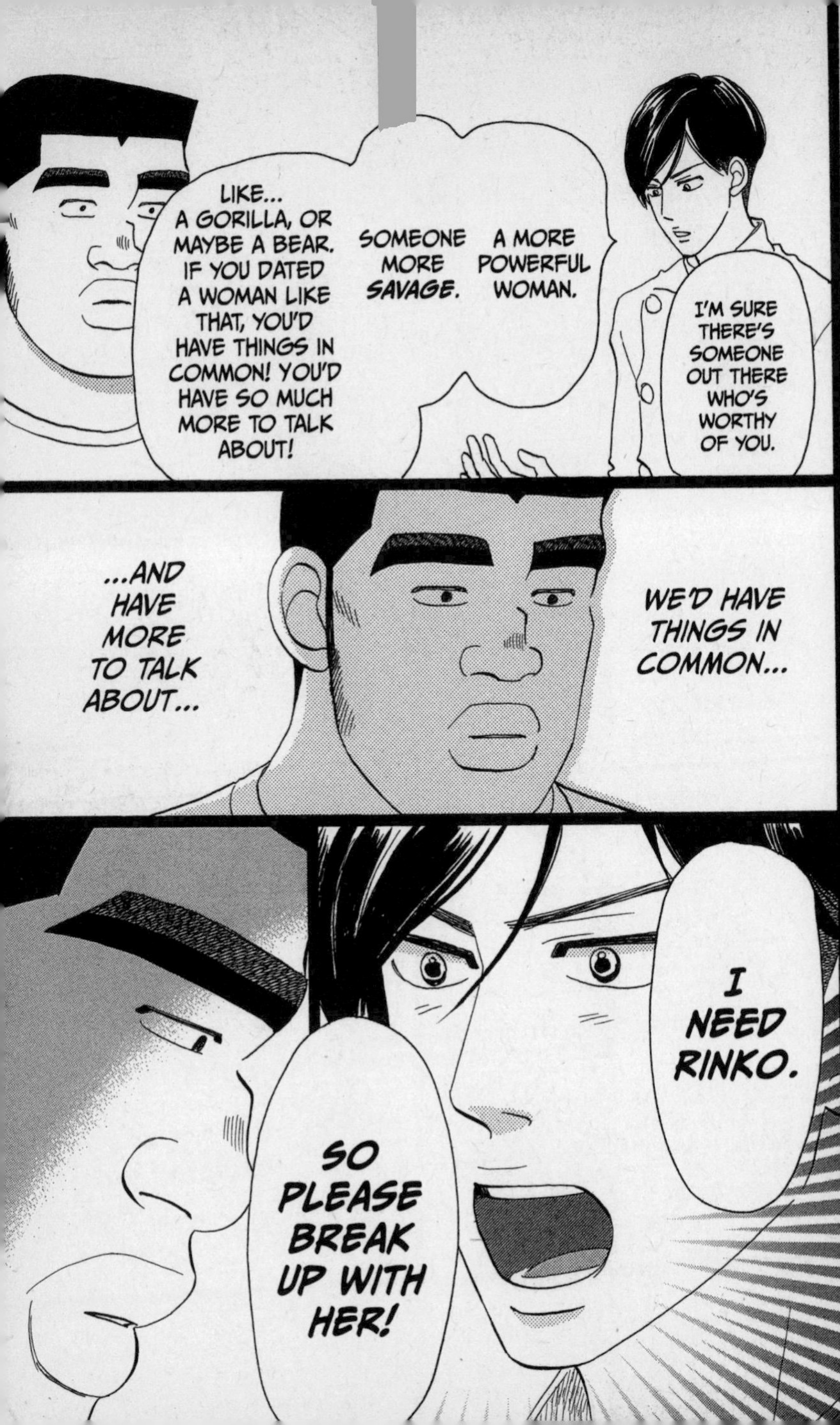
I'M SURE THERE'S SOMEONE OUT THERE WHO'S WORTHY OF YOU.
A MORE POWERFUL WOMAN.
SOMEONE MORE SAVAGE.
LIKE... A GORILLA, OR MAYBE A BEAR. IF YOU DATED A WOMAN LIKE THAT, YOU'D HAVE THINGS IN COMMON! YOU'D HAVE SO MUCH MORE TO TALK ABOUT!
WE'D HAVE THINGS IN COMMON...
...AND HAVE MORE TO TALK ABOUT...
I NEED RINKO.
SO PLEASE BREAK UP WITH HER!

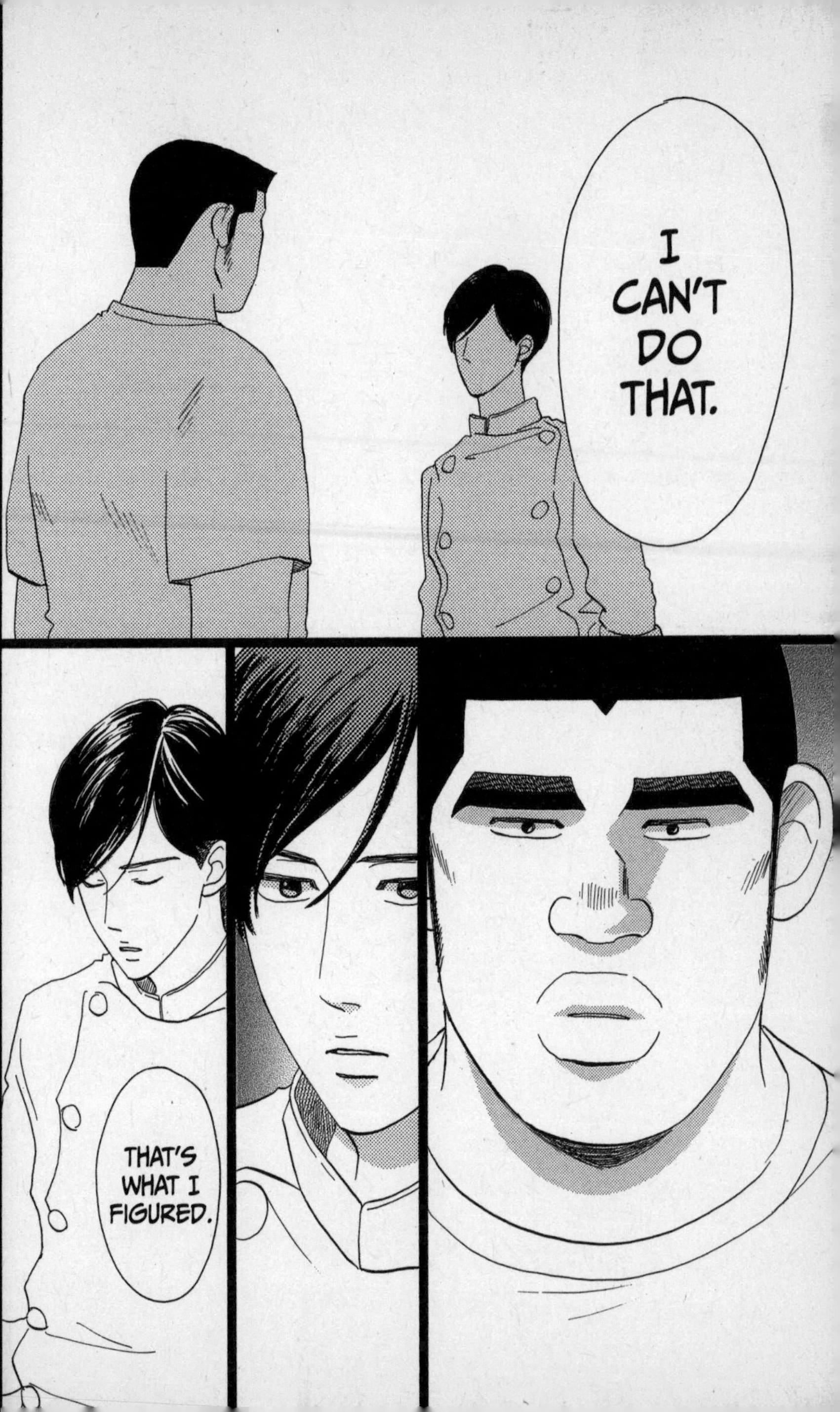
I CAN'T DO THAT.
THAT'S WHAT I FIGURED.

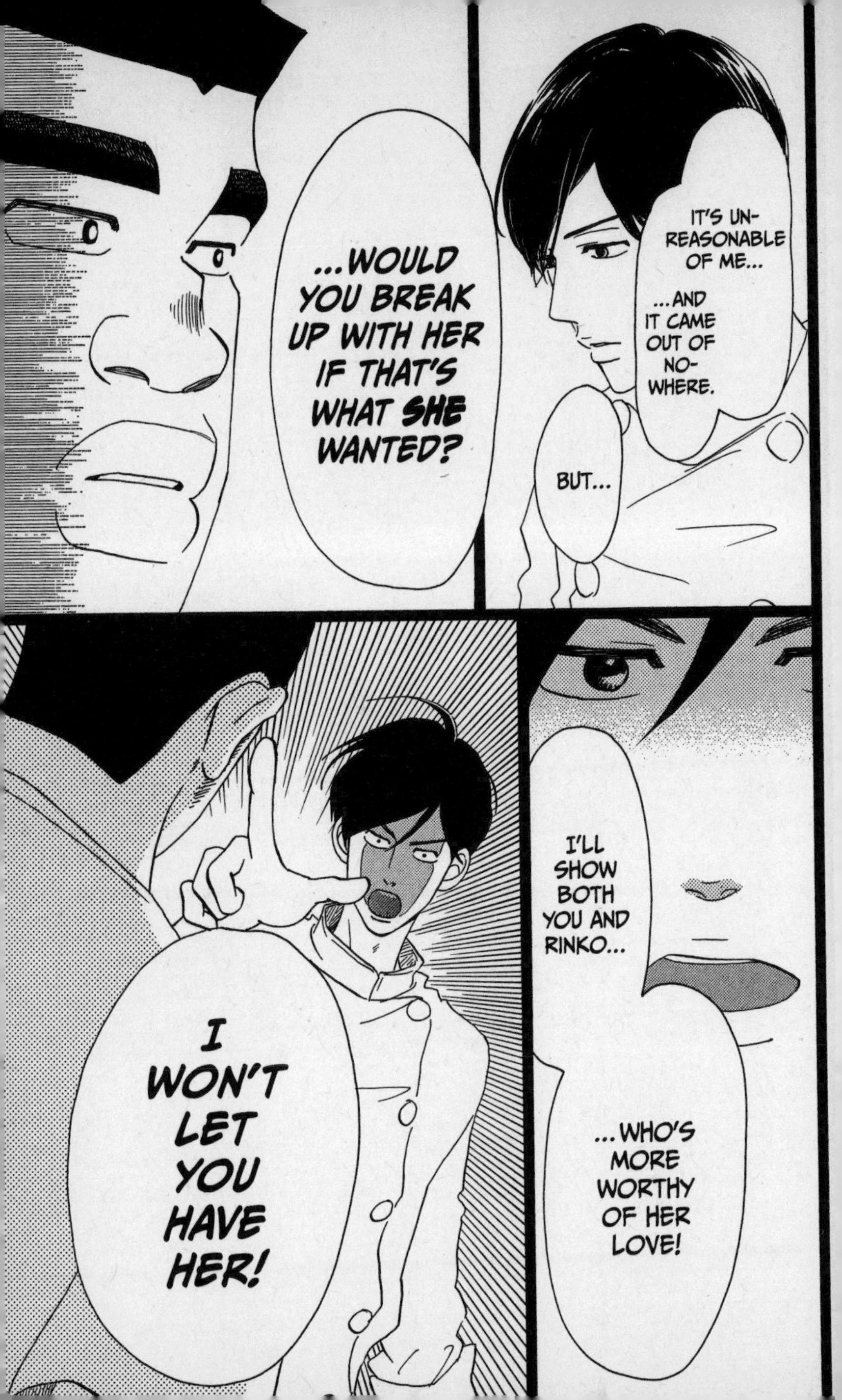
IT'S UN-REASONABLE OF ME... ...AND IT CAME OUT OF NO-WHERE.
BUT...
...WOULD YOU BREAK UP WITH HER IF THAT'S WHAT SHE WANTED?
I'LL SHOW BOTH YOU AND RINKO...
...WHO'S MORE WORTHY OF HER LOVE!
I WON'T LET YOU HAVE HER!

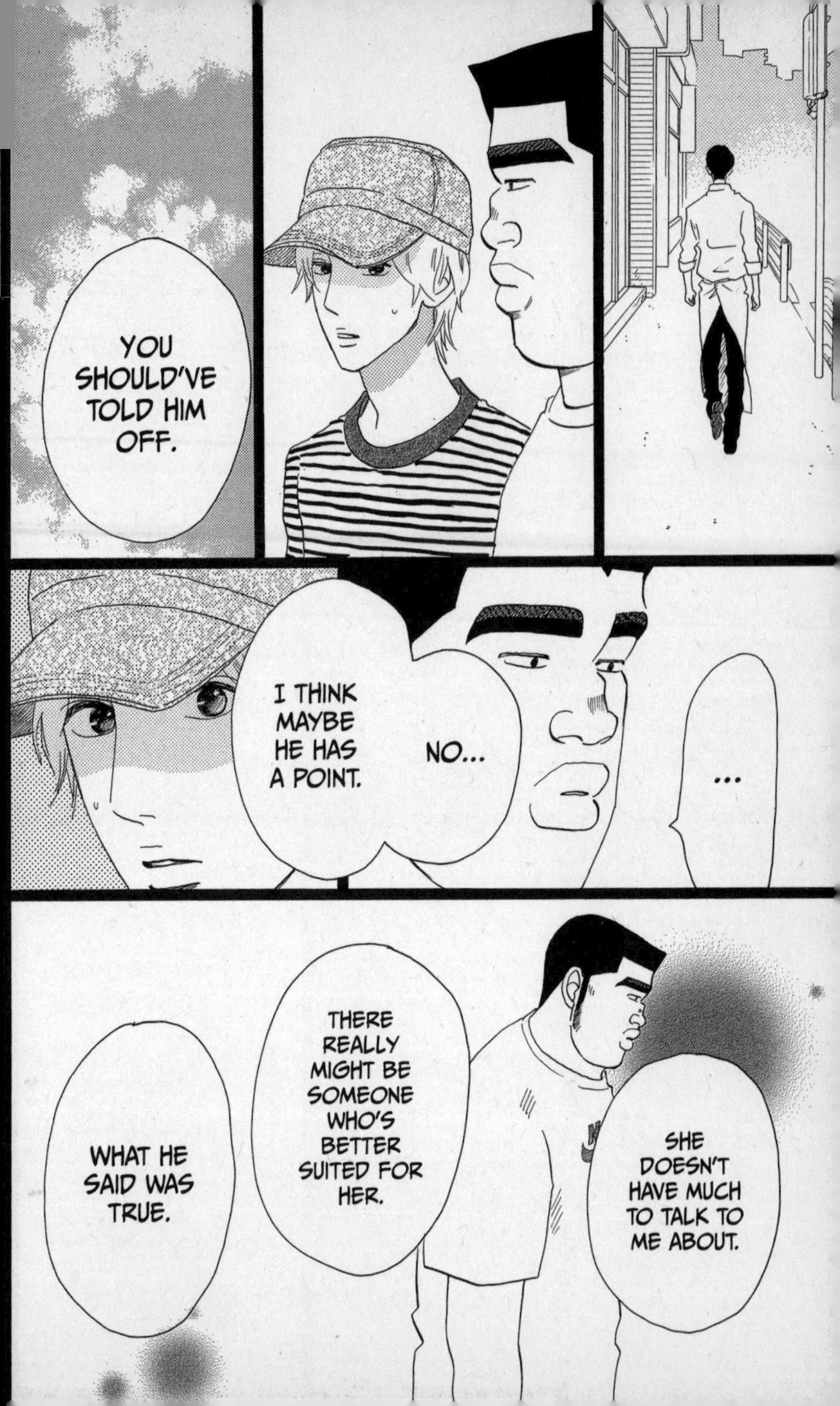
YOU SHOULD'VE TOLD HIM OFF.
...
NO...
I THINK MAYBE HE HAS A POINT.
SHE DOESN'T HAVE MUCH TO TALK TO ME ABOUT.
THERE REALLY MIGHT BE SOMEONE WHO'S BETTER SUITED FOR HER.
WHAT HE SAID WAS TRUE.

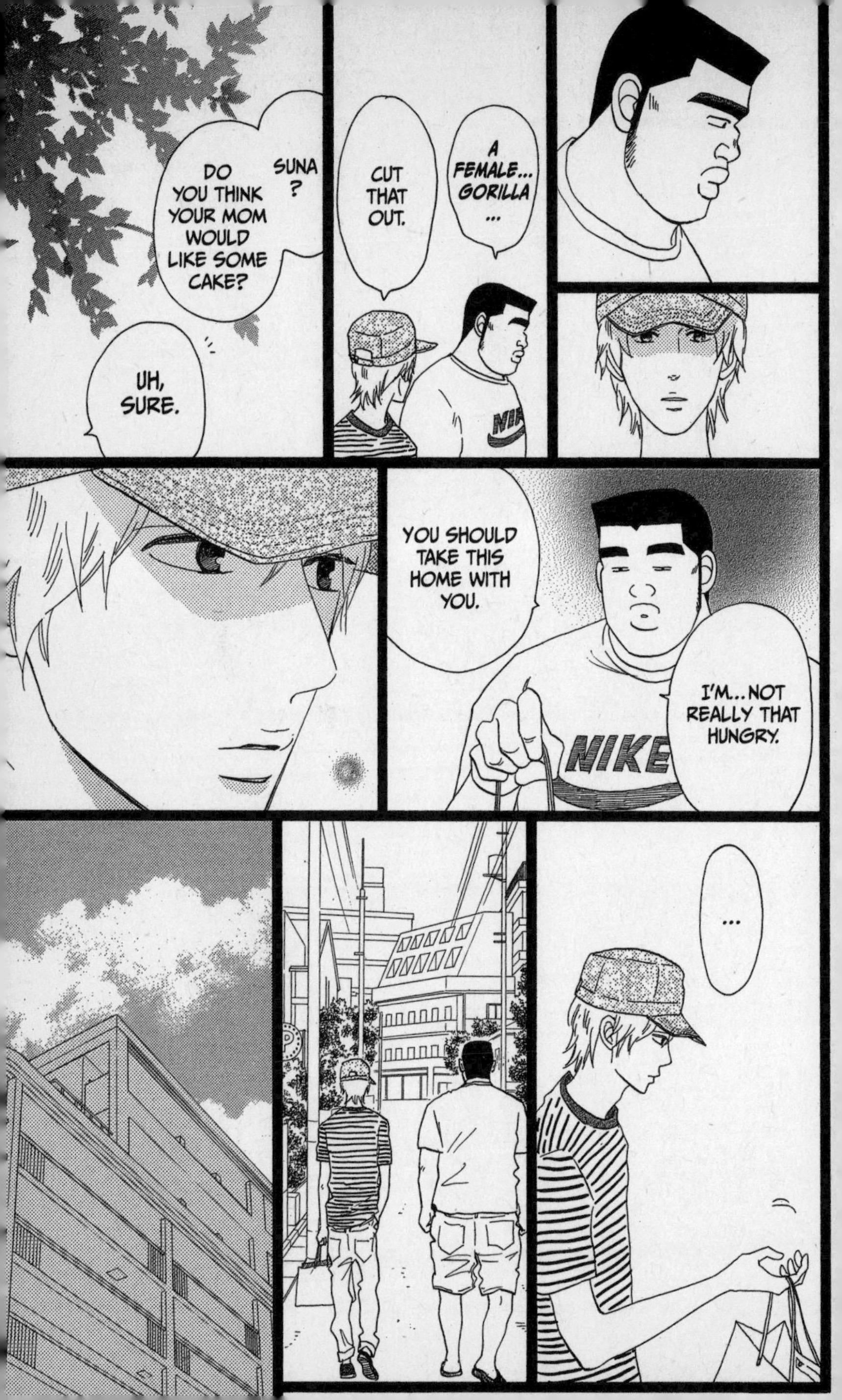
A FEMALE... GORILLA ...
CUT THAT OUT.
SUNA ?
DO YOU THINK YOUR MOM WOULD LIKE SOME CAKE?
UH, SURE.
I'M...NOT REALLY THAT HUNGRY.
YOU SHOULD TAKE THIS HOME WITH YOU.
...

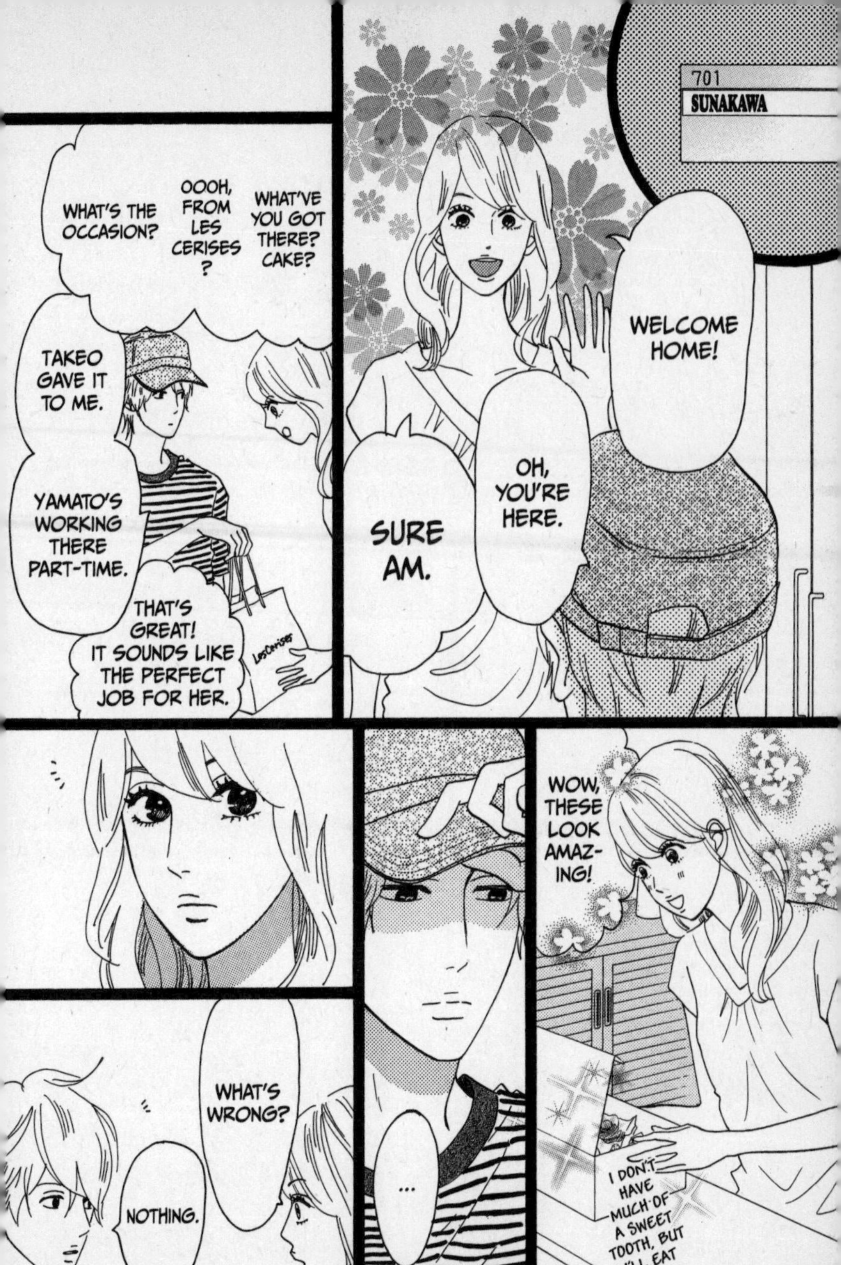
701
SUNAKAWA
WELCOME HOME!
OH, YOU'RE HERE.
SURE AM.
WHAT'VE YOU GOT THERE? CAKE?
OOOH, FROM LES CERISES?
WHAT'S THE OCCASION?
TAKEO GAVE IT TO ME.
YAMATO'S WORKING THERE PART-TIME.
THAT'S GREAT! IT SOUNDS LIKE THE PERFECT JOB FOR HER.
LesCerises
WOW, THESE LOOK AMAZ-ING!
I DON'T HAVE MUCH OF A SWEET TOOTH, BUT I'LL EAT ONE.
...
WHAT'S WRONG?
NOTHING.

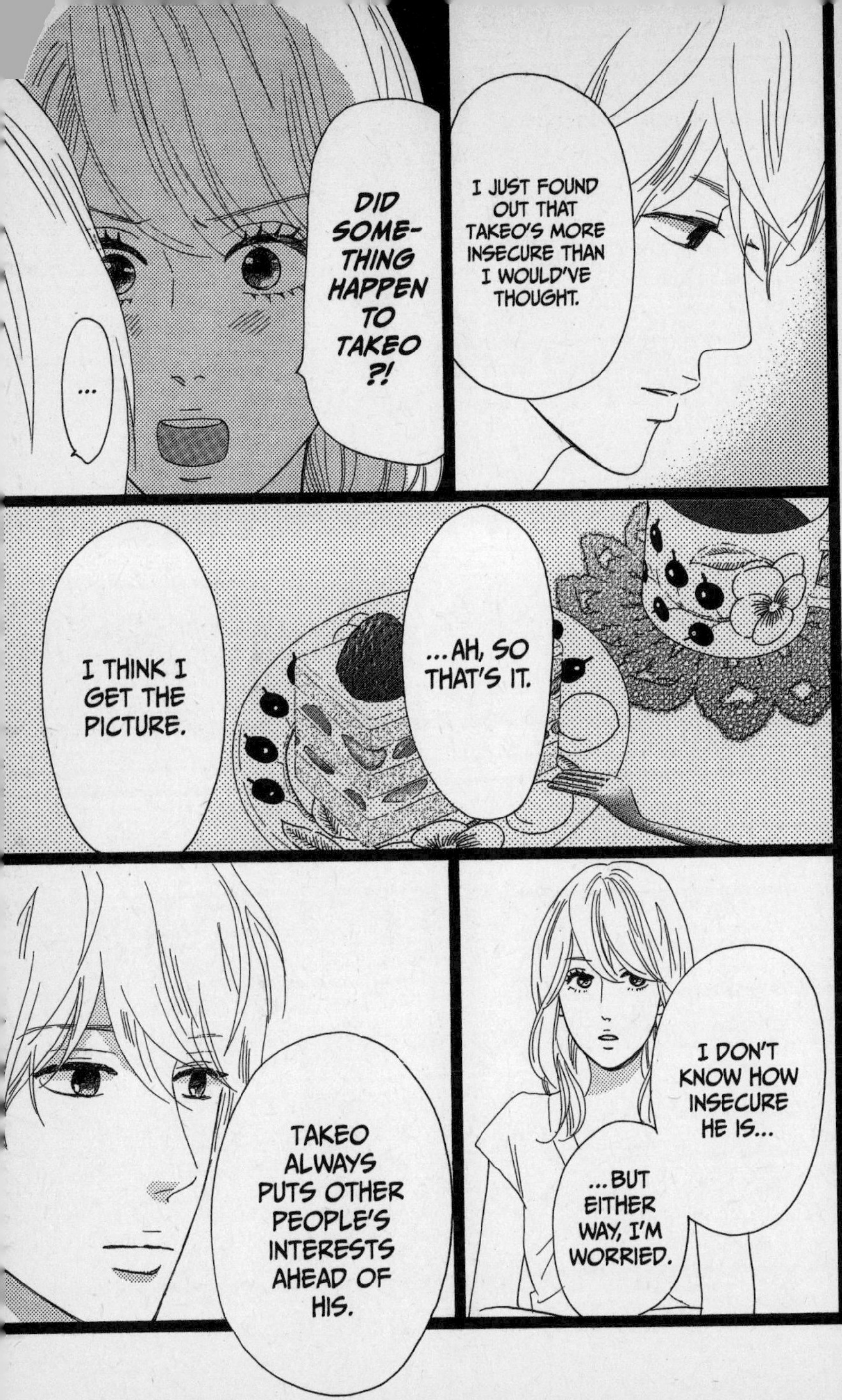
I JUST FOUND OUT THAT TAKEO'S MORE INSECURE THAN I WOULD'VE THOUGHT.
DID SOMETHING HAPPEN TO TAKEO?!
...
...AH, SO THAT'S IT.
I THINK I GET THE PICTURE.
I DON'T KNOW HOW INSECURE HE IS...
...BUT EITHER WAY, I'M WORRIED.
TAKEO ALWAYS PUTS OTHER PEOPLE'S INTERESTS AHEAD OF HIS.

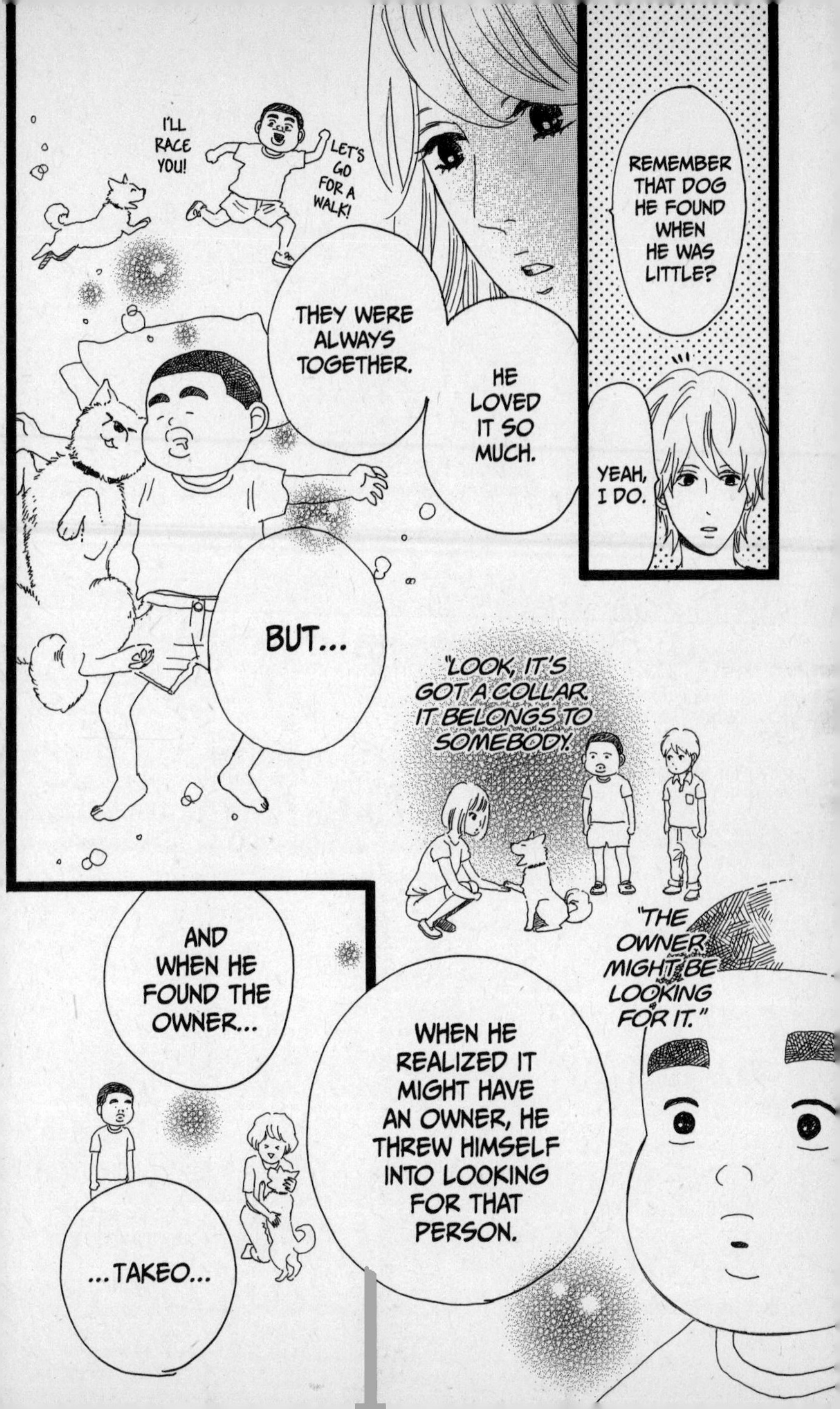
REMEMBER THAT DOG HE FOUND WHEN HE WAS LITTLE?
YEAH, I DO.
LET'S GO FOR A WALK!
I'LL RACE YOU!
THEY WERE ALWAYS TOGETHER.
HE LOVED IT SO MUCH.
BUT...
"LOOK, IT'S GOT A COLLAR. IT BELONGS TO SOMEBODY.
"THE OWNER MIGHT BE LOOKING FOR IT."
WHEN HE REALIZED IT MIGHT HAVE AN OWNER, HE THREW HIMSELF INTO LOOKING FOR THAT PERSON.
AND WHEN HE FOUND THE OWNER...
...TAKEO...

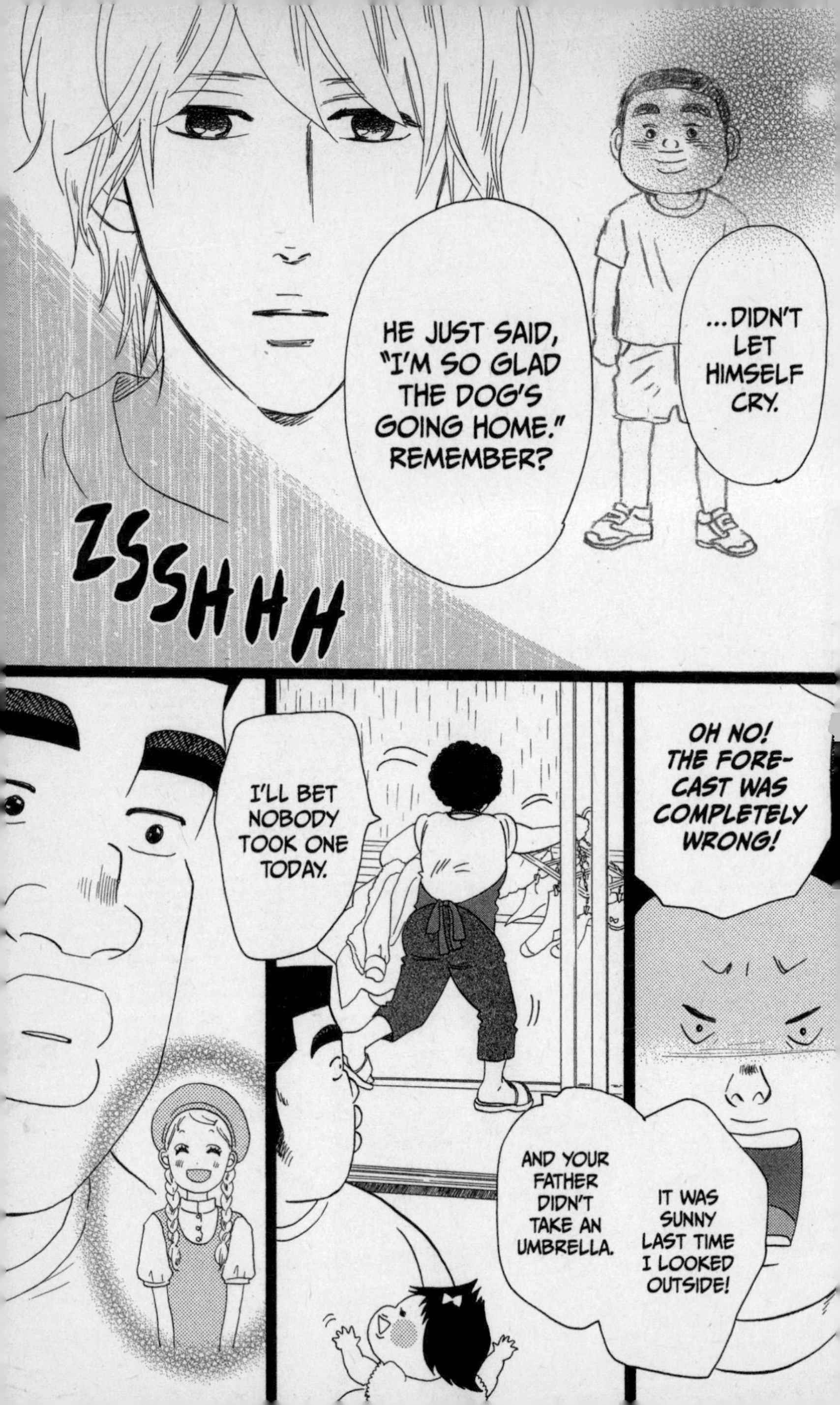
...DIDN'T LET HIMSELF CRY.
HE JUST SAID, "I'M SO GLAD THE DOG'S GOING HOME." REMEMBER?
ZSSHHH
OH NO! THE FORE-CAST WAS COMPLETELY WRONG!
IT WAS SUNNY LAST TIME I LOOKED OUTSIDE!
AND YOUR FATHER DIDN'T TAKE AN UMBRELLA.
I'LL BET NOBODY TOOK ONE TODAY.

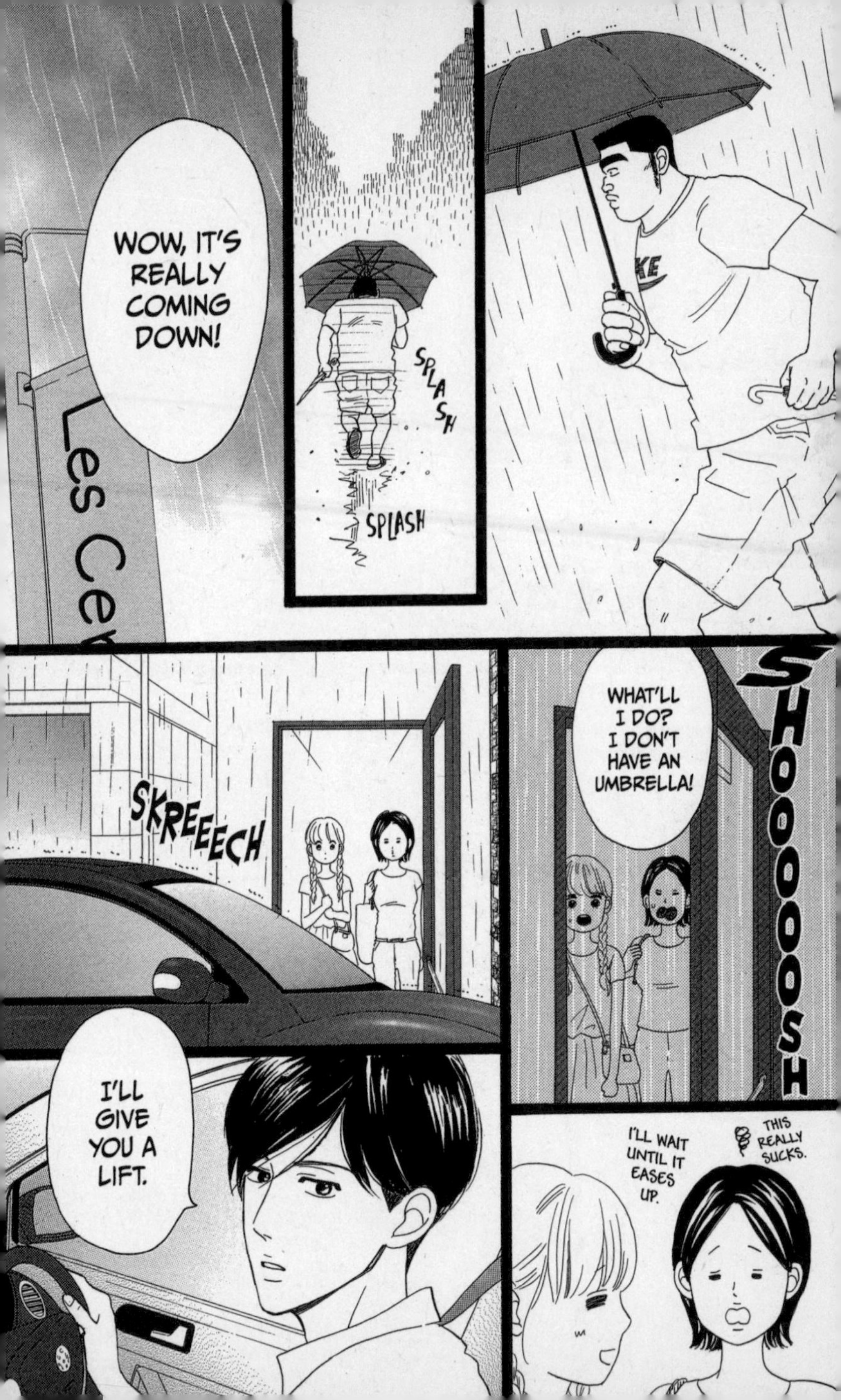
SPLASH
SPLASH
WOW, IT'S REALLY COMING DOWN!
SHOOOOOOSH
WHAT'LL I DO? I DON'T HAVE AN UMBRELLA!
I'LL WAIT UNTIL IT EASES UP.
THIS REALLY SUCKS.
SKREEECH
I'LL GIVE YOU A LIFT.

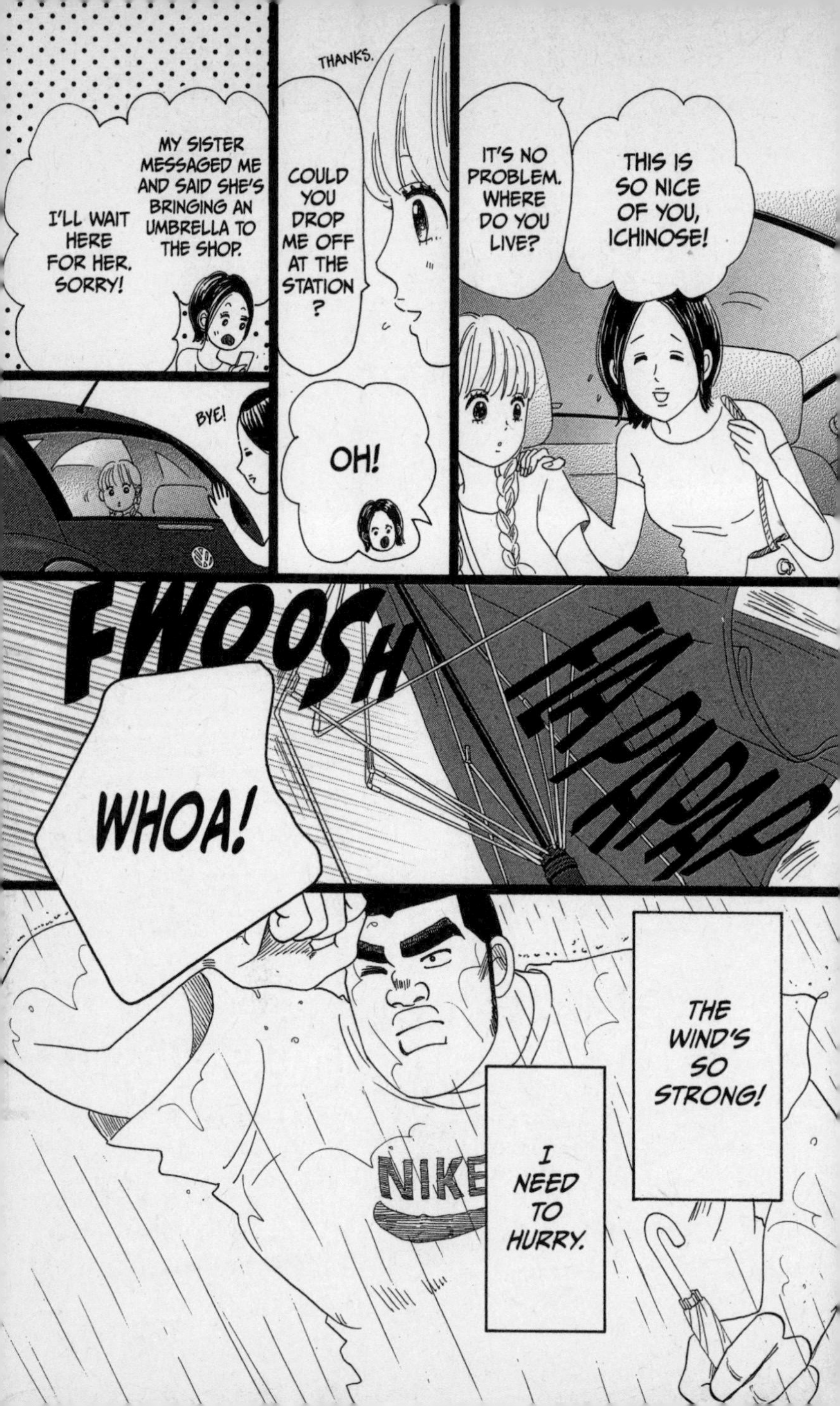
THIS IS SO NICE OF YOU, ICHINOSE!
IT'S NO PROBLEM. WHERE DO YOU LIVE?
THANKS.
COULD YOU DROP ME OFF AT THE STATION?
OH!
MY SISTER MESSAGED ME AND SAID SHE'S BRINGING AN UMBRELLA TO THE SHOP.
I'LL WAIT HERE FOR HER. SORRY!
BYE!
FAPAPP
FWOOSH
WHOA!
THE WIND'S SO STRONG!
I NEED TO HURRY.
NIKE

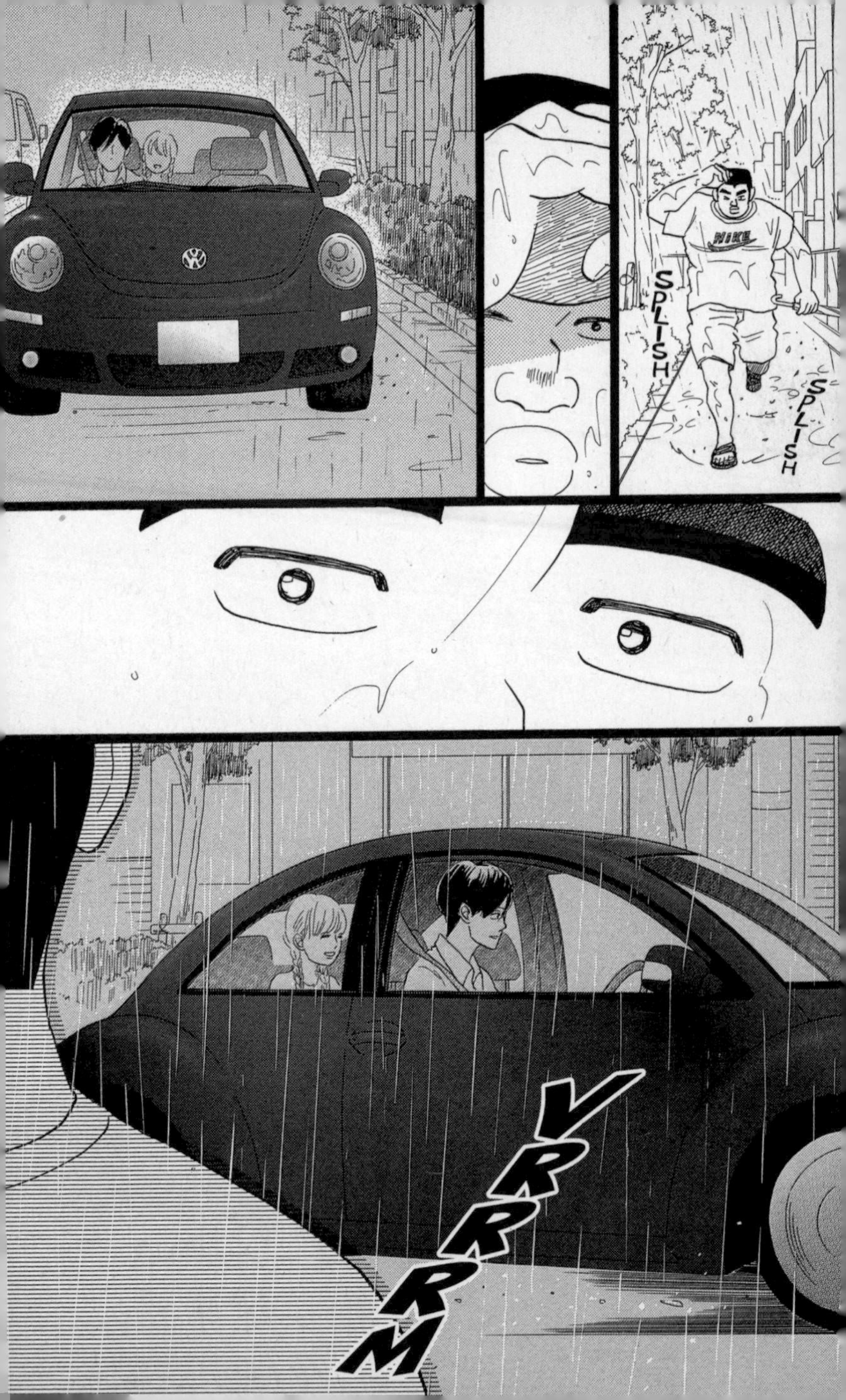
NIKE
SPLISH
SPLISH
VRRRM

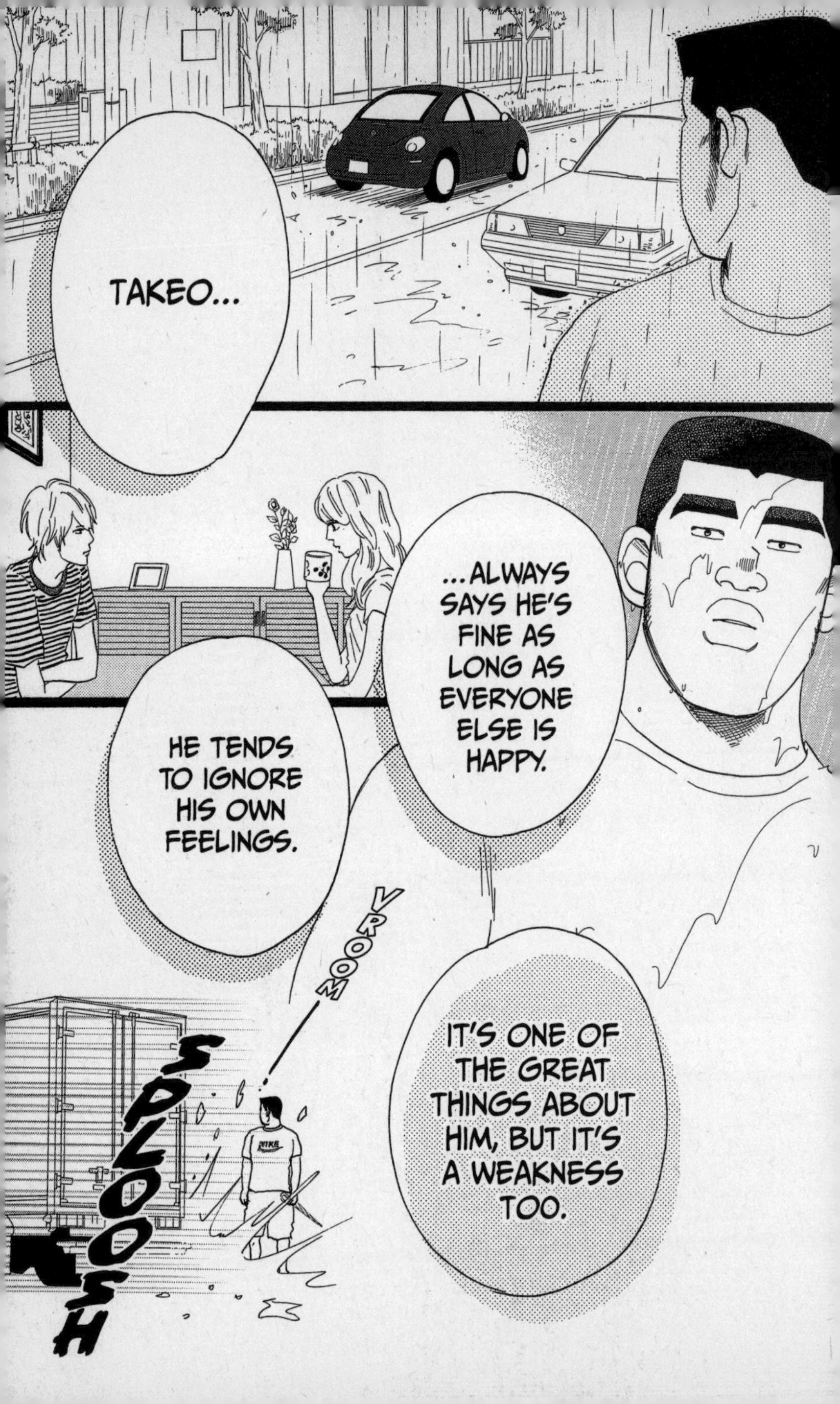
TAKEO...
...ALWAYS SAYS HE'S FINE AS LONG AS EVERYONE ELSE IS HAPPY.
HE TENDS TO IGNORE HIS OWN FEELINGS.
IT'S ONE OF THE GREAT THINGS ABOUT HIM, BUT IT'S A WEAKNESS TOO.
VROOM
SPLOOSH
NIKE

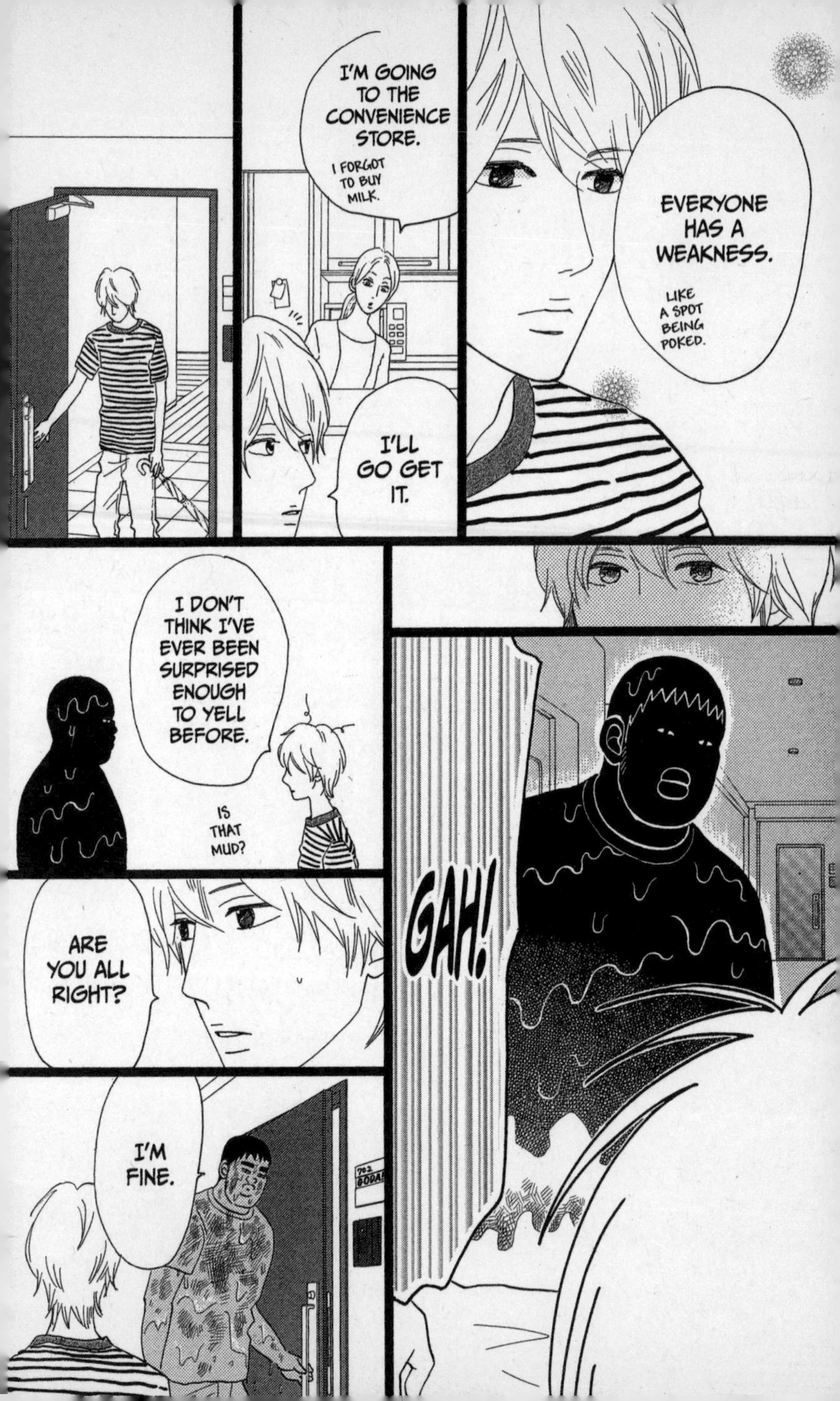
EVERYONE HAS A WEAKNESS.
LIKE A SPOT BEING POKED.
I'M GOING TO THE CONVENIENCE STORE.
I FORGOT TO BUY MILK.
I'LL GO GET IT.
GAH!
I DON'T THINK I'VE EVER BEEN SURPRISED ENOUGH TO YELL BEFORE.
IS THAT MUD?
ARE YOU ALL RIGHT?
I'M FINE.

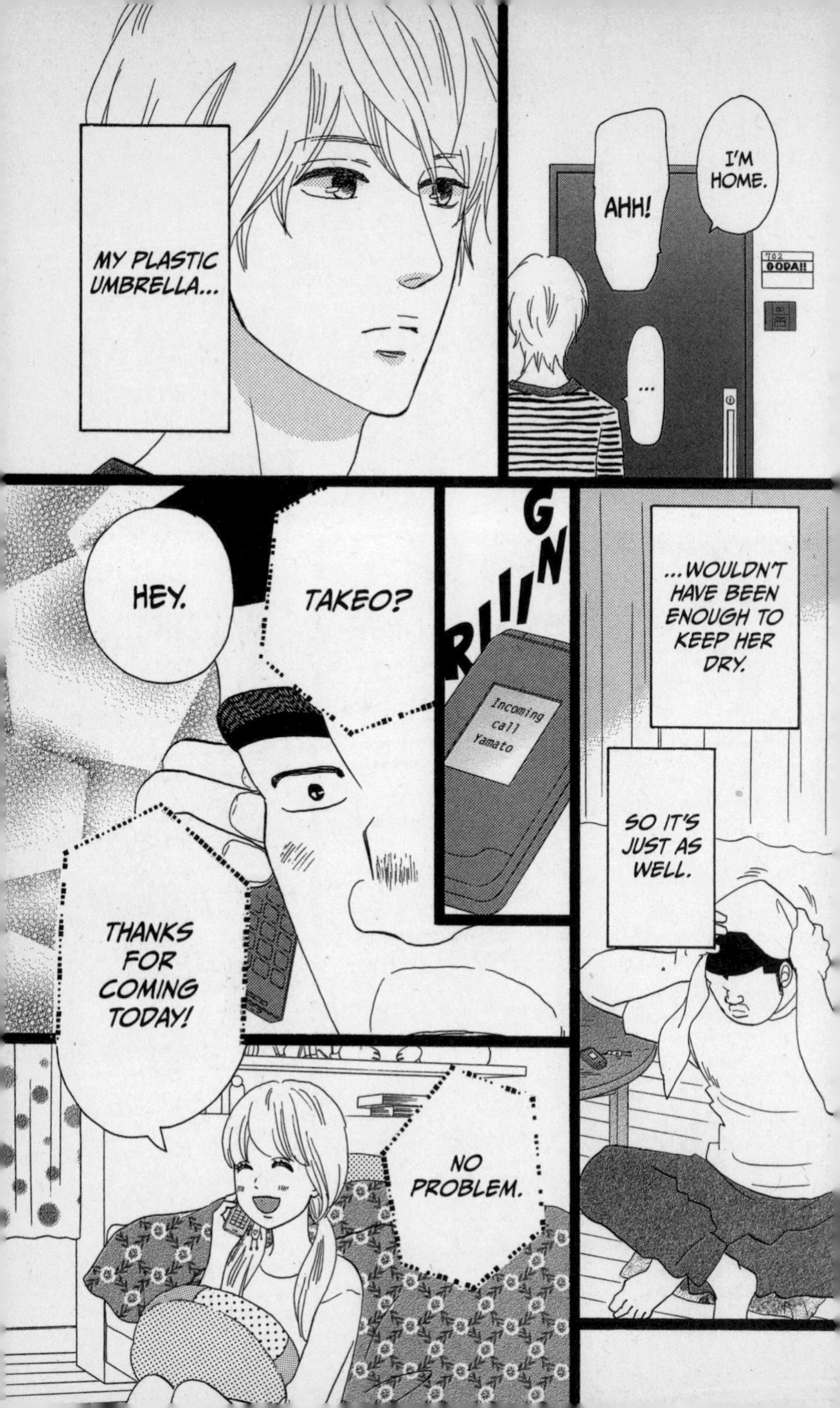
I'M HOME.
AHH!
...
GODA
MY PLASTIC UMBRELLA...
...WOULDN'T HAVE BEEN ENOUGH TO KEEP HER DRY.
SO IT'S JUST AS WELL.
RIIING
Incoming call Yamato
TAKEO?
HEY.
THANKS FOR COMING TODAY!
NO PROBLEM.

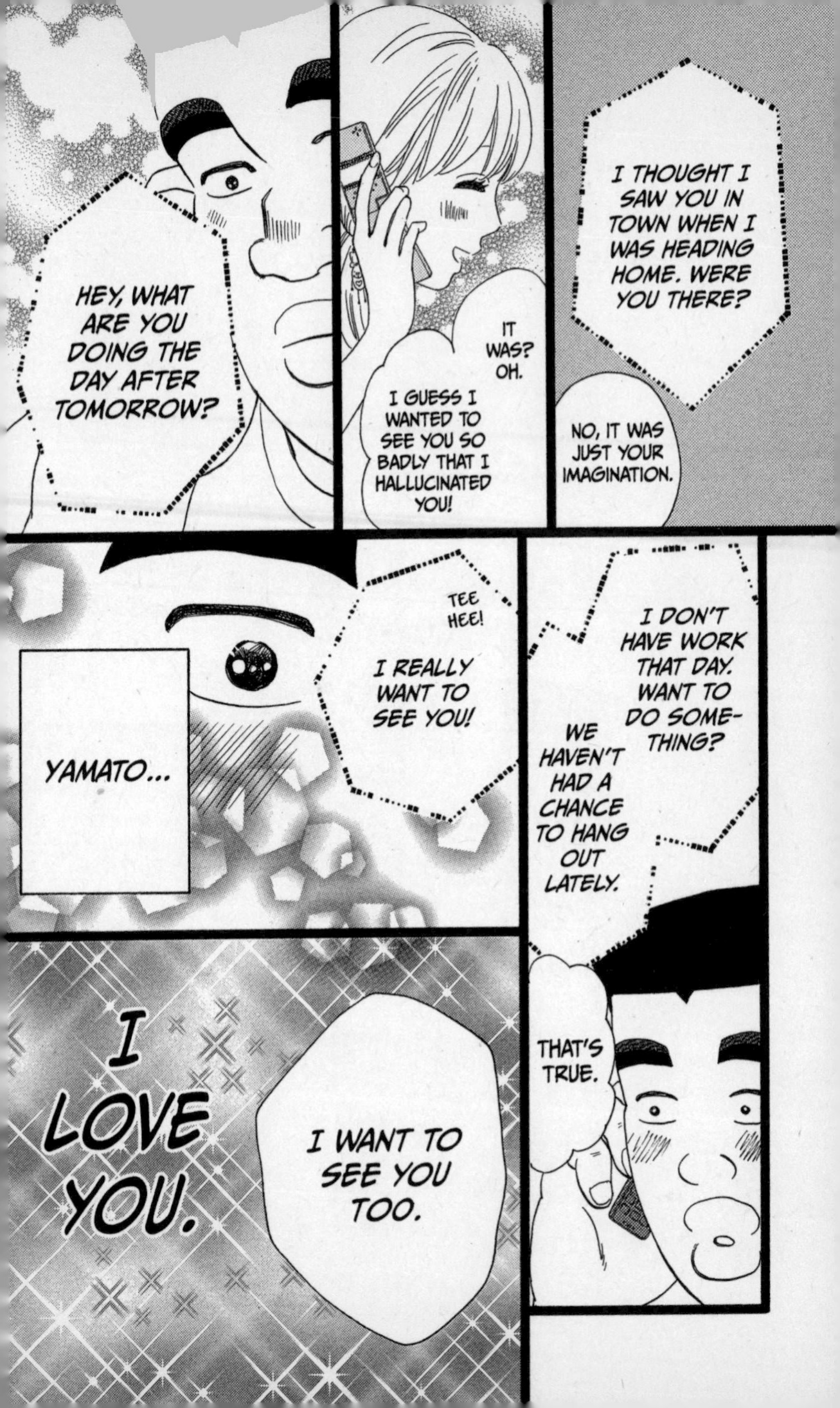
I THOUGHT I SAW YOU IN TOWN WHEN I WAS HEADING HOME. WERE YOU THERE?
NO, IT WAS JUST YOUR IMAGINATION.
IT WAS? OH.
I GUESS I WANTED TO SEE YOU SO BADLY THAT I HALLUCINATED YOU!
HEY, WHAT ARE YOU DOING THE DAY AFTER TOMORROW?
I DON'T HAVE WORK THAT DAY. WANT TO DO SOME-THING?
WE HAVEN'T HAD A CHANCE TO HANG OUT LATELY.
THAT'S TRUE.
TEE HEE!
I REALLY WANT TO SEE YOU!
YAMATO...
I WANT TO SEE YOU TOO.
I LOVE YOU.

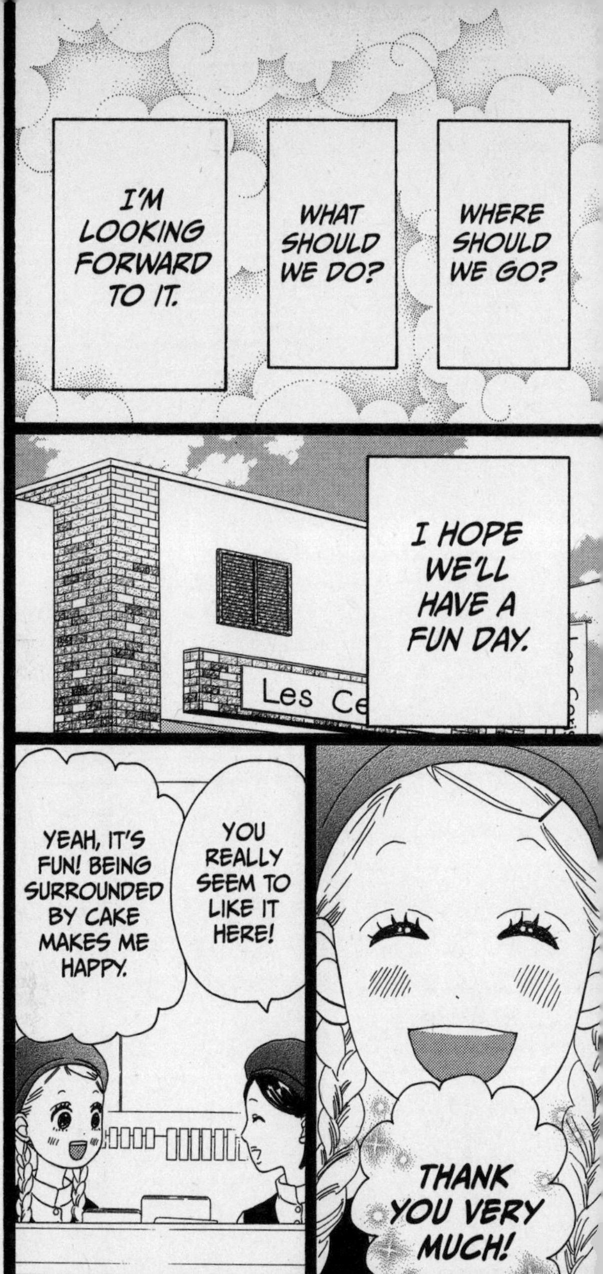
WHERE SHOULD WE GO?
WHAT SHOULD WE DO?
I'M LOOKING FORWARD TO IT.
I HOPE WE'LL HAVE A FUN DAY.
Les Ce
THANK YOU VERY MUCH!
YOU REALLY SEEM TO LIKE IT HERE!
YEAH, IT'S FUN! BEING SURROUNDED BY CAKE MAKES ME HAPPY.

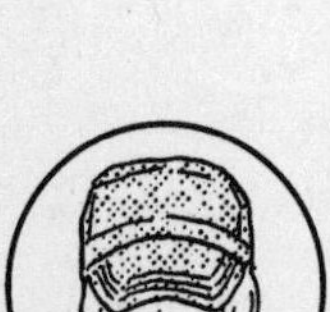

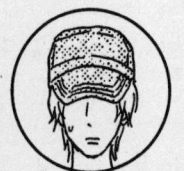

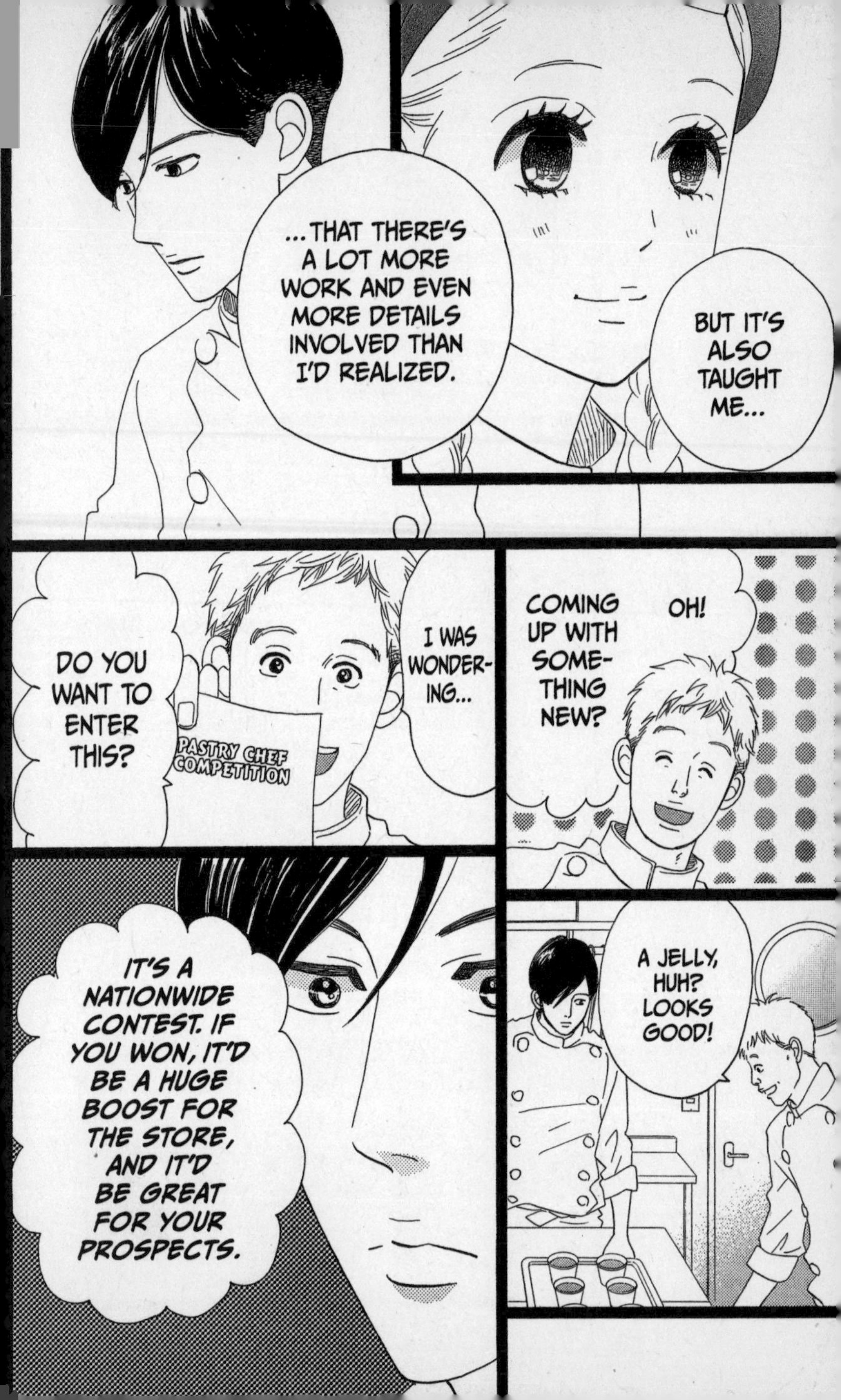
BUT IT'S ALSO TAUGHT ME...
...THAT THERE'S A LOT MORE WORK AND EVEN MORE DETAILS INVOLVED THAN I'D REALIZED.
OH!
COMING UP WITH SOME-THING NEW?
I WAS WONDER-ING...
DO YOU WANT TO ENTER THIS?
PASTRY CHEF COMPETITION
A JELLY, HUH? LOOKS GOOD!
IT'S A NATIONWIDE CONTEST. IF YOU WON, IT'D BE A HUGE BOOST FOR THE STORE, AND IT'D BE GREAT FOR YOUR PROSPECTS.

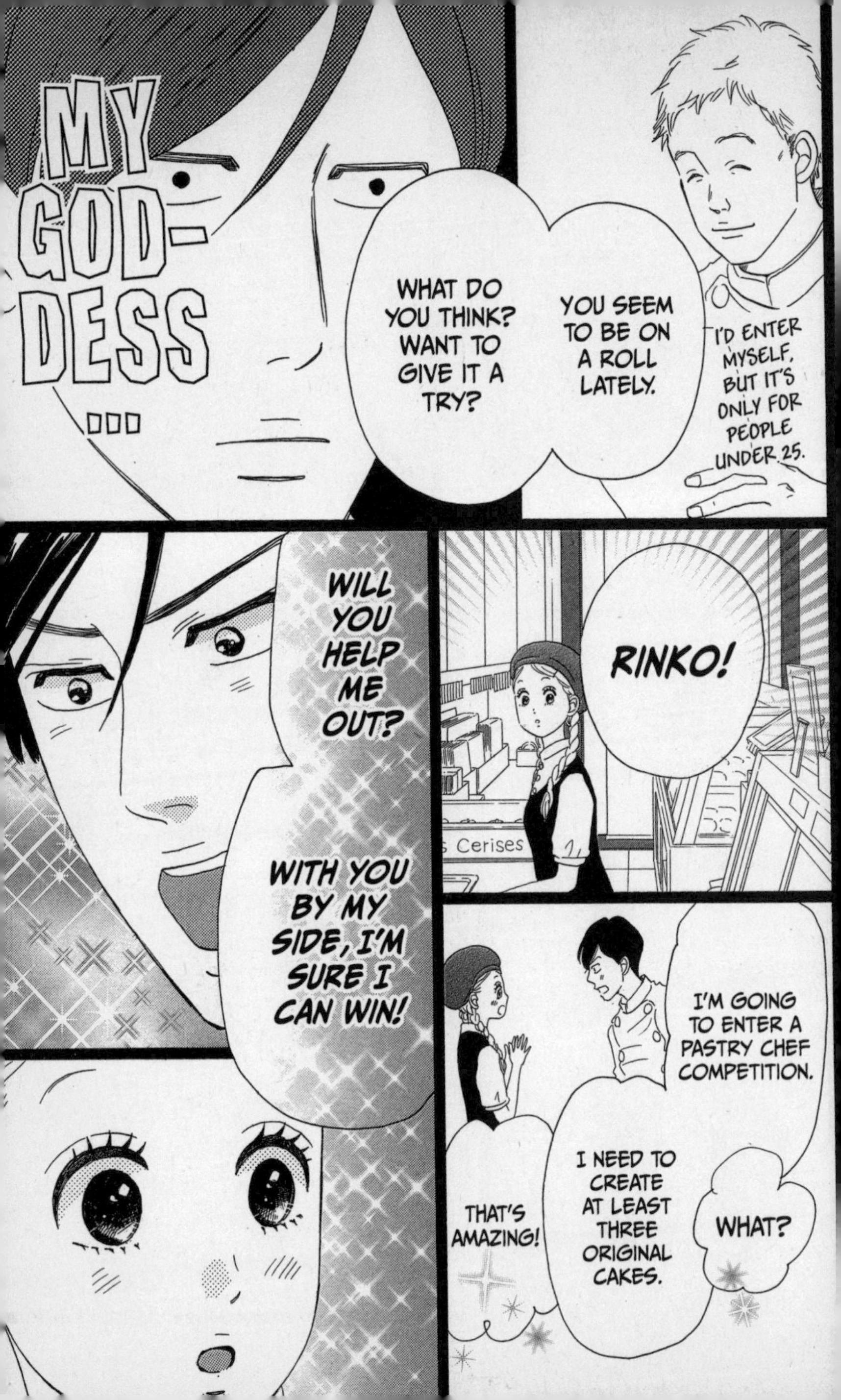
I'D ENTER MYSELF, BUT IT'S ONLY FOR PEOPLE UNDER 25.
YOU SEEM TO BE ON A ROLL LATELY.
WHAT DO YOU THINK? WANT TO GIVE IT A TRY?
MY GOD-DESS...
RINKO!
I'M GOING TO ENTER A PASTRY CHEF COMPETITION.
WHAT?
I NEED TO CREATE AT LEAST THREE ORIGINAL CAKES.
THAT'S AMAZING!
WILL YOU HELP ME OUT?
WITH YOU BY MY SIDE, I'M SURE I CAN WIN!
s Cerises

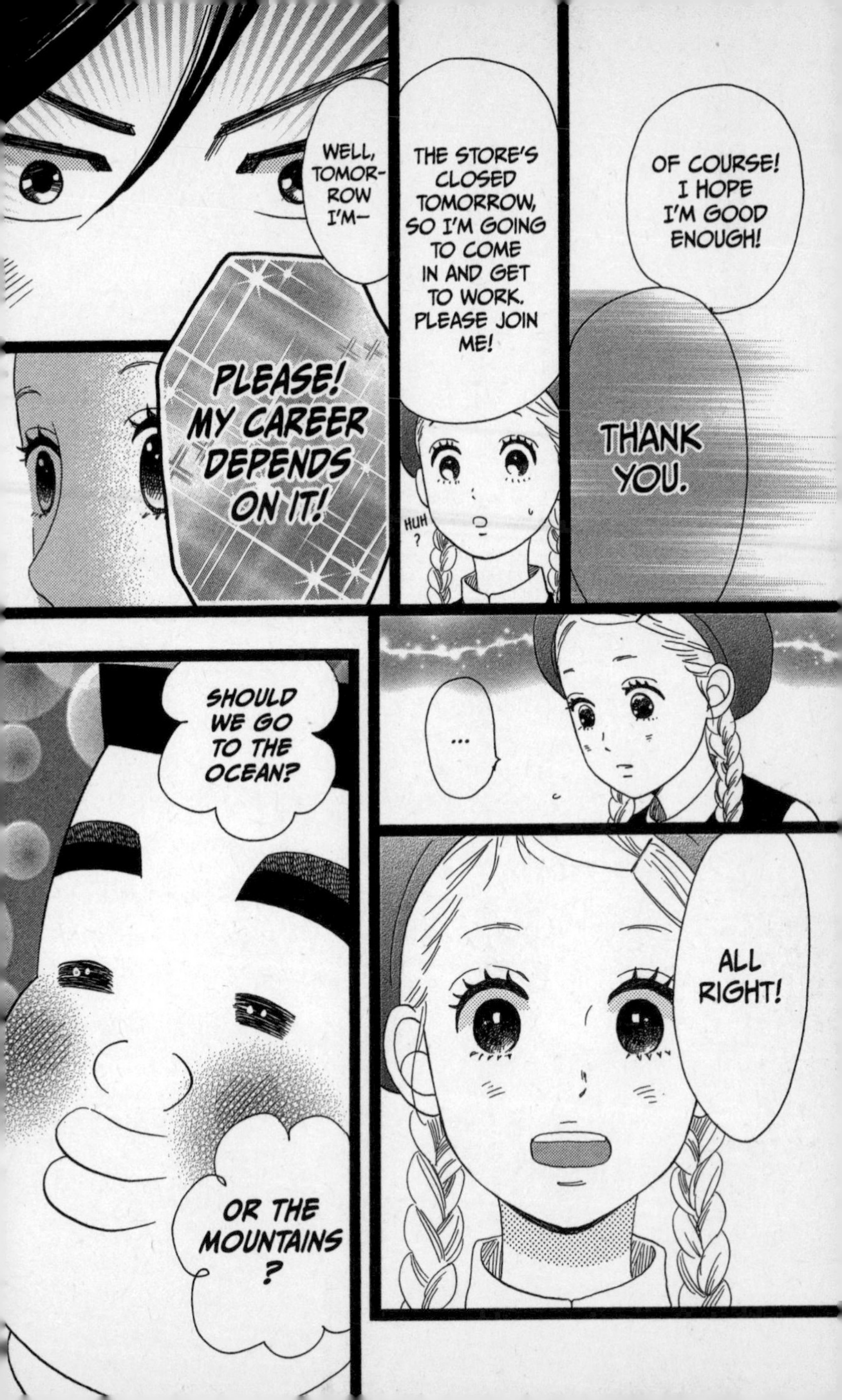
OF COURSE! I HOPE I'M GOOD ENOUGH!
THANK YOU.
THE STORE'S CLOSED TOMORROW, SO I'M GOING TO COME IN AND GET TO WORK. PLEASE JOIN ME!
HUH ?
WELL, TOMORROW I'M—
PLEASE! MY CAREER DEPENDS ON IT!
...
ALL RIGHT!
SHOULD WE GO TO THE OCEAN?
OR THE MOUNTAINS ?

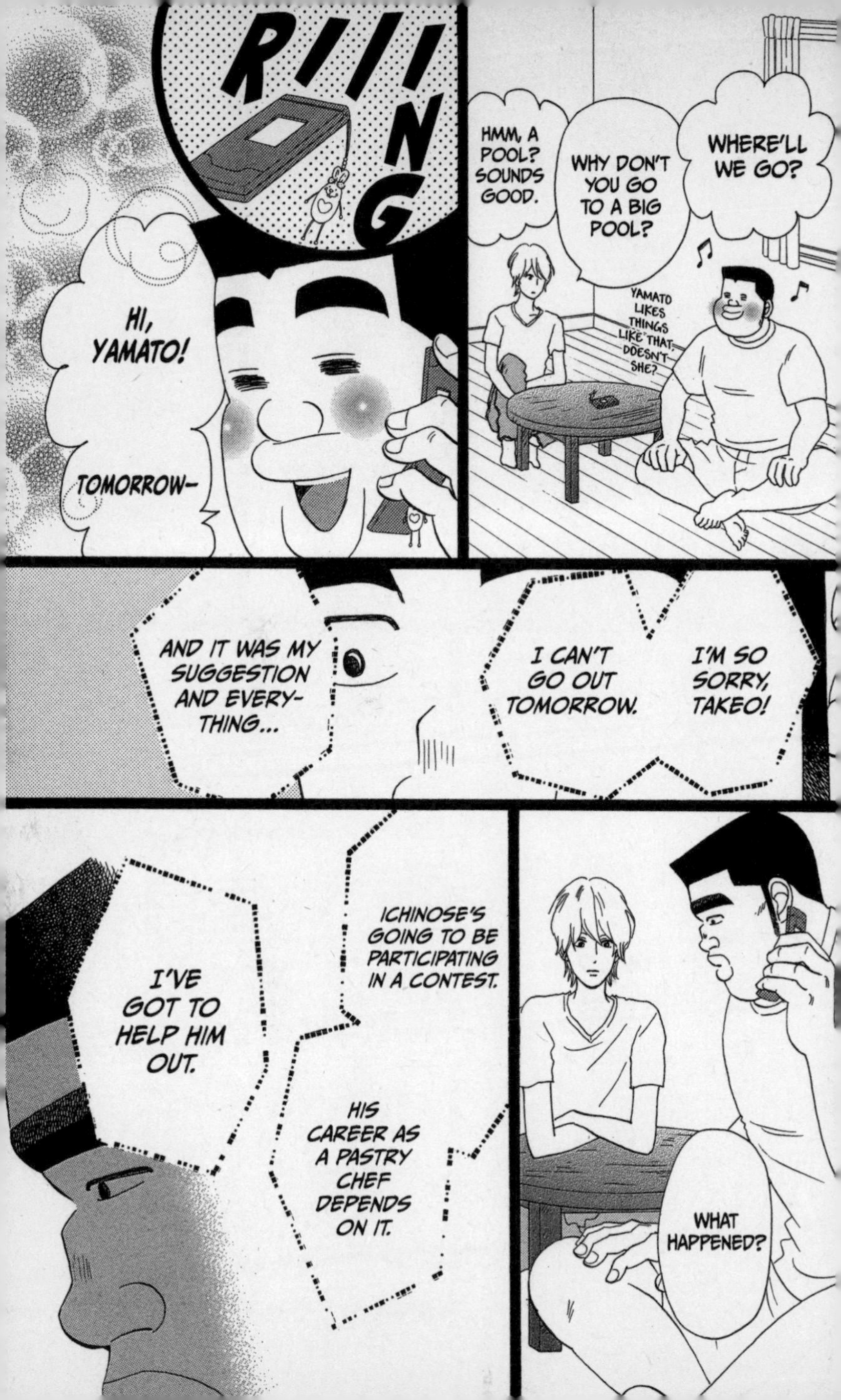
WHERE'LL WE GO?
WHY DON'T YOU GO TO A BIG POOL?
HMM, A POOL? SOUNDS GOOD.
YAMATO LIKES THINGS LIKE THAT, DOESN'T SHE?
RIIING
HI, YAMATO!
TOMORROW-
I'M SO SORRY, TAKEO!
I CAN'T GO OUT TOMORROW.
AND IT WAS MY SUGGESTION AND EVERY-THING...
WHAT HAPPENED?
ICHINOSE'S GOING TO BE PARTICIPATING IN A CONTEST.
HIS CAREER AS A PASTRY CHEF DEPENDS ON IT.
I'VE GOT TO HELP HIM OUT.

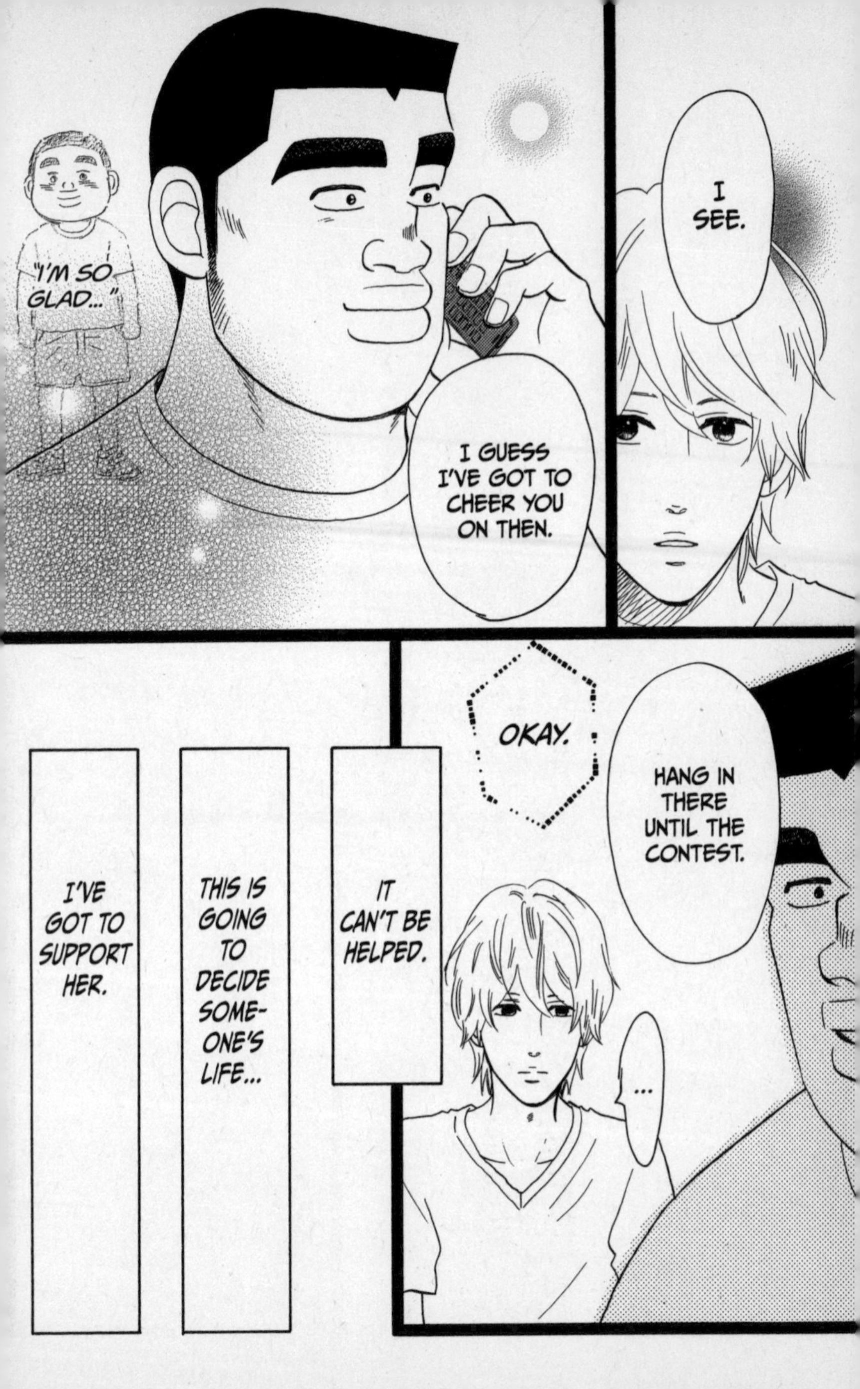
I SEE.
I GUESS I'VE GOT TO CHEER YOU ON THEN.
"I'M SO GLAD..."
HANG IN THERE UNTIL THE CONTEST.
OKAY.
...
IT CAN'T BE HELPED.
THIS IS GOING TO DECIDE SOME-ONE'S LIFE...
I'VE GOT TO SUPPORT HER.

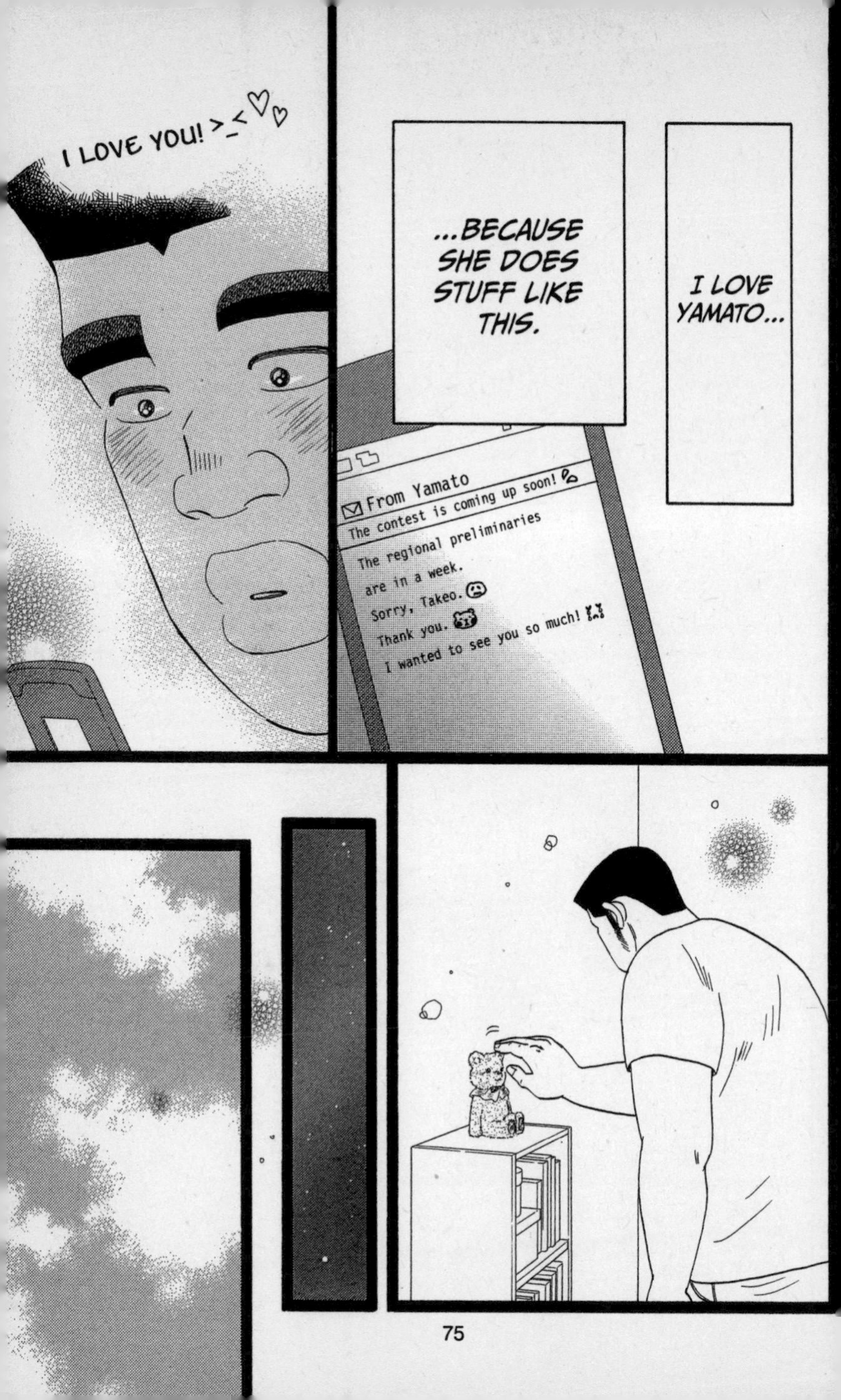
I LOVE YAMATO...
...BECAUSE SHE DOES STUFF LIKE THIS.
From Yamato
The contest is coming up soon!
The regional preliminaries are in a week.
Sorry, Takeo.
Thank you.
I wanted to see you so much!
I LOVE YOU! >_<

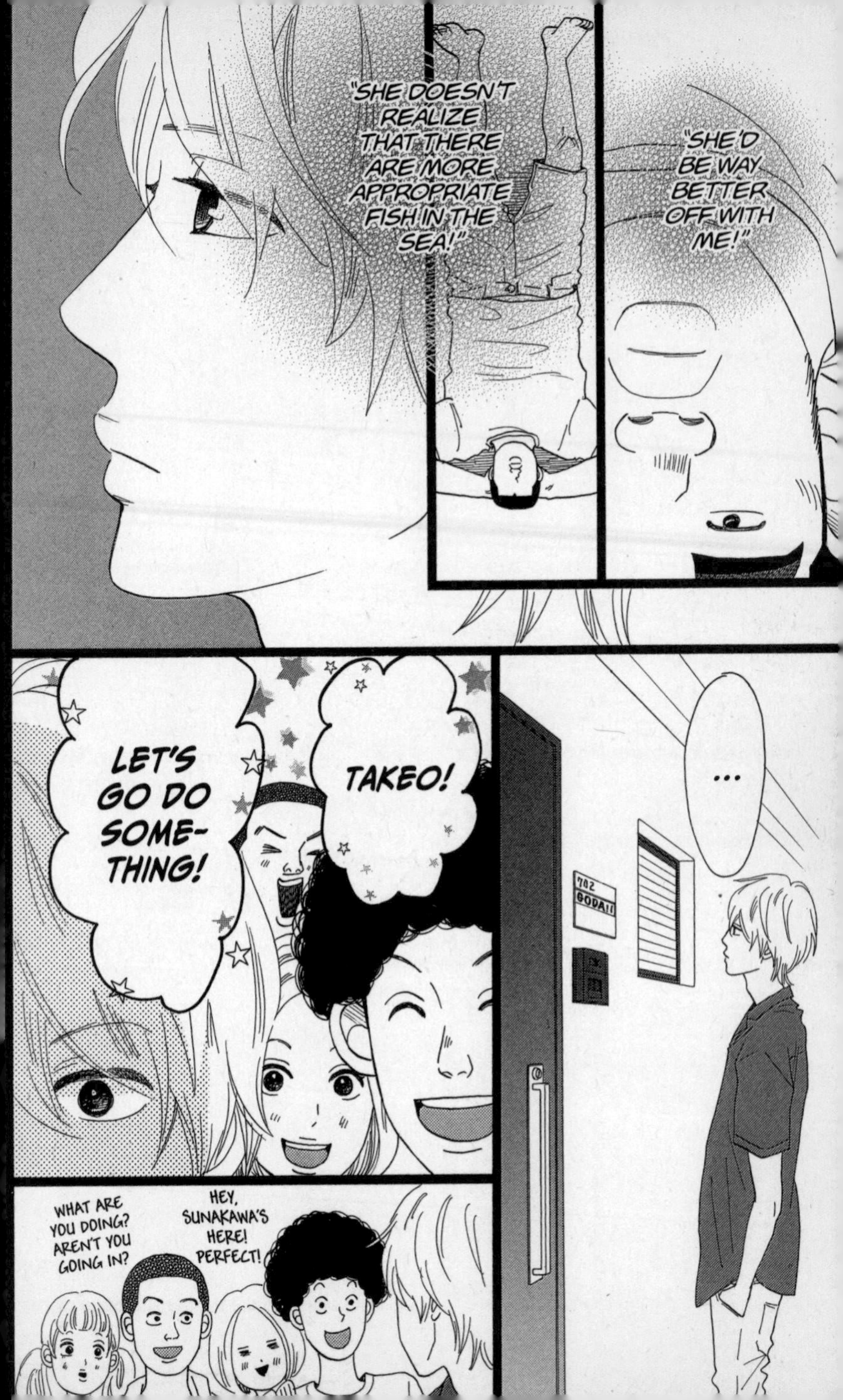
"SHE'D BE WAY BETTER OFF WITH ME!"
"SHE DOESN'T REALIZE THAT THERE ARE MORE APPROPRIATE FISH IN THE SEA!"
...
702 GODA
TAKEO!
LET'S GO DO SOME-THING!
HEY, SUNAKAWA'S HERE! PERFECT!
WHAT ARE YOU DOING? AREN'T YOU GOING IN?

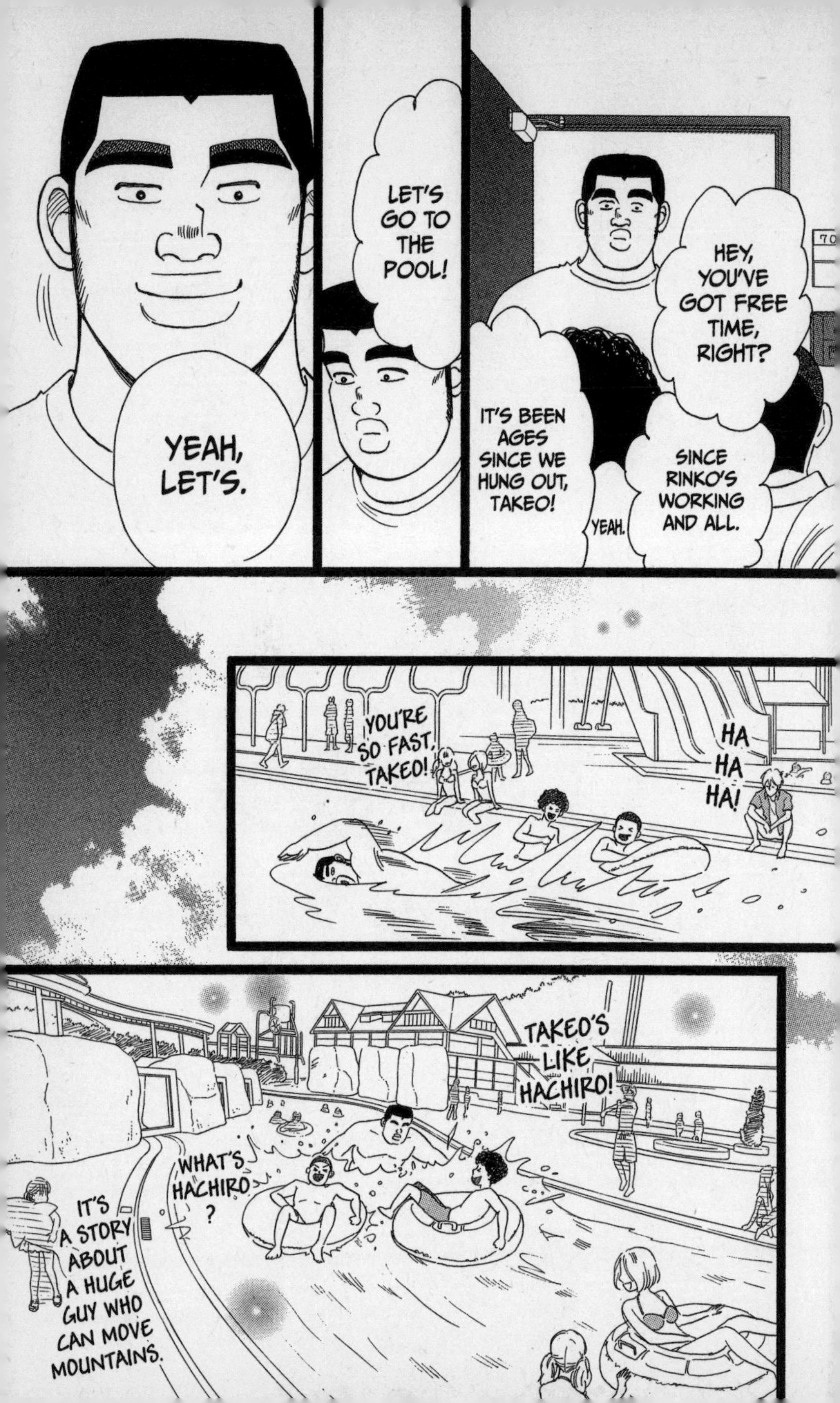
HEY, YOU'VE GOT FREE TIME, RIGHT?
SINCE RINKO'S WORKING AND ALL.
IT'S BEEN AGES SINCE WE HUNG OUT, TAKEO!
YEAH.
LET'S GO TO THE POOL!
YEAH, LET'S.
HA HA HA!
YOU'RE SO FAST, TAKEO!
TAKEO'S LIKE HACHIRO!
WHAT'S HACHIRO?
IT'S A STORY ABOUT A HUGE GUY WHO CAN MOVE MOUNTAINS.

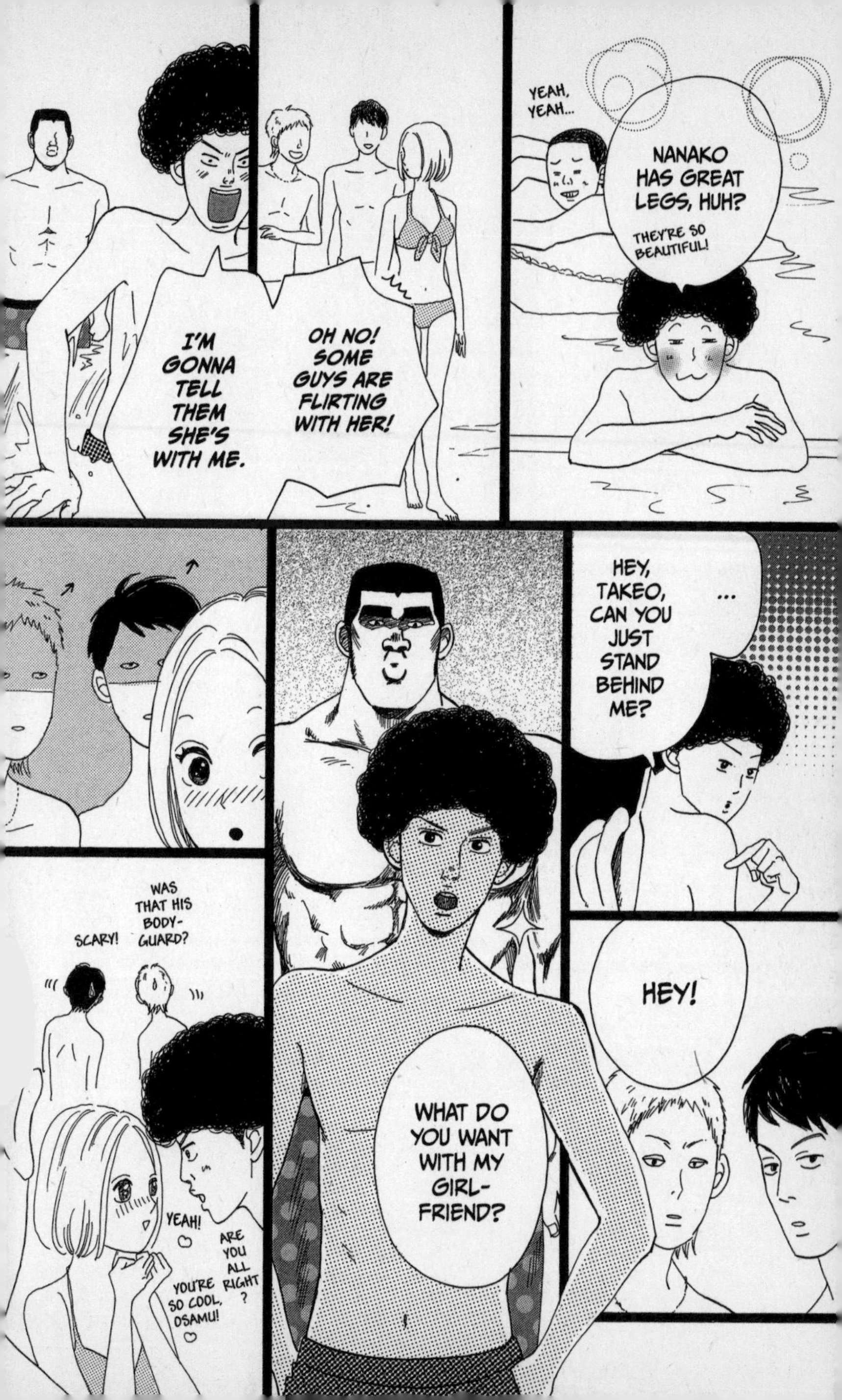
NANAKO HAS GREAT LEGS, HUH?
THEY'RE SO BEAUTIFUL!
YEAH, YEAH...
OH NO! SOME GUYS ARE FLIRTING WITH HER!
I'M GONNA TELL THEM SHE'S WITH ME.
HEY, TAKEO, CAN YOU JUST STAND BEHIND ME?
...
HEY!
WHAT DO YOU WANT WITH MY GIRL-FRIEND?
WAS THAT HIS BODY-GUARD?
SCARY!
ARE YOU ALL RIGHT?
YEAH!
YOU'RE SO COOL, OSAMU!

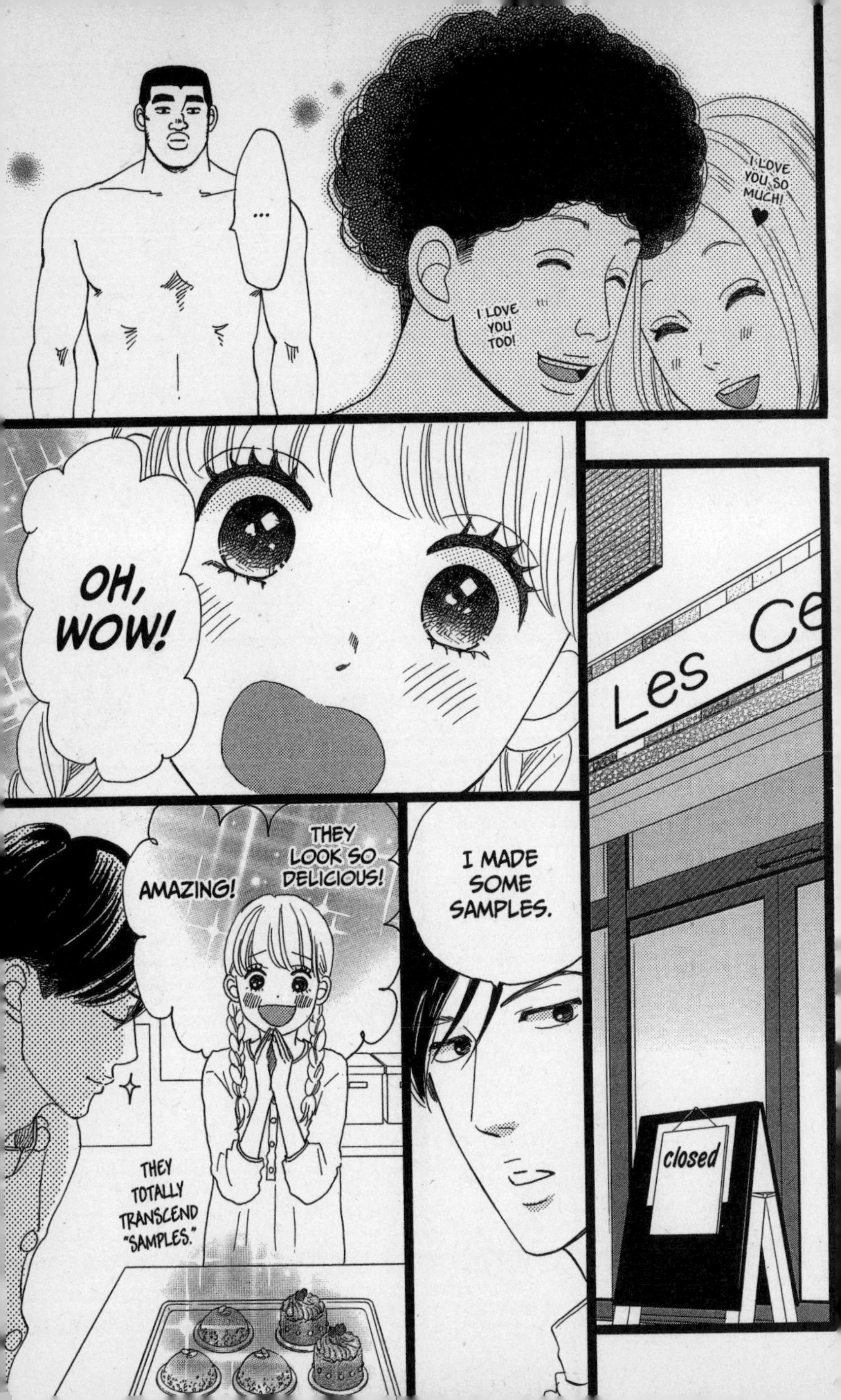

I LOVE YOU SO MUCH! ♥
I LOVE YOU TOO!
...
Les Ce
closed
OH, WOW!
I MADE SOME SAMPLES.
THEY LOOK SO DELICIOUS!
AMAZING!
THEY TOTALLY TRANSCEND "SAMPLES."

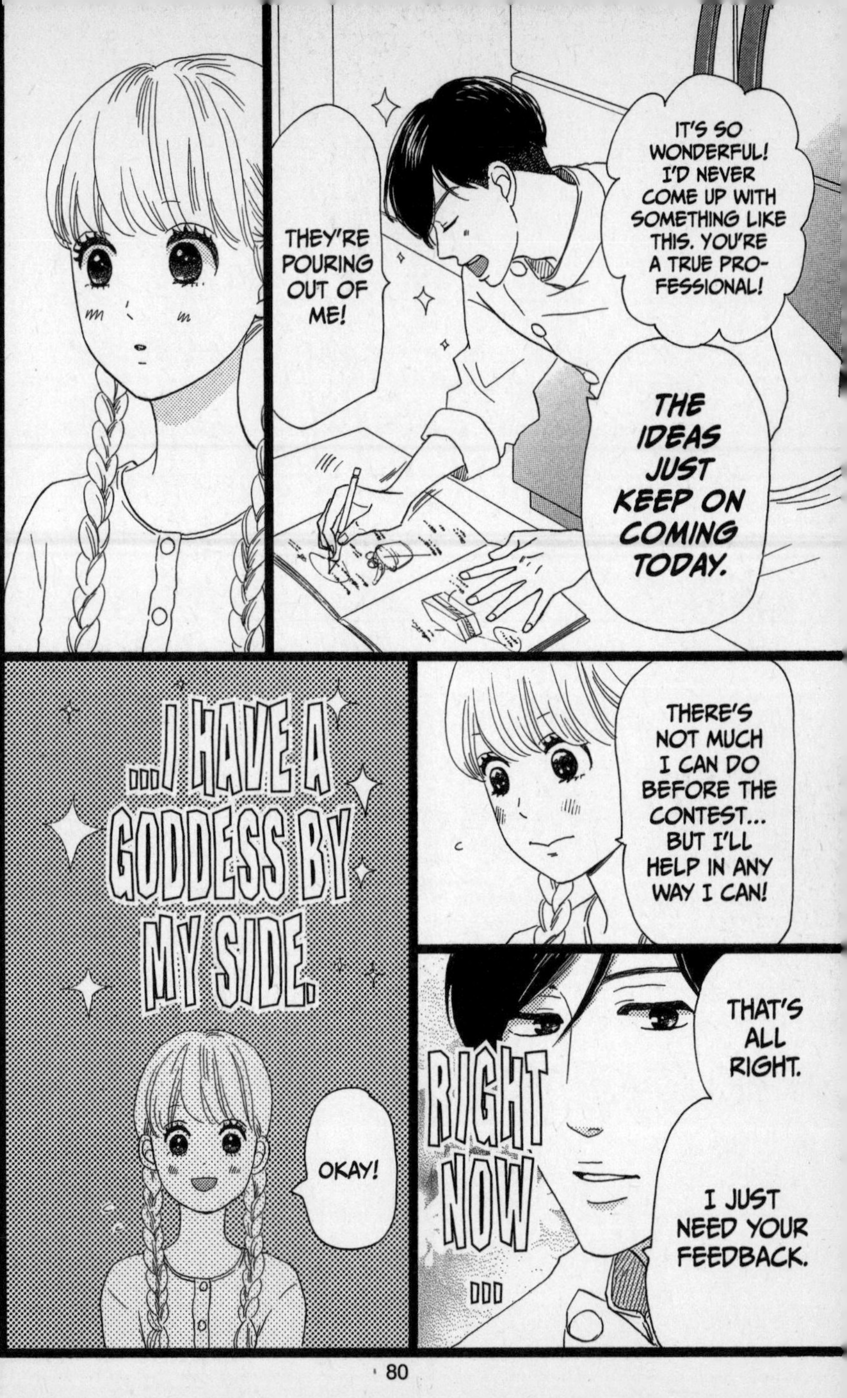
IT'S SO WONDERFUL! I'D NEVER COME UP WITH SOMETHING LIKE THIS. YOU'RE A TRUE PRO-FESSIONAL!
THE IDEAS JUST KEEP ON COMING TODAY.
THEY'RE POURING OUT OF ME!
THERE'S NOT MUCH I CAN DO BEFORE THE CONTEST... BUT I'LL HELP IN ANY WAY I CAN!
THAT'S ALL RIGHT.
I JUST NEED YOUR FEEDBACK.
RIGHT NOW...
...I HAVE A GODDESS BY MY SIDE.
OKAY!

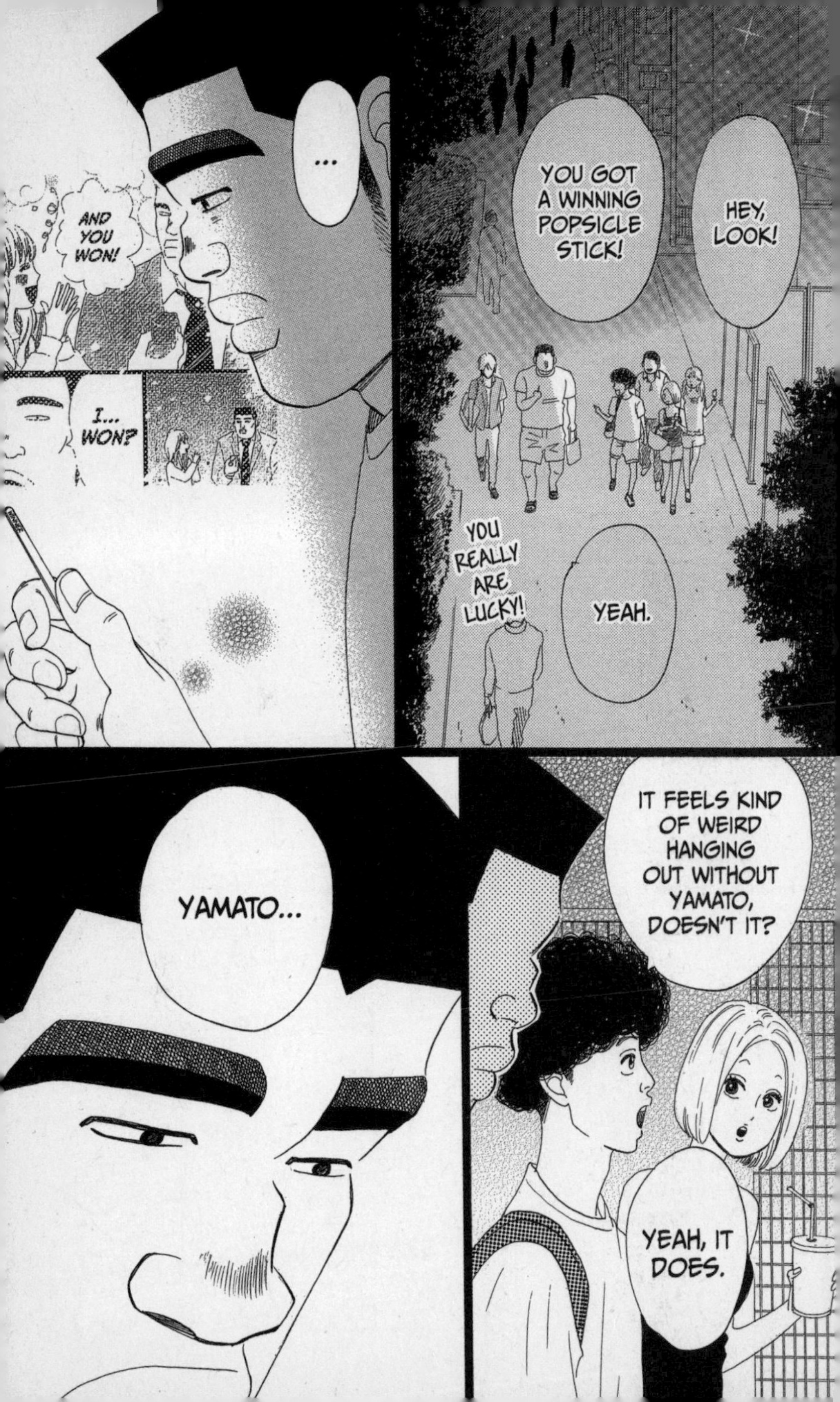

HEY, LOOK!
YOU GOT A WINNING POPSICLE STICK!
YEAH.
YOU REALLY ARE LUCKY!
...
AND YOU WON!
I... WON?
IT FEELS KIND OF WEIRD HANGING OUT WITHOUT YAMATO, DOESN'T IT?
YEAH, IT DOES.
YAMATO...

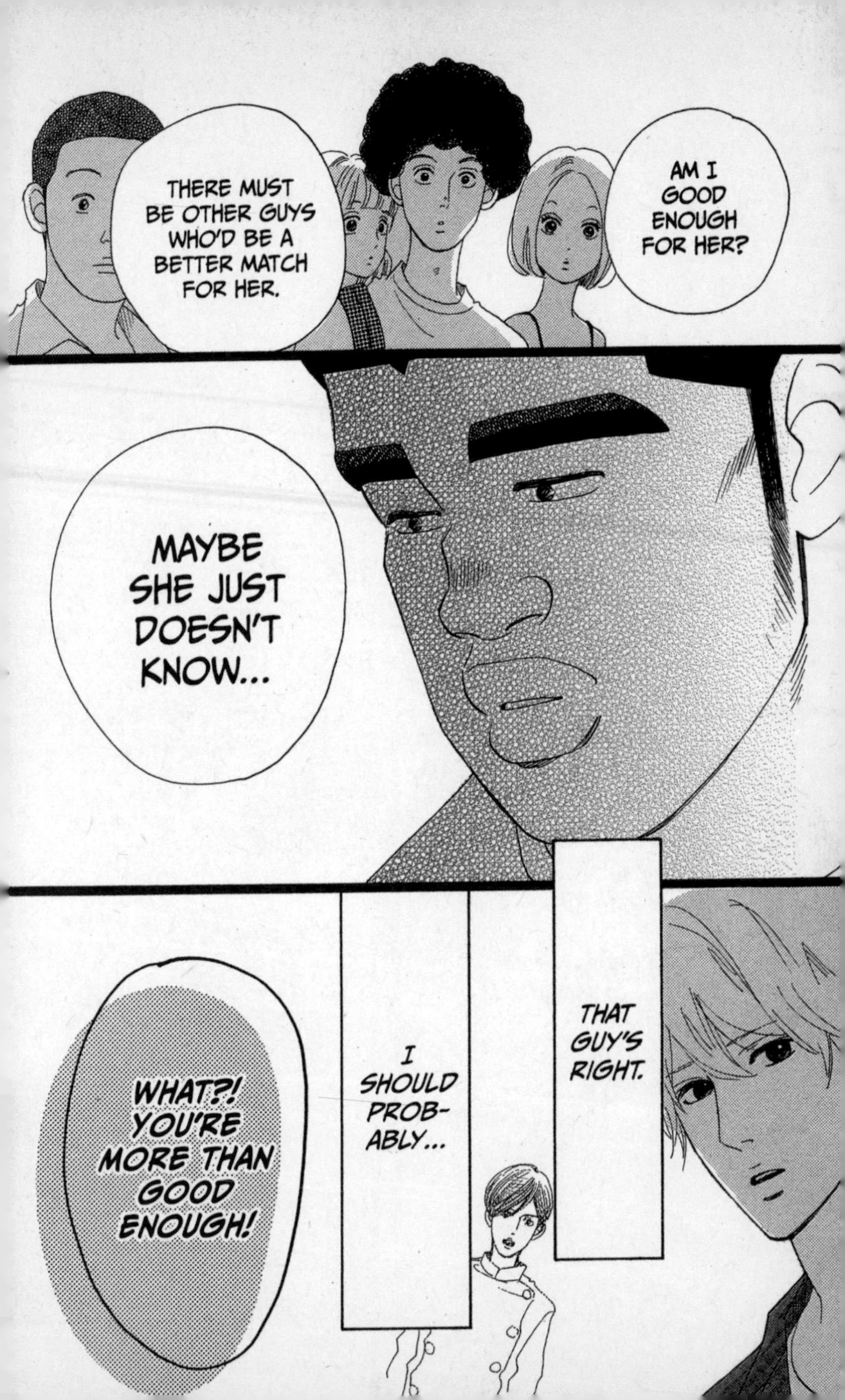
AM I GOOD ENOUGH FOR HER?
THERE MUST BE OTHER GUYS WHO'D BE A BETTER MATCH FOR HER.
MAYBE SHE JUST DOESN'T KNOW...
THAT GUY'S RIGHT.
I SHOULD PROB-ABLY...
WHAT?! YOU'RE MORE THAN GOOD ENOUGH!

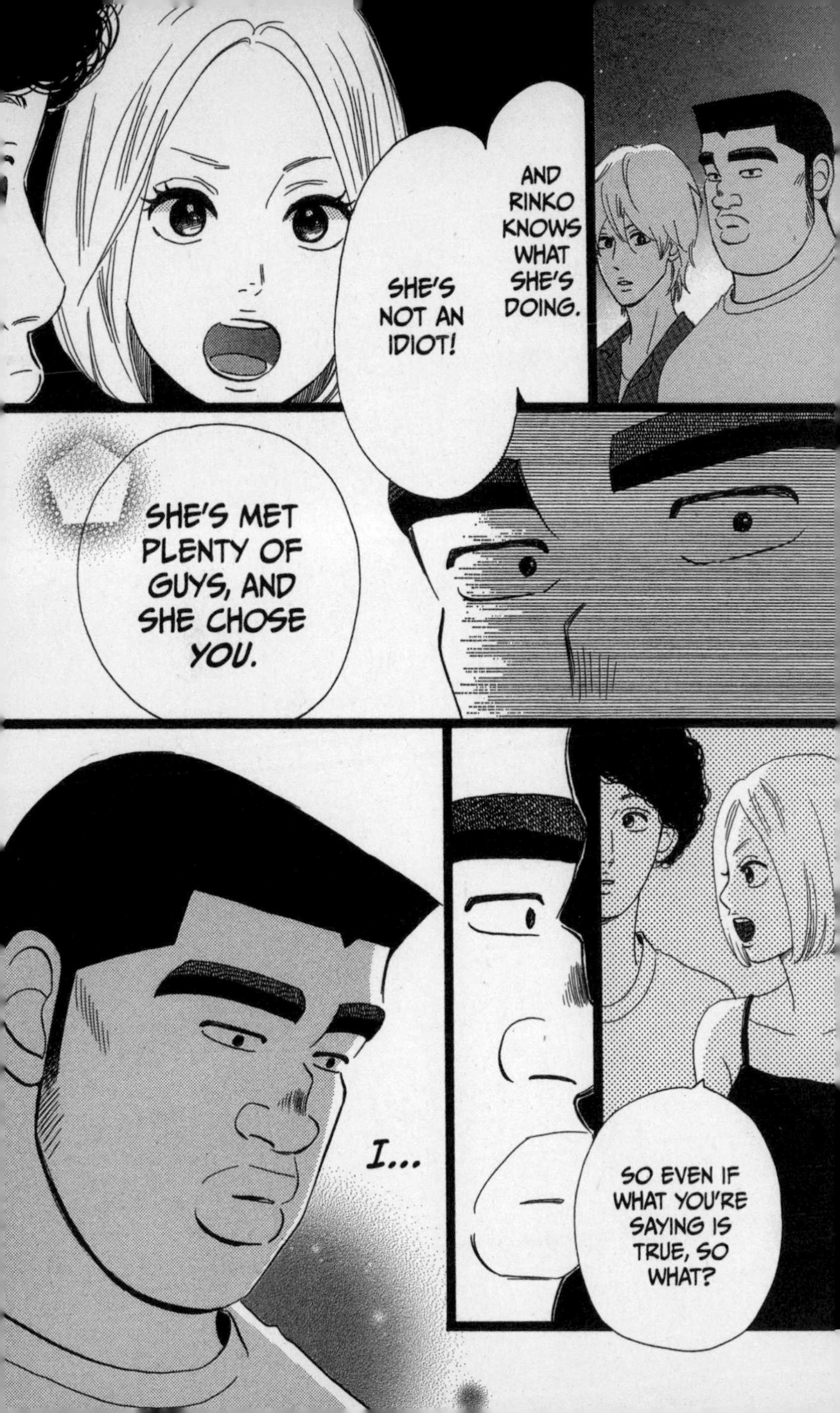
AND RINKO KNOWS WHAT SHE'S DOING.
SHE'S NOT AN IDIOT!
SHE'S MET PLENTY OF GUYS, AND SHE CHOSE *YOU*.
SO EVEN IF WHAT YOU'RE SAYING IS TRUE, SO WHAT?
*I...*

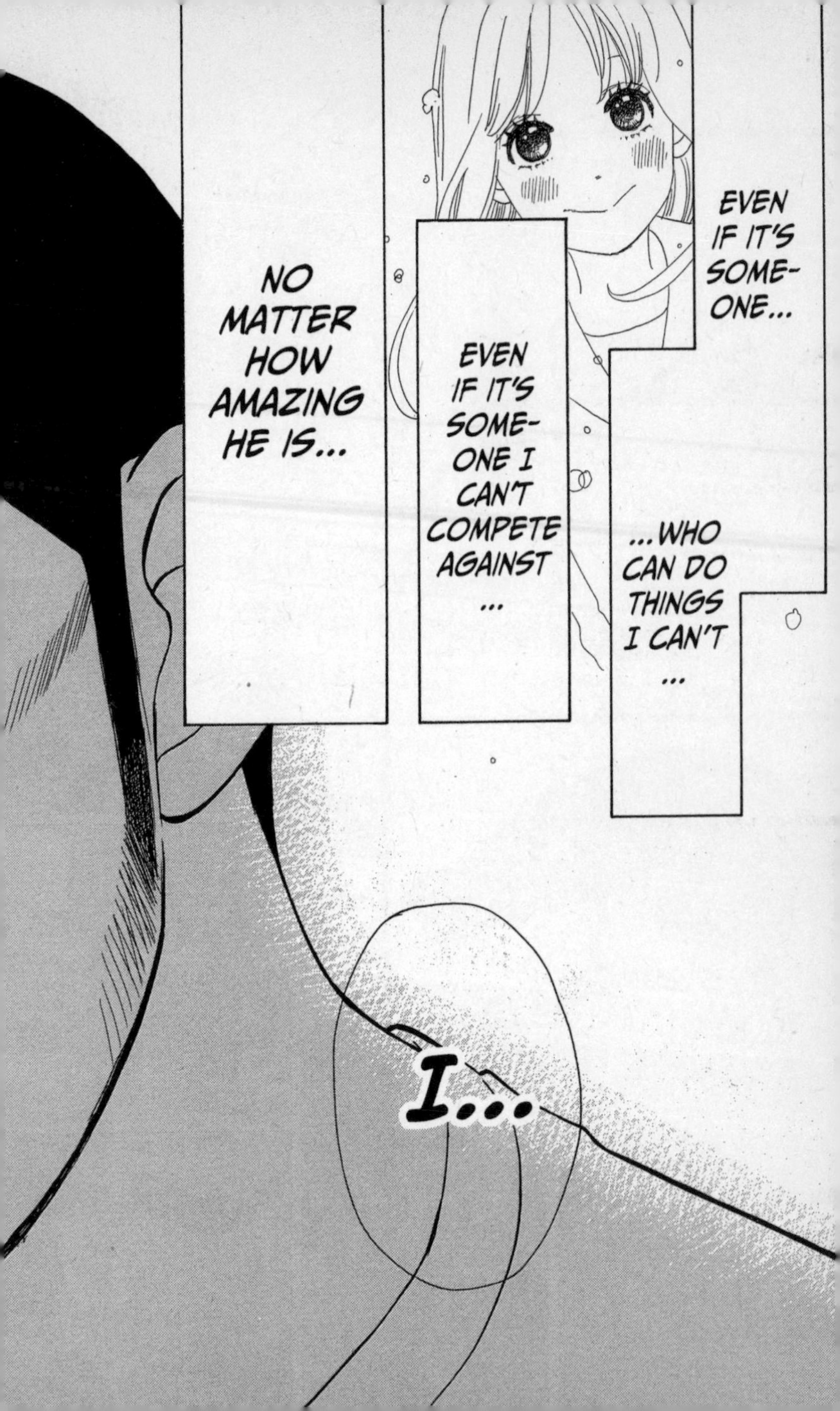
EVEN IF IT'S SOME-ONE...
...WHO CAN DO THINGS I CAN'T ...
EVEN IF IT'S SOME-ONE I CAN'T COMPETE AGAINST ...
NO MATTER HOW AMAZING HE IS...
I...

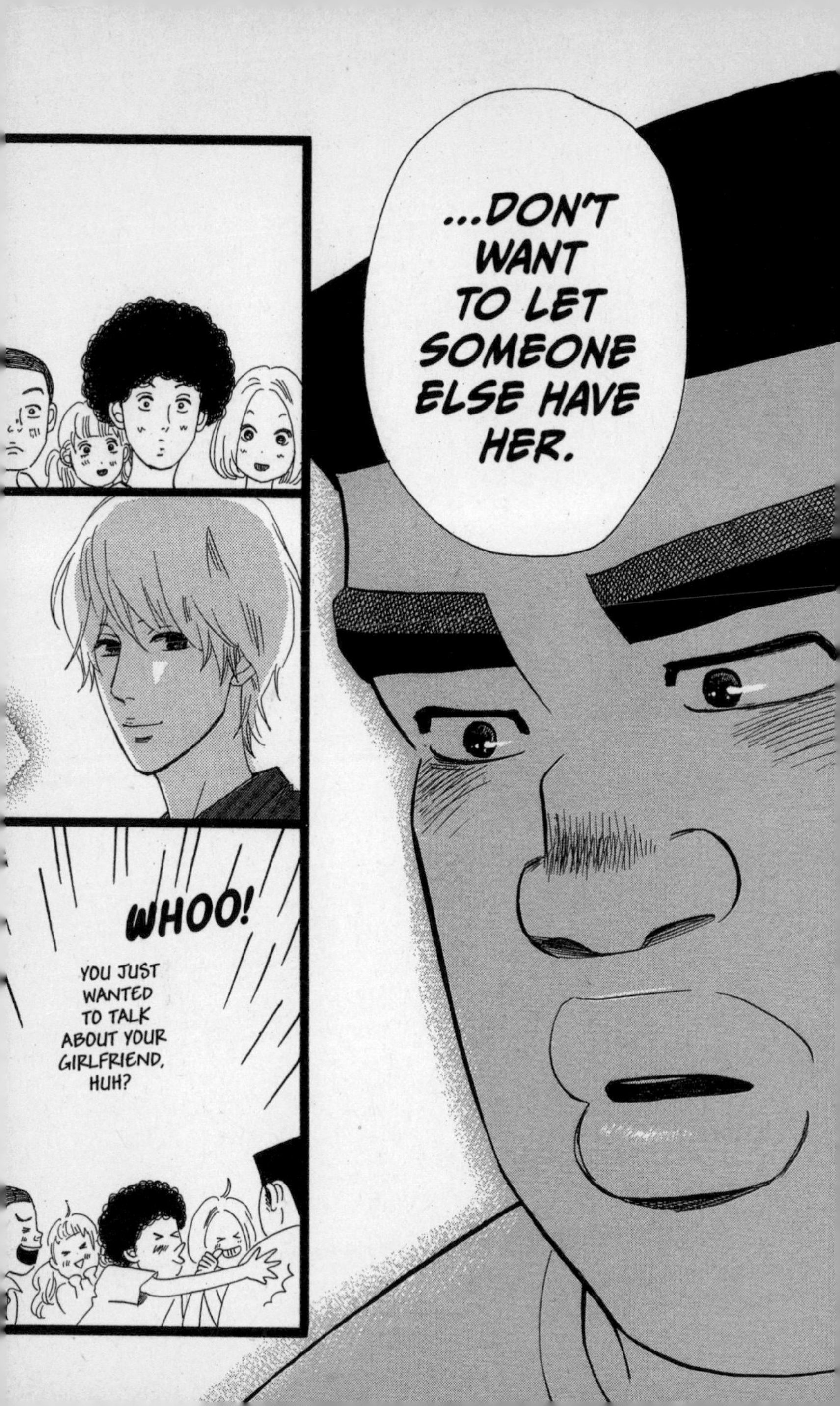
...DON'T WANT TO LET SOMEONE ELSE HAVE HER.
WHOO!
YOU JUST WANTED TO TALK ABOUT YOUR GIRLFRIEND, HUH?

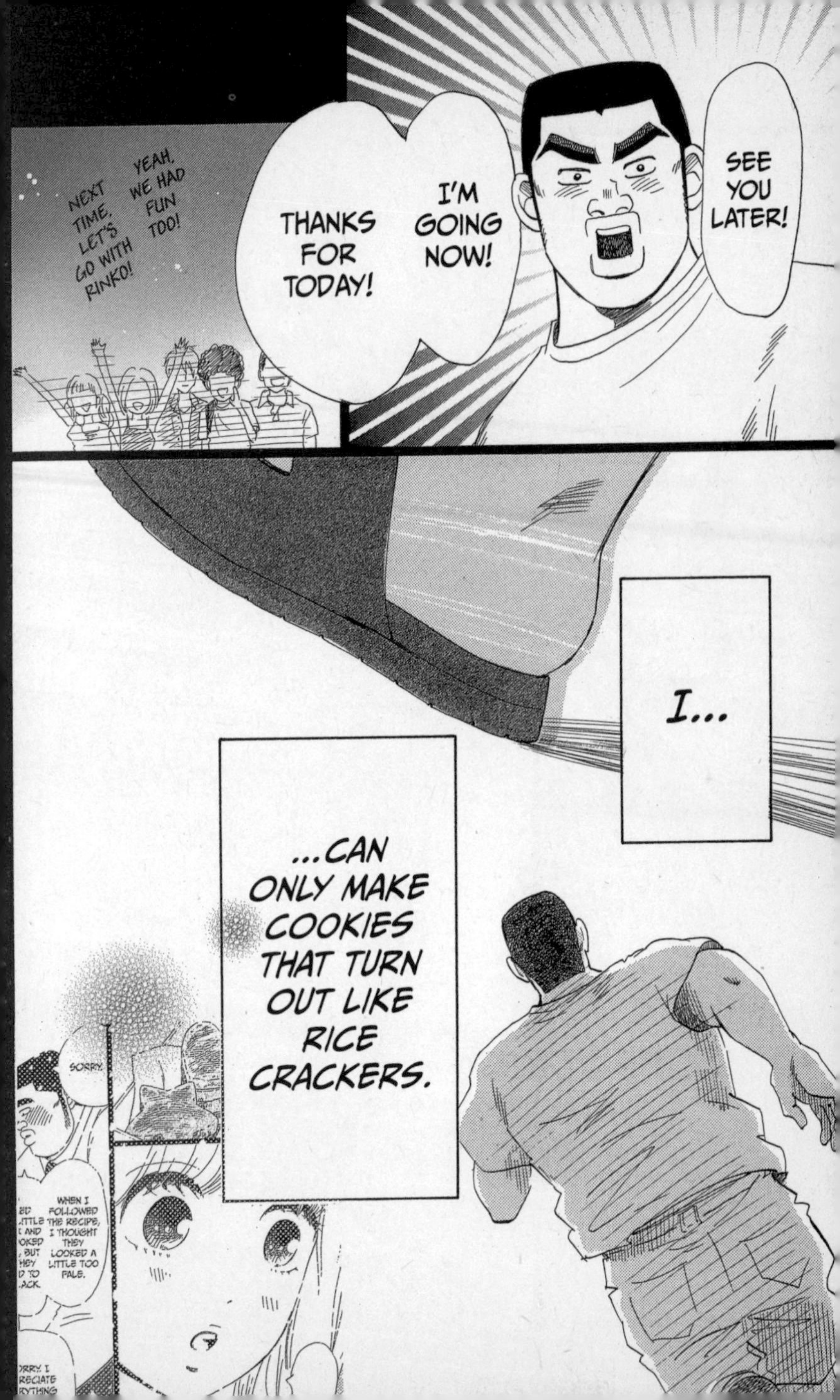
SEE YOU LATER!
I'M GOING NOW!
THANKS FOR TODAY!
YEAH, WE HAD FUN TOO!
NEXT TIME, LET'S GO WITH RINKO!
I...
...CAN ONLY MAKE COOKIES THAT TURN OUT LIKE RICE CRACKERS.
SORRY.
WHEN I FOLLOWED THE RECIPE, I THOUGHT THEY LOOKED A LITTLE TOO PALE.

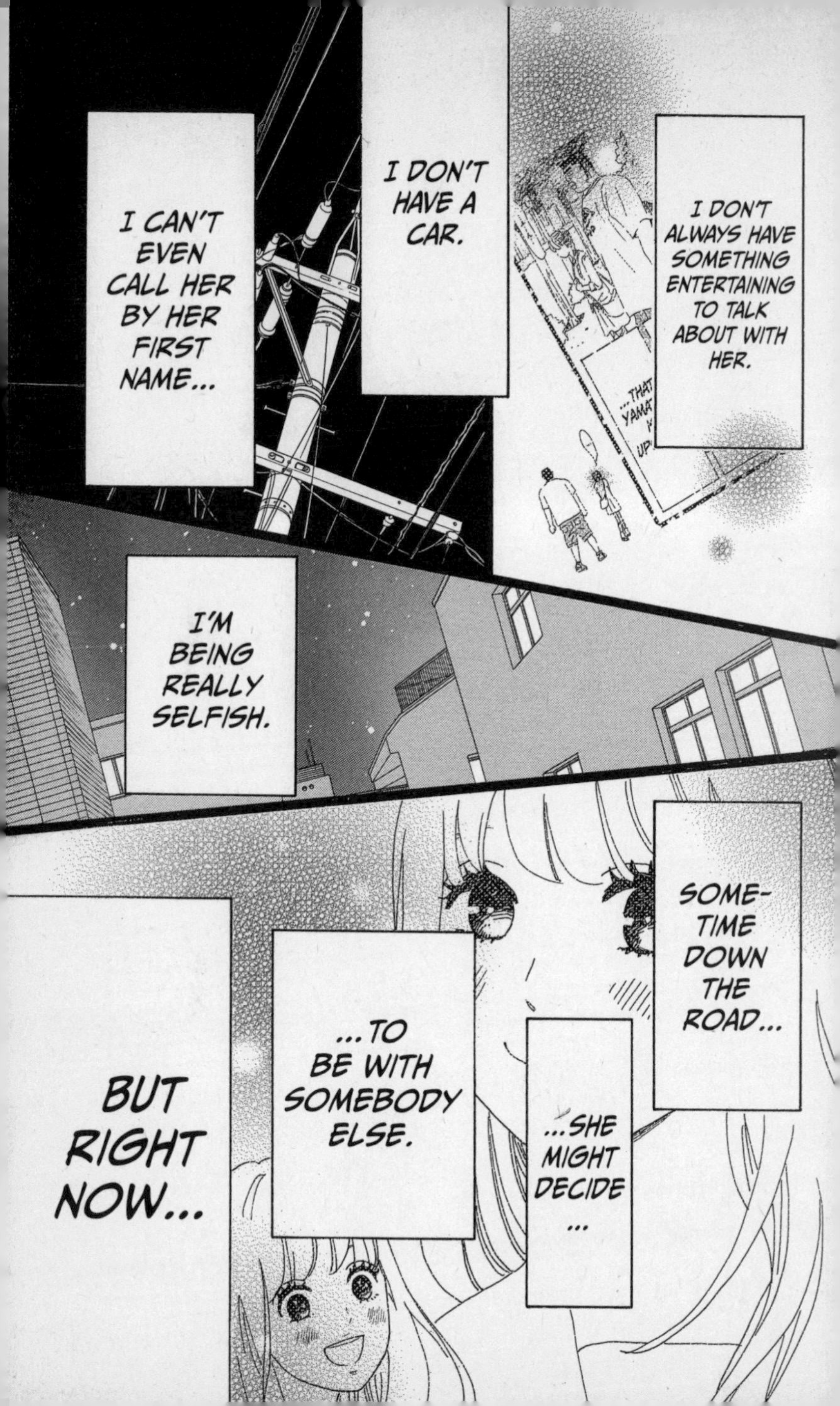
I DON'T ALWAYS HAVE SOMETHING ENTERTAINING TO TALK ABOUT WITH HER.
I DON'T HAVE A CAR.
I CAN'T EVEN CALL HER BY HER FIRST NAME...
I'M BEING REALLY SELFISH.
SOME-TIME DOWN THE ROAD...
...SHE MIGHT DECIDE ...
...TO BE WITH SOMEBODY ELSE.
BUT RIGHT NOW...

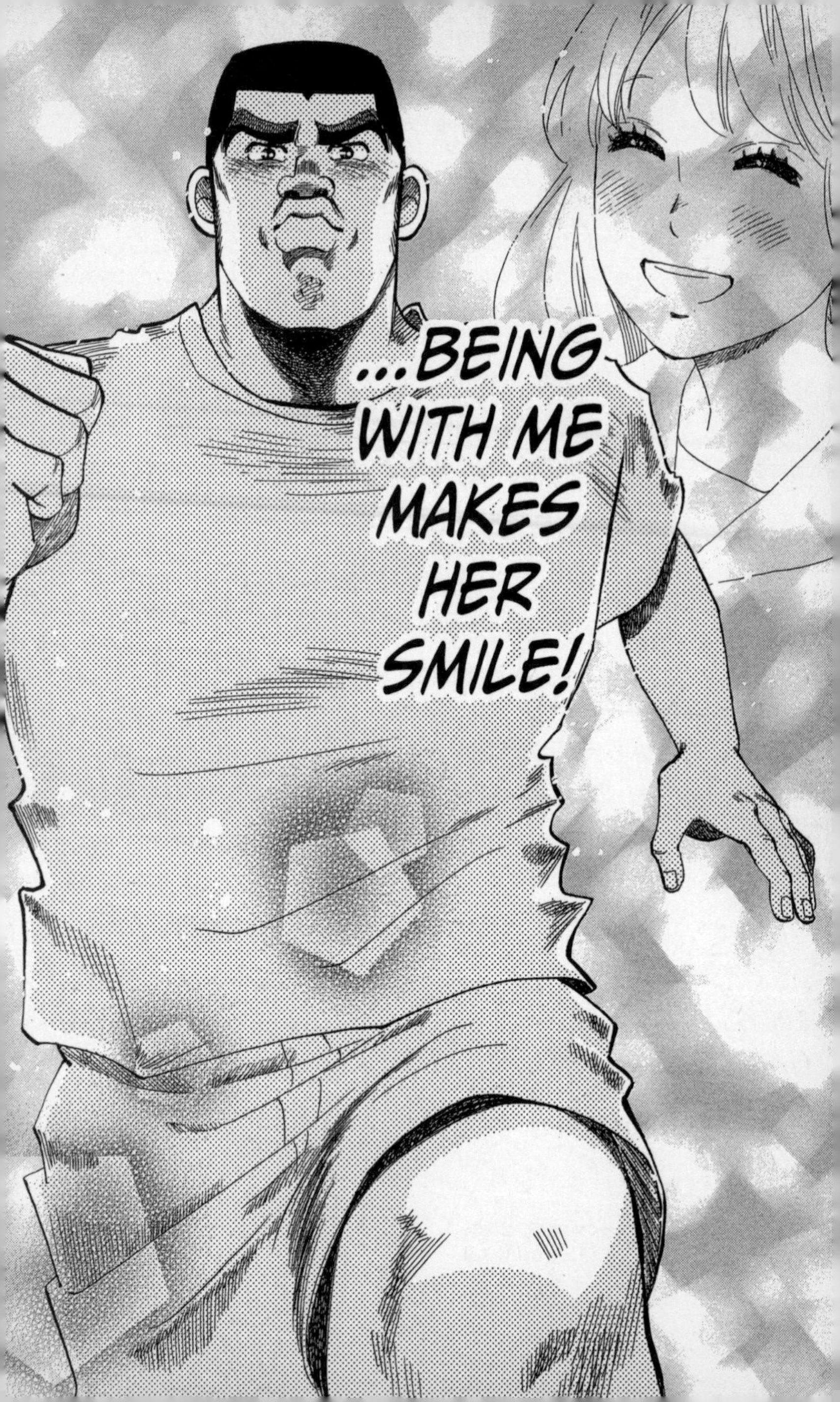
...BEING WITH ME MAKES HER SMILE!

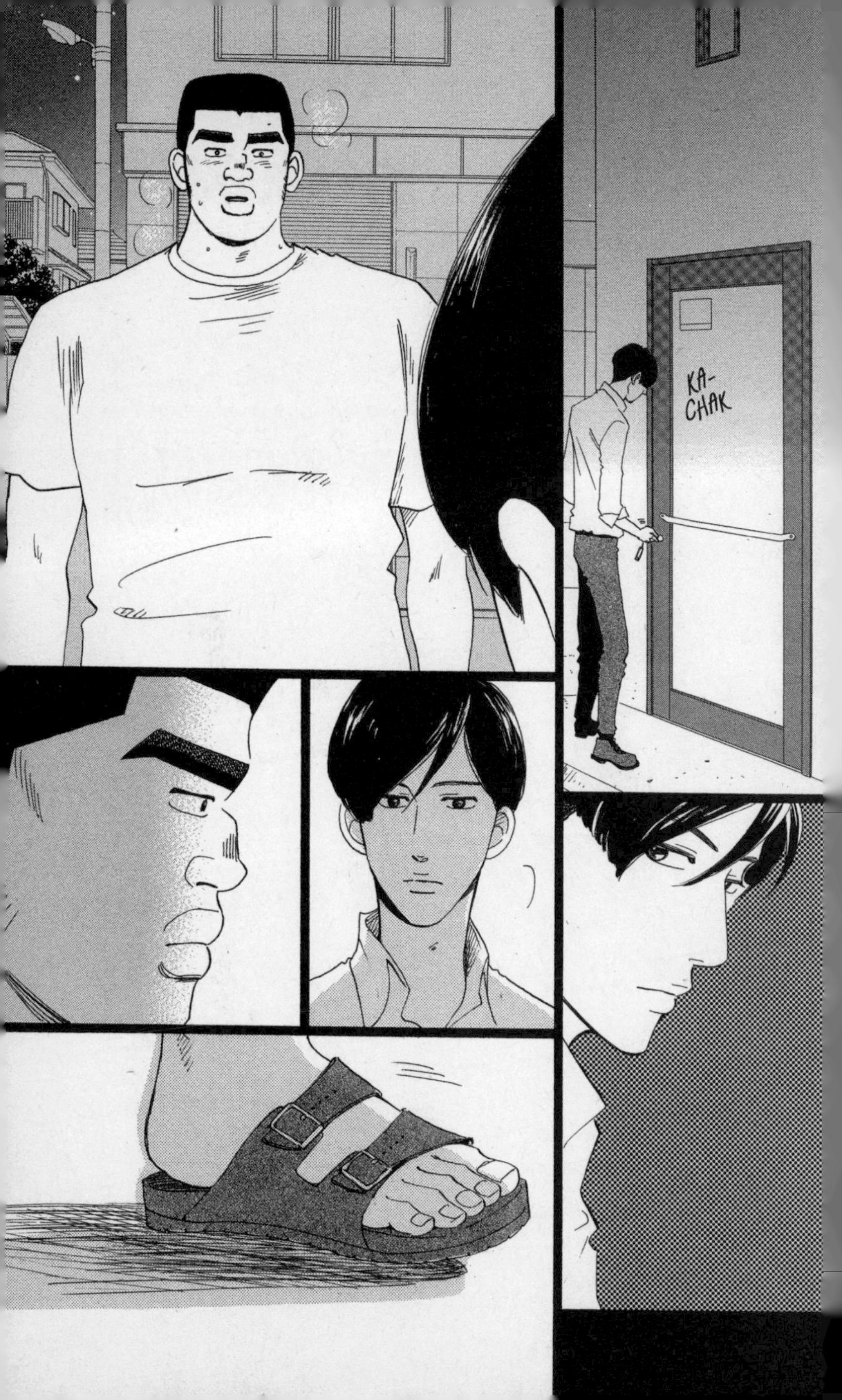
KA-CHAK

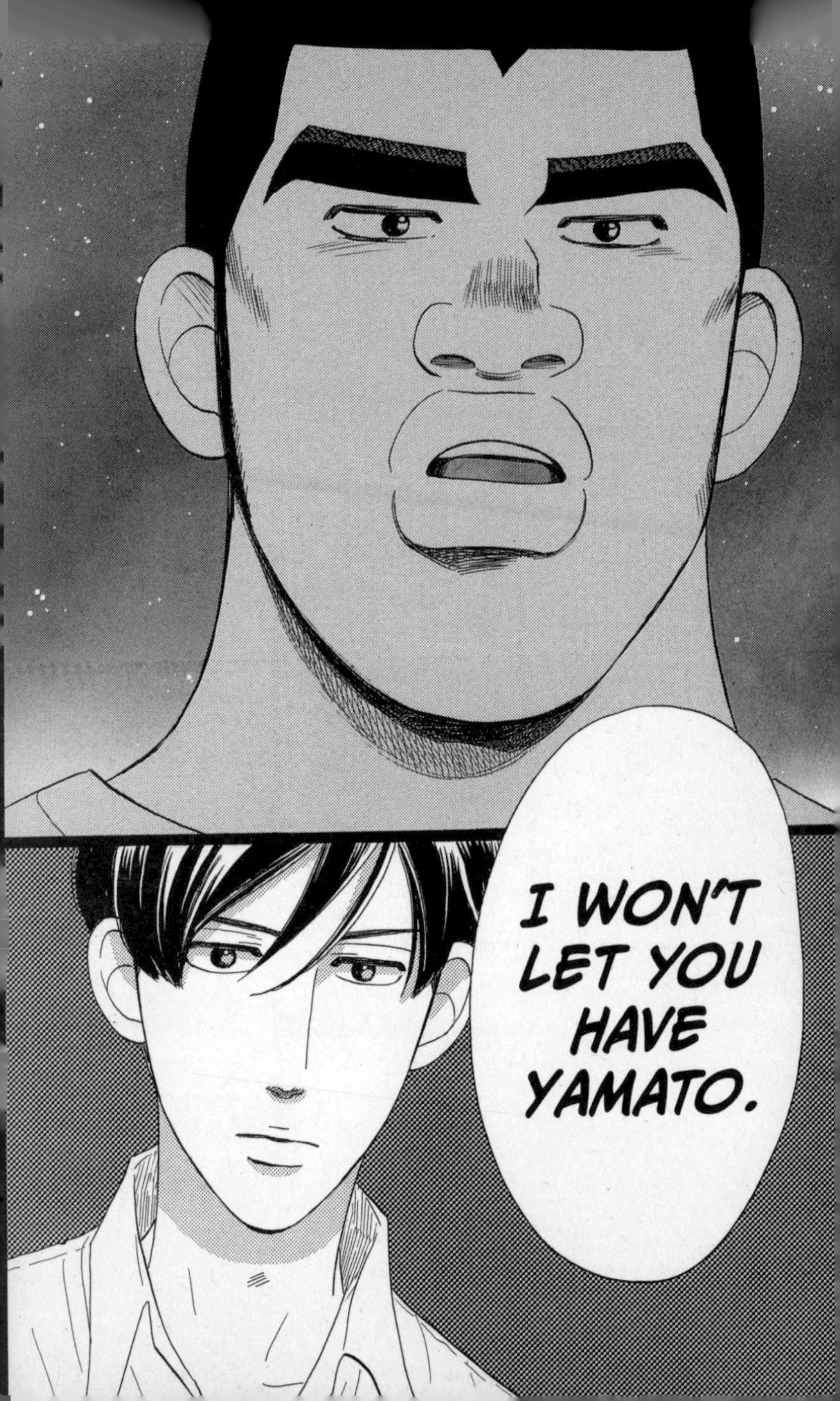
I WON'T LET YOU HAVE YAMATO.

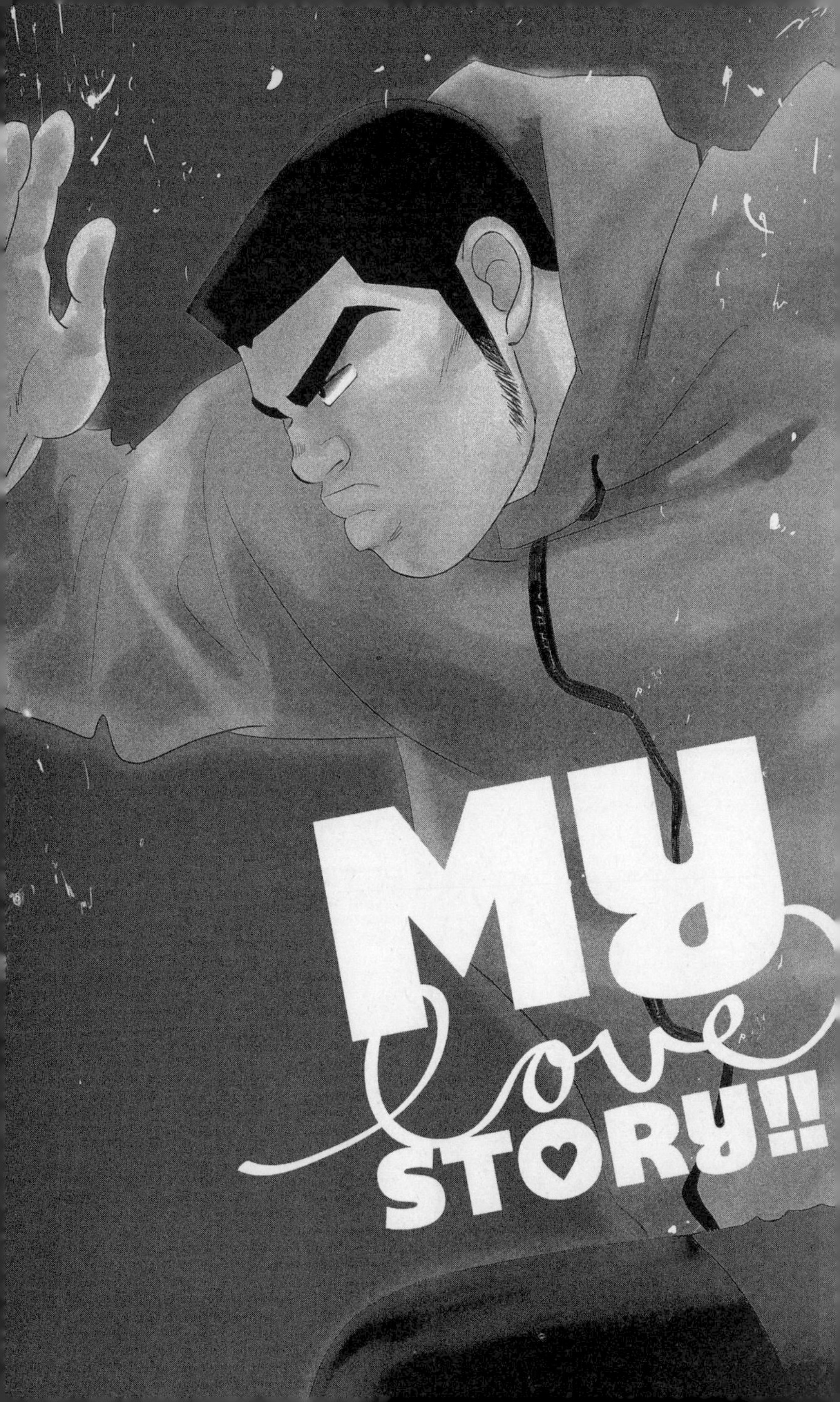
MY
love
STORY!!

Hello! This is Kawahara, the *My Love Story!!* writer. Thank you for continuing to support our story! Somehow we're already on volume 9. It's really flown by! And now *My Love Story!!* is getting an anime! The opening and closing songs are wonderful, and I love the lyrics!

The art, the acting, the music, the directing... Everything about the anime is great. They've even created some scenes that don't exist in the manga. I think you'll enjoy it whether you've read the manga or not, so please check it out if you haven't already! It's so cool seeing Takeo in motion. Yamato's so cute! Sunakawa's so cool, and you feel bad for him in a good way. (laugh) And don't the desserts look delicious? I hope you'll enjoy the anime!

By the way, Main* is all grown up now. I recently saw her as a Sui Girl!** She's as cute as always. The current hosts and the previous hosts are all adorable. Wait, what am I talking about? Girls are so cute... or something like that.

*Haruka Fukuhara played a character known as Main on a children's cooking show called *Cooking Idol Mai! Mai! Main!*

**Short for Suiensaa Girl, the hosts of *Suiensaa*, a scientific variety show.

I have a smartphone. Three years after I made the switch, it's basically a miniature gaming device.

I hope to see you again in volume 10!

Thank you for all your help, Aruko! ♡

This was Kazune Kawahara.

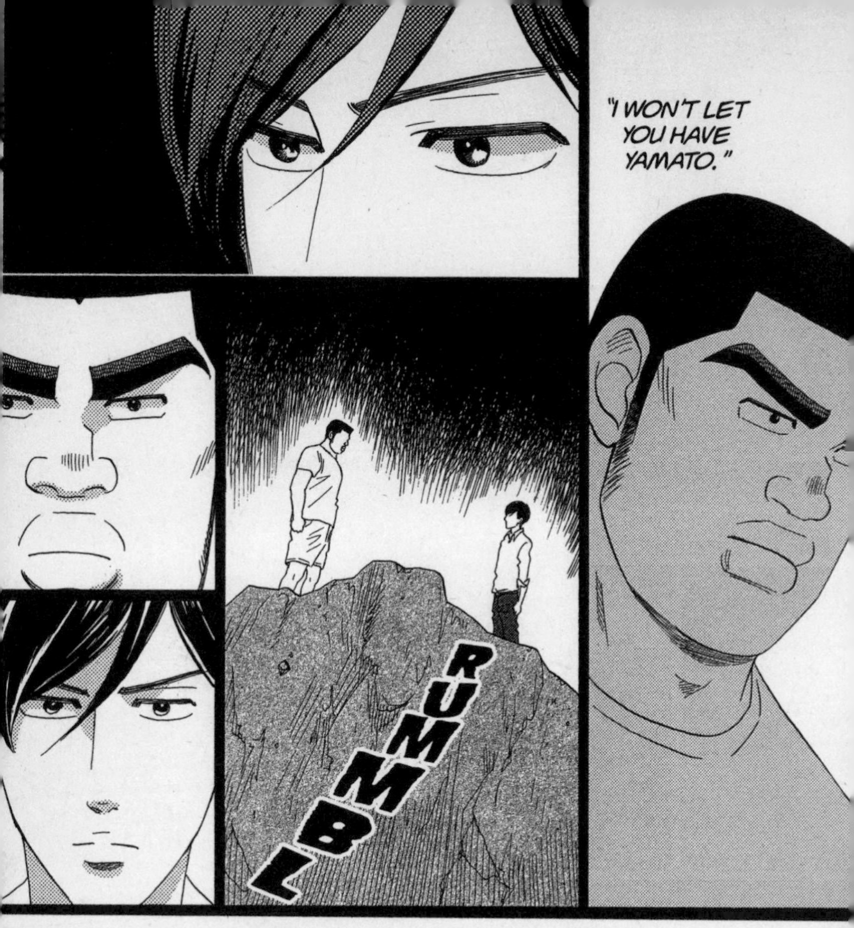
"I WON'T LET YOU HAVE YAMATO."
RUMMBL

# MY love STORY!!

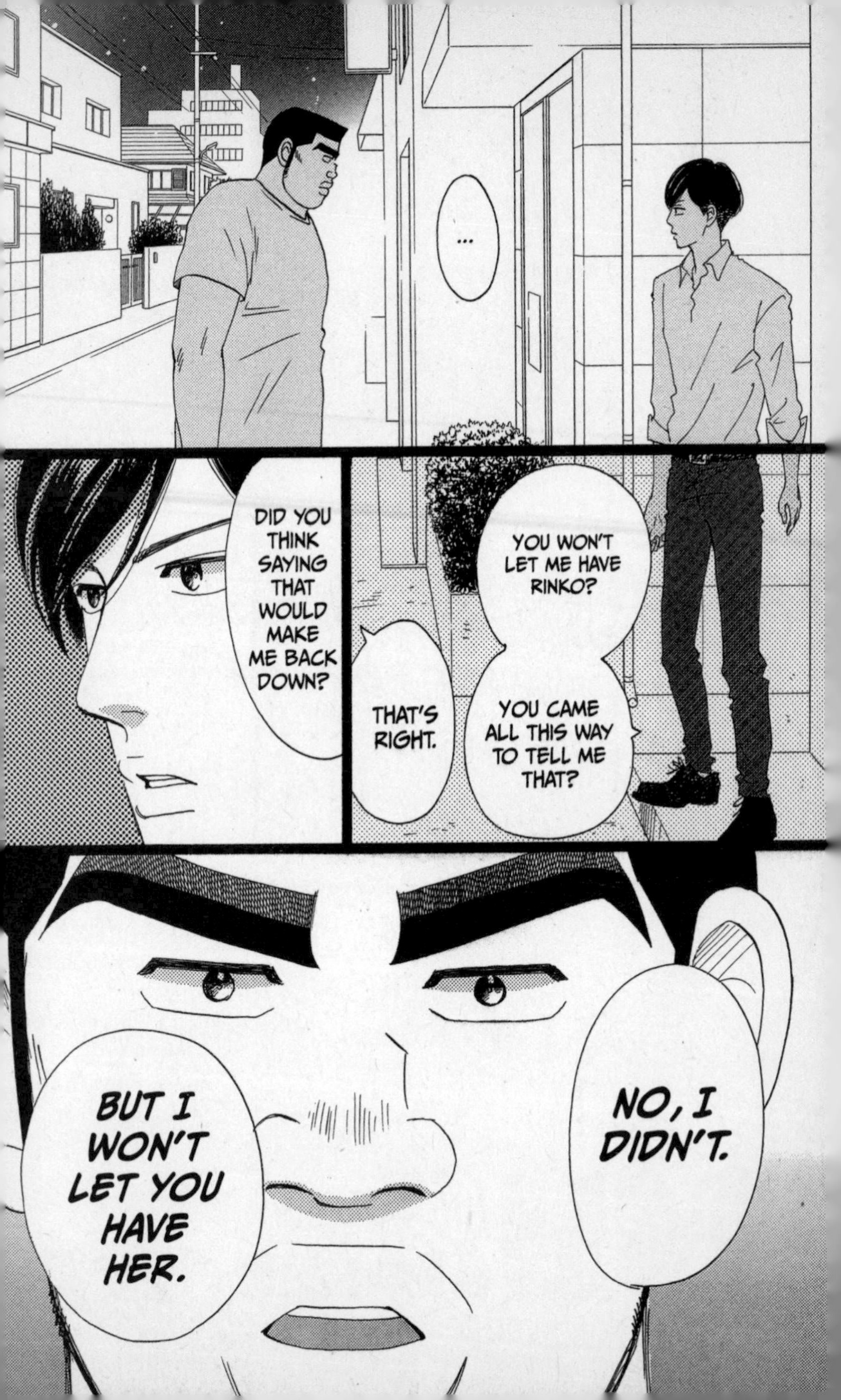
...
YOU WON'T LET ME HAVE RINKO?
YOU CAME ALL THIS WAY TO TELL ME THAT?
THAT'S RIGHT.
DID YOU THINK SAYING THAT WOULD MAKE ME BACK DOWN?
NO, I DIDN'T.
BUT I WON'T LET YOU HAVE HER.

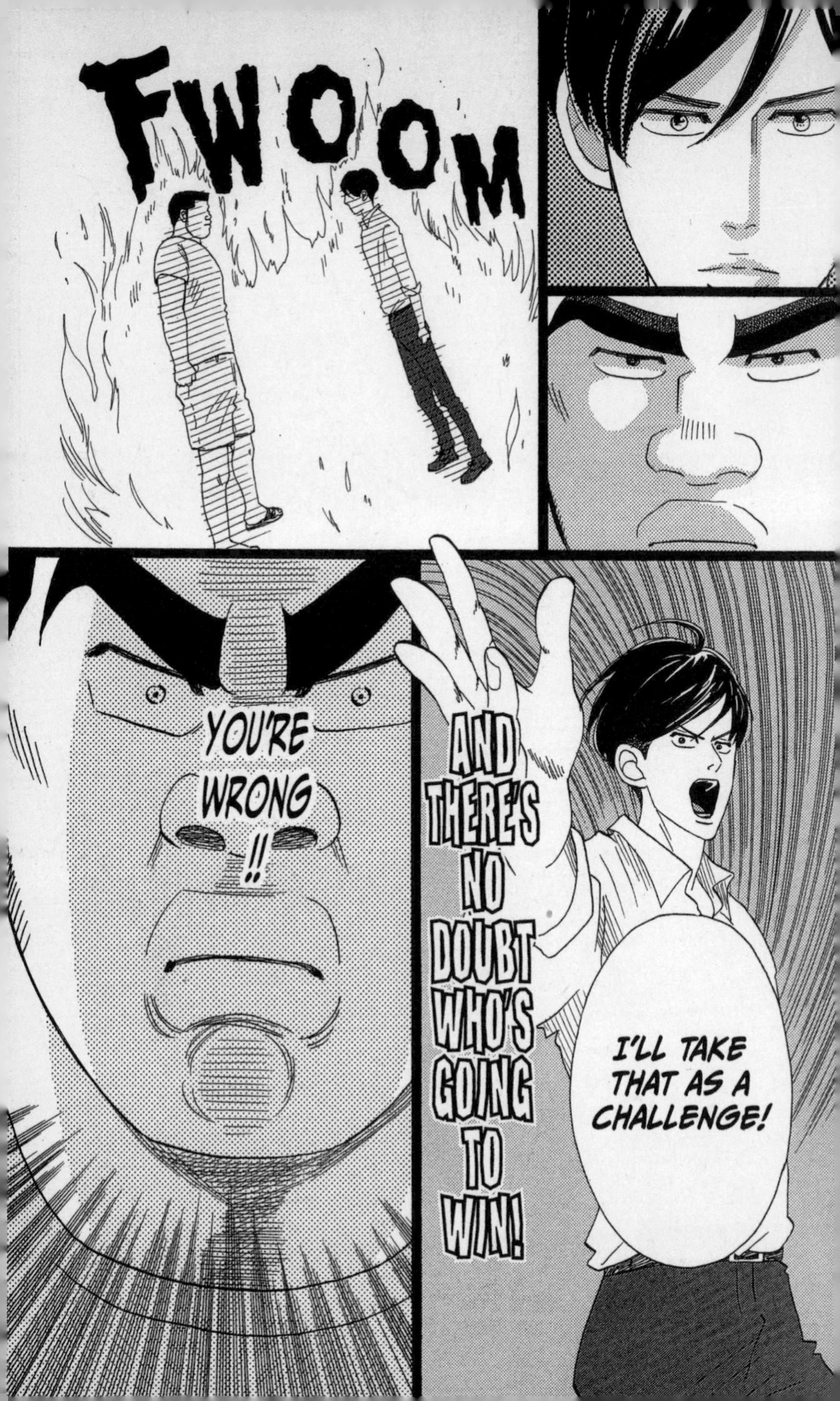
FWOOOM
I'LL TAKE THAT AS A CHALLENGE!
AND THERE'S NO DOUBT WHO'S GOING TO WIN!
YOU'RE WRONG!!

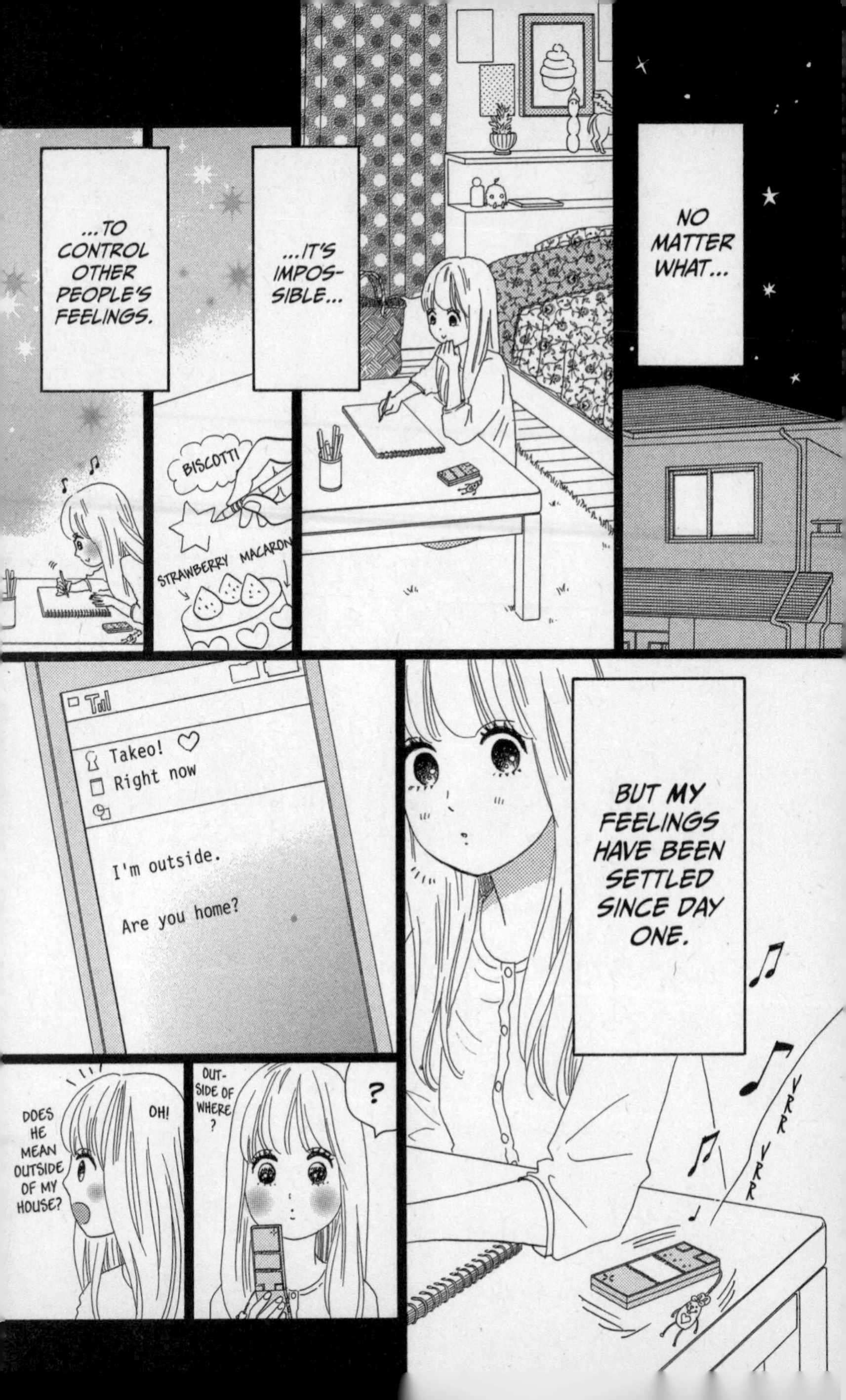
NO MATTER WHAT...
...IT'S IMPOS-SIBLE...
...TO CONTROL OTHER PEOPLE'S FEELINGS.
BISCOTTI
STRAWBERRY
MACARON
BUT MY FEELINGS HAVE BEEN SETTLED SINCE DAY ONE.
VRR VRR
Takeo!
Right now
I'm outside.
Are you home?
?
OUT-SIDE OF WHERE?
OH!
DOES HE MEAN OUTSIDE OF MY HOUSE?

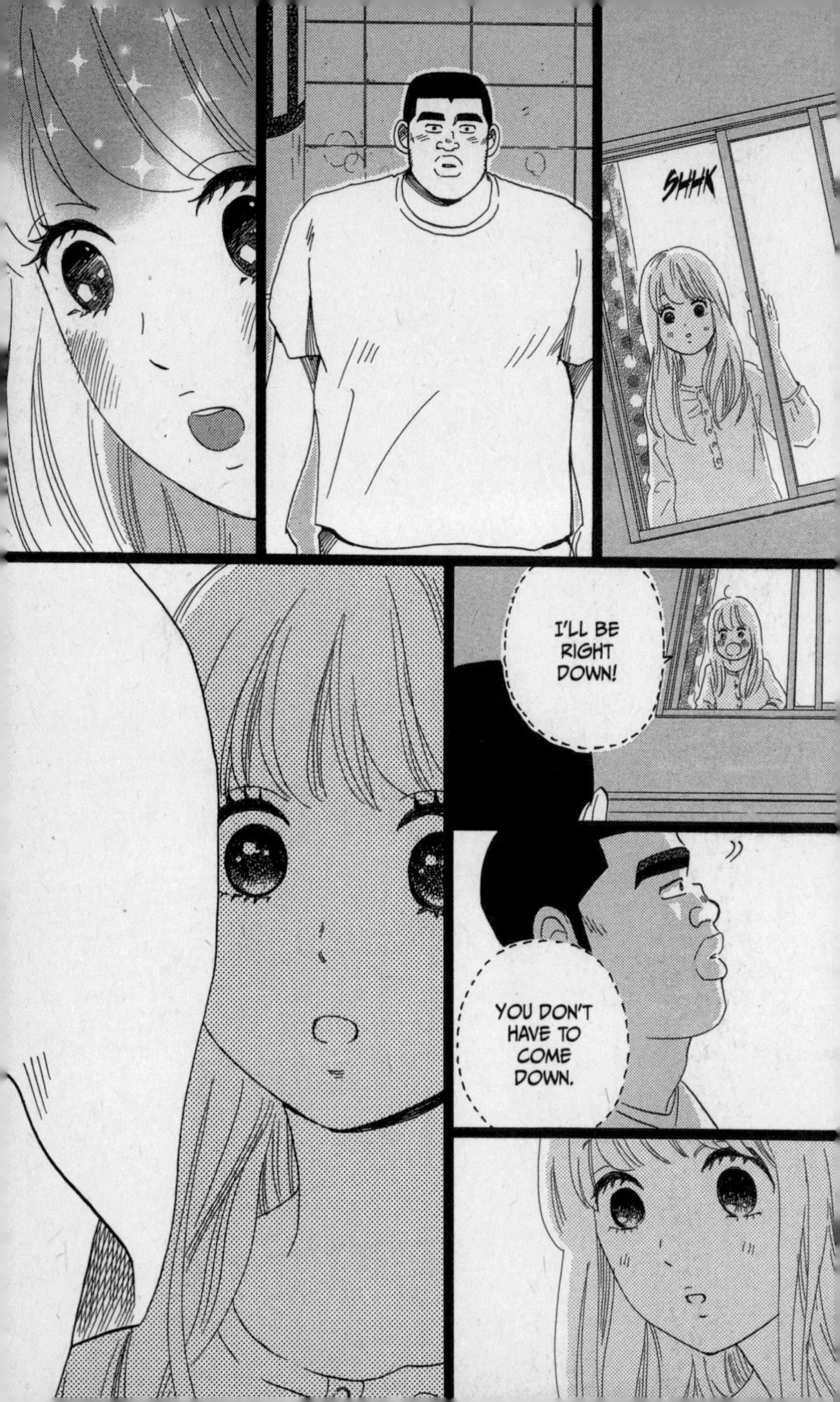
SHHK
I'LL BE RIGHT DOWN!
YOU DON'T HAVE TO COME DOWN.

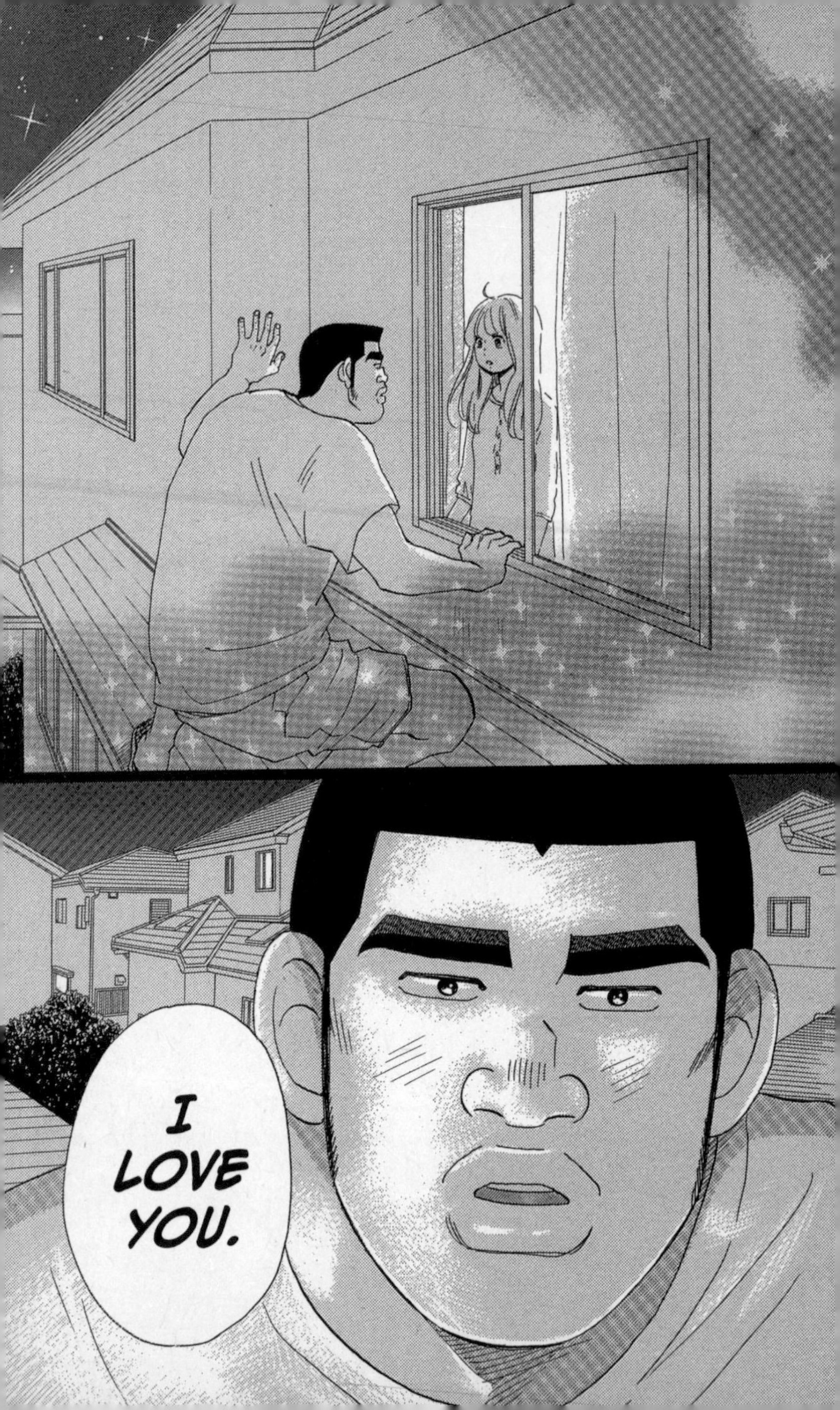
I LOVE YOU.

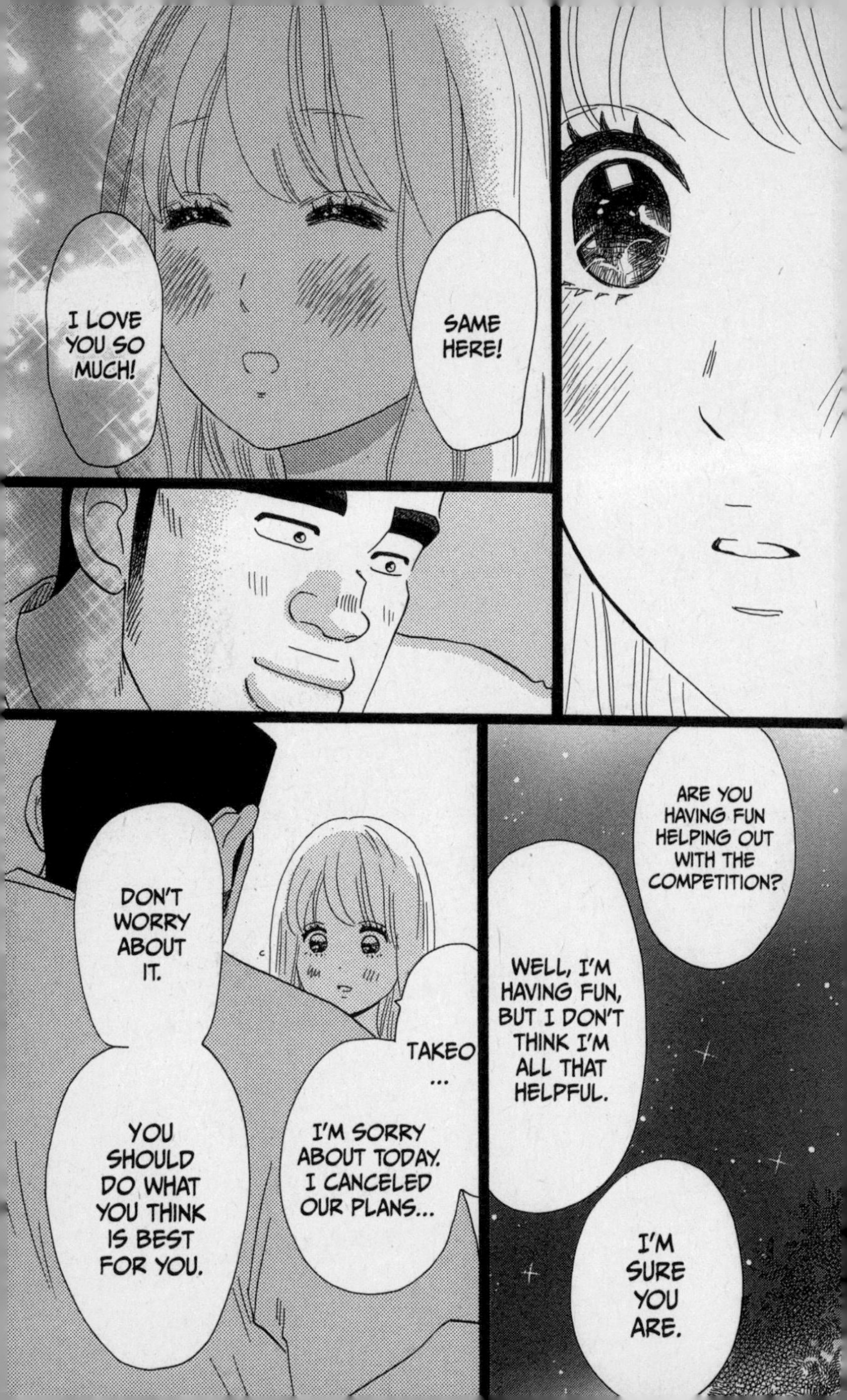
SAME HERE!
I LOVE YOU SO MUCH!
ARE YOU HAVING FUN HELPING OUT WITH THE COMPETITION?
WELL, I'M HAVING FUN, BUT I DON'T THINK I'M ALL THAT HELPFUL.
I'M SURE YOU ARE.
TAKEO...
I'M SORRY ABOUT TODAY. I CANCELED OUR PLANS...
DON'T WORRY ABOUT IT.
YOU SHOULD DO WHAT YOU THINK IS BEST FOR YOU.

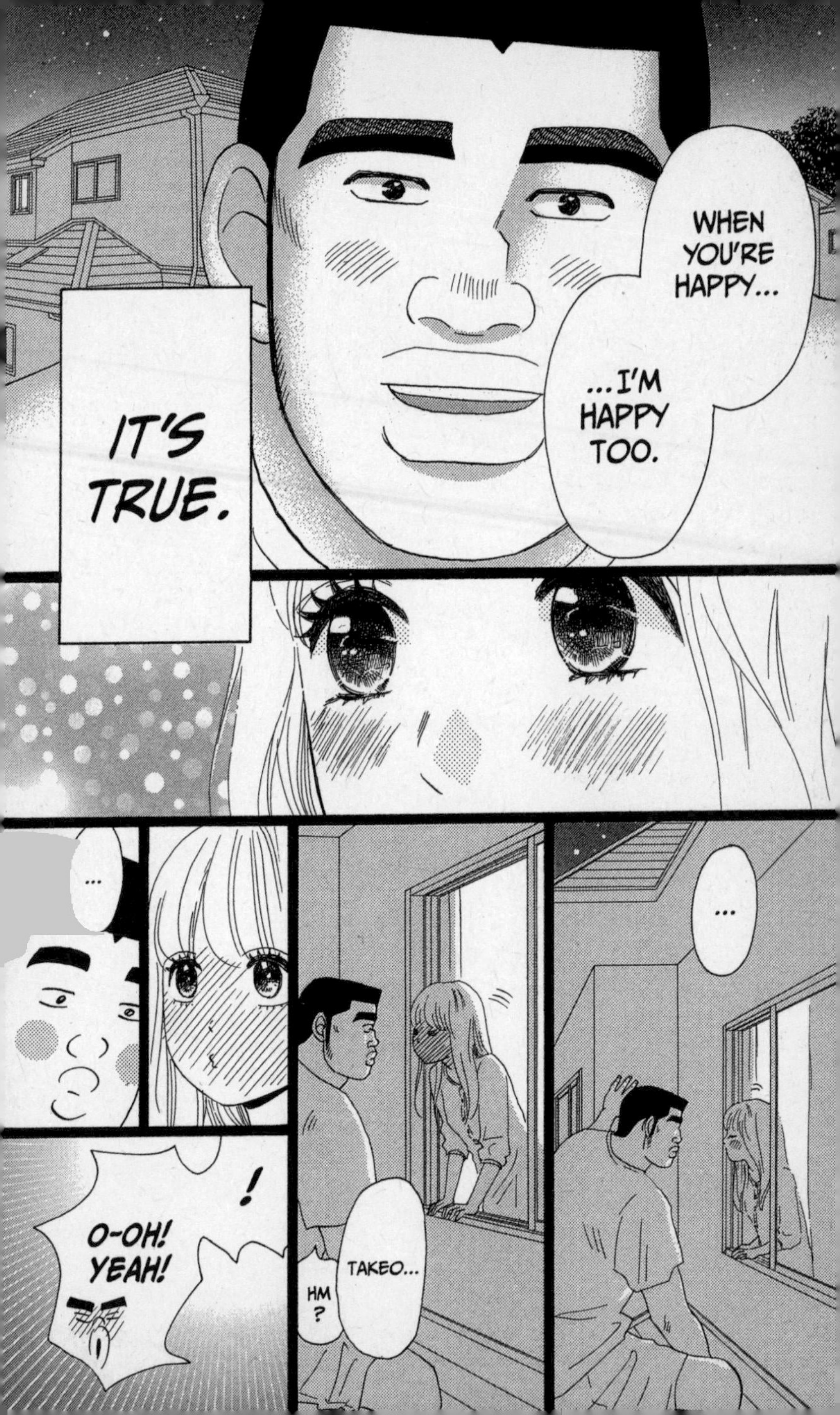
WHEN YOU'RE HAPPY...
...I'M HAPPY TOO.
IT'S TRUE.
...
TAKEO...
HM ?
...
!
O-OH! YEAH!

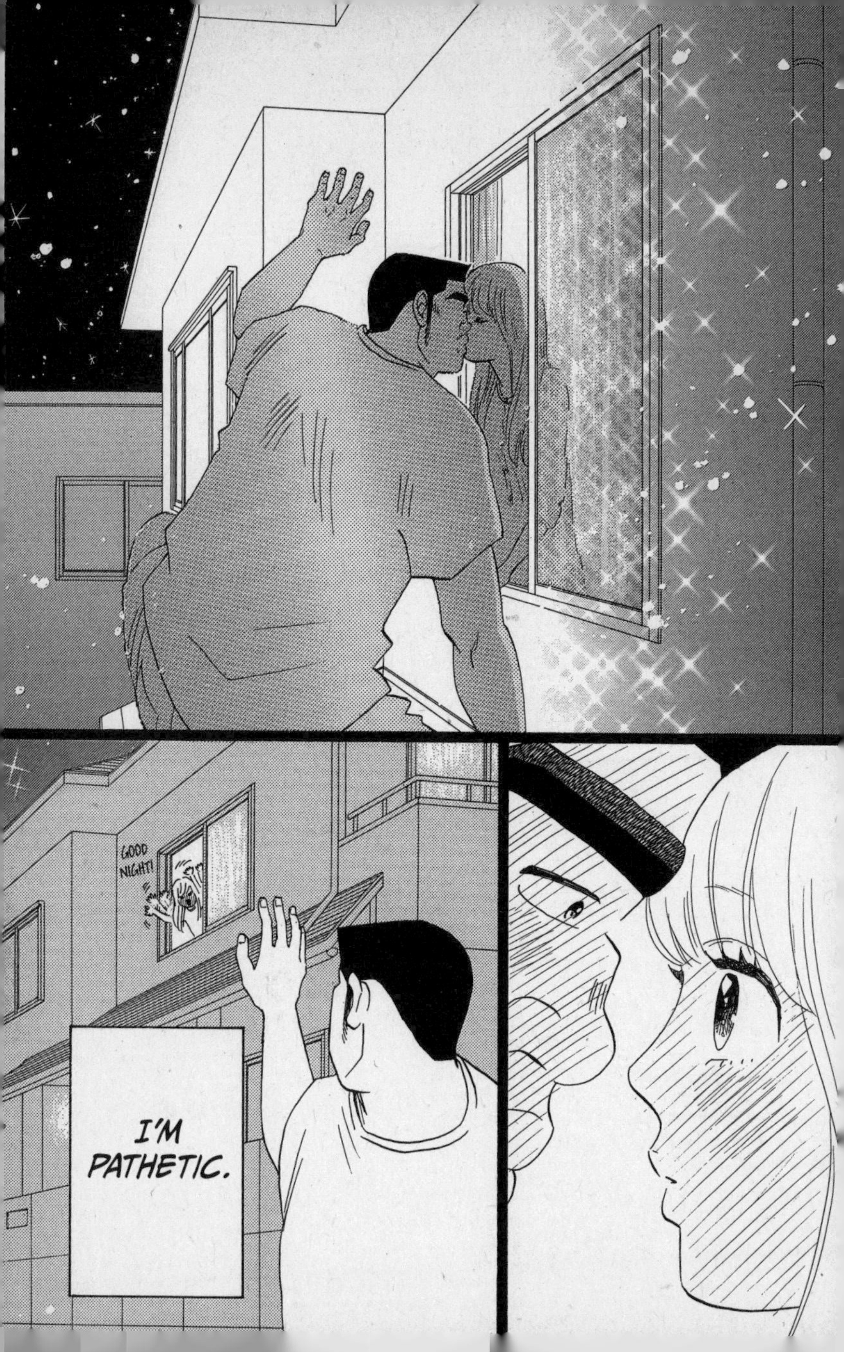
GOOD NIGHT!
I'M PATHETIC.

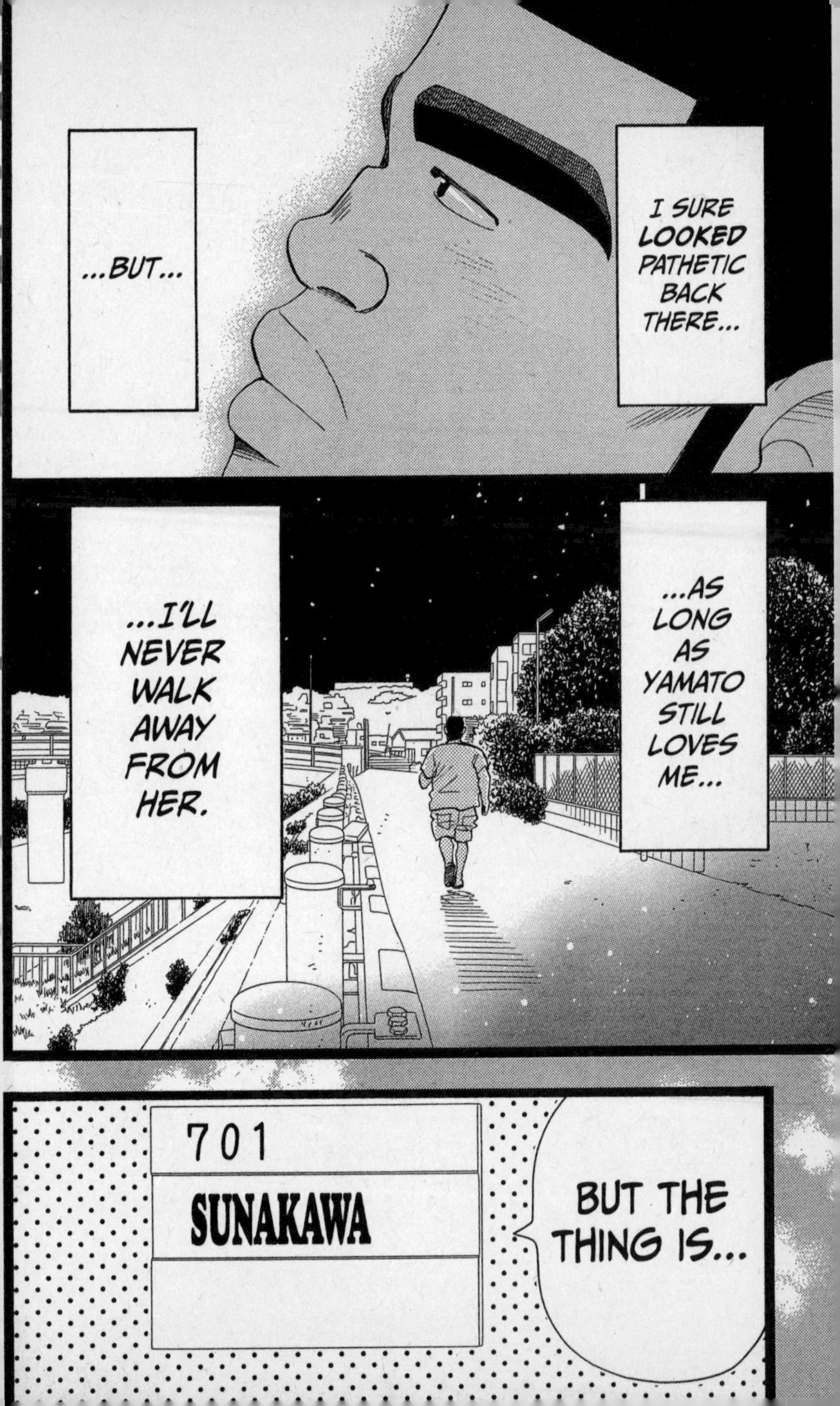
I SURE LOOKED PATHETIC BACK THERE...
...BUT...
...AS LONG AS YAMATO STILL LOVES ME...
...I'LL NEVER WALK AWAY FROM HER.
BUT THE THING IS...
701
SUNAKAWA

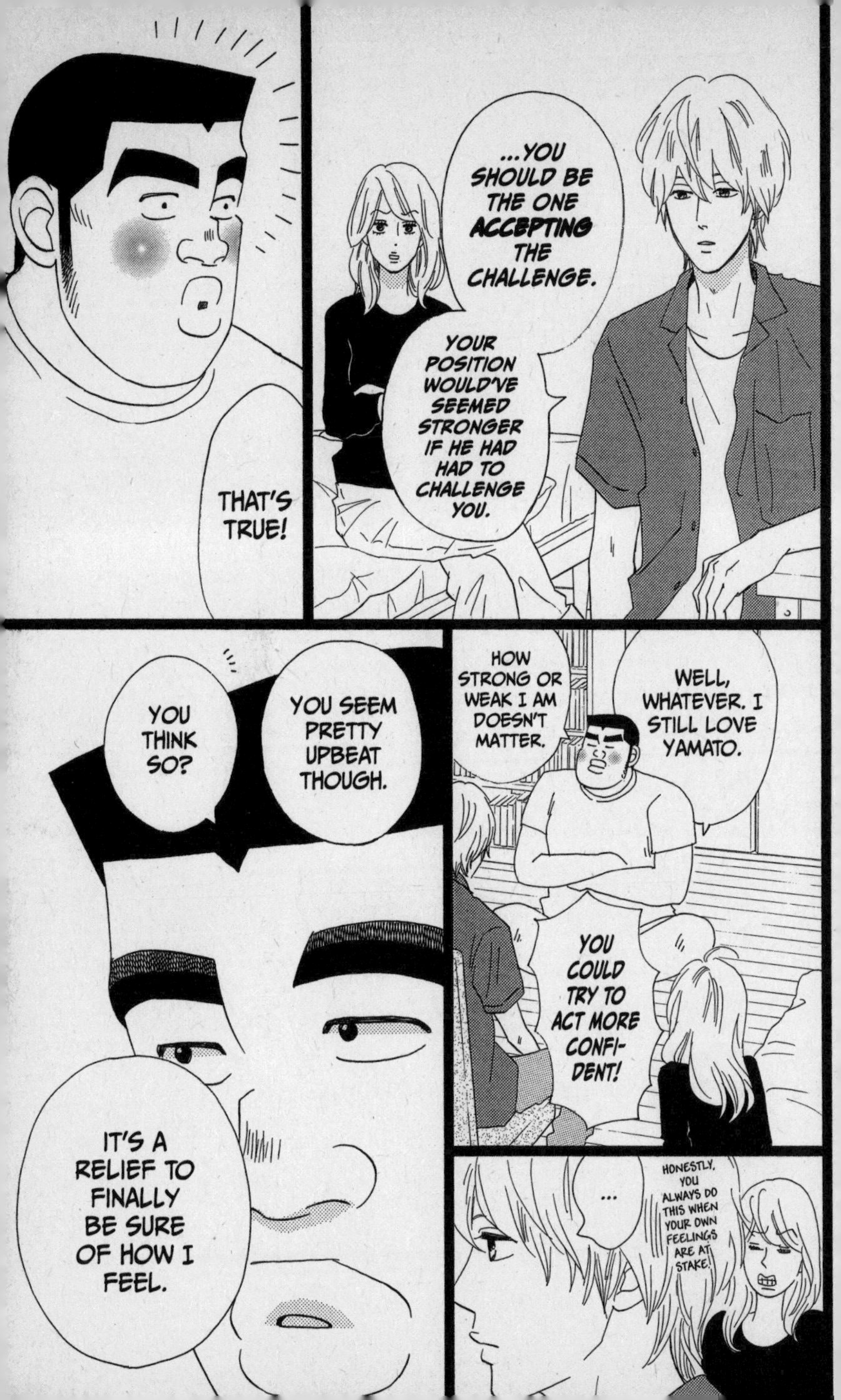

...YOU SHOULD BE THE ONE ACCEPTING THE CHALLENGE.
YOUR POSITION WOULD'VE SEEMED STRONGER IF HE HAD HAD TO CHALLENGE YOU.
THAT'S TRUE!
WELL, WHATEVER. I STILL LOVE YAMATO.
HOW STRONG OR WEAK I AM DOESN'T MATTER.
YOU COULD TRY TO ACT MORE CONFI-DENT!
HONESTLY, YOU ALWAYS DO THIS WHEN YOUR OWN FEELINGS ARE AT STAKE.
...
YOU SEEM PRETTY UPBEAT THOUGH.
YOU THINK SO?
IT'S A RELIEF TO FINALLY BE SURE OF HOW I FEEL.

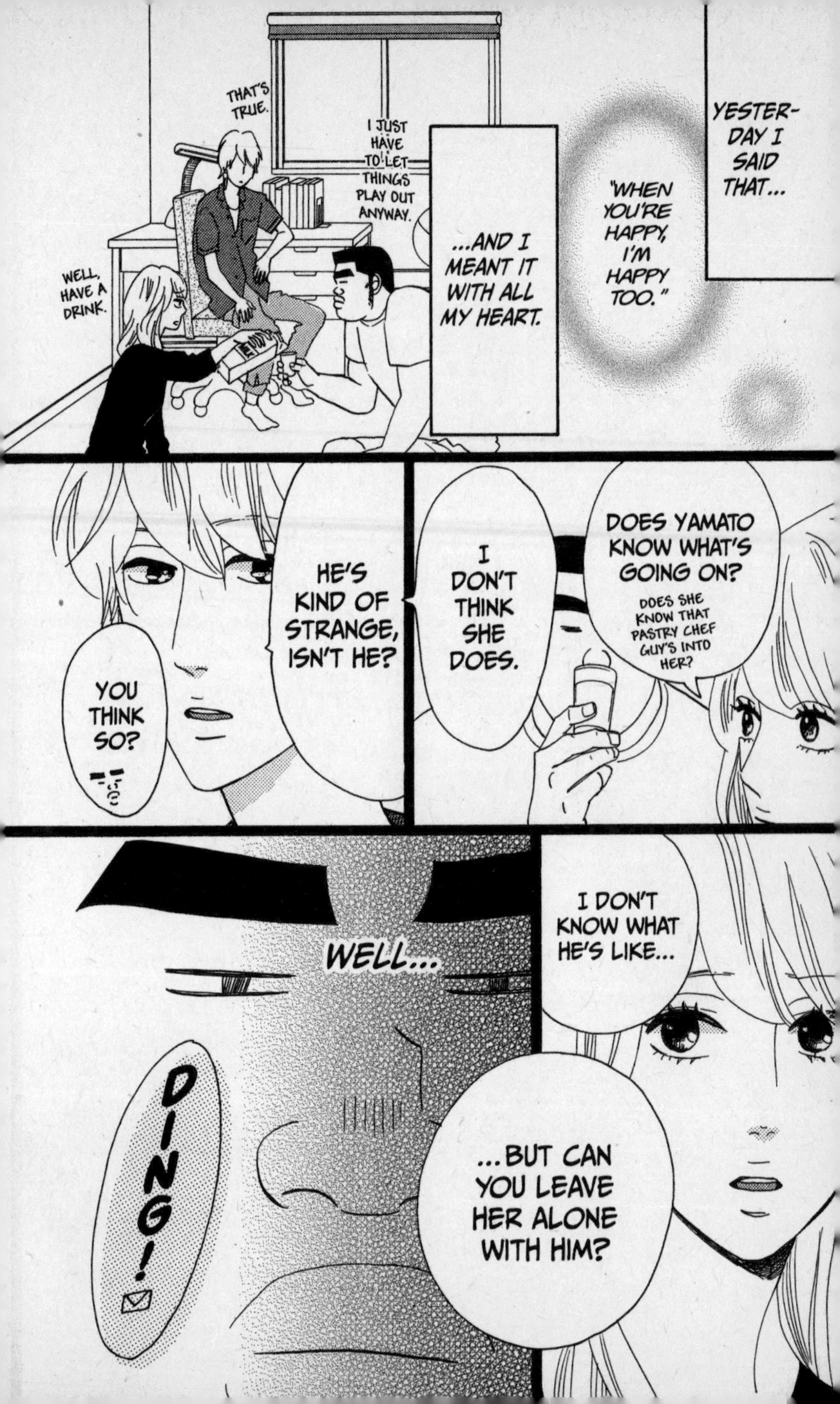
YESTERDAY I SAID THAT...
"WHEN YOU'RE HAPPY, I'M HAPPY TOO."
...AND I MEANT IT WITH ALL MY HEART.
I JUST HAVE TO LET THINGS PLAY OUT ANYWAY.
THAT'S TRUE.
WELL, HAVE A DRINK.
DOES YAMATO KNOW WHAT'S GOING ON?
DOES SHE KNOW THAT PASTRY CHEF GUY'S INTO HER?
I DON'T THINK SHE DOES.
HE'S KIND OF STRANGE, ISN'T HE?
YOU THINK SO?
I DON'T KNOW WHAT HE'S LIKE...
...BUT CAN YOU LEAVE HER ALONE WITH HIM?
WELL...
DING!

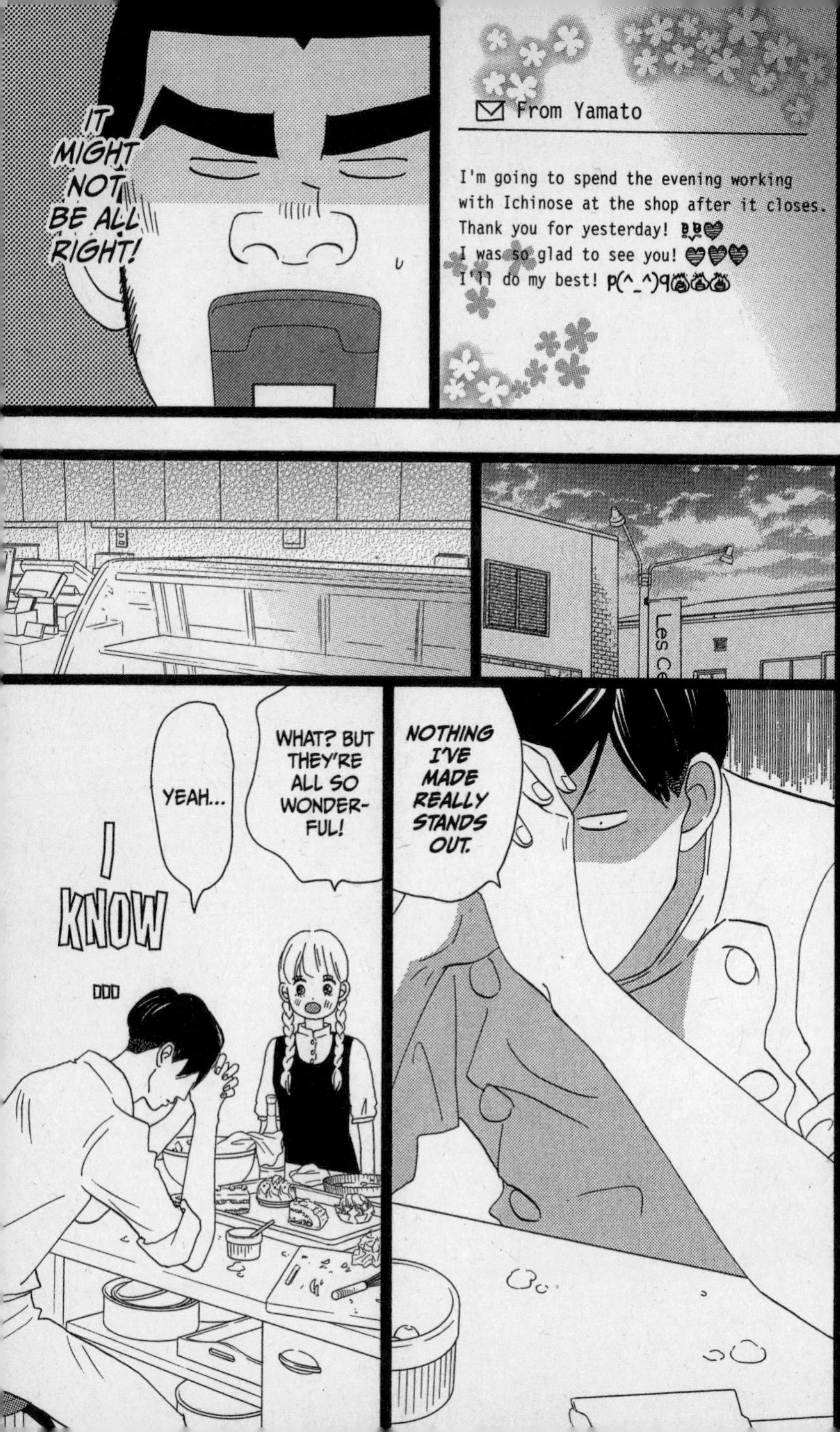
From Yamato
I'm going to spend the evening working with Ichinose at the shop after it closes.
Thank you for yesterday!
I was so glad to see you!
I'll do my best! p(^_^)q
IT MIGHT NOT BE ALL RIGHT!
NOTHING I'VE MADE REALLY STANDS OUT.
WHAT? BUT THEY'RE ALL SO WONDERFUL!
YEAH...
I KNOW

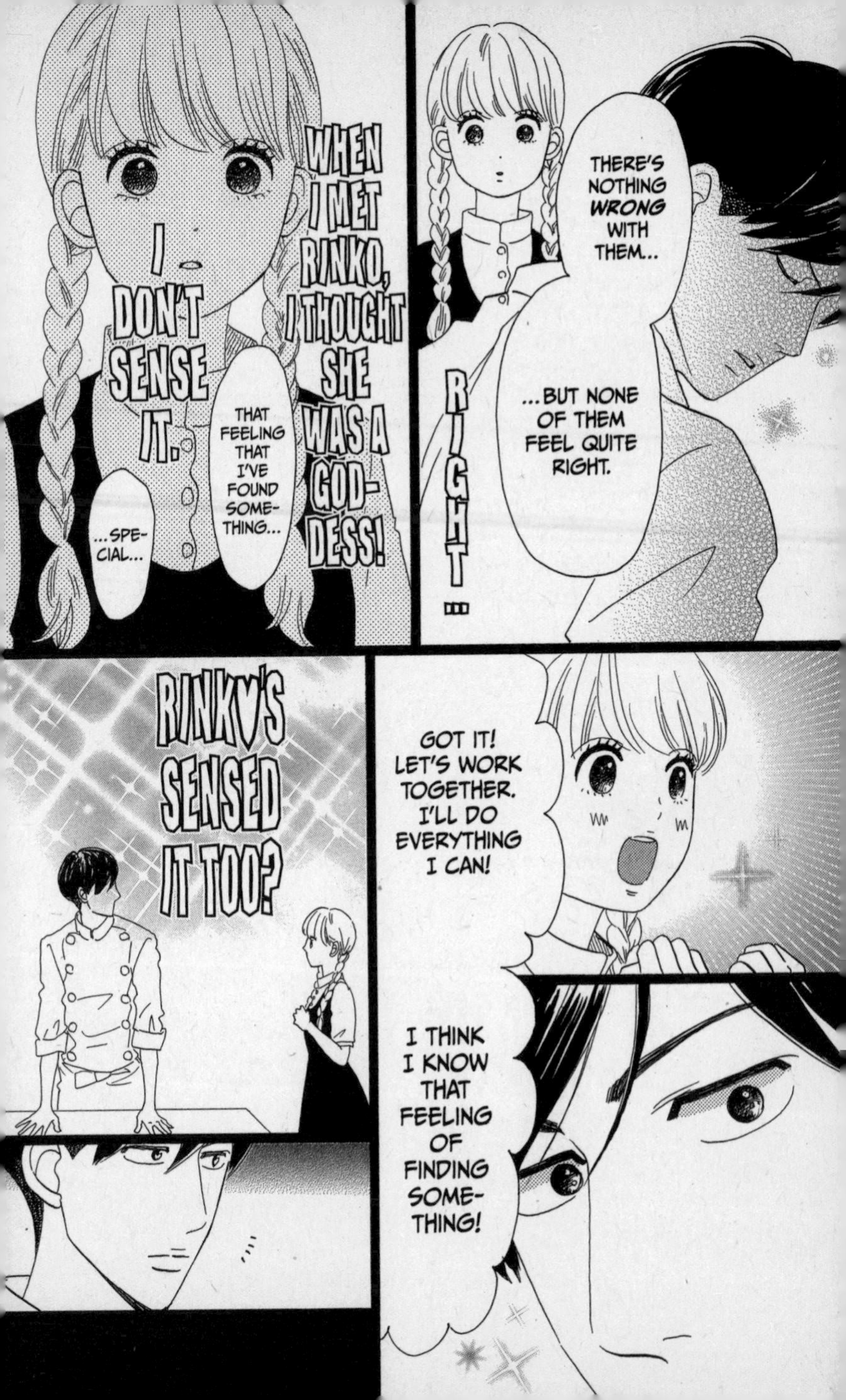

THERE'S NOTHING *WRONG* WITH THEM...
...BUT NONE OF THEM FEEL QUITE RIGHT.
RIGHT...
WHEN I MET RINKO, I THOUGHT SHE WAS A GOD-DESS!
I DON'T SENSE IT.
THAT FEELING THAT I'VE FOUND SOME-THING...
...SPE-CIAL...
GOT IT! LET'S WORK TOGETHER. I'LL DO EVERYTHING I CAN!
I THINK I KNOW THAT FEELING OF FINDING SOME-THING!
RINK♥'S SENSED IT TOO?

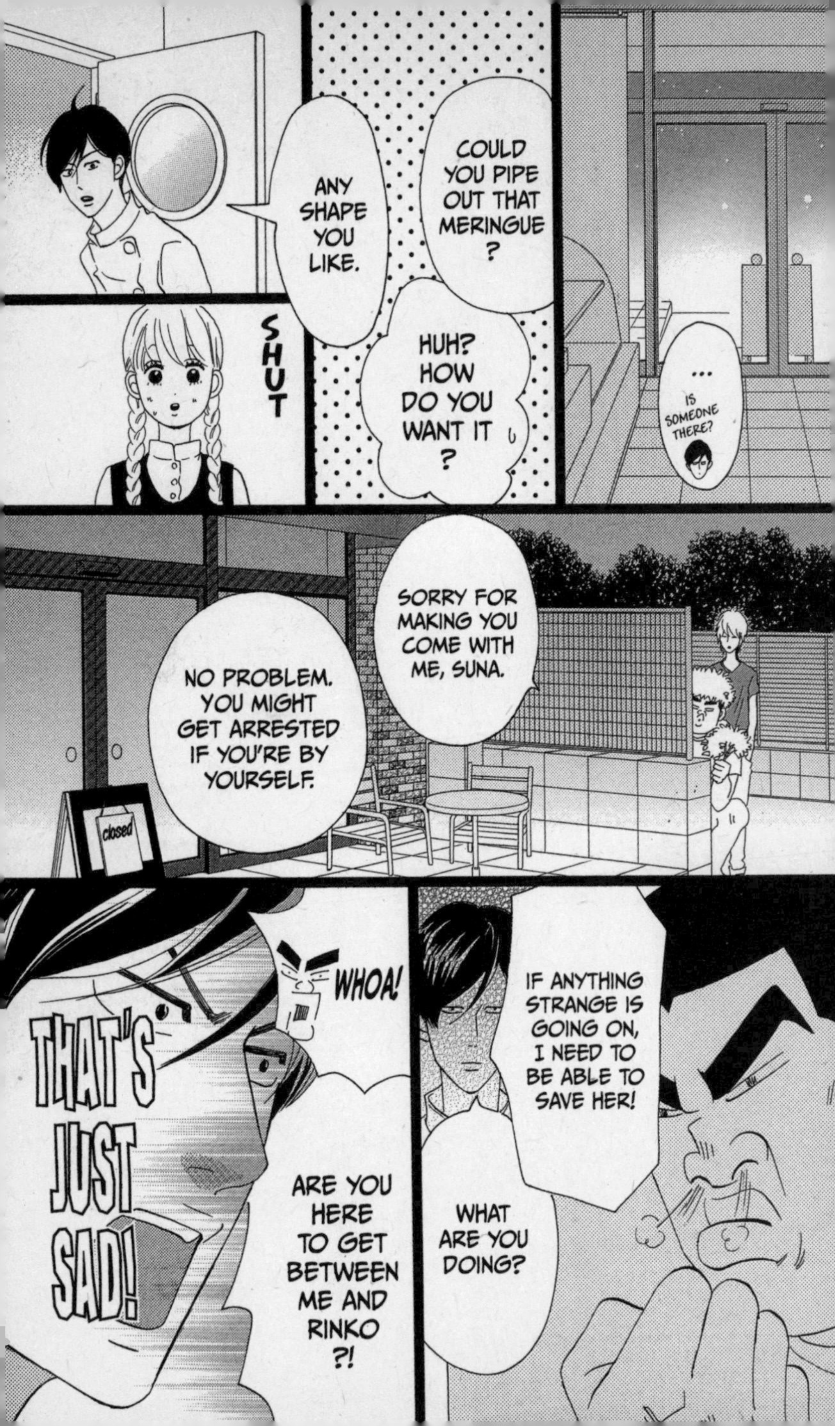
...
IS SOMEONE THERE?
COULD YOU PIPE OUT THAT MERINGUE?
ANY SHAPE YOU LIKE.
HUH? HOW DO YOU WANT IT?
SHUT
SORRY FOR MAKING YOU COME WITH ME, SUNA.
NO PROBLEM. YOU MIGHT GET ARRESTED IF YOU'RE BY YOURSELF.
closed
IF ANYTHING STRANGE IS GOING ON, I NEED TO BE ABLE TO SAVE HER!
WHAT ARE YOU DOING?
ARE YOU HERE TO GET BETWEEN ME AND RINKO?!
WHOA!
THAT'S JUST SAD!

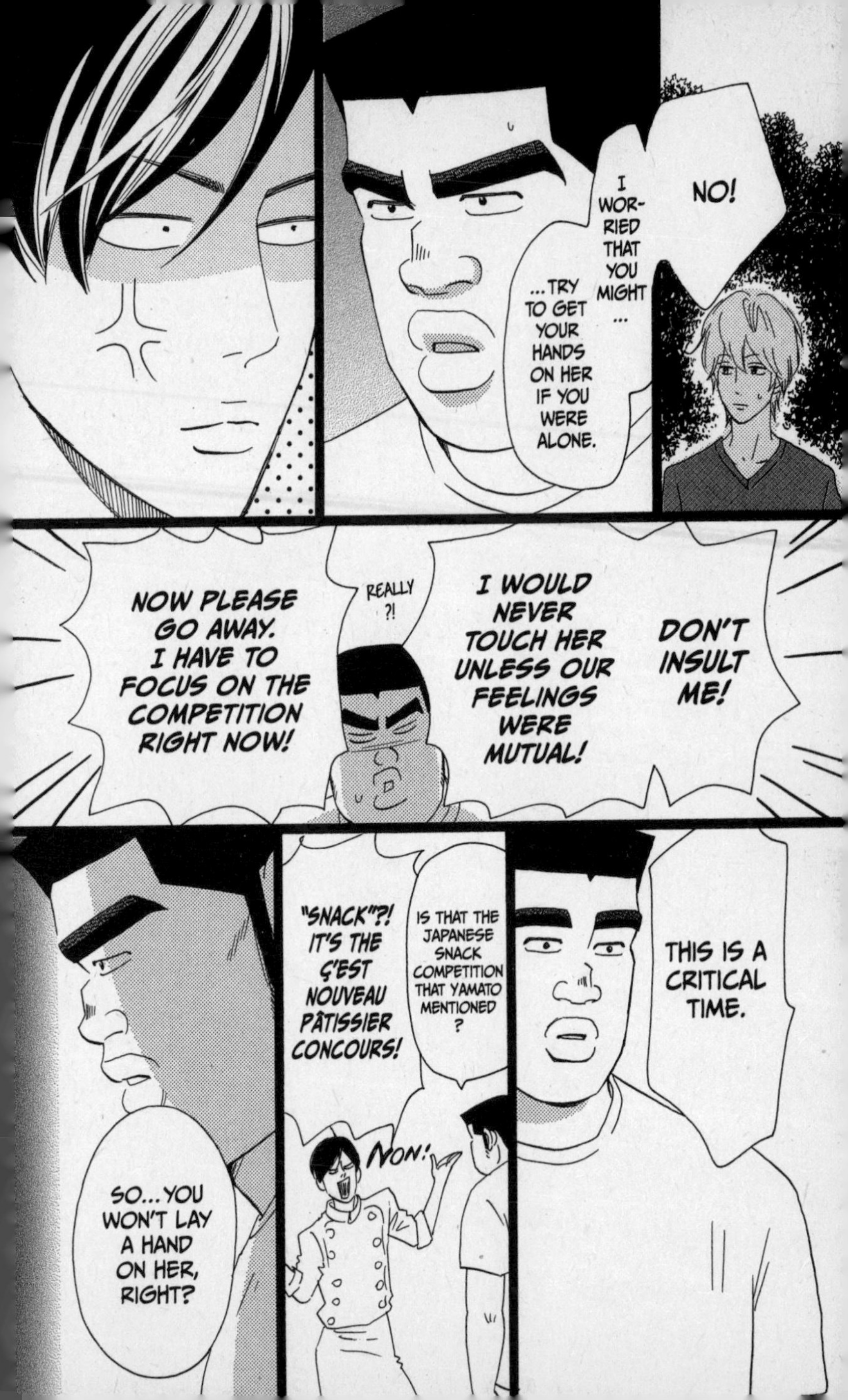
NO!
I WOR-RIED THAT YOU MIGHT...
...TRY TO GET YOUR HANDS ON HER IF YOU WERE ALONE.
DON'T INSULT ME!
I WOULD NEVER TOUCH HER UNLESS OUR FEELINGS WERE MUTUAL!
REALLY?!
NOW PLEASE GO AWAY. I HAVE TO FOCUS ON THE COMPETITION RIGHT NOW!
THIS IS A CRITICAL TIME.
IS THAT THE JAPANESE SNACK COMPETITION THAT YAMATO MENTIONED?
"SNACK"?! IT'S THE Ç'EST NOUVEAU PÂTISSIER CONCOURS!
NON!
SO...YOU WON'T LAY A HAND ON HER, RIGHT?

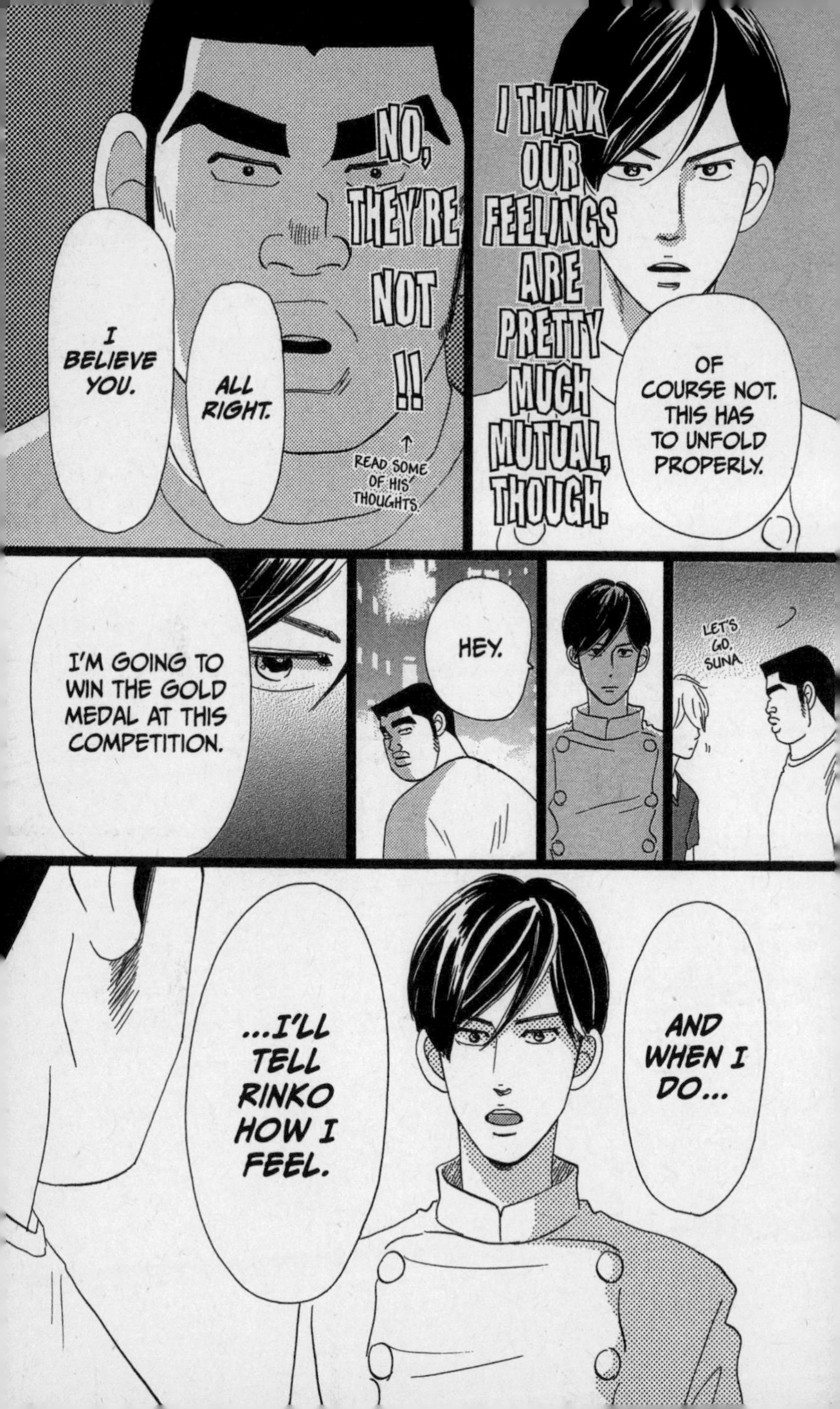
OF COURSE NOT. THIS HAS TO UNFOLD PROPERLY.
I THINK OUR FEELINGS ARE PRETTY MUCH MUTUAL, THOUGH.
NO, THEY'RE NOT!!
↑ READ SOME OF HIS THOUGHTS.
ALL RIGHT.
I BELIEVE YOU.
LET'S GO, SUNA.
HEY.
I'M GOING TO WIN THE GOLD MEDAL AT THIS COMPETITION.
AND WHEN I DO...
...I'LL TELL RINKO HOW I FEEL.

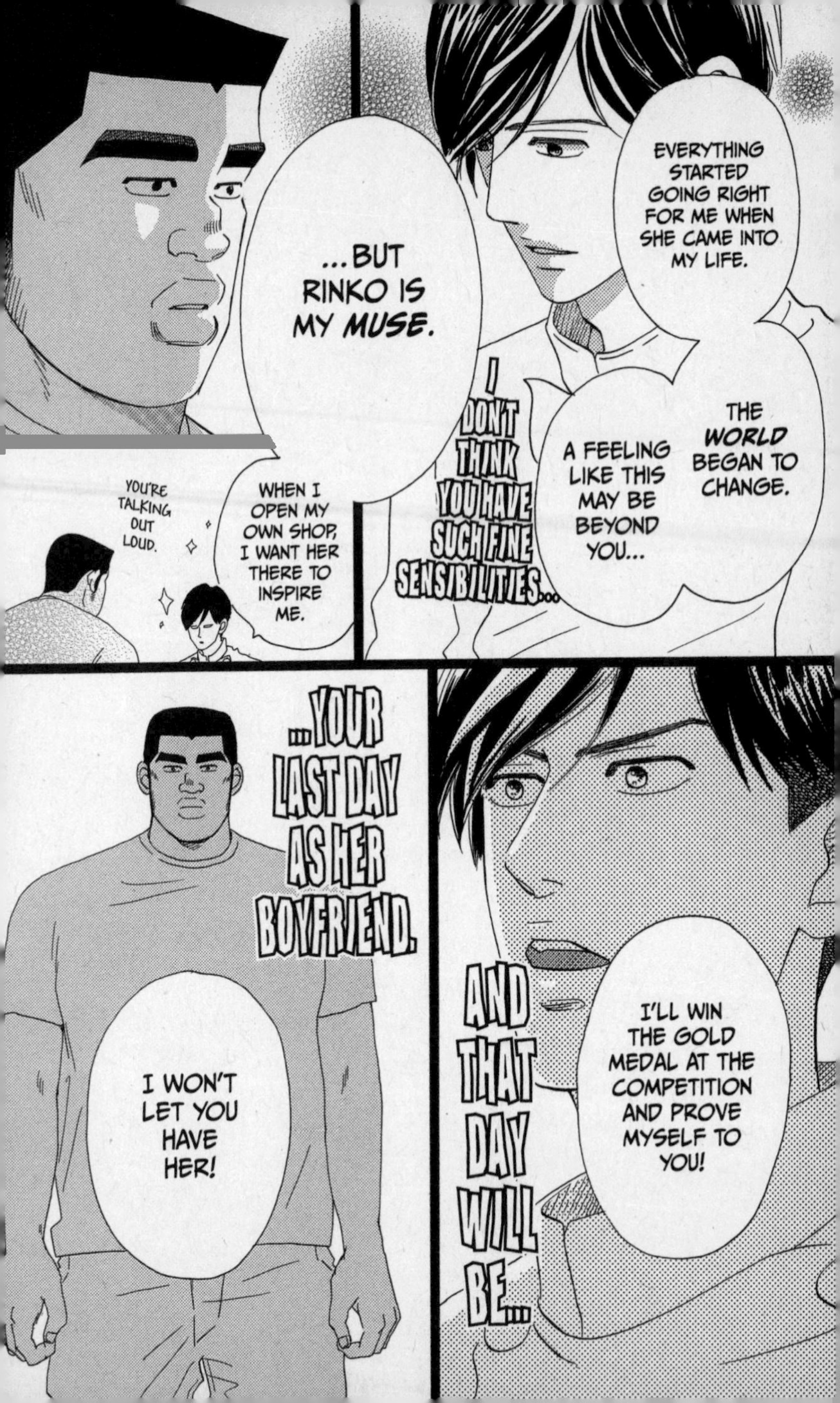
EVERYTHING STARTED GOING RIGHT FOR ME WHEN SHE CAME INTO MY LIFE.
THE *WORLD* BEGAN TO CHANGE.
A FEELING LIKE THIS MAY BE BEYOND YOU...
I DON'T THINK YOU HAVE SUCH FINE SENSIBILITIES...
...BUT RINKO IS MY *MUSE*.
WHEN I OPEN MY OWN SHOP, I WANT HER THERE TO INSPIRE ME.
YOU'RE TALKING OUT LOUD.
I'LL WIN THE GOLD MEDAL AT THE COMPETITION AND PROVE MYSELF TO YOU!
AND THAT DAY WILL BE...
...YOUR LAST DAY AS HER BOYFRIEND.
I WON'T LET YOU HAVE HER!

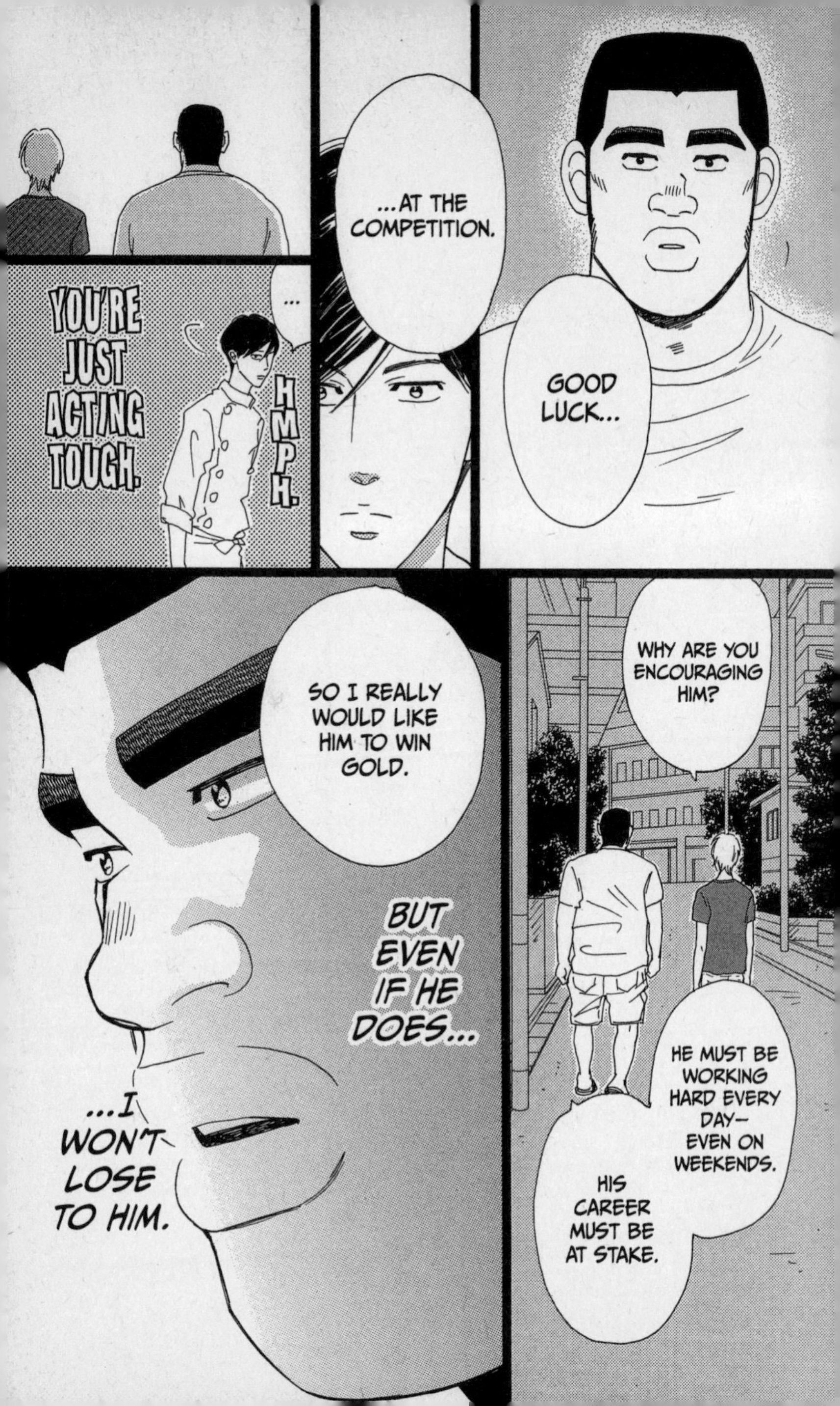
GOOD LUCK...
...AT THE COMPETITION.
...
HMPH.
YOU'RE JUST ACTING TOUGH.
WHY ARE YOU ENCOURAGING HIM?
HE MUST BE WORKING HARD EVERY DAY— EVEN ON WEEKENDS.
HIS CAREER MUST BE AT STAKE.
SO I REALLY WOULD LIKE HIM TO WIN GOLD.
BUT EVEN IF HE DOES...
...I WON'T LOSE TO HIM.

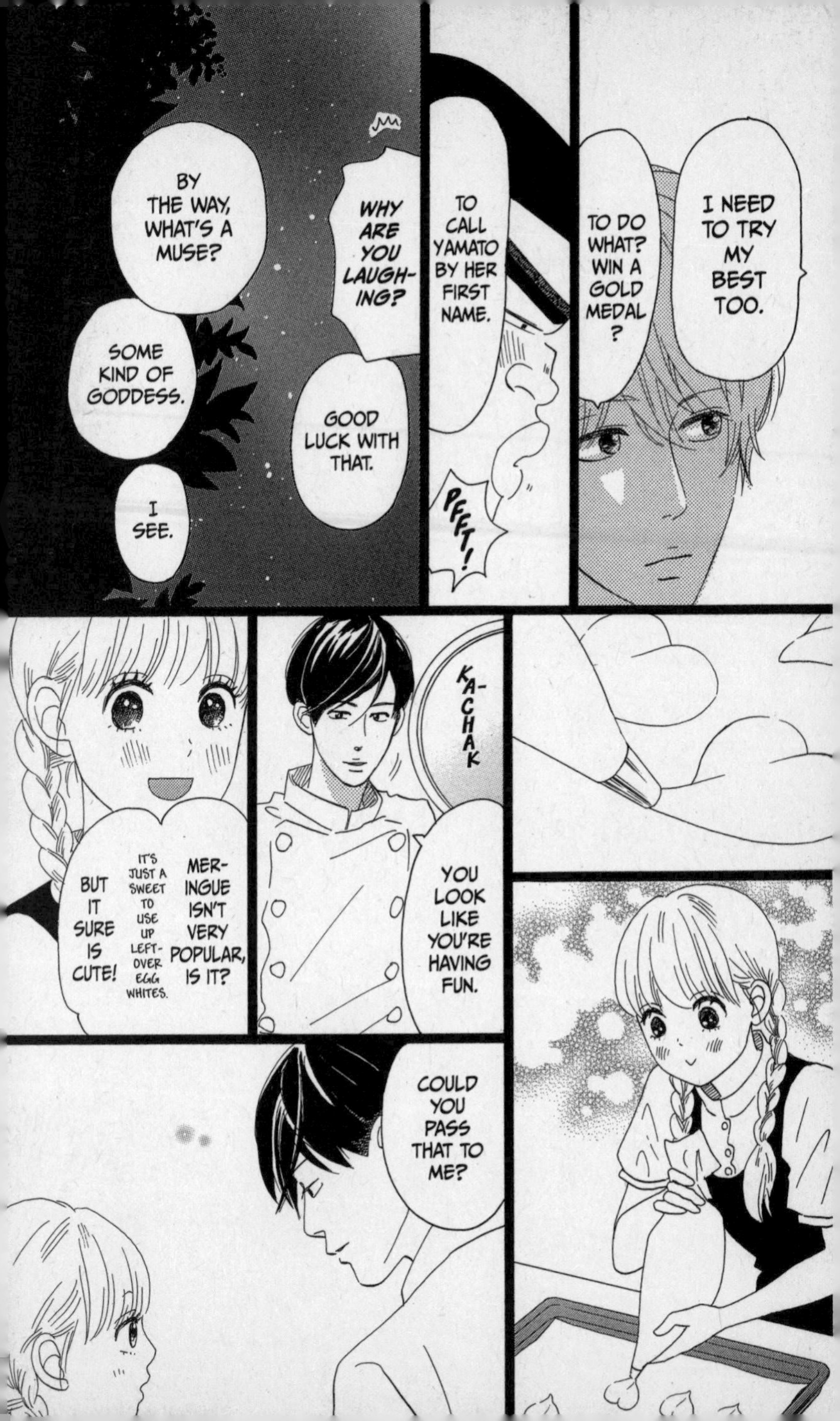
I NEED TO TRY MY BEST TOO.
TO DO WHAT? WIN A GOLD MEDAL?
TO CALL YAMATO BY HER FIRST NAME.
PFFT!
WHY ARE YOU LAUGHING?
GOOD LUCK WITH THAT.
BY THE WAY, WHAT'S A MUSE?
SOME KIND OF GODDESS.
I SEE.
KA-CHAK
YOU LOOK LIKE YOU'RE HAVING FUN.
MERINGUE ISN'T VERY POPULAR, IS IT?
IT'S JUST A SWEET TO USE UP LEFTOVER EGG WHITES.
BUT IT SURE IS CUTE!
COULD YOU PASS THAT TO ME?

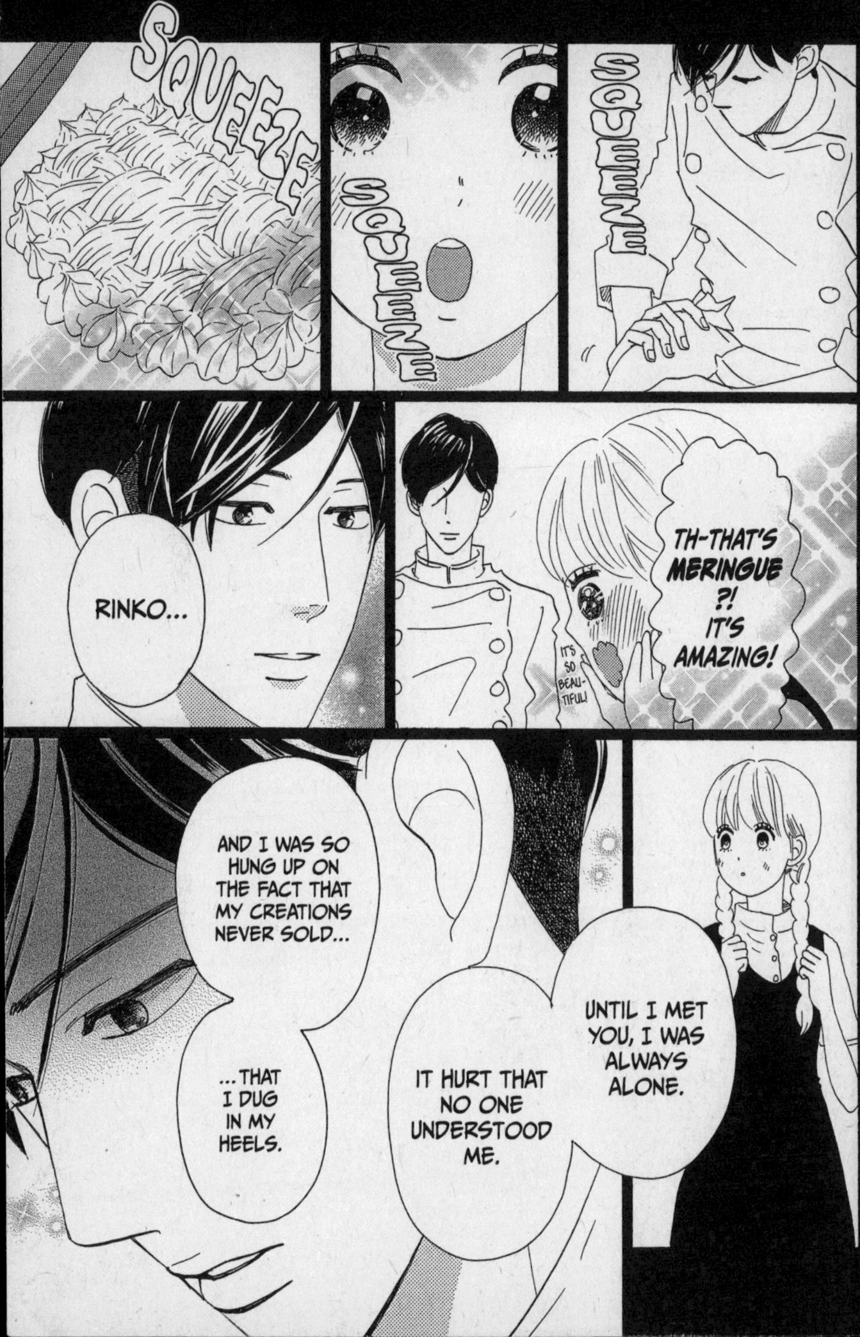
SQUEEZE
SQUEEZE
SQUEEZE
TH-THAT'S MERINGUE?! IT'S AMAZING!
IT'S SO BEAU-TIFUL!
RINKO...
UNTIL I MET YOU, I WAS ALWAYS ALONE.
IT HURT THAT NO ONE UNDERSTOOD ME.
AND I WAS SO HUNG UP ON THE FACT THAT MY CREATIONS NEVER SOLD...
...THAT I DUG IN MY HEELS.

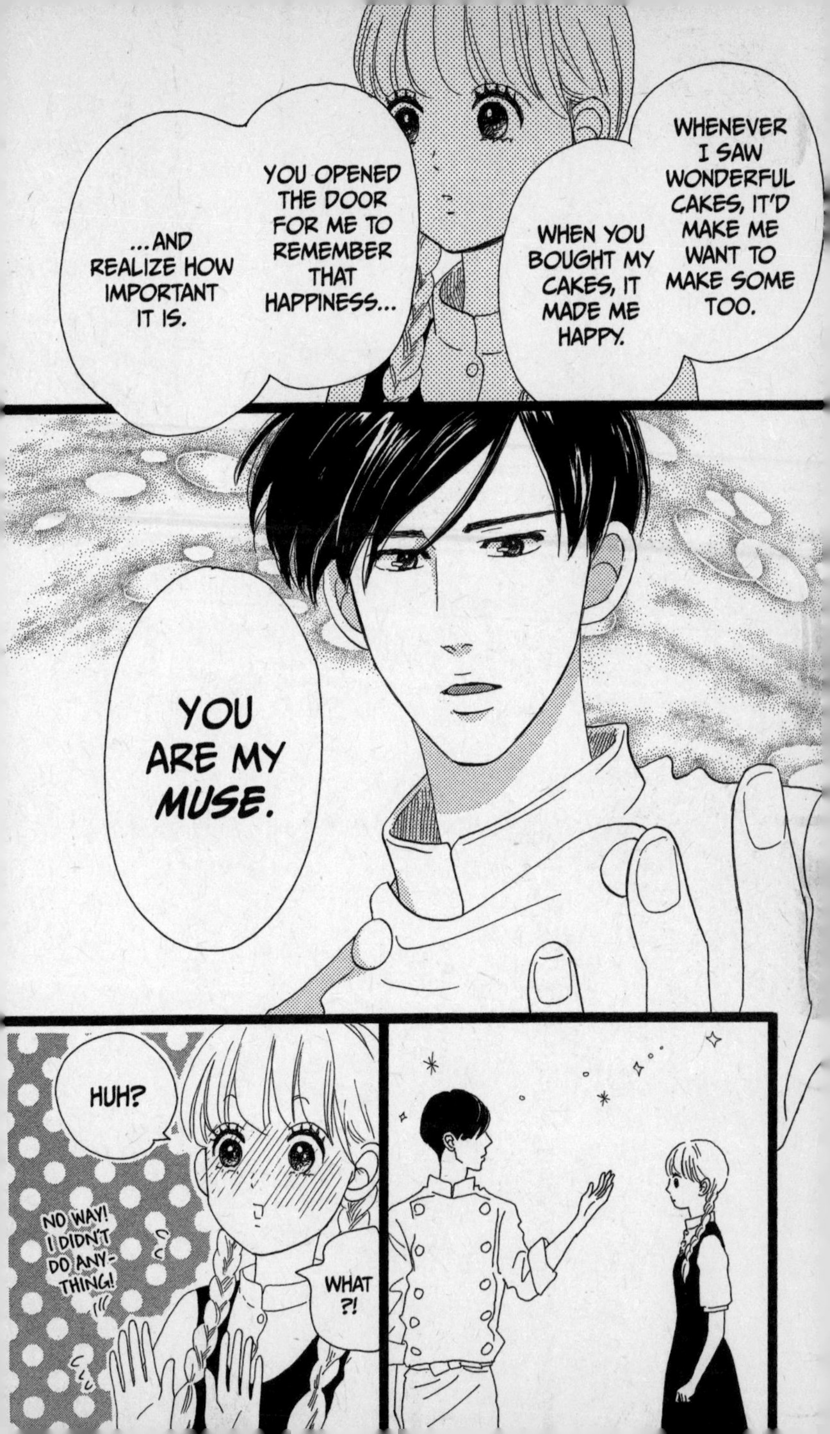
WHENEVER I SAW WONDERFUL CAKES, IT'D MAKE ME WANT TO MAKE SOME TOO.
WHEN YOU BOUGHT MY CAKES, IT MADE ME HAPPY.
YOU OPENED THE DOOR FOR ME TO REMEMBER THAT HAPPINESS...
...AND REALIZE HOW IMPORTANT IT IS.
YOU ARE MY *MUSE*.
HUH?
WHAT ?!
NO WAY! I DIDN'T DO ANY-THING!

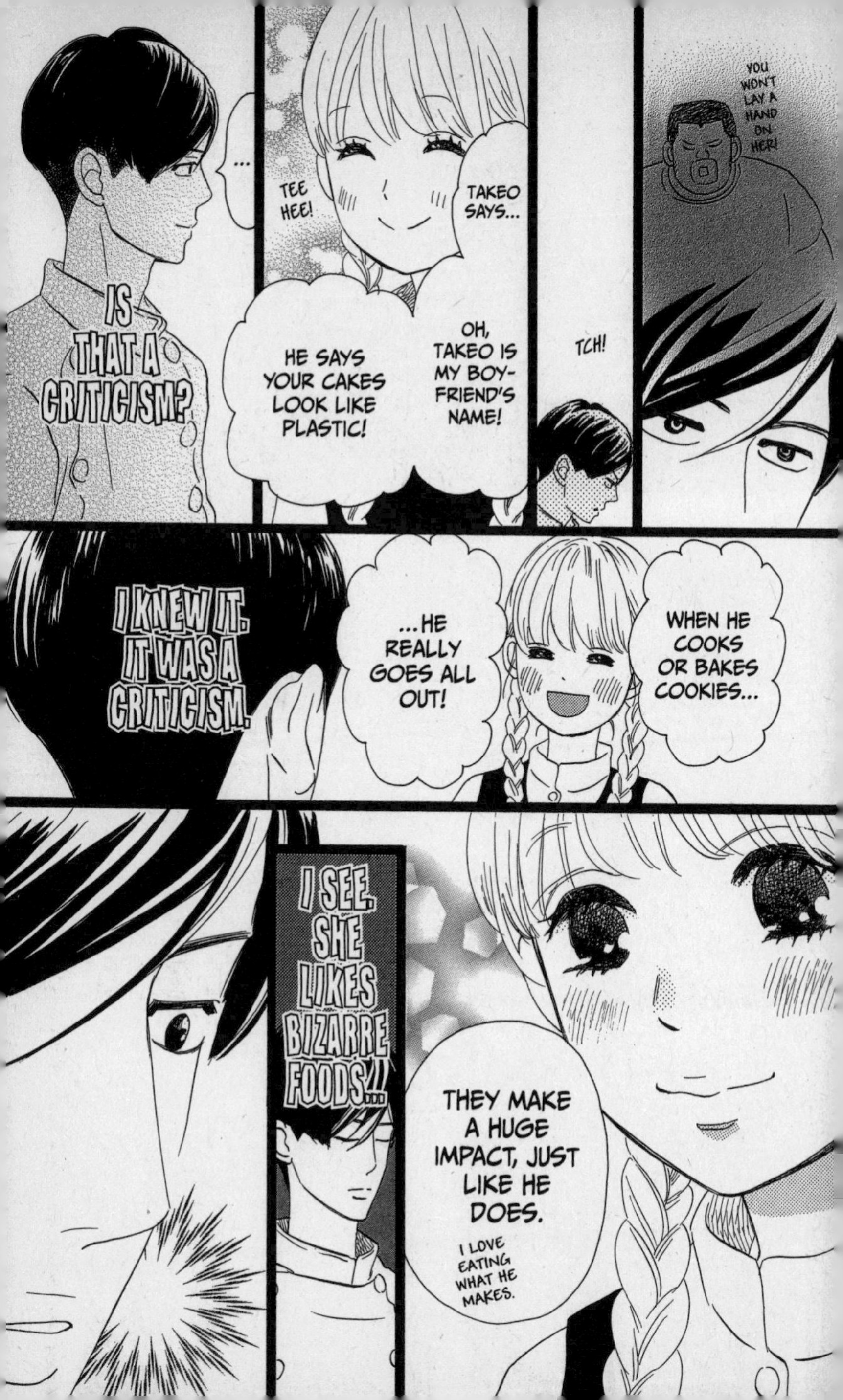
YOU WON'T LAY A HAND ON HER!
TCH!
TAKEO SAYS...
TEE HEE!
OH, TAKEO IS MY BOY-FRIEND'S NAME!
HE SAYS YOUR CAKES LOOK LIKE PLASTIC!
...
IS THAT A CRITICISM?
WHEN HE COOKS OR BAKES COOKIES...
...HE REALLY GOES ALL OUT!
I KNEW IT. IT WAS A CRITICISM.
THEY MAKE A HUGE IMPACT, JUST LIKE HE DOES.
I LOVE EATING WHAT HE MAKES.
I SEE. SHE LIKES BIZARRE FOODS...!!

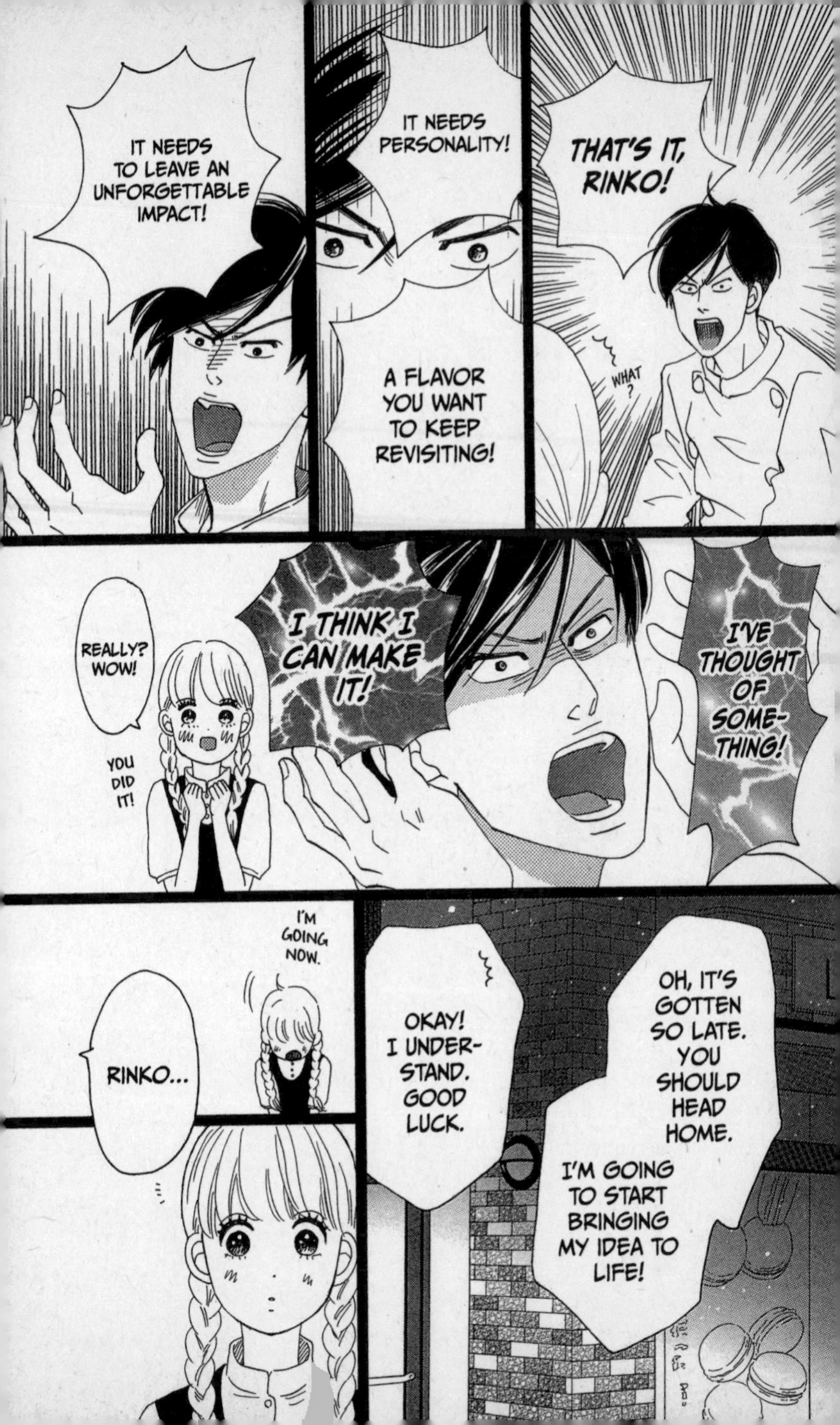
THAT'S IT, RINKO!
WHAT?
IT NEEDS PERSONALITY!
A FLAVOR YOU WANT TO KEEP REVISITING!
IT NEEDS TO LEAVE AN UNFORGETTABLE IMPACT!
I'VE THOUGHT OF SOME-THING!
I THINK I CAN MAKE IT!
REALLY? WOW!
YOU DID IT!
OH, IT'S GOTTEN SO LATE. YOU SHOULD HEAD HOME.
I'M GOING TO START BRINGING MY IDEA TO LIFE!
OKAY! I UNDER-STAND. GOOD LUCK.
I'M GOING NOW.
RINKO...

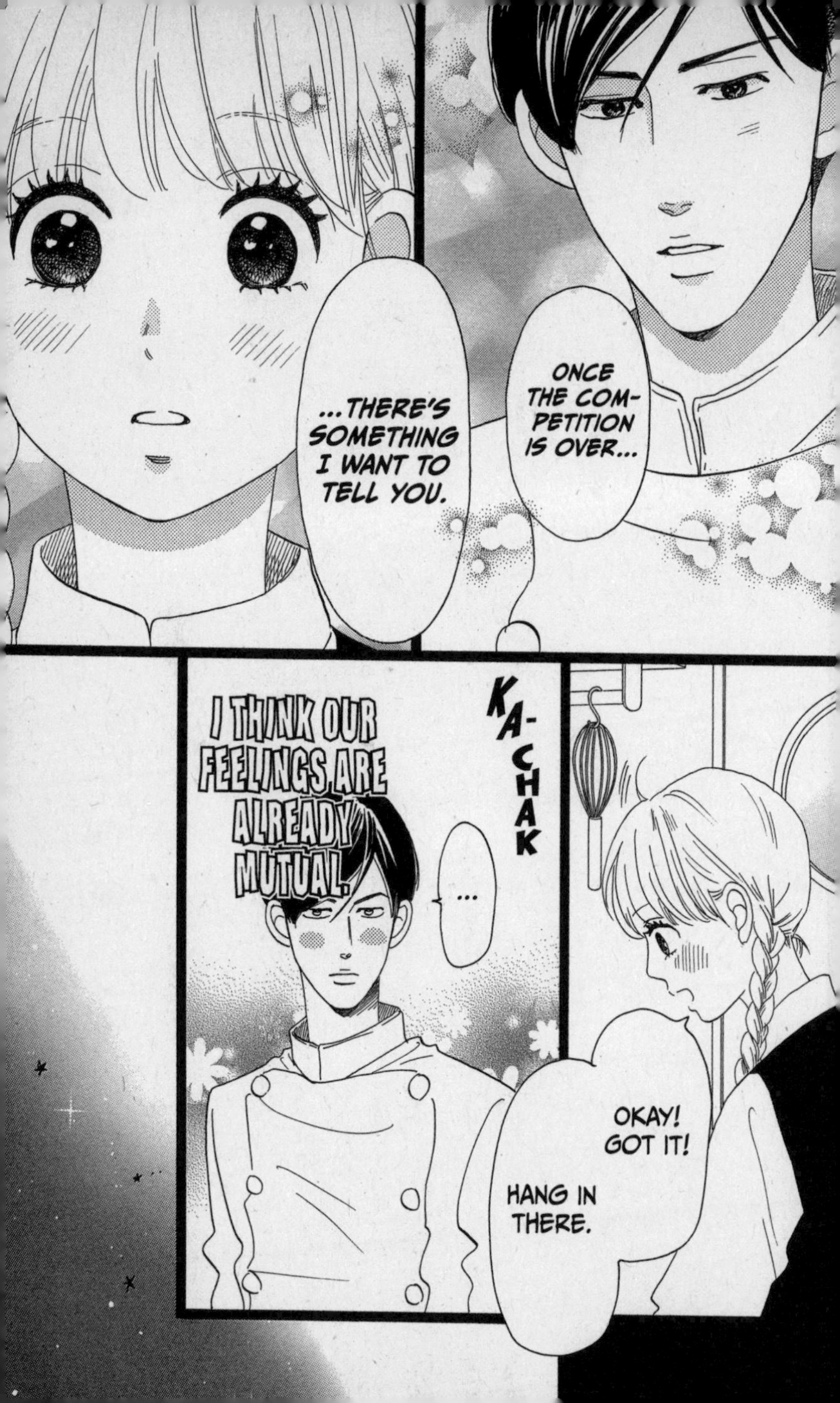
ONCE THE COM-PETITION IS OVER...
...THERE'S SOMETHING I WANT TO TELL YOU.
OKAY! GOT IT!
HANG IN THERE.
KA-CHAK
...
I THINK OUR FEELINGS ARE ALREADY MUTUAL.

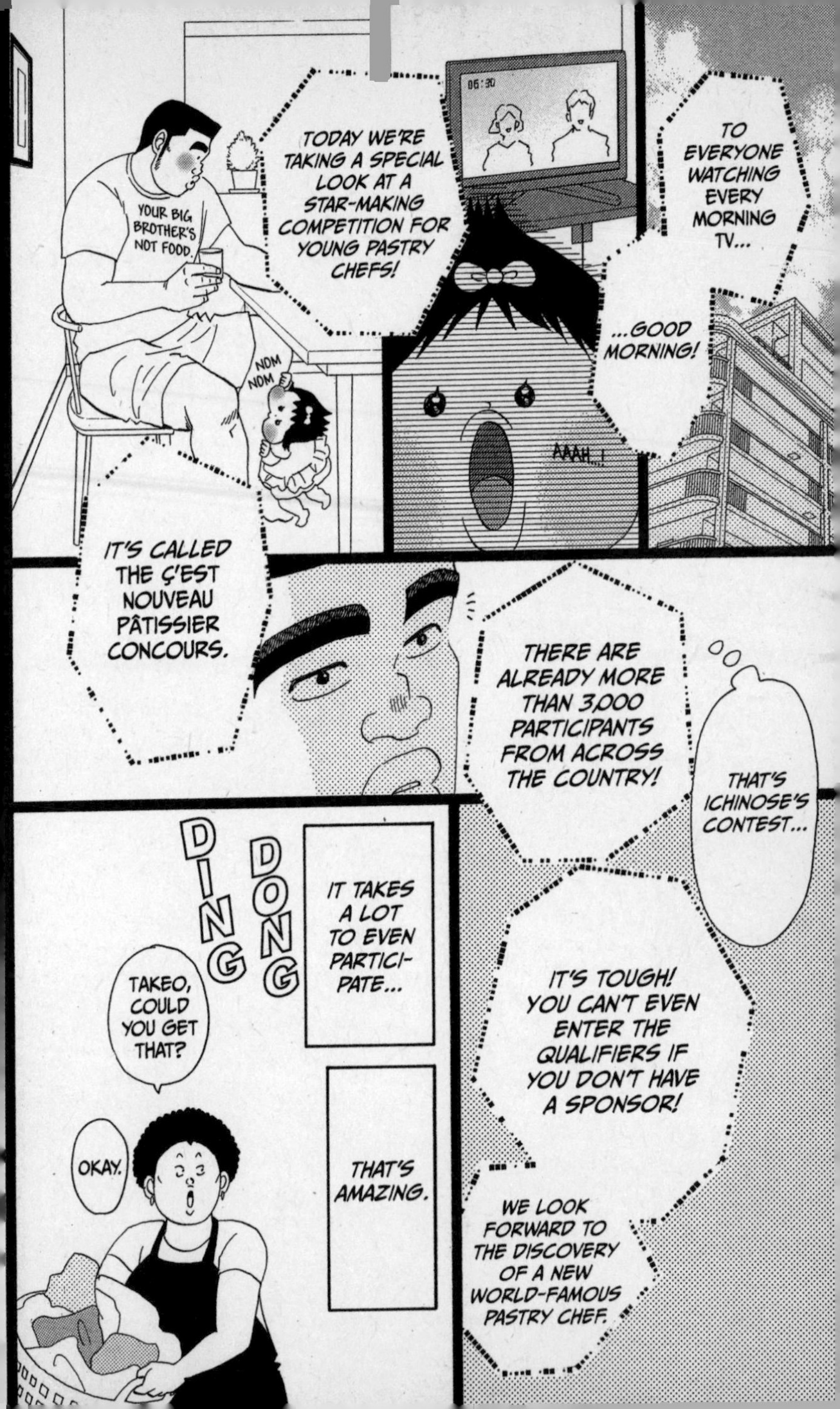
TO EVERYONE WATCHING EVERY MORNING TV...
...GOOD MORNING!
AAAH...!
06:30
TODAY WE'RE TAKING A SPECIAL LOOK AT A STAR-MAKING COMPETITION FOR YOUNG PASTRY CHEFS!
YOUR BIG BROTHER'S NOT FOOD.
NOM NOM
IT'S CALLED THE Ç'EST NOUVEAU PÂTISSIER CONCOURS.
THERE ARE ALREADY MORE THAN 3,000 PARTICIPANTS FROM ACROSS THE COUNTRY!
THAT'S ICHINOSE'S CONTEST...
IT'S TOUGH! YOU CAN'T EVEN ENTER THE QUALIFIERS IF YOU DON'T HAVE A SPONSOR!
WE LOOK FORWARD TO THE DISCOVERY OF A NEW WORLD-FAMOUS PASTRY CHEF.
IT TAKES A LOT TO EVEN PARTICIPATE...
THAT'S AMAZING.
DING DONG
TAKEO, COULD YOU GET THAT?
OKAY.

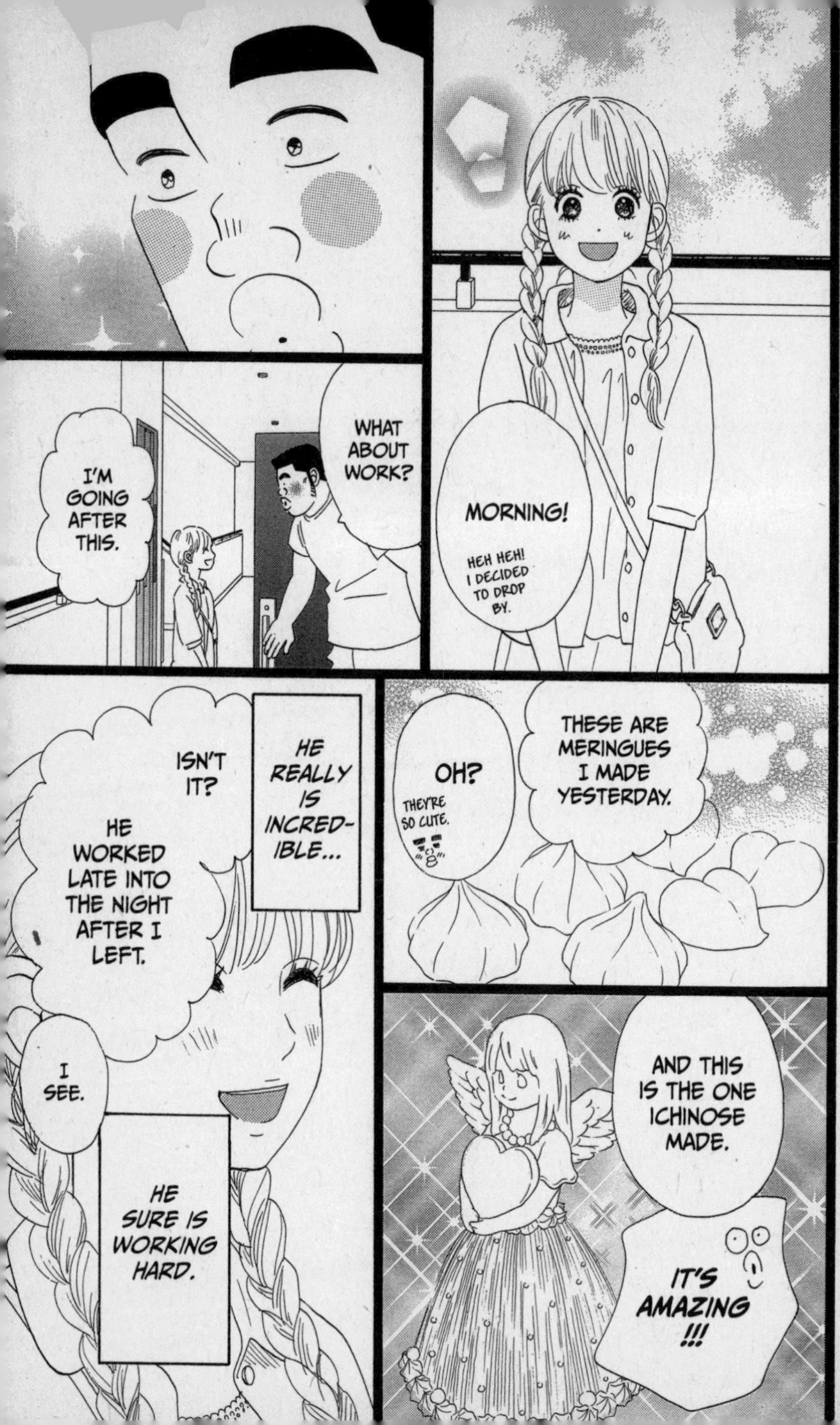
MORNING!
HEH HEH! I DECIDED TO DROP BY.
WHAT ABOUT WORK?
I'M GOING AFTER THIS.
THESE ARE MERINGUES I MADE YESTERDAY.
OH?
THEY'RE SO CUTE.
AND THIS IS THE ONE ICHINOSE MADE.
IT'S AMAZING!!!
HE REALLY IS INCREDIBLE...
ISN'T IT?
HE WORKED LATE INTO THE NIGHT AFTER I LEFT.
I SEE.
HE SURE IS WORKING HARD.

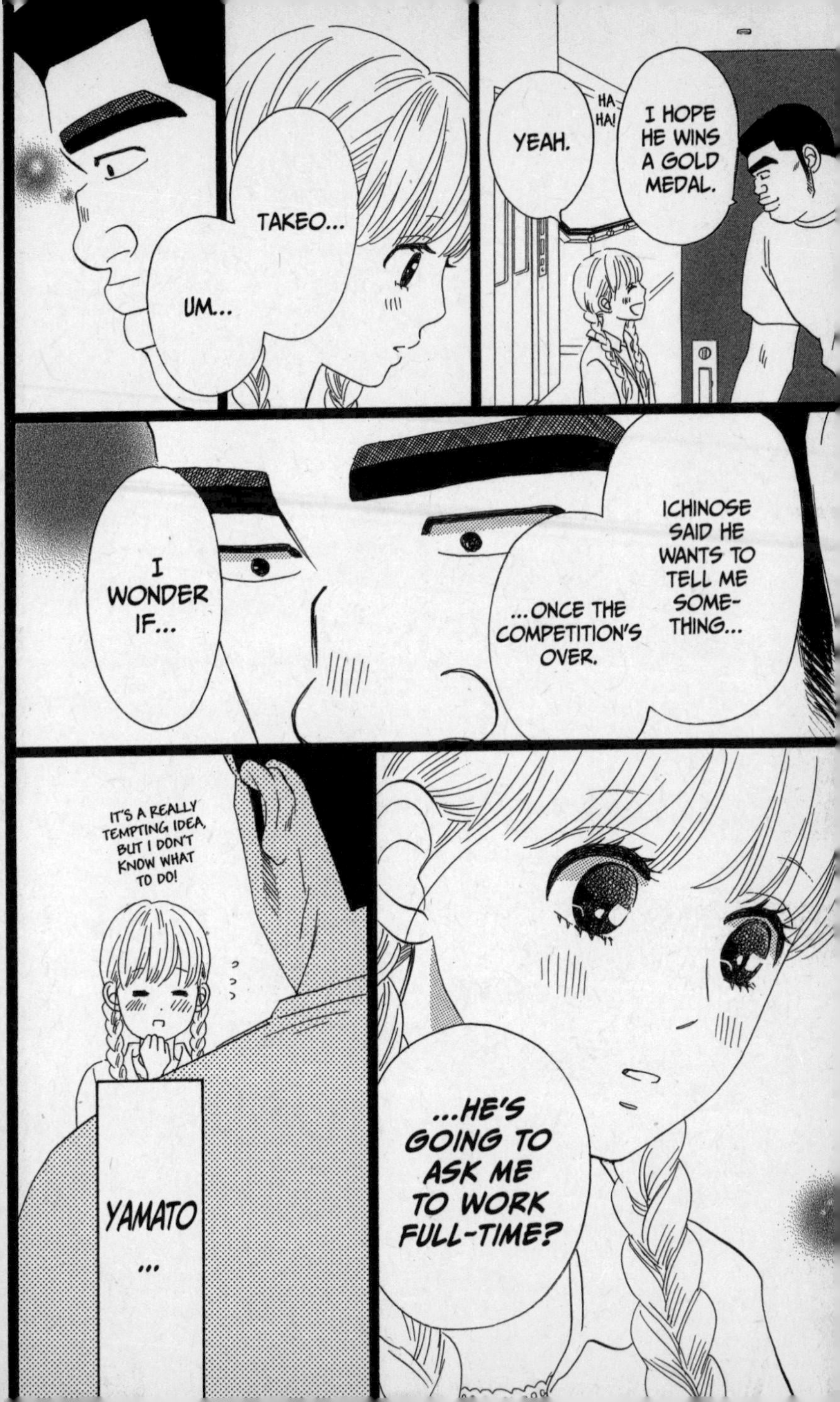
I HOPE HE WINS A GOLD MEDAL.
HA HA!
YEAH.
TAKEO...
UM...
ICHINOSE SAID HE WANTS TO TELL ME SOME-THING...
...ONCE THE COMPETITION'S OVER.
I WONDER IF...
...HE'S GOING TO ASK ME TO WORK FULL-TIME?
IT'S A REALLY TEMPTING IDEA, BUT I DON'T KNOW WHAT TO DO!
YAMATO ...

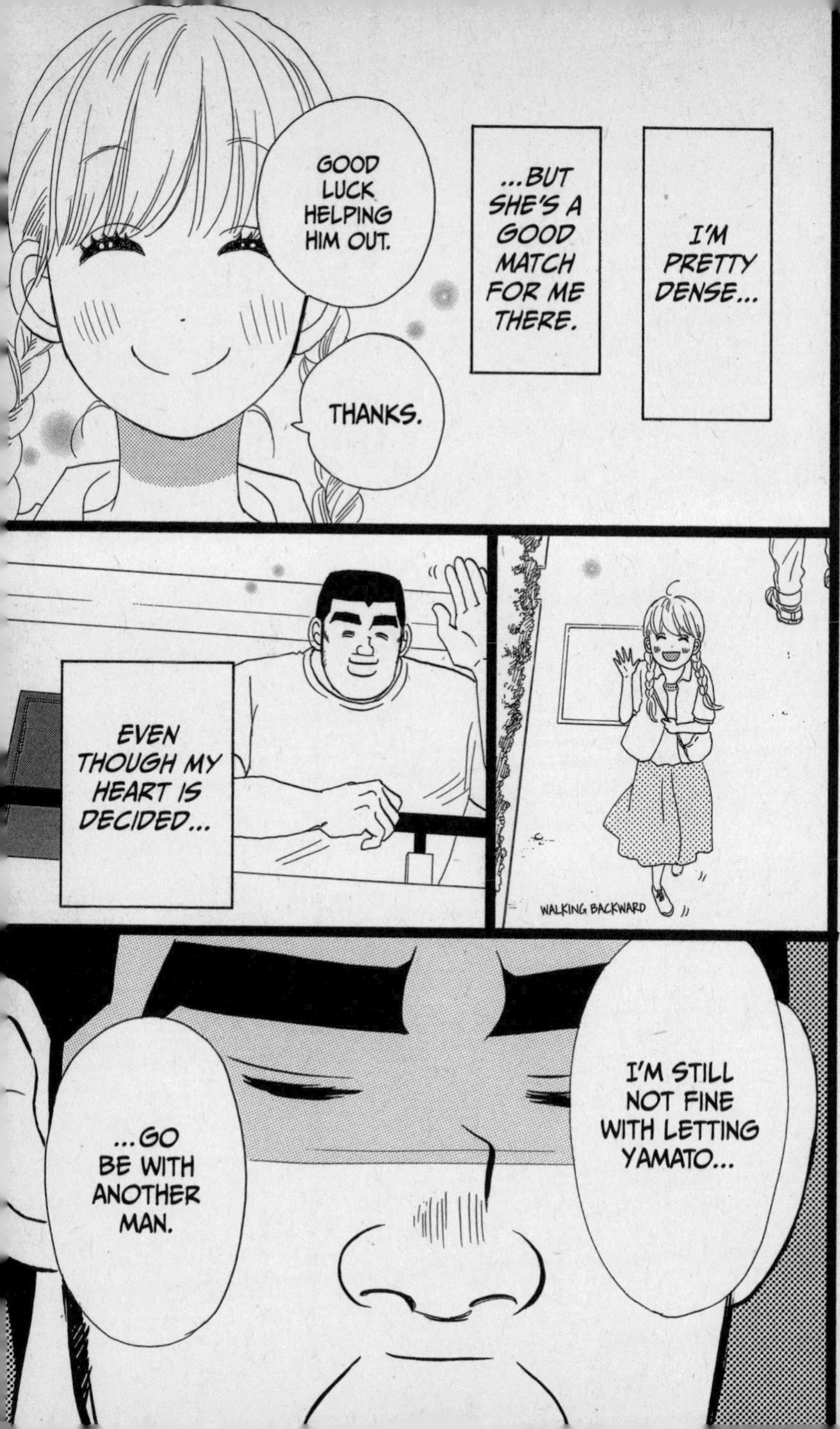
I'M PRETTY DENSE...
...BUT SHE'S A GOOD MATCH FOR ME THERE.
GOOD LUCK HELPING HIM OUT.
THANKS.
WALKING BACKWARD
EVEN THOUGH MY HEART IS DECIDED...
I'M STILL NOT FINE WITH LETTING YAMATO...
...GO BE WITH ANOTHER MAN.

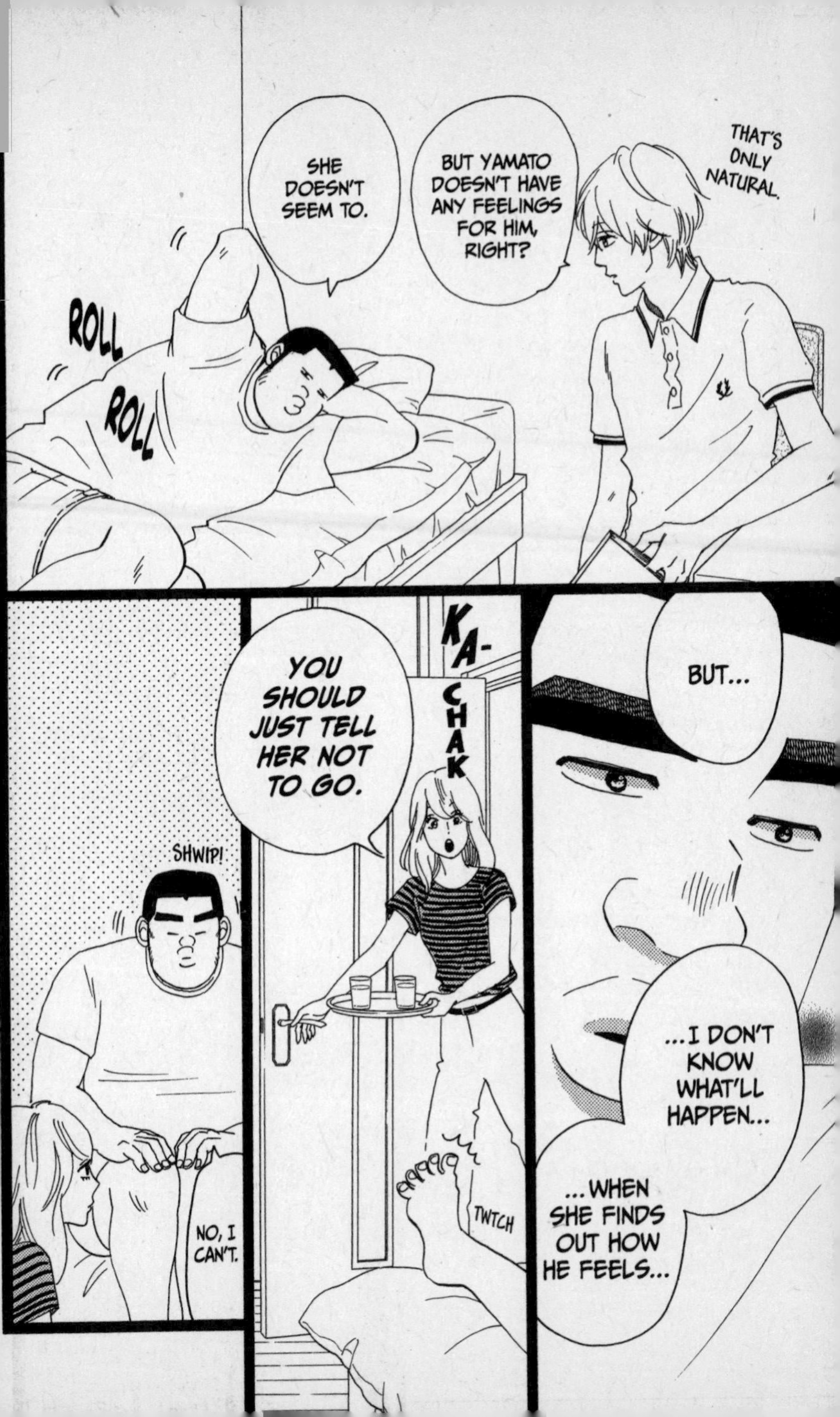
THAT'S ONLY NATURAL.
BUT YAMATO DOESN'T HAVE ANY FEELINGS FOR HIM, RIGHT?
SHE DOESN'T SEEM TO.
ROLL
ROLL
BUT...
...I DON'T KNOW WHAT'LL HAPPEN...
...WHEN SHE FINDS OUT HOW HE FEELS...
KA-CHAK
YOU SHOULD JUST TELL HER NOT TO GO.
TWTCH
SHWIP!
NO, I CAN'T.

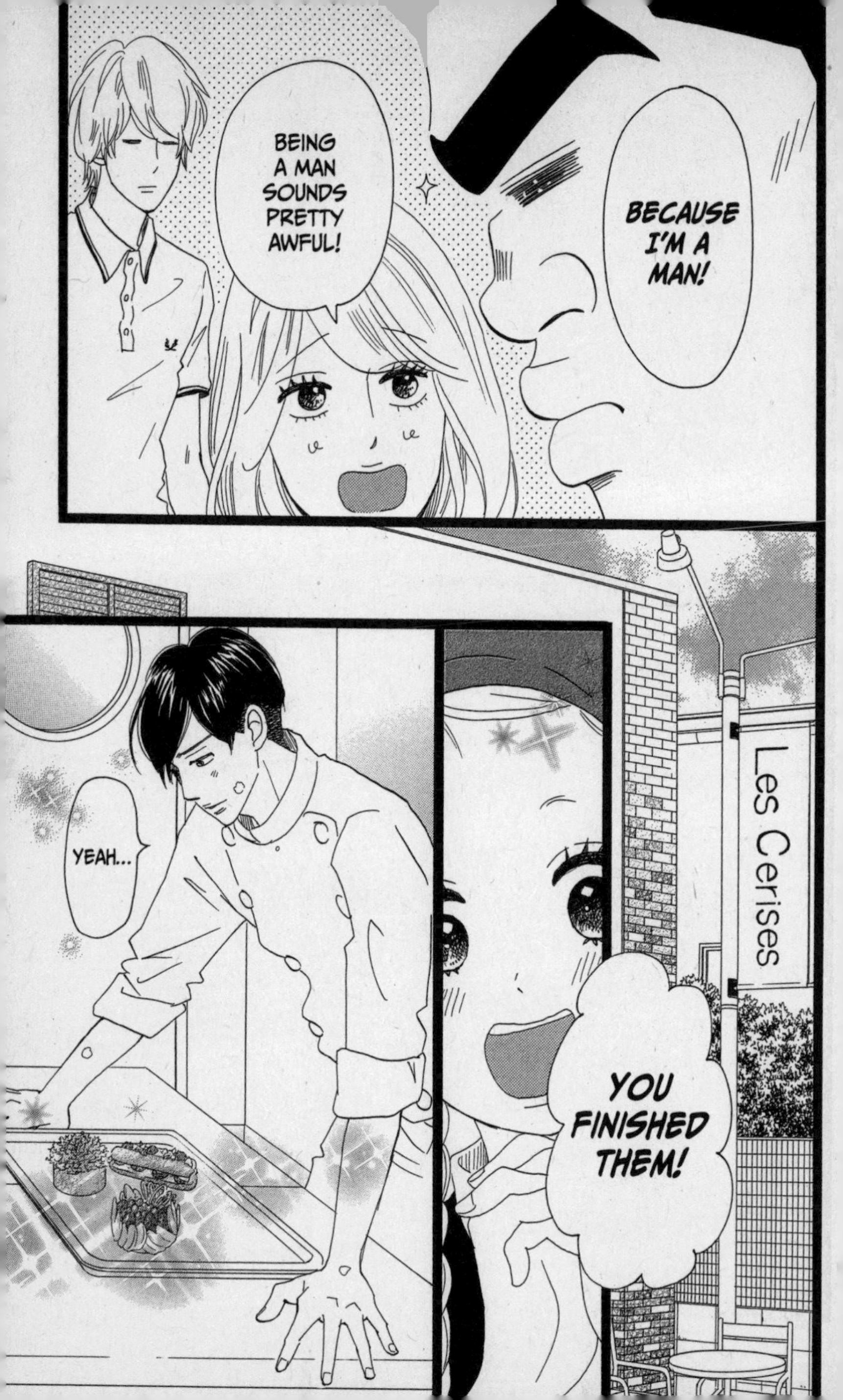
BECAUSE I'M A MAN!
BEING A MAN SOUNDS PRETTY AWFUL!
Les Cerises
YOU FINISHED THEM!
YEAH...

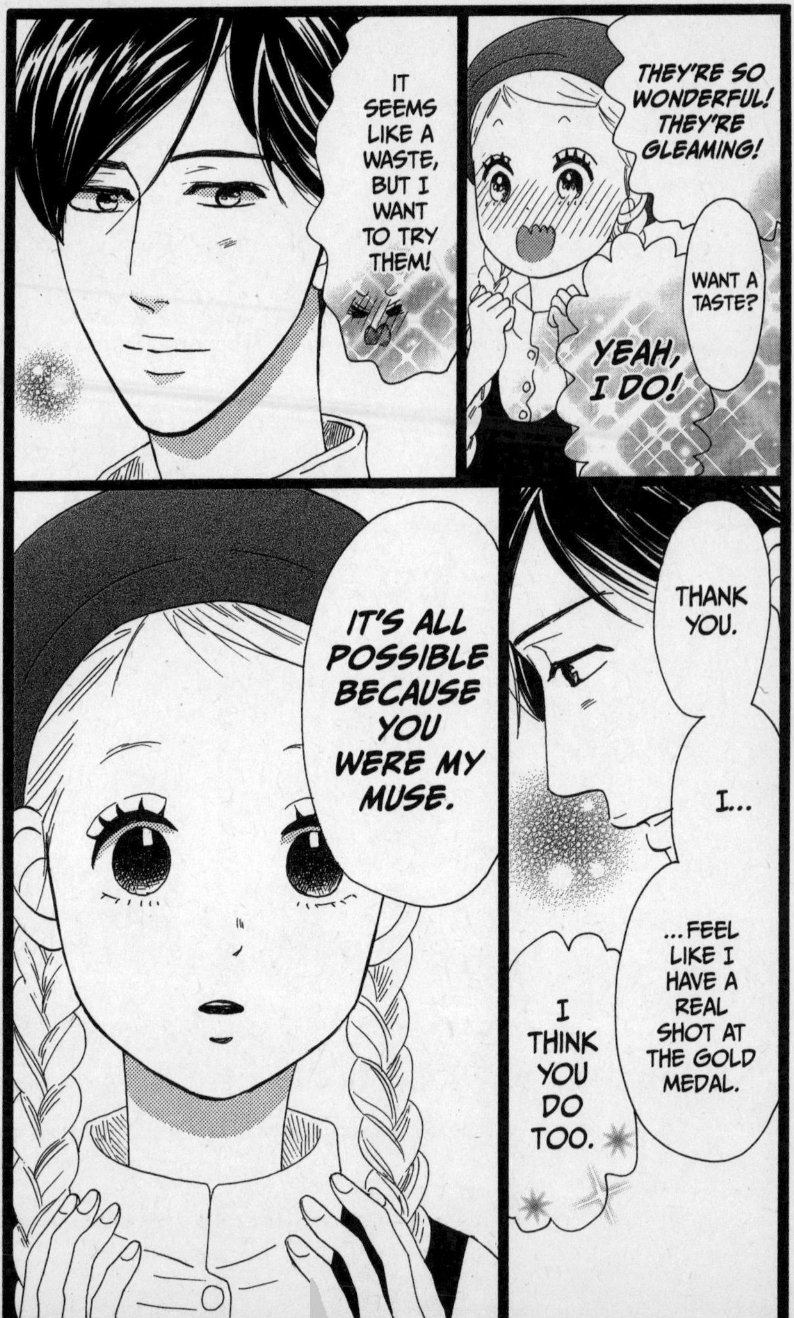
THEY'RE SO WONDERFUL! THEY'RE GLEAMING!
WANT A TASTE?
YEAH, I DO!
IT SEEMS LIKE A WASTE, BUT I WANT TO TRY THEM!
THANK YOU.
I...
...FEEL LIKE I HAVE A REAL SHOT AT THE GOLD MEDAL.
I THINK YOU DO TOO.
IT'S ALL POSSIBLE BECAUSE YOU WERE MY MUSE.

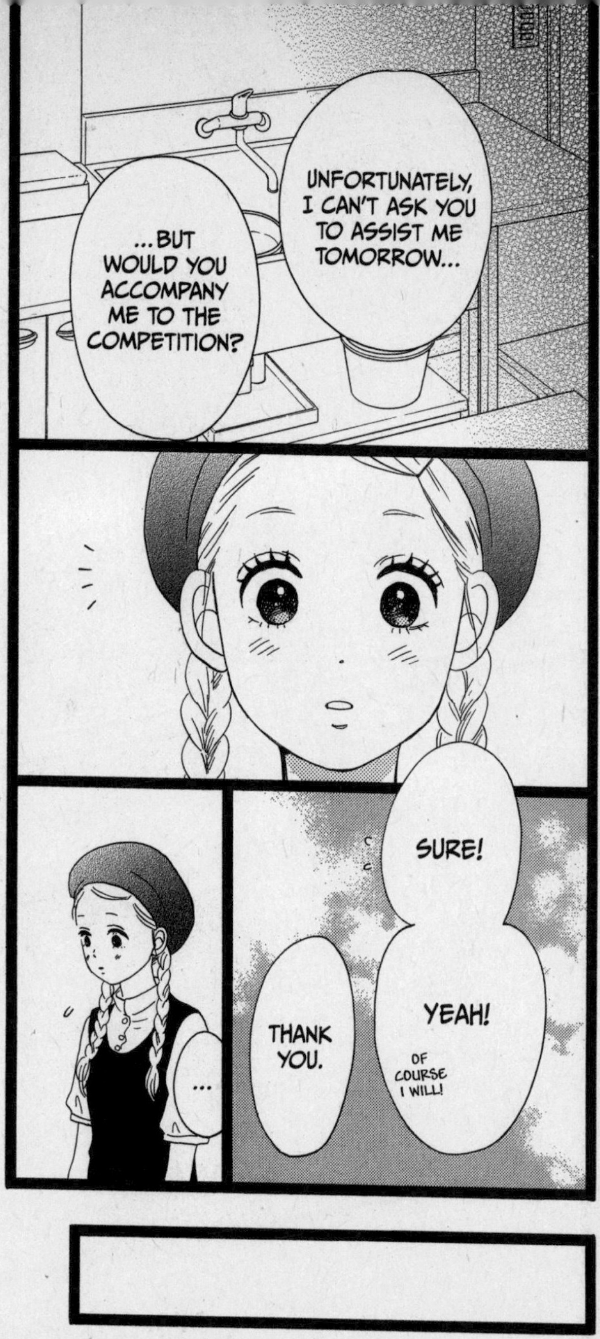
UNFORTUNATELY, I CAN'T ASK YOU TO ASSIST ME TOMORROW...
...BUT WOULD YOU ACCOMPANY ME TO THE COMPETITION?
SURE!
YEAH!
OF COURSE I WILL!
THANK YOU.
...

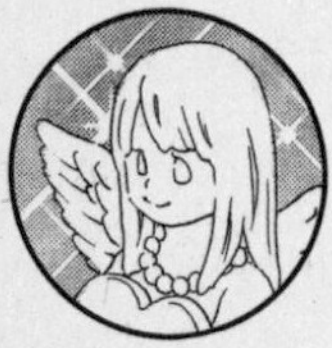

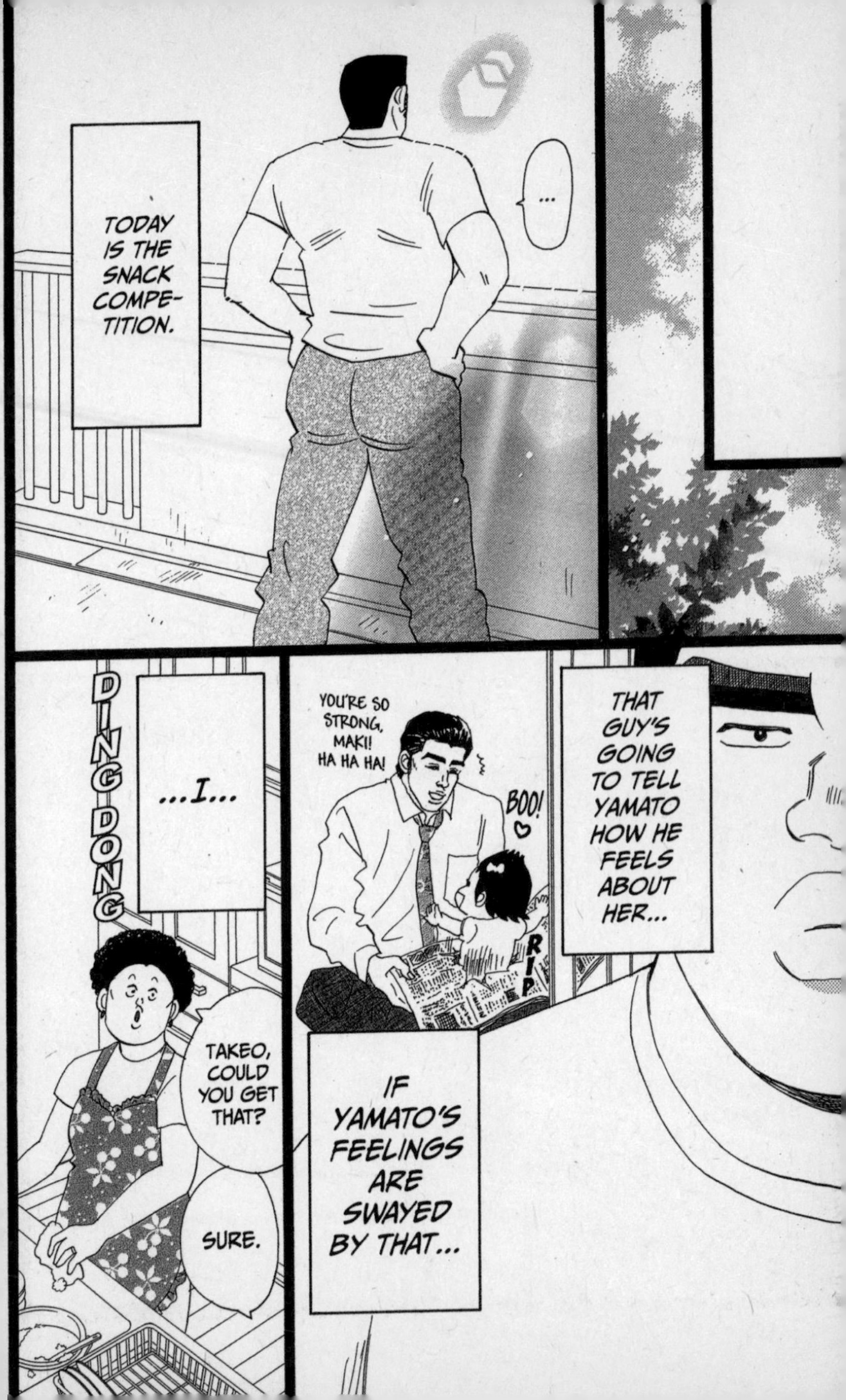
...
TODAY IS THE SNACK COMPETITION.
THAT GUY'S GOING TO TELL YAMATO HOW HE FEELS ABOUT HER...
BOO!
YOU'RE SO STRONG, MAKI! HA HA HA!
RIP
IF YAMATO'S FEELINGS ARE SWAYED BY THAT...
...I...
DING DONG
TAKEO, COULD YOU GET THAT?
SURE.

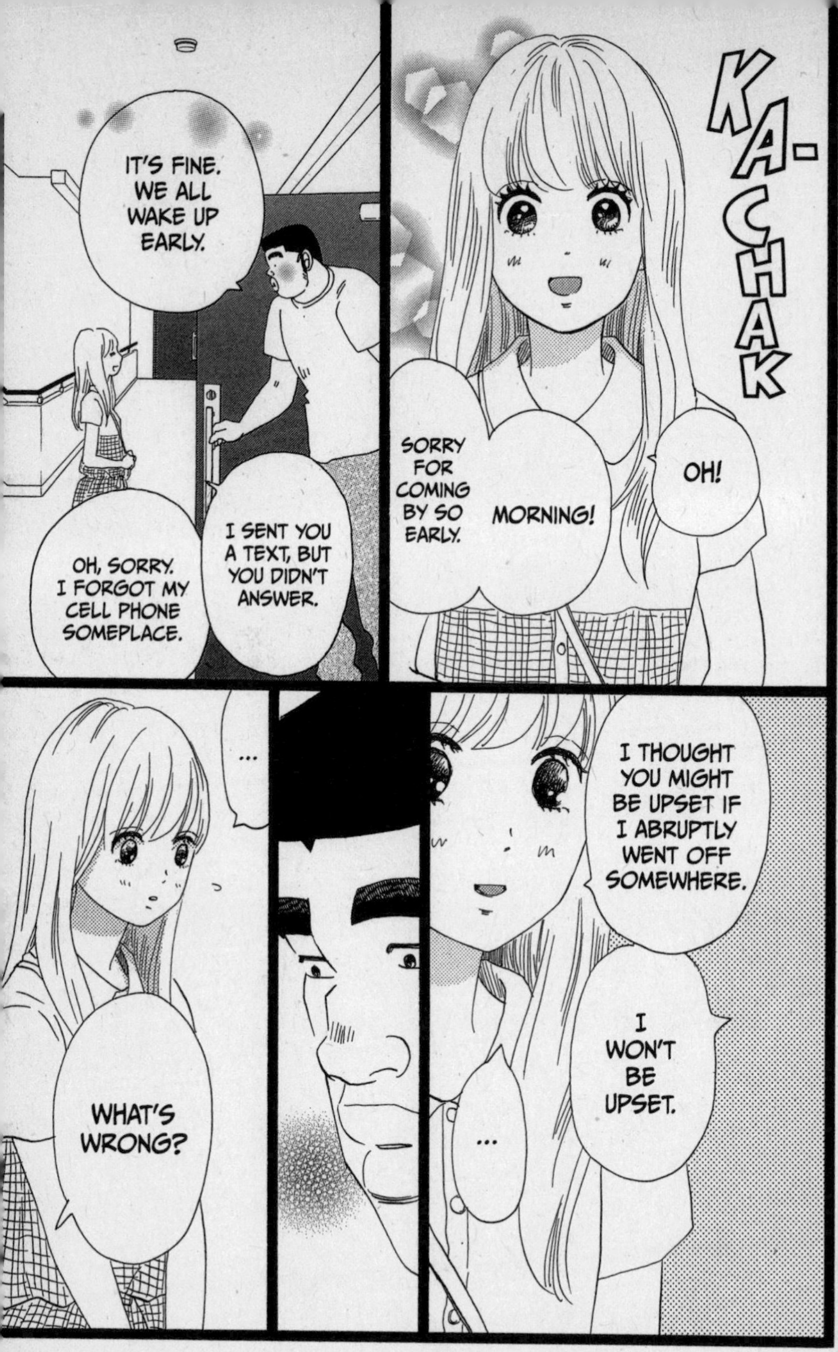

KA-CHAK
OH!
MORNING!
SORRY FOR COMING BY SO EARLY.
IT'S FINE. WE ALL WAKE UP EARLY.
I SENT YOU A TEXT, BUT YOU DIDN'T ANSWER.
OH, SORRY. I FORGOT MY CELL PHONE SOMEPLACE.
I THOUGHT YOU MIGHT BE UPSET IF I ABRUPTLY WENT OFF SOMEWHERE.
I WON'T BE UPSET.
...
...
WHAT'S WRONG?

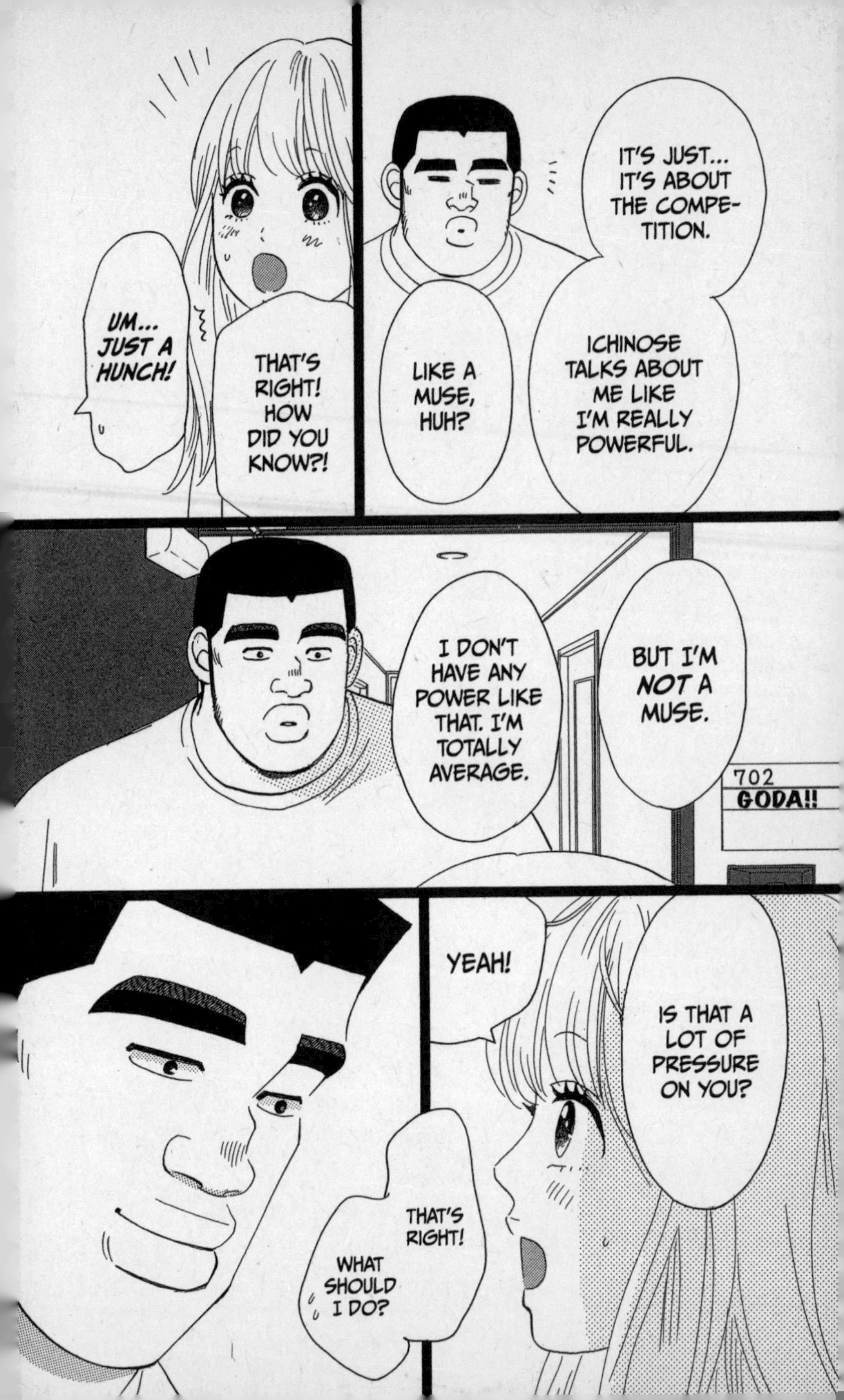
IT'S JUST... IT'S ABOUT THE COMPE-TITION.
ICHINOSE TALKS ABOUT ME LIKE I'M REALLY POWERFUL.
LIKE A MUSE, HUH?
THAT'S RIGHT! HOW DID YOU KNOW?!
UM... JUST A HUNCH!
BUT I'M *NOT* A MUSE.
I DON'T HAVE ANY POWER LIKE THAT. I'M TOTALLY AVERAGE.
702
GODA!!
IS THAT A LOT OF PRESSURE ON YOU?
YEAH!
THAT'S RIGHT!
WHAT SHOULD I DO?

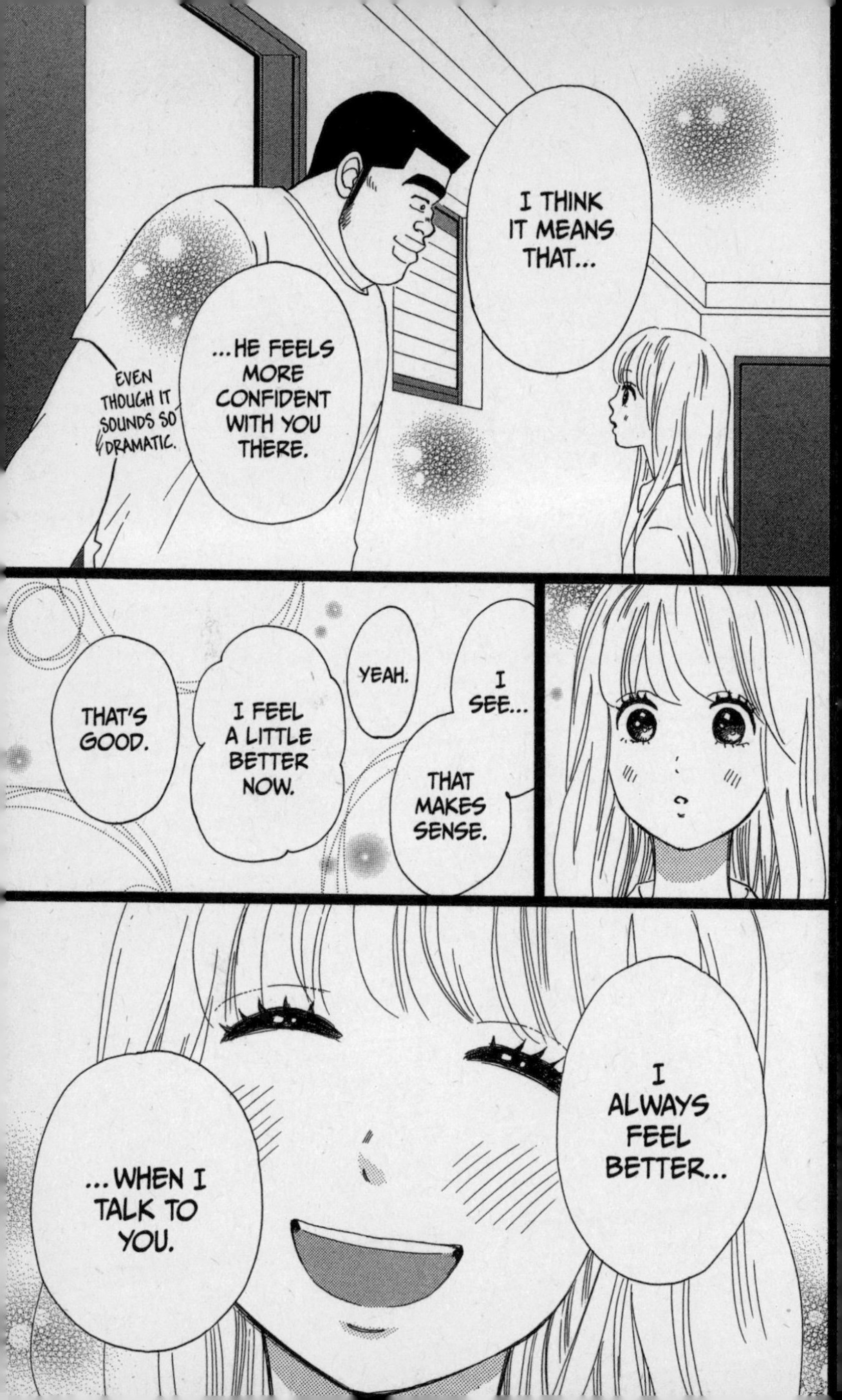
I THINK IT MEANS THAT...
...HE FEELS MORE CONFIDENT WITH YOU THERE.
EVEN THOUGH IT SOUNDS SO DRAMATIC.
I SEE...
THAT MAKES SENSE.
YEAH.
I FEEL A LITTLE BETTER NOW.
THAT'S GOOD.
I ALWAYS FEEL BETTER...
...WHEN I TALK TO YOU.

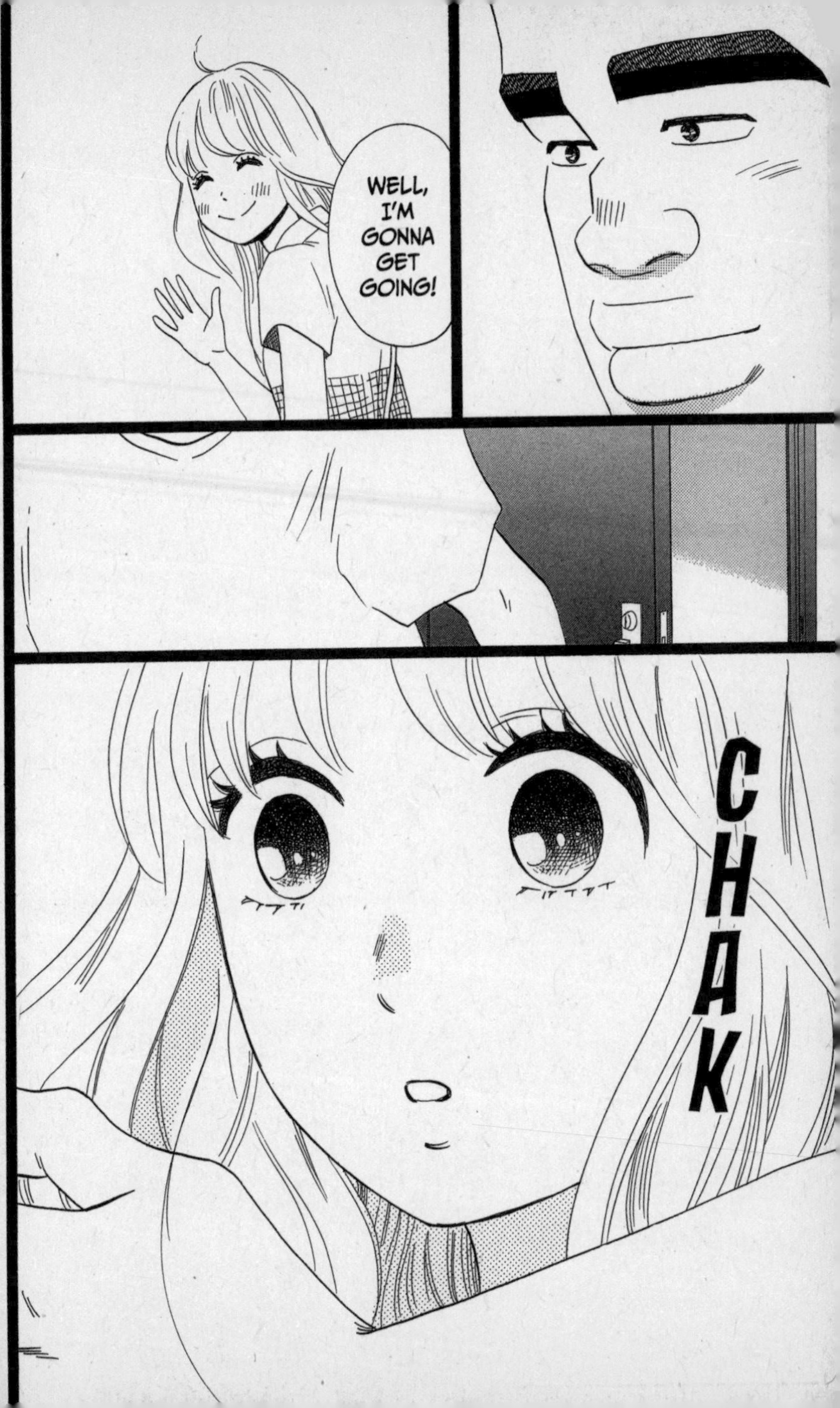
WELL, I'M GONNA GET GOING!
CHAK

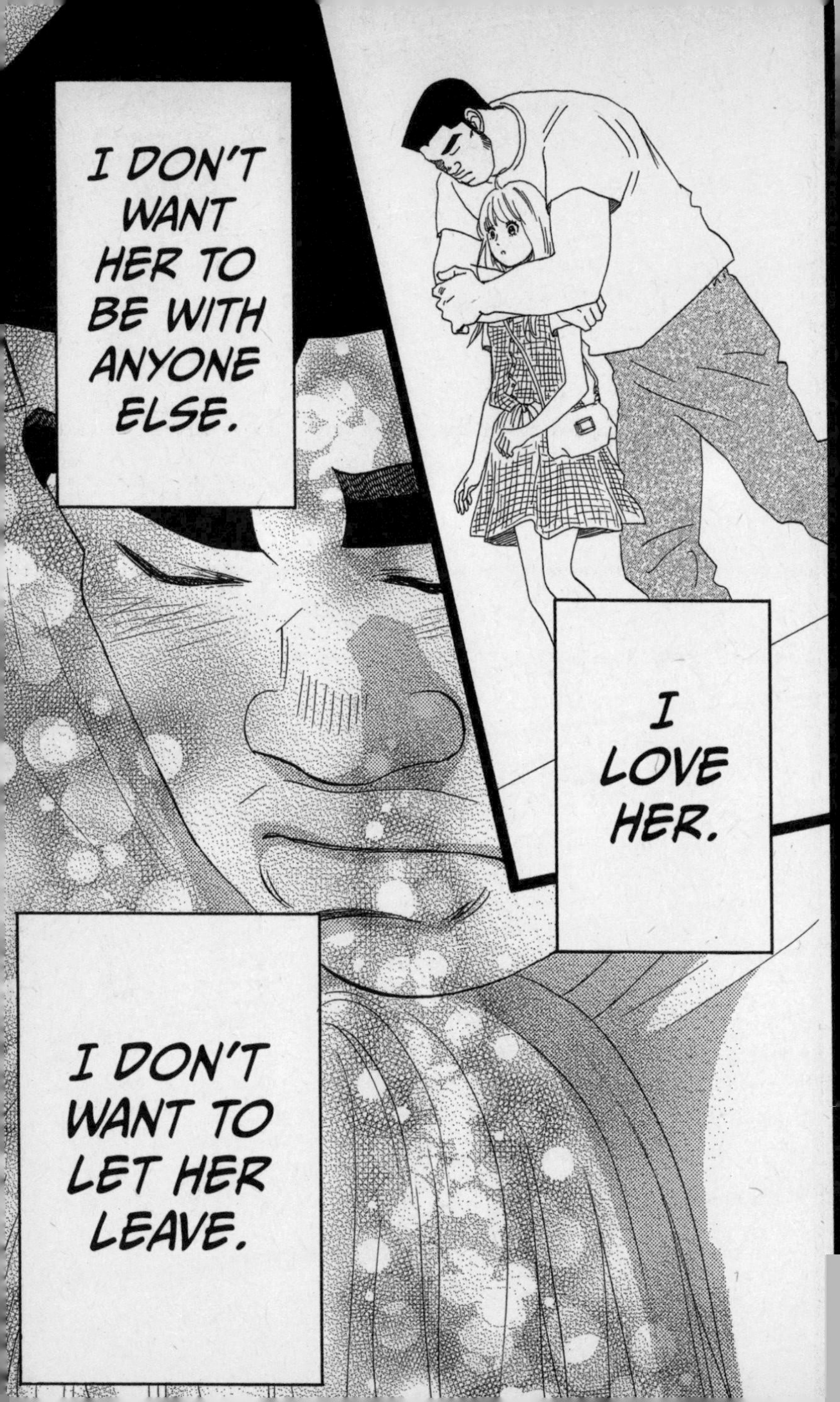
I LOVE HER.
I DON'T WANT HER TO BE WITH ANYONE ELSE.
I DON'T WANT TO LET HER LEAVE.

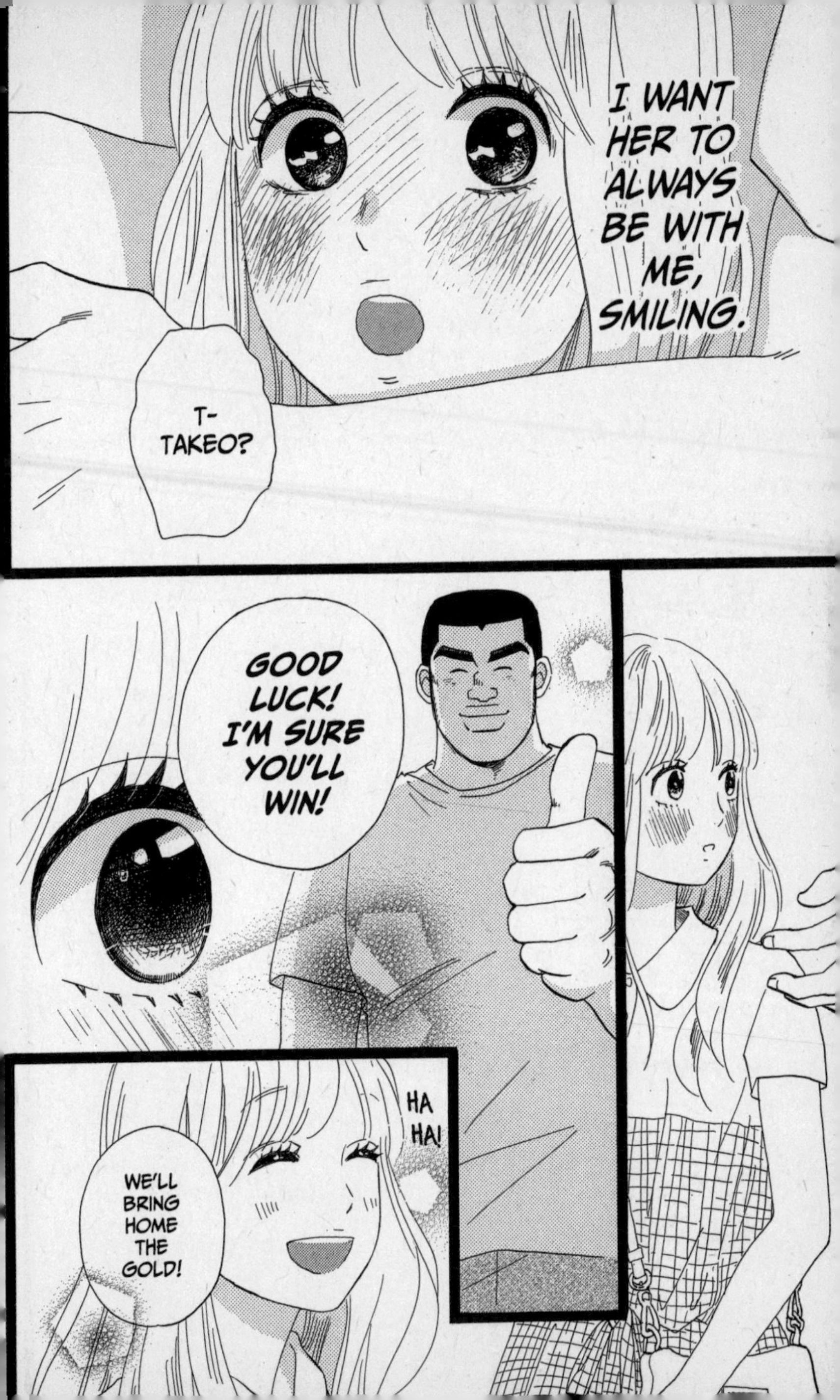
I WANT HER TO ALWAYS BE WITH ME, SMILING.
T- TAKEO?
GOOD LUCK! I'M SURE YOU'LL WIN!
HA HA!
WE'LL BRING HOME THE GOLD!

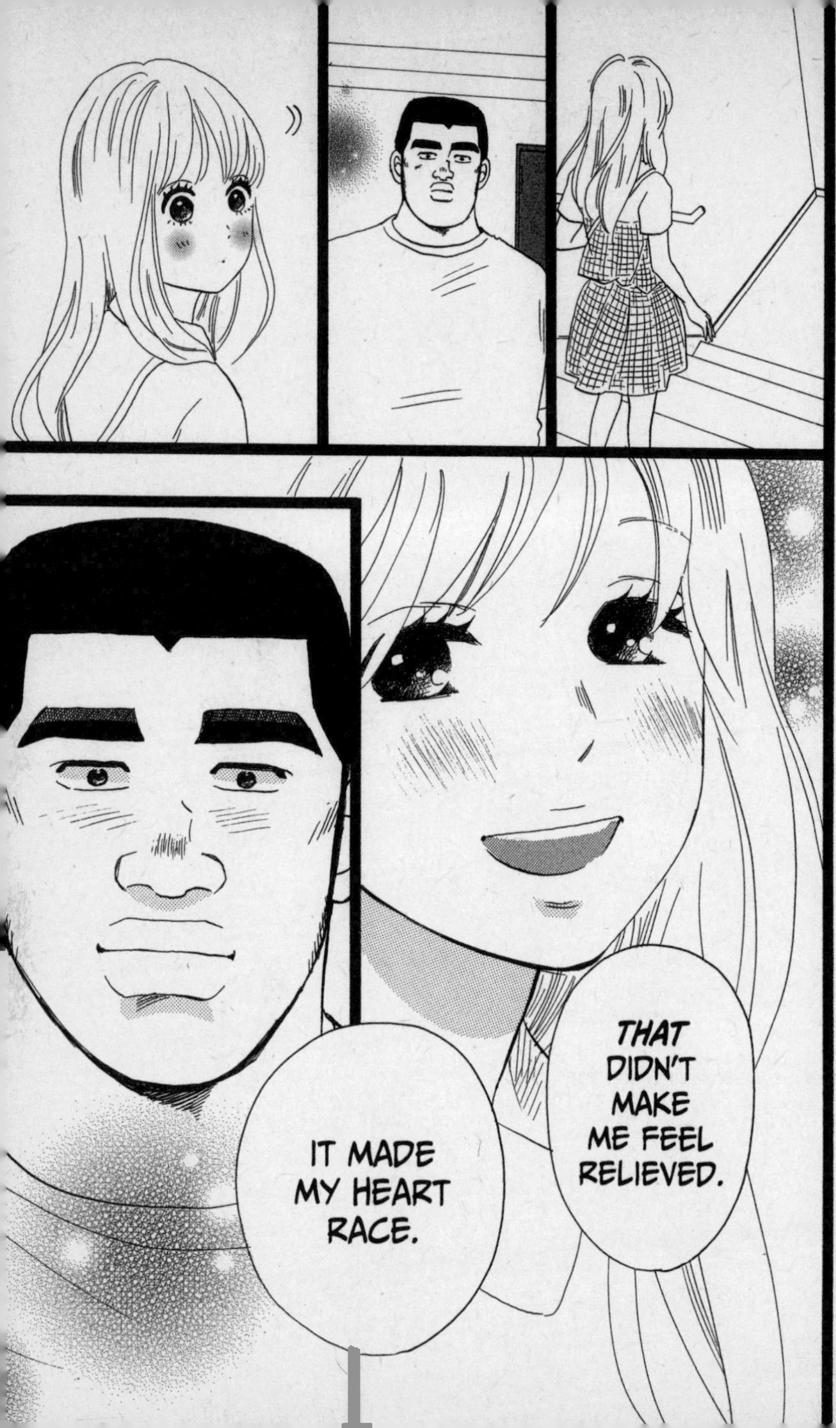
THAT DIDN'T MAKE ME FEEL RELIEVED.
IT MADE MY HEART RACE.

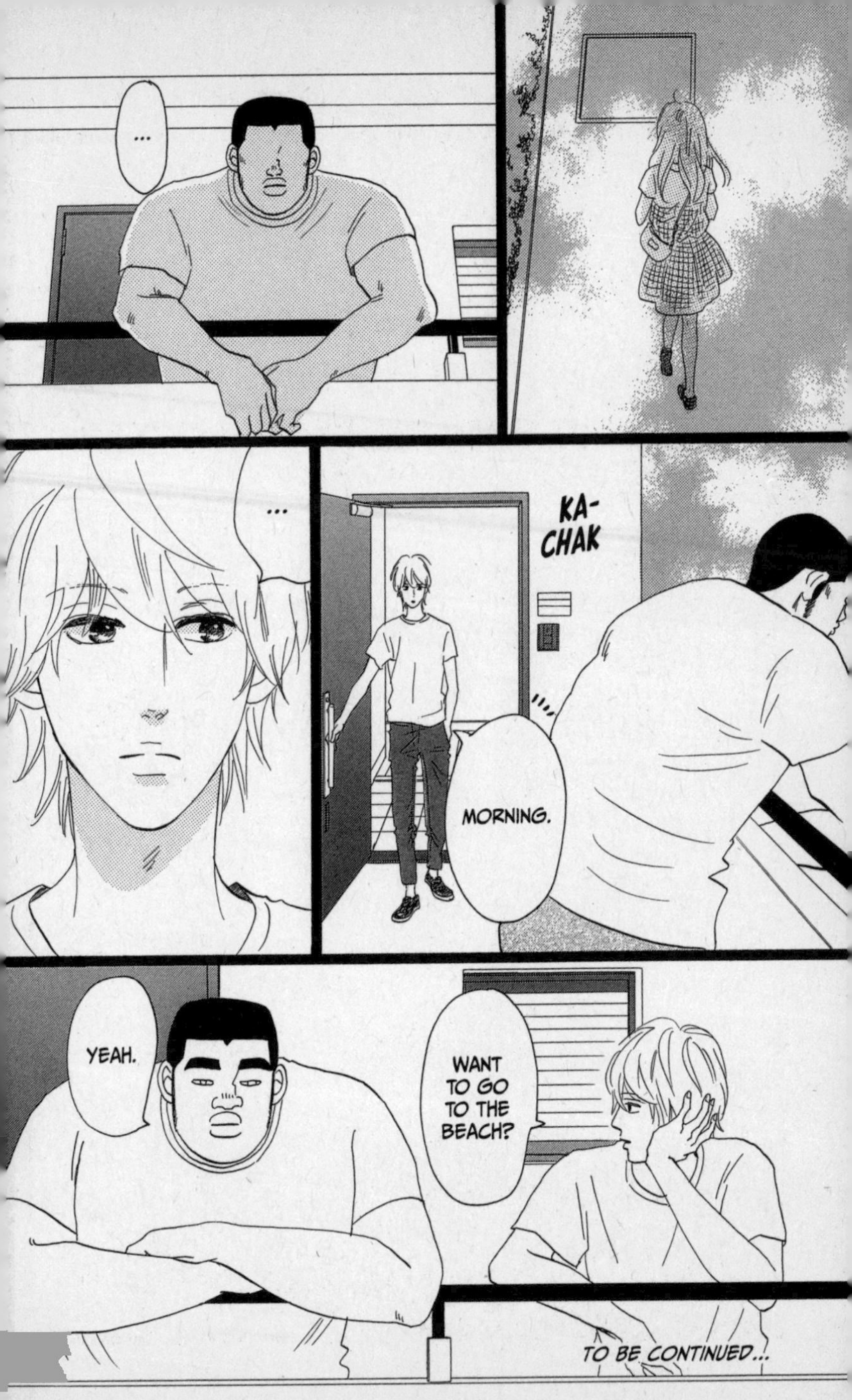
...
KA-CHAK
MORNING.
...
WANT TO GO TO THE BEACH?
YEAH.
TO BE CONTINUED...

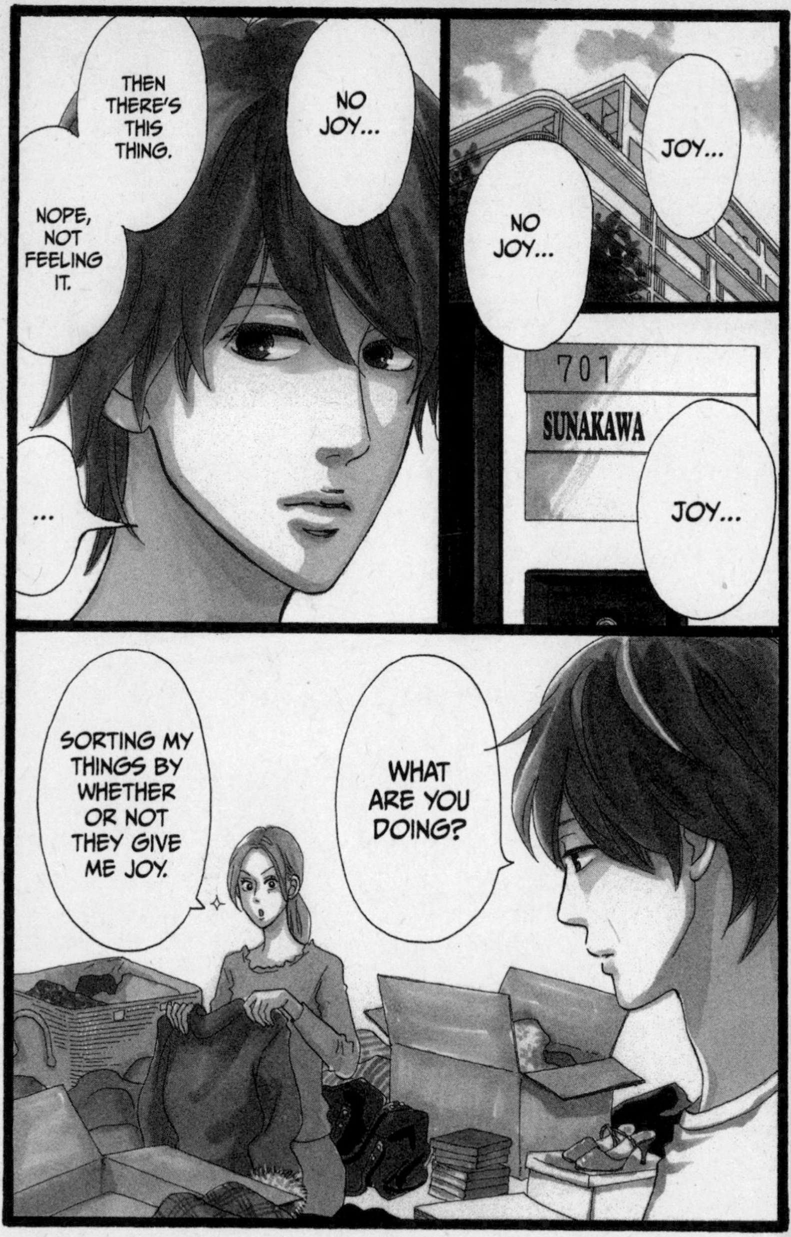
JOY...
NO JOY...
701
SUNAKAWA
JOY...
NO JOY...
THEN THERE'S THIS THING.
NOPE, NOT FEELING IT.
...
WHAT ARE YOU DOING?
SORTING MY THINGS BY WHETHER OR NOT THEY GIVE ME JOY.

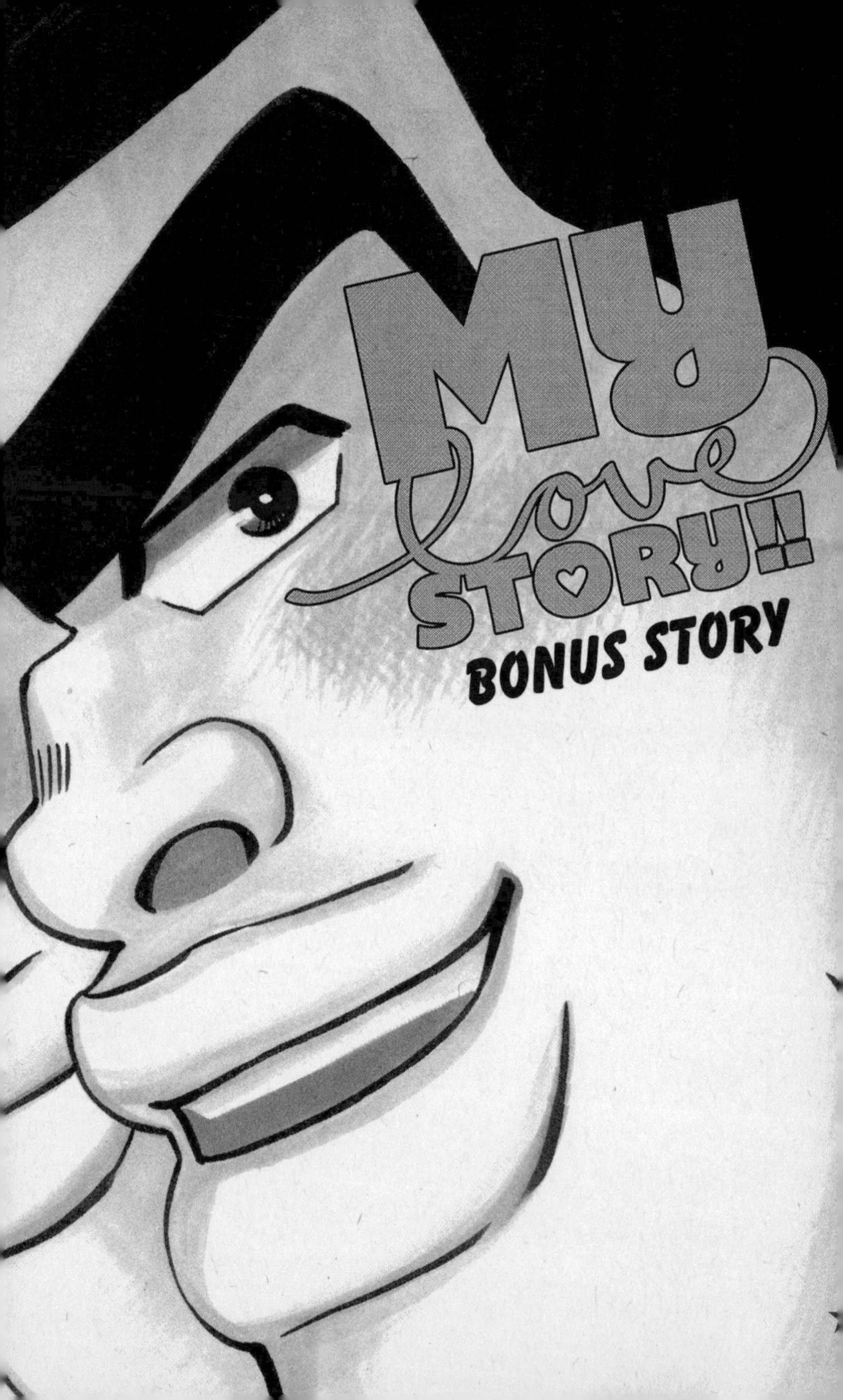
MY Love STORY!!
BONUS STORY

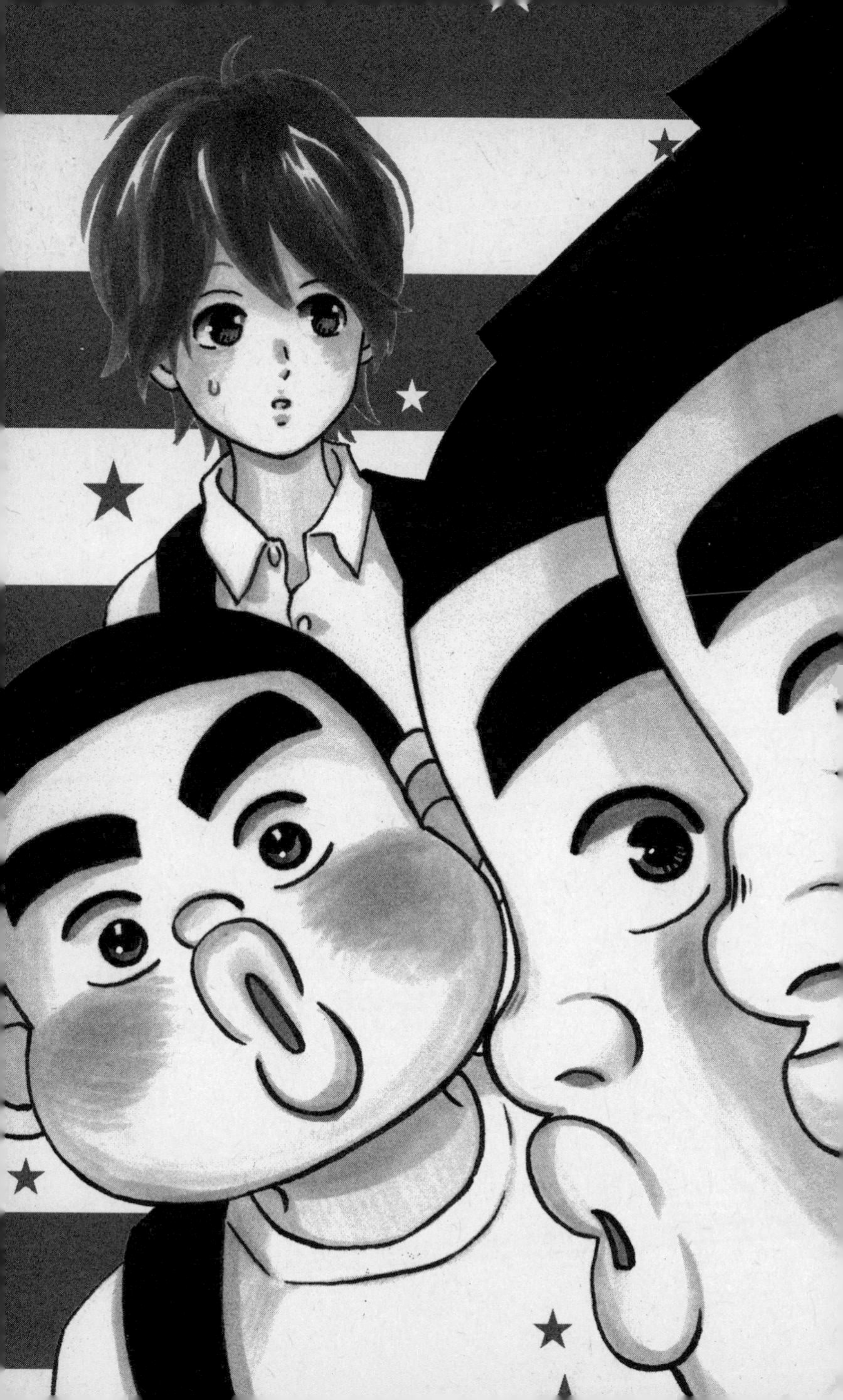

MY love STORY!!

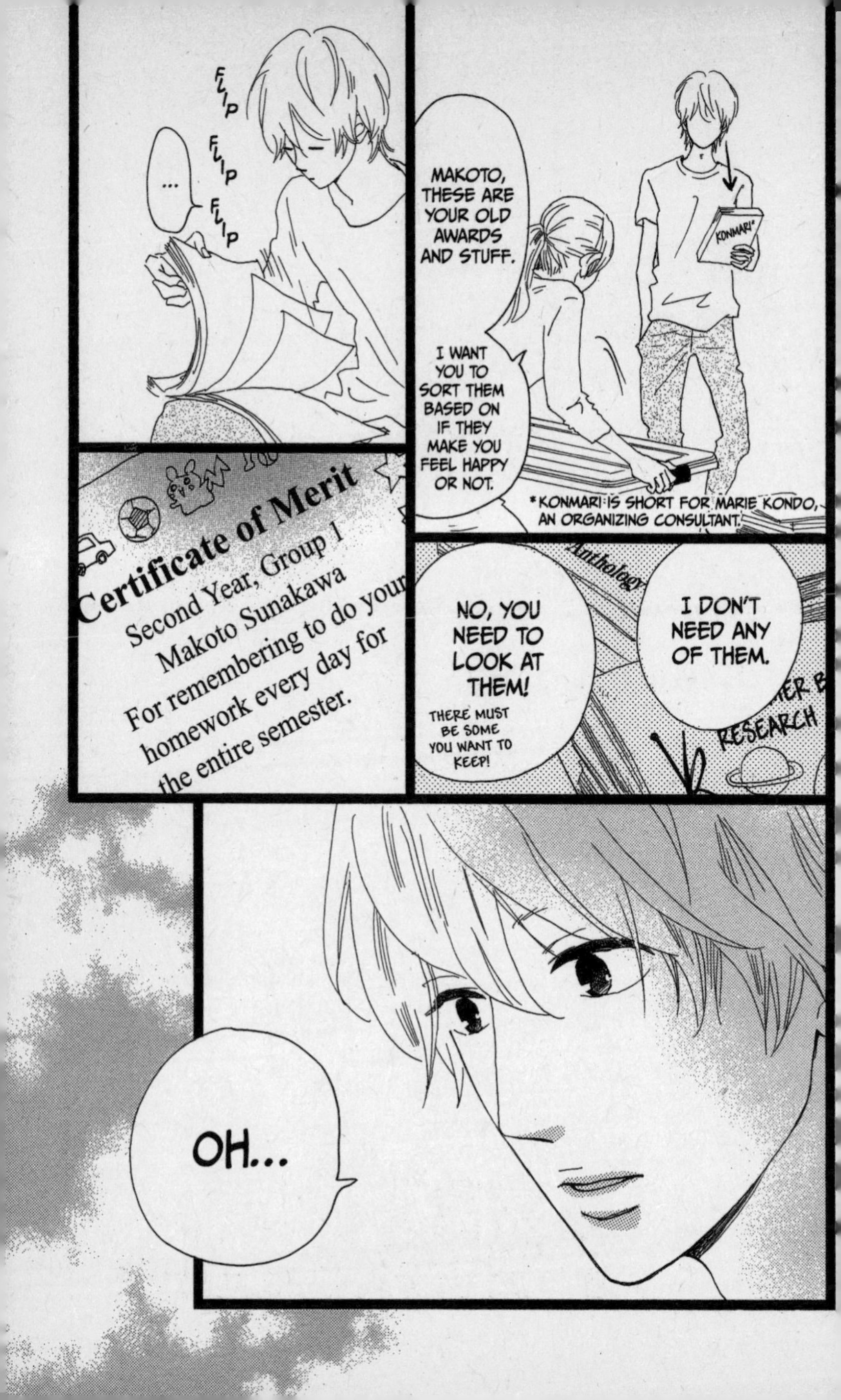
KONMARI*
MAKOTO, THESE ARE YOUR OLD AWARDS AND STUFF.
I WANT YOU TO SORT THEM BASED ON IF THEY MAKE YOU FEEL HAPPY OR NOT.
*KONMARI IS SHORT FOR MARIE KONDO, AN ORGANIZING CONSULTANT.
FLIP FLIP FLIP
...
Anthology
RESEARCH
I DON'T NEED ANY OF THEM.
NO, YOU NEED TO LOOK AT THEM!
THERE MUST BE SOME YOU WANT TO KEEP!
Certificate of Merit
Second Year, Group 1
Makoto Sunakawa
For remembering to do your homework every day for the entire semester.
OH...

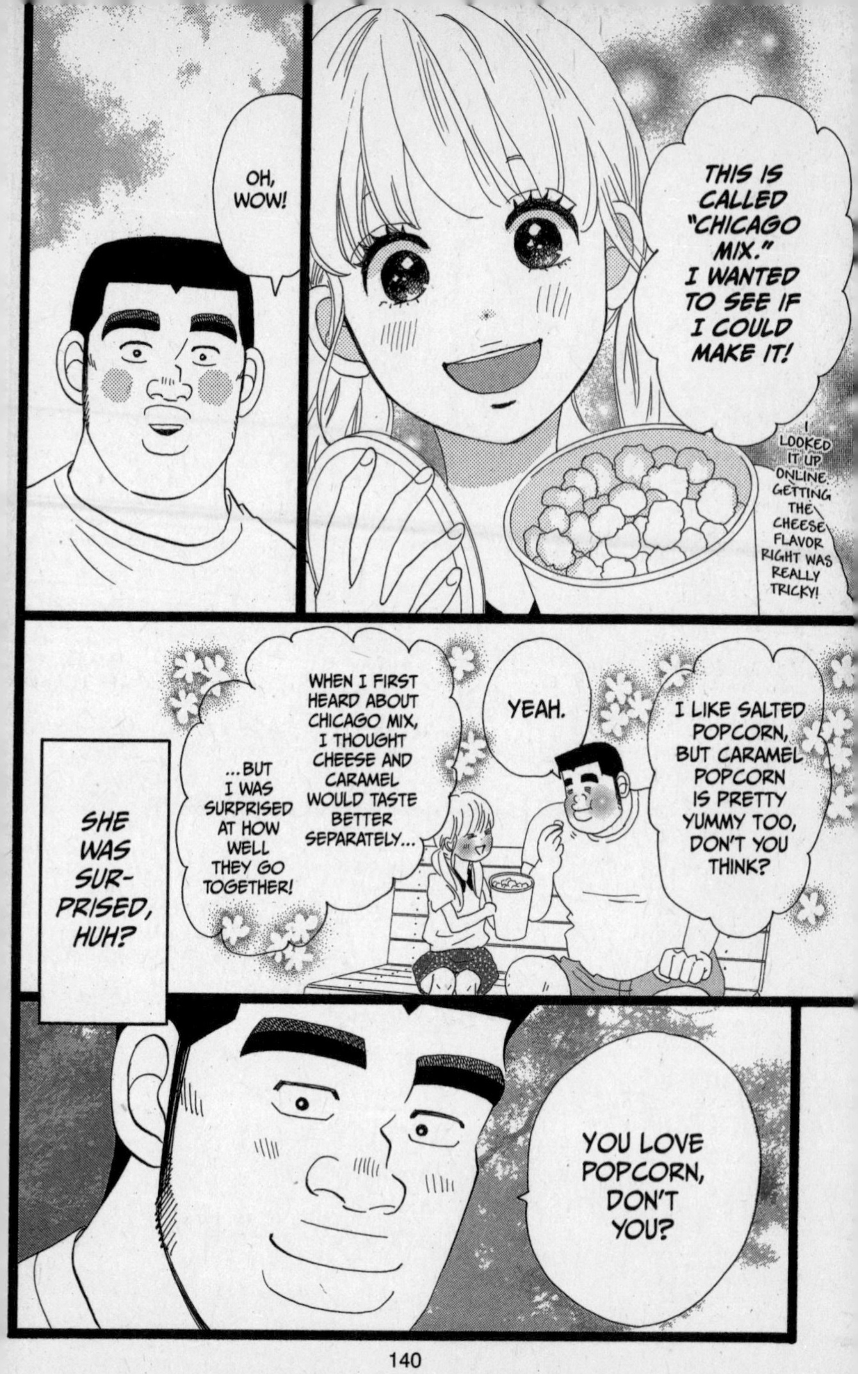
THIS IS CALLED "CHICAGO MIX." I WANTED TO SEE IF I COULD MAKE IT!
I LOOKED IT UP ONLINE. GETTING THE CHEESE FLAVOR RIGHT WAS REALLY TRICKY!
OH, WOW!
I LIKE SALTED POPCORN, BUT CARAMEL POPCORN IS PRETTY YUMMY TOO, DON'T YOU THINK?
YEAH.
WHEN I FIRST HEARD ABOUT CHICAGO MIX, I THOUGHT CHEESE AND CARAMEL WOULD TASTE BETTER SEPARATELY...
...BUT I WAS SURPRISED AT HOW WELL THEY GO TOGETHER!
SHE WAS SUR-PRISED, HUH?
YOU LOVE POPCORN, DON'T YOU?

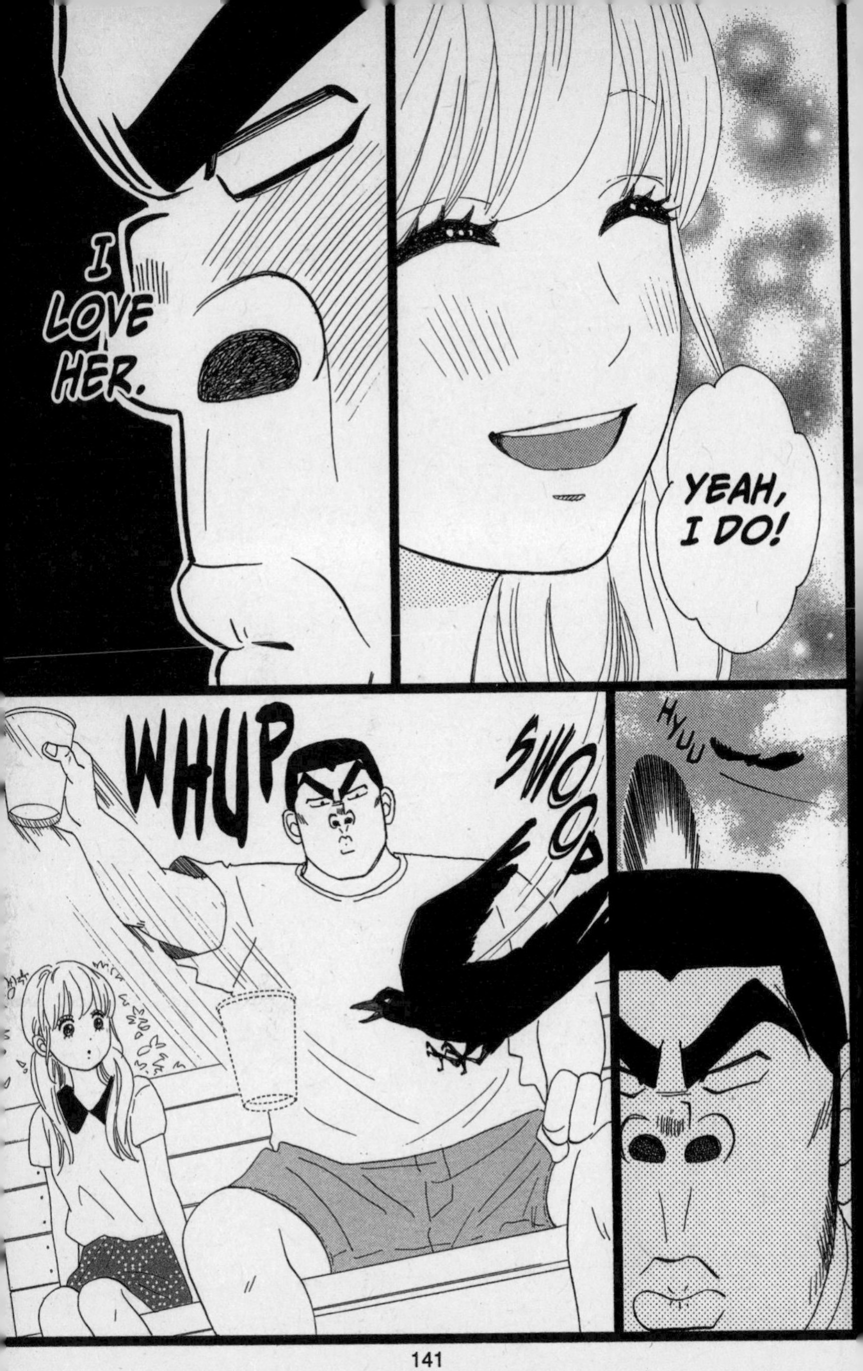
YEAH, I DO!
I LOVE HER.
HYUU
SWOOP
WHUP

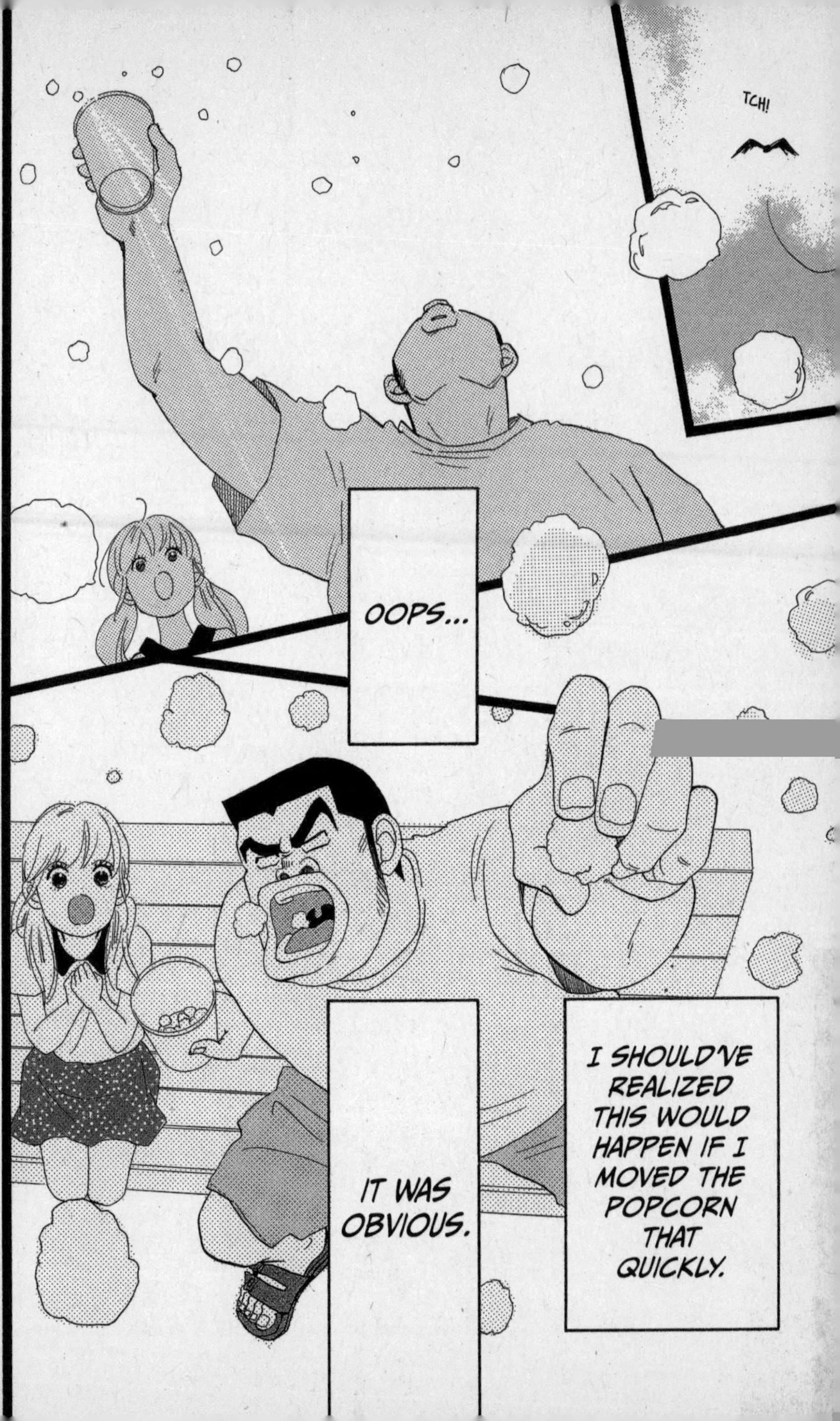
TCH!
OOPS...
I SHOULD'VE REALIZED THIS WOULD HAPPEN IF I MOVED THE POPCORN THAT QUICKLY.
IT WAS OBVIOUS.

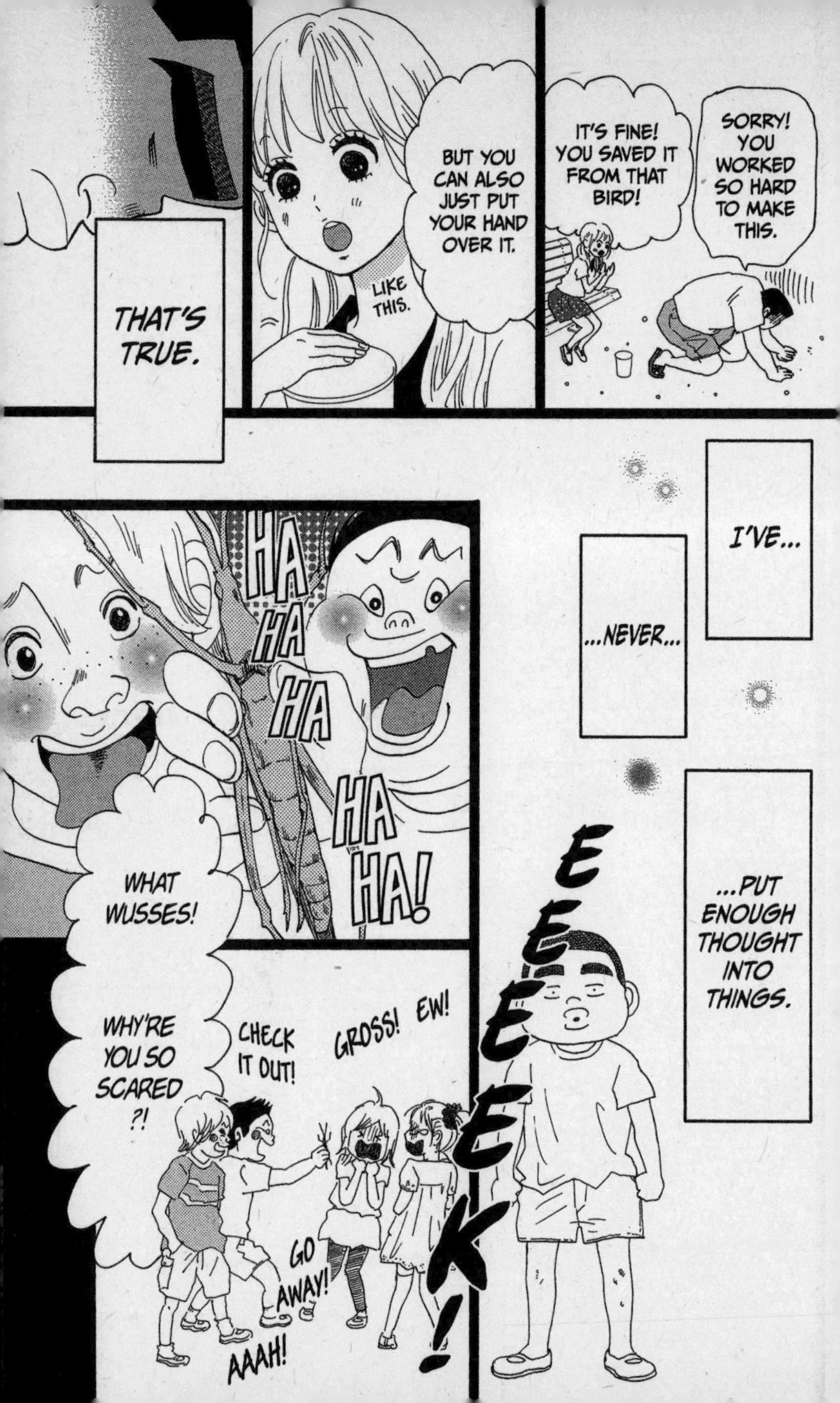
SORRY! YOU WORKED SO HARD TO MAKE THIS.
IT'S FINE! YOU SAVED IT FROM THAT BIRD!
BUT YOU CAN ALSO JUST PUT YOUR HAND OVER IT.
LIKE THIS.
THAT'S TRUE.
I'VE...
...NEVER...
...PUT ENOUGH THOUGHT INTO THINGS.
EEEEEEEK!
HA HA HA HA HA!
WHAT WUSSES!
WHY'RE YOU SO SCARED?!
EW!
GROSS!
CHECK IT OUT!
GO AWAY!
AAAH!

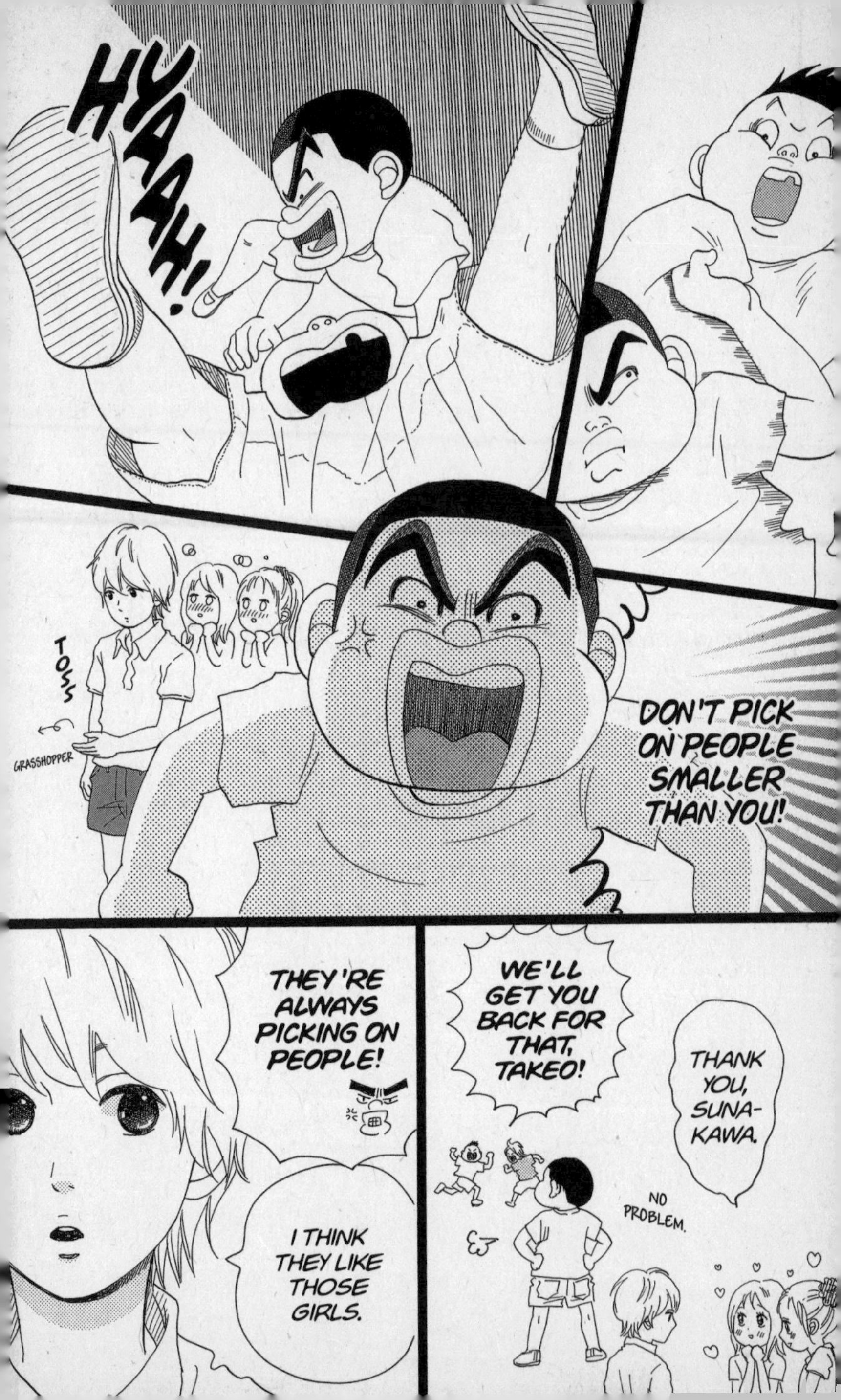
HYAAAH!
DON'T PICK ON PEOPLE SMALLER THAN YOU!
TOSS
GRASSHOPPER
WE'LL GET YOU BACK FOR THAT, TAKEO!
THANK YOU, SUNA-KAWA.
NO PROBLEM.
THEY'RE ALWAYS PICKING ON PEOPLE!
I THINK THEY LIKE THOSE GIRLS.

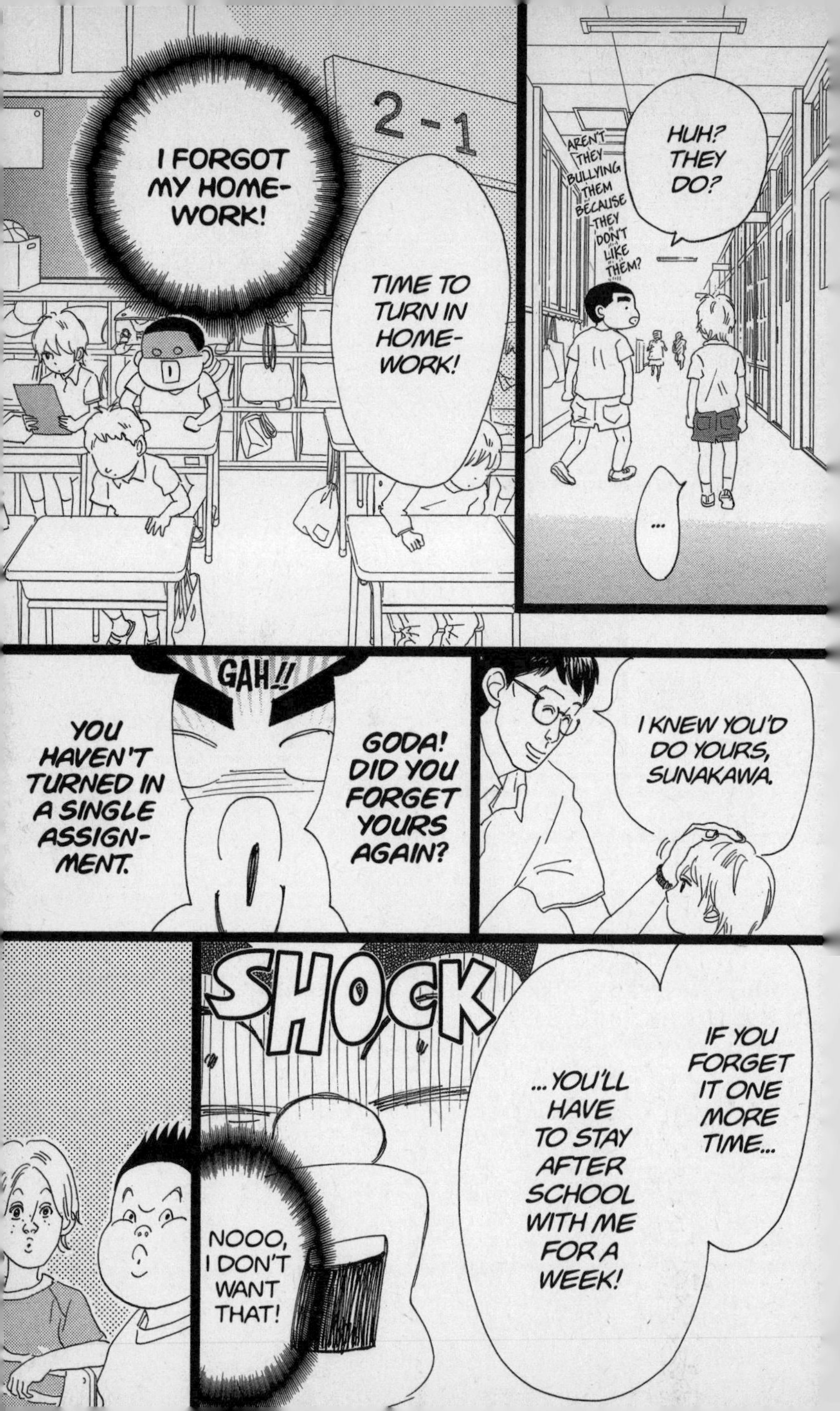
HUH? THEY DO?
AREN'T THEY BULLYING THEM BECAUSE THEY DON'T LIKE THEM?
...
2-1
TIME TO TURN IN HOME-WORK!
I FORGOT MY HOME-WORK!
I KNEW YOU'D DO YOURS, SUNAKAWA.
GAH!!
GODA! DID YOU FORGET YOURS AGAIN?
YOU HAVEN'T TURNED IN A SINGLE ASSIGN-MENT.
IF YOU FORGET IT ONE MORE TIME...
...YOU'LL HAVE TO STAY AFTER SCHOOL WITH ME FOR A WEEK!
SHOCK
NOOO, I DON'T WANT THAT!

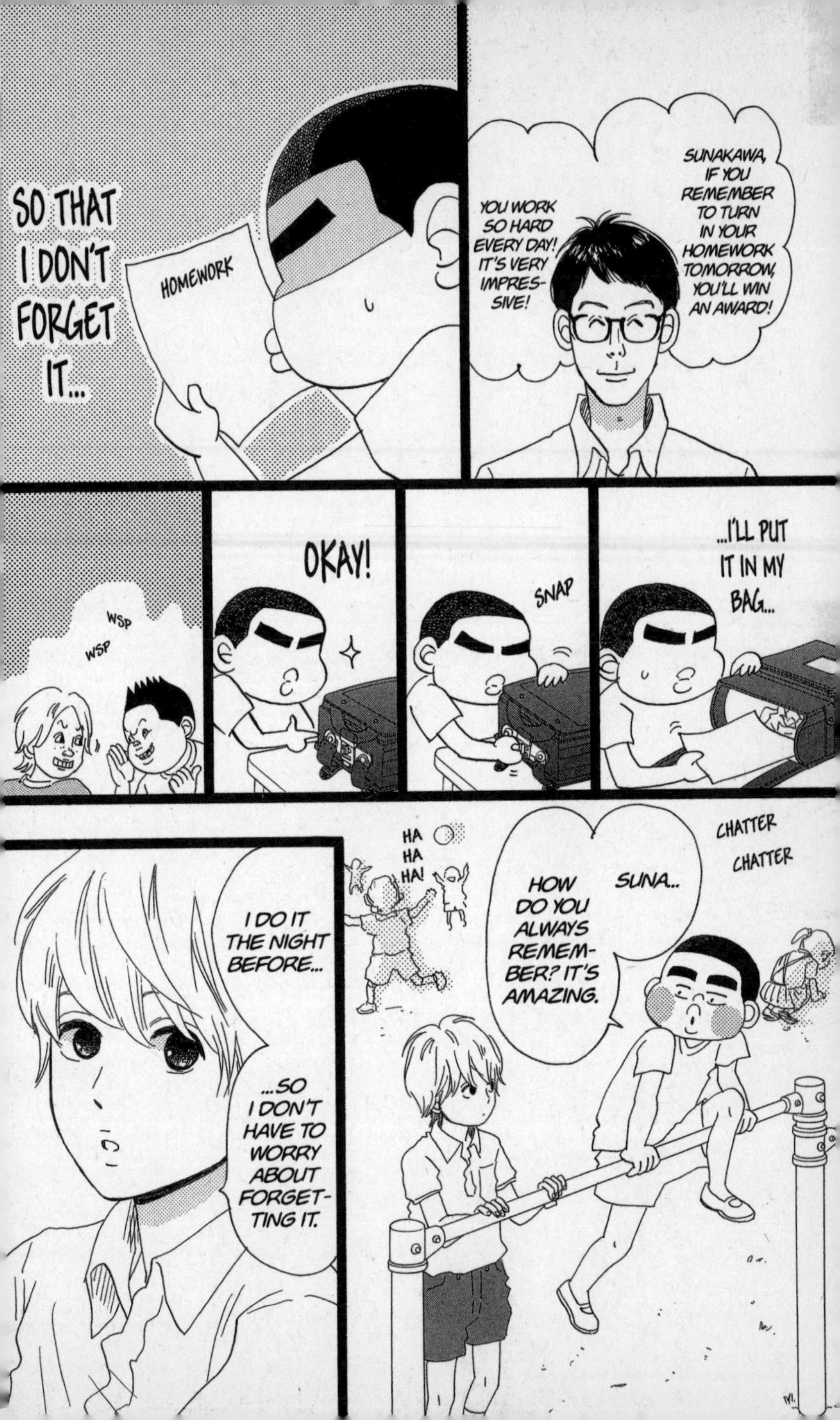
SUNAKAWA, IF YOU REMEMBER TO TURN IN YOUR HOMEWORK TOMORROW, YOU'LL WIN AN AWARD!
YOU WORK SO HARD EVERY DAY! IT'S VERY IMPRES-SIVE!
HOMEWORK
SO THAT I DON'T FORGET IT...
...I'LL PUT IT IN MY BAG...
SNAP
OKAY!
WSP
WSP
CHATTER
CHATTER
SUNA...
HOW DO YOU ALWAYS REMEM-BER? IT'S AMAZING.
HA HA HA!
I DO IT THE NIGHT BEFORE...
...SO I DON'T HAVE TO WORRY ABOUT FORGET-TING IT.

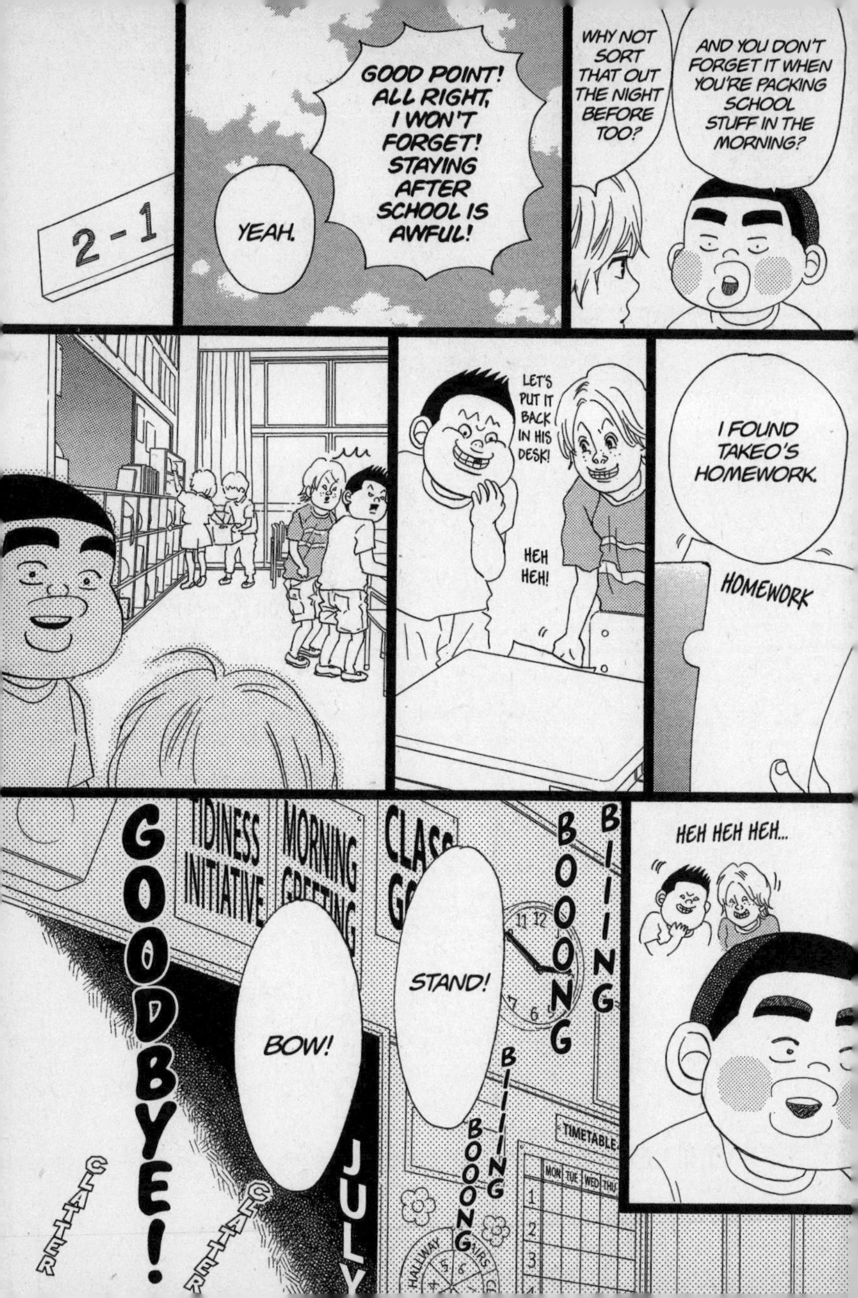
AND YOU DON'T FORGET IT WHEN YOU'RE PACKING SCHOOL STUFF IN THE MORNING?
WHY NOT SORT THAT OUT THE NIGHT BEFORE TOO?
GOOD POINT! ALL RIGHT, I WON'T FORGET! STAYING AFTER SCHOOL IS AWFUL!
YEAH.
2-1
I FOUND TAKEO'S HOMEWORK.
HOMEWORK
LET'S PUT IT BACK IN HIS DESK!
HEH HEH!
HEH HEH HEH...
BIIING
BOOONG
CLASS
STAND!
TIMETABLE
MON TUE WED THU
BIIING
BOOONG
MORNING GREETING
TIDINESS INITIATIVE
BOW!
JULY
GOODBYE!
CLATTER
CLATTER

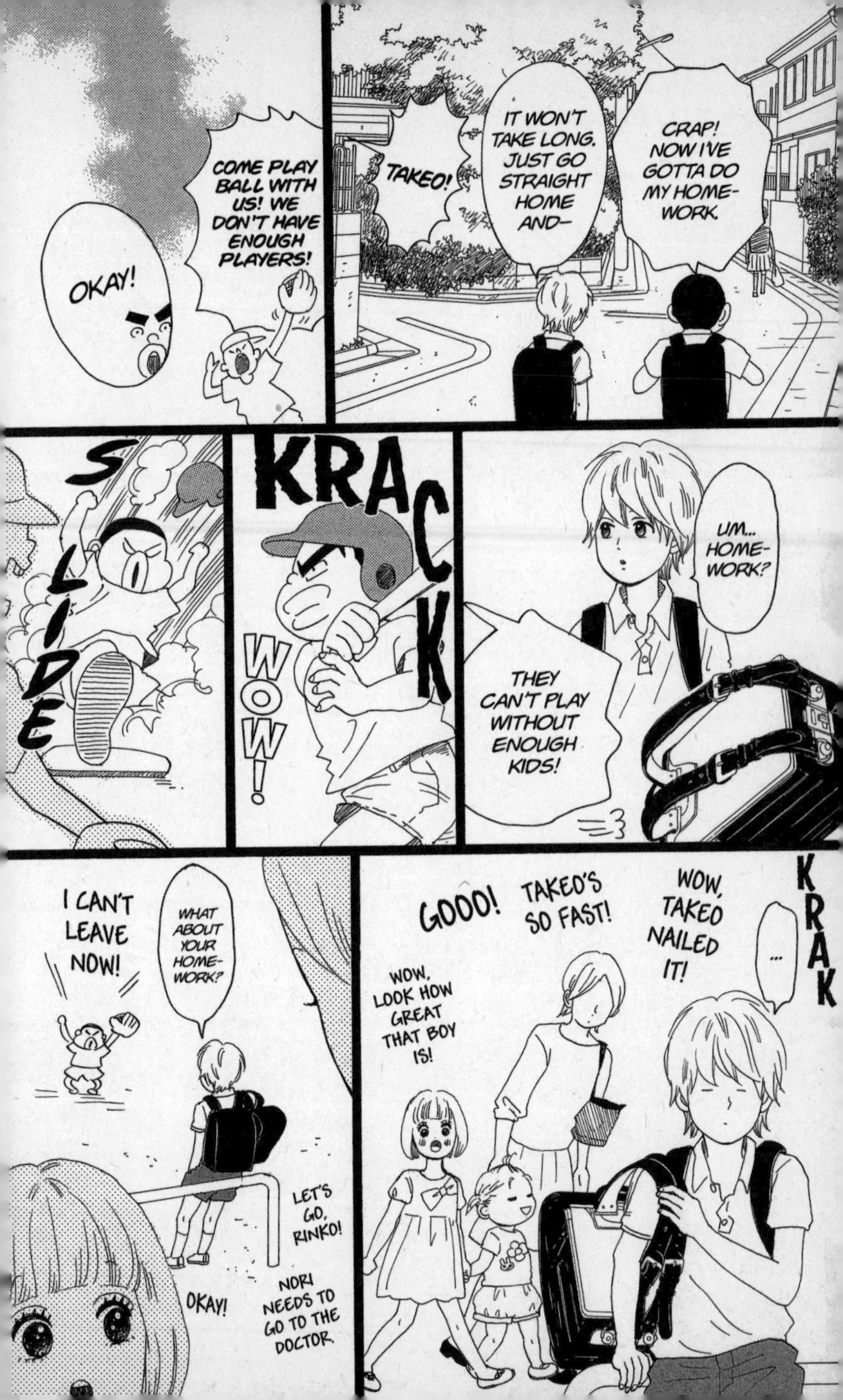

CRAP! NOW I'VE GOTTA DO MY HOME-WORK.
IT WON'T TAKE LONG. JUST GO STRAIGHT HOME AND—
TAKEO!
COME PLAY BALL WITH US! WE DON'T HAVE ENOUGH PLAYERS!
OKAY!
UM... HOME-WORK?
THEY CAN'T PLAY WITHOUT ENOUGH KIDS!
KRACK
WOW!
SLIDE
KRAK
...
WOW, TAKEO NAILED IT!
TAKEO'S SO FAST!
GOOO!
WOW, LOOK HOW GREAT THAT BOY IS!
WHAT ABOUT YOUR HOME-WORK?
I CAN'T LEAVE NOW!
LET'S GO, RINKO!
OKAY!
NORI NEEDS TO GO TO THE DOCTOR.

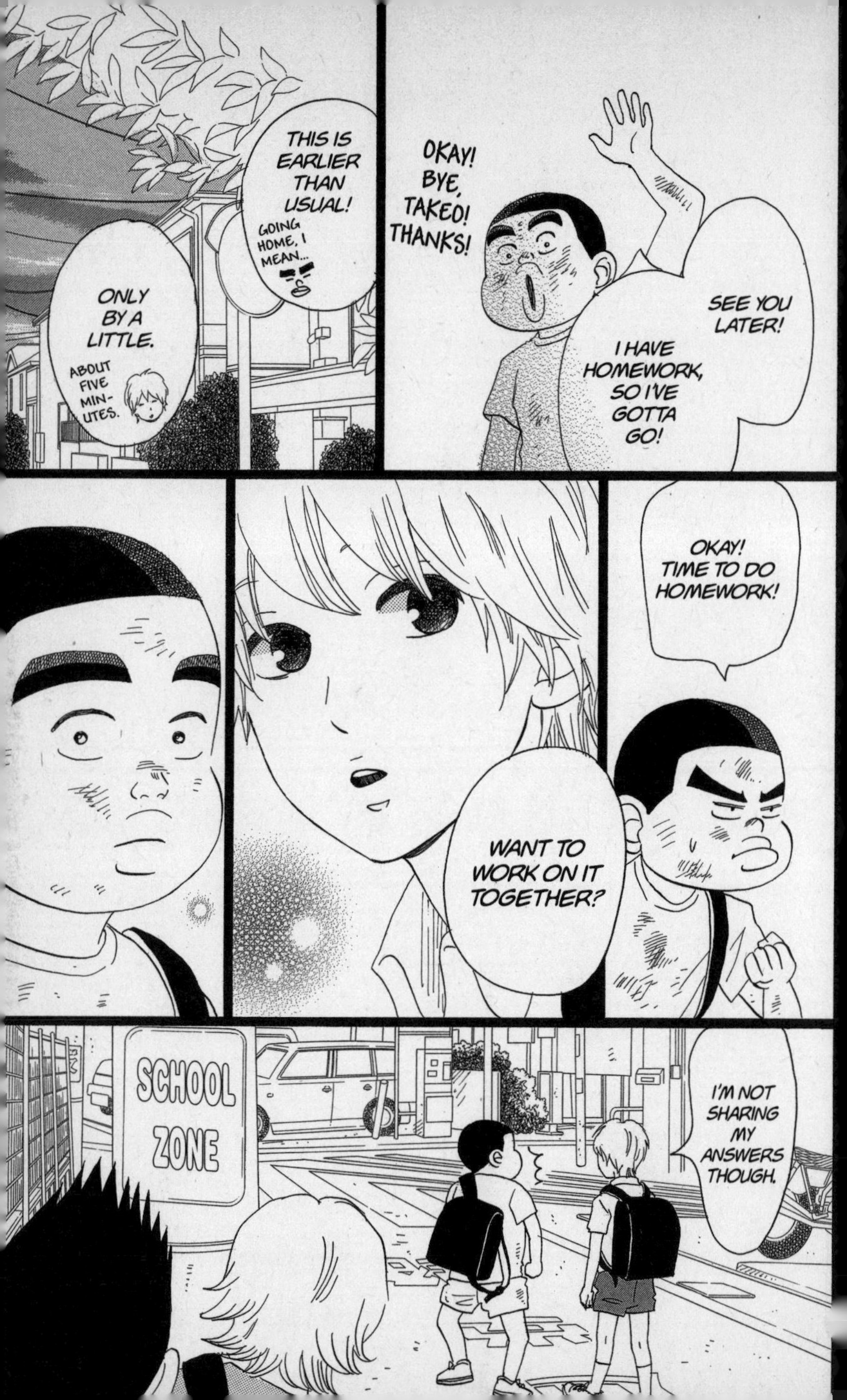
OKAY! BYE, TAKEO! THANKS!
SEE YOU LATER!
I HAVE HOMEWORK, SO I'VE GOTTA GO!
THIS IS EARLIER THAN USUAL!
GOING HOME, I MEAN...
ONLY BY A LITTLE.
ABOUT FIVE MIN-UTES.
OKAY! TIME TO DO HOMEWORK!
WANT TO WORK ON IT TOGETHER?
I'M NOT SHARING MY ANSWERS THOUGH.
SCHOOL ZONE

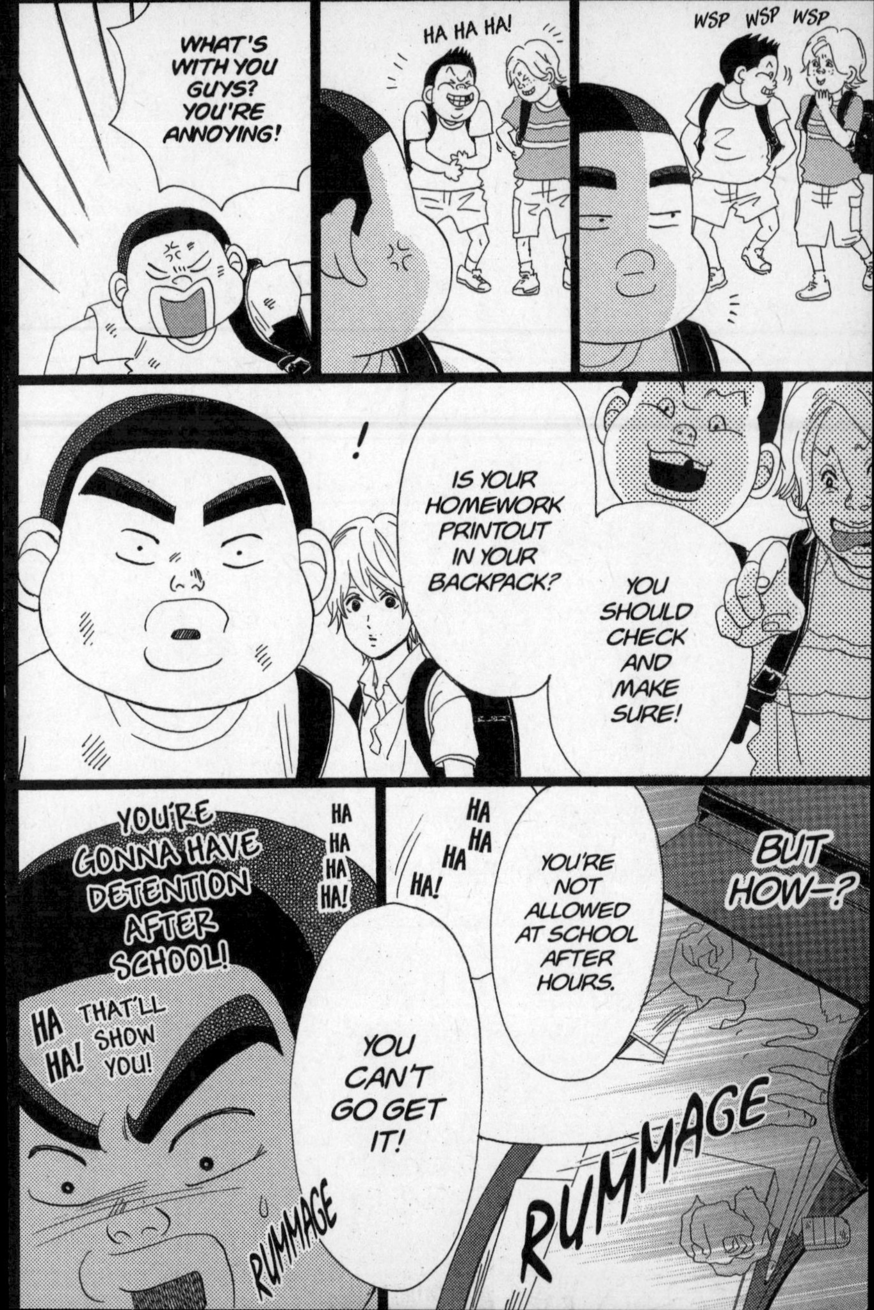
WSP WSP WSP
HA HA HA!
WHAT'S WITH YOU GUYS? YOU'RE ANNOYING!
!
IS YOUR HOMEWORK PRINTOUT IN YOUR BACKPACK?
YOU SHOULD CHECK AND MAKE SURE!
BUT HOW--?
HA HA HA HA!
YOU'RE NOT ALLOWED AT SCHOOL AFTER HOURS.
YOU CAN'T GO GET IT!
RUMMAGE
HA HA HA HA!
YOU'RE GONNA HAVE DETENTION AFTER SCHOOL!
HA HA!
THAT'LL SHOW YOU!
RUMMAGE

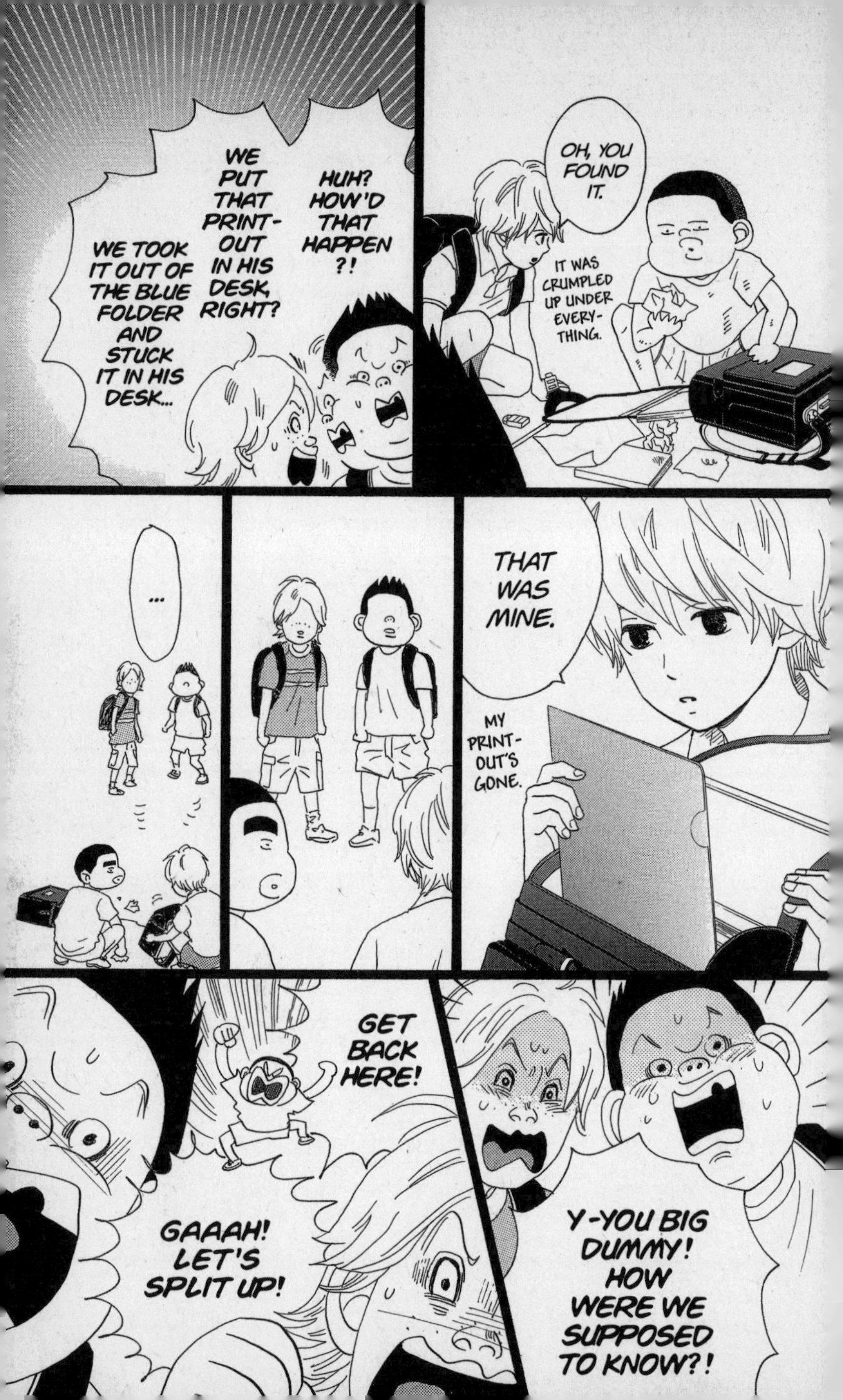
OH, YOU FOUND IT.
IT WAS CRUMPLED UP UNDER EVERYTHING.
HUH? HOW'D THAT HAPPEN?!
WE PUT THAT PRINT-OUT IN HIS DESK, RIGHT?
WE TOOK IT OUT OF THE BLUE FOLDER AND STUCK IT IN HIS DESK...
THAT WAS MINE.
MY PRINT-OUT'S GONE.
...
Y-YOU BIG DUMMY! HOW WERE WE SUPPOSED TO KNOW?!
GET BACK HERE!
GAAAH! LET'S SPLIT UP!

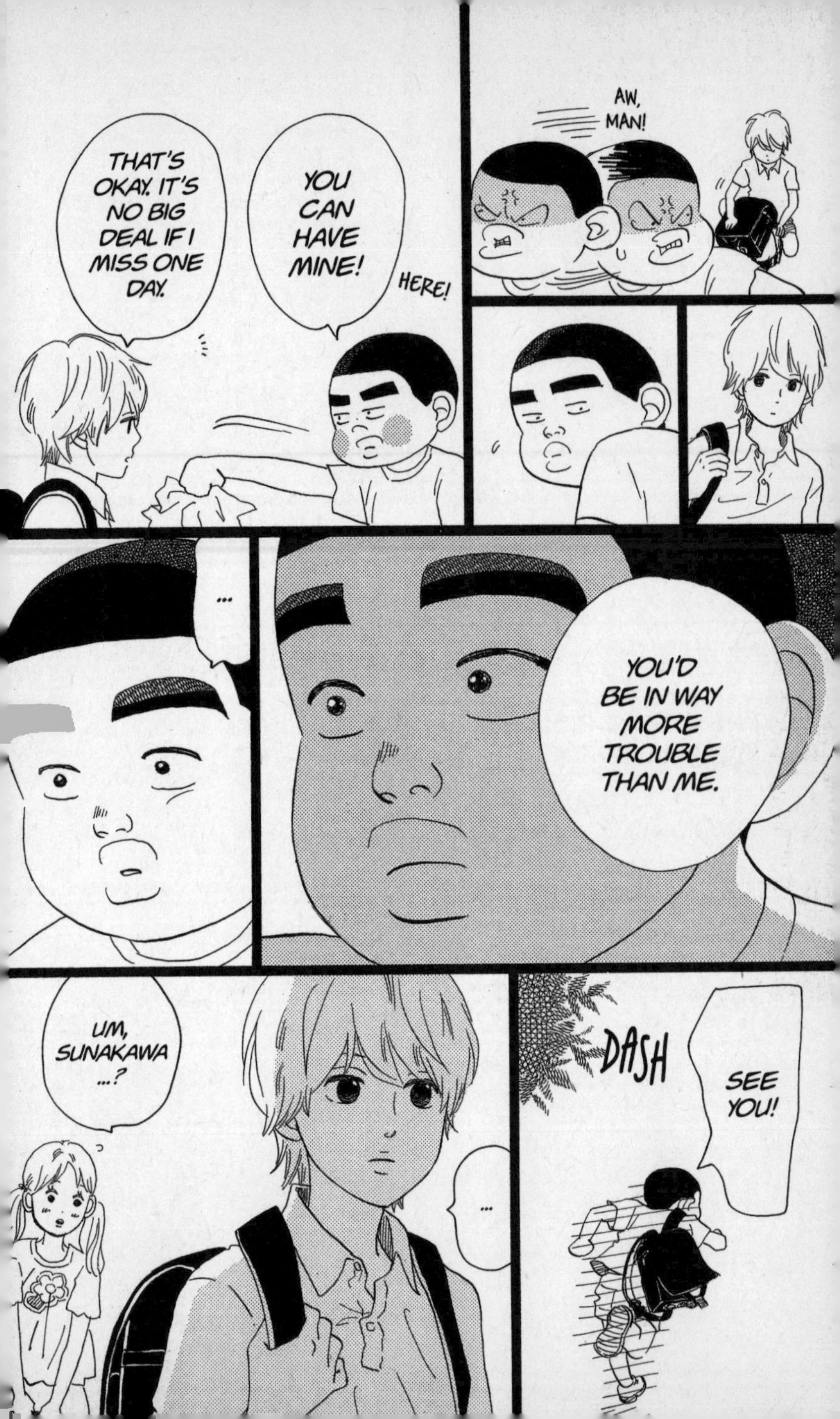
AW, MAN!
YOU CAN HAVE MINE!
HERE!
THAT'S OKAY. IT'S NO BIG DEAL IF I MISS ONE DAY.
YOU'D BE IN WAY MORE TROUBLE THAN ME.
...
SEE YOU!
DASH
...
UM, SUNAKAWA ...?

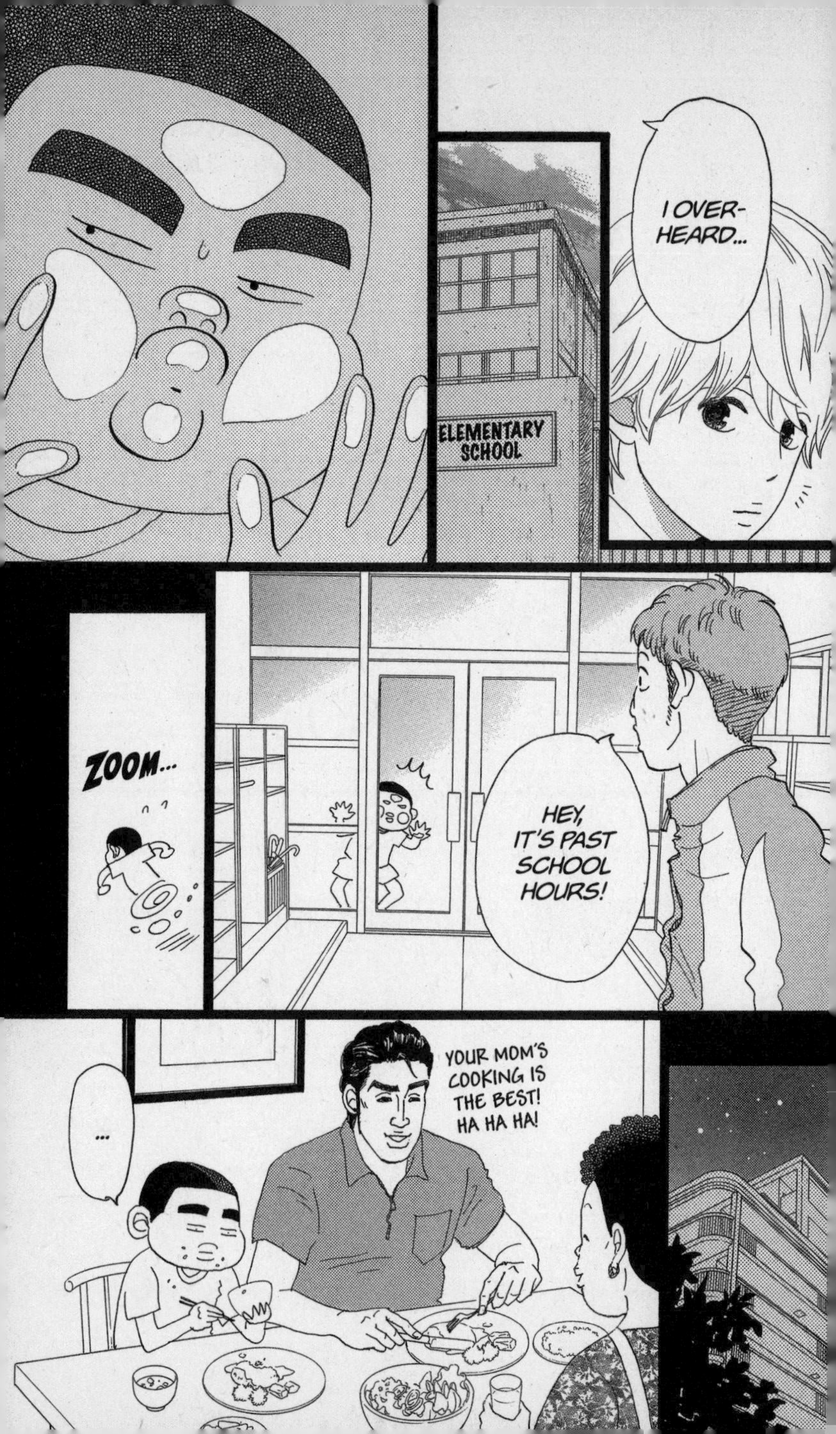
I OVER-HEARD...
ELEMENTARY SCHOOL
HEY, IT'S PAST SCHOOL HOURS!
ZOOM...
YOUR MOM'S COOKING IS THE BEST! HA HA HA!
...

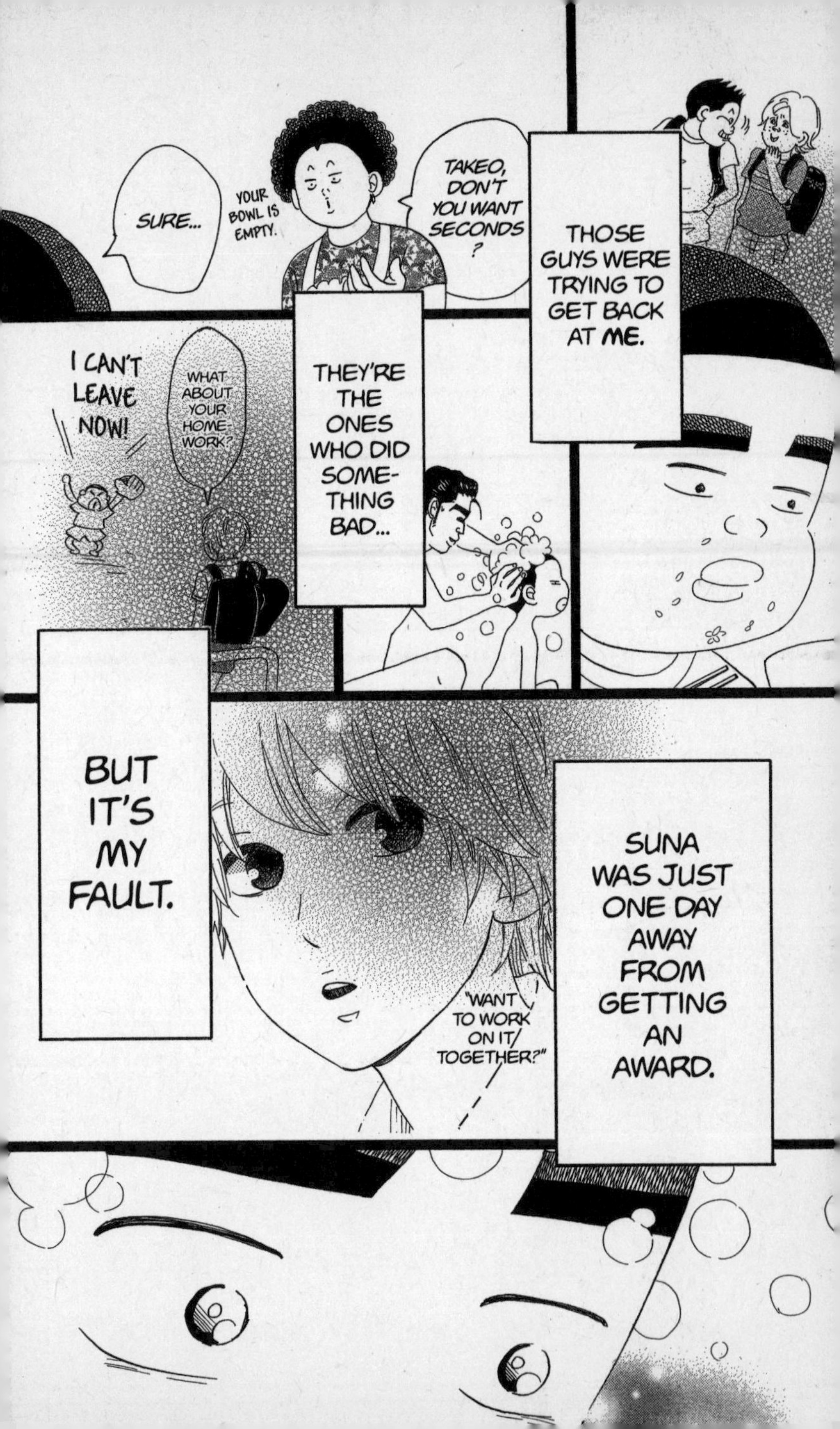
THOSE GUYS WERE TRYING TO GET BACK AT ME.
TAKEO, DON'T YOU WANT SECONDS?
YOUR BOWL IS EMPTY.
SURE...
THEY'RE THE ONES WHO DID SOME-THING BAD...
WHAT ABOUT YOUR HOME-WORK?
I CAN'T LEAVE NOW!
SUNA WAS JUST ONE DAY AWAY FROM GETTING AN AWARD.
"WANT TO WORK ON IT/ TOGETHER?"
BUT IT'S MY FAULT.

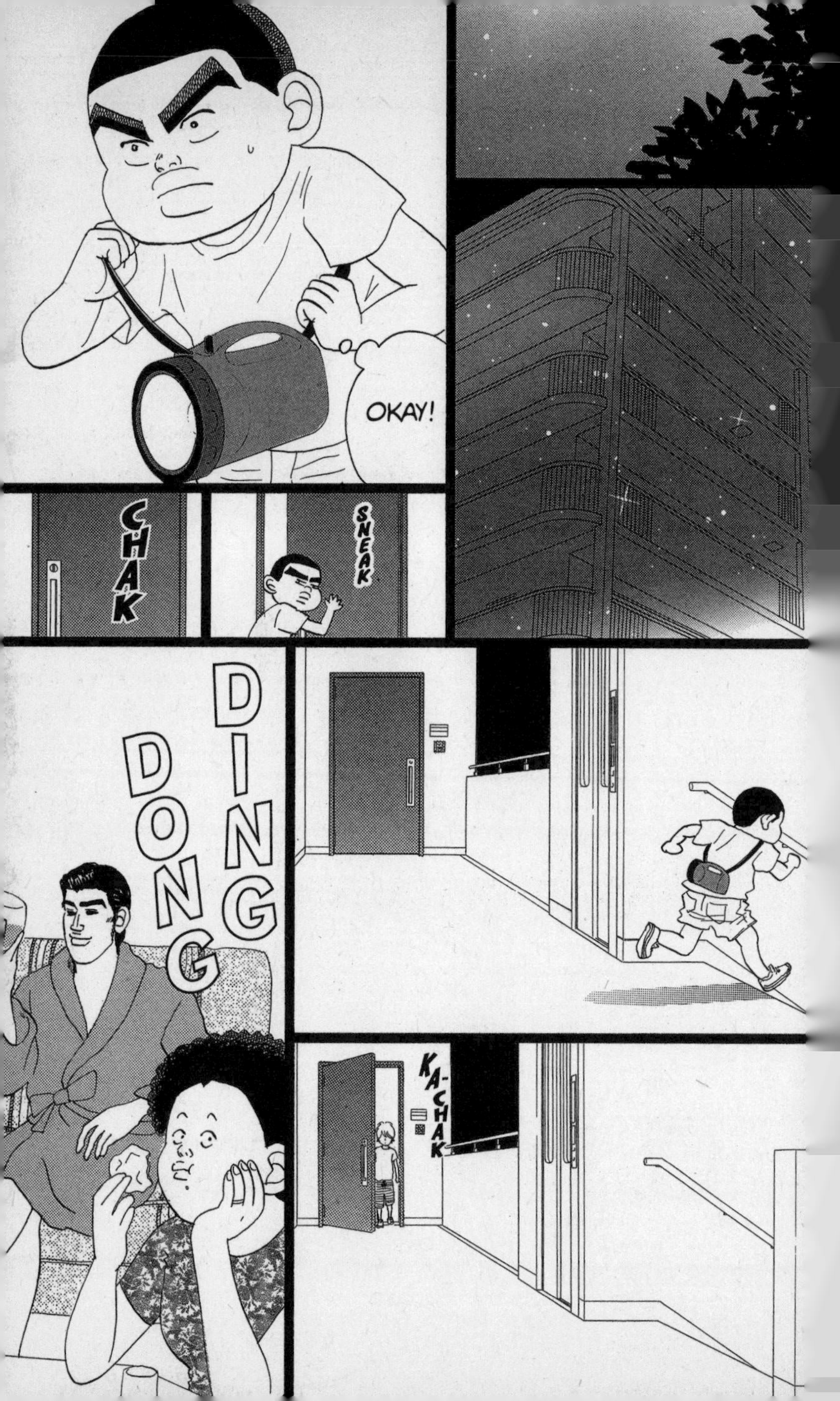
OKAY!
SNEAK
CHAK
KA-CHAK
DING DONG

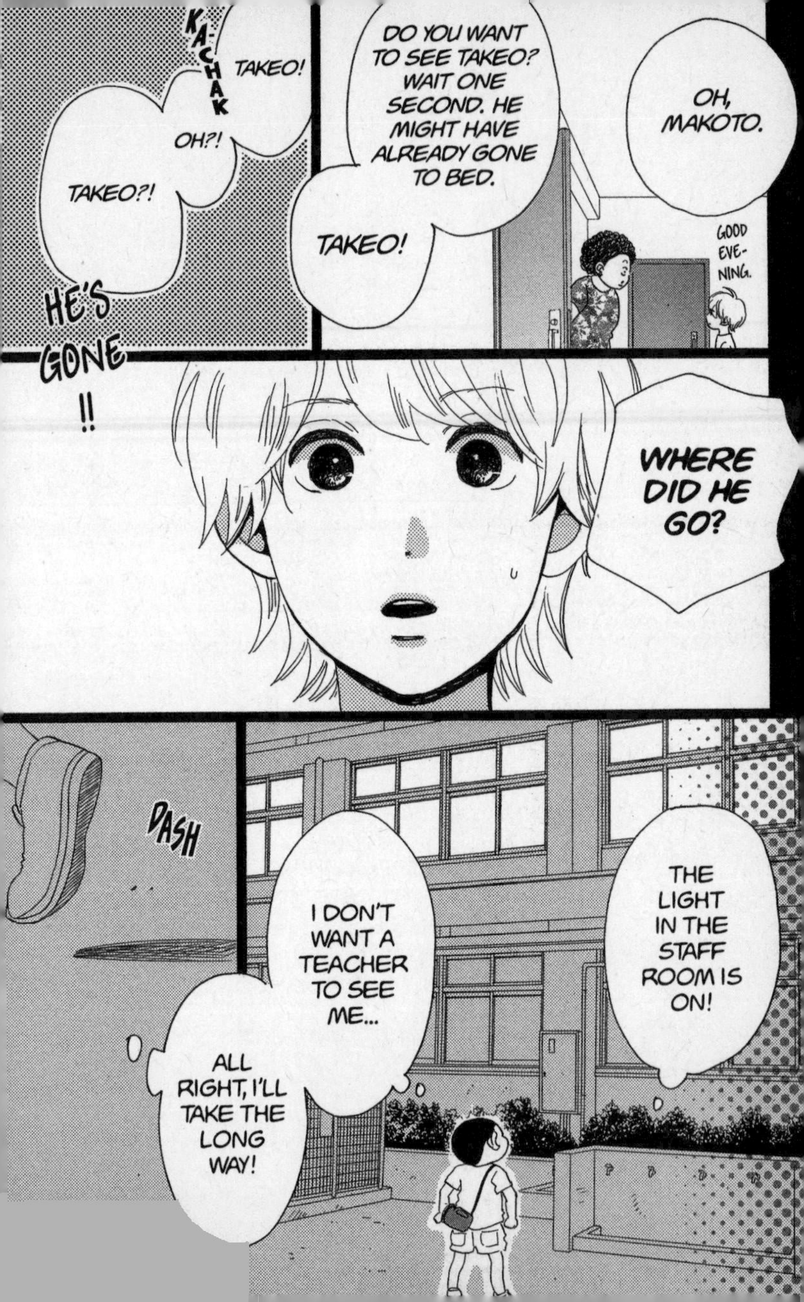
OH, MAKOTO.
GOOD EVENING.
DO YOU WANT TO SEE TAKEO? WAIT ONE SECOND. HE MIGHT HAVE ALREADY GONE TO BED.
TAKEO!
TAKEO!
KA-CHAK
OH?!
TAKEO?!
HE'S GONE !!
WHERE DID HE GO?
THE LIGHT IN THE STAFF ROOM IS ON!
I DON'T WANT A TEACHER TO SEE ME...
ALL RIGHT, I'LL TAKE THE LONG WAY!
DASH

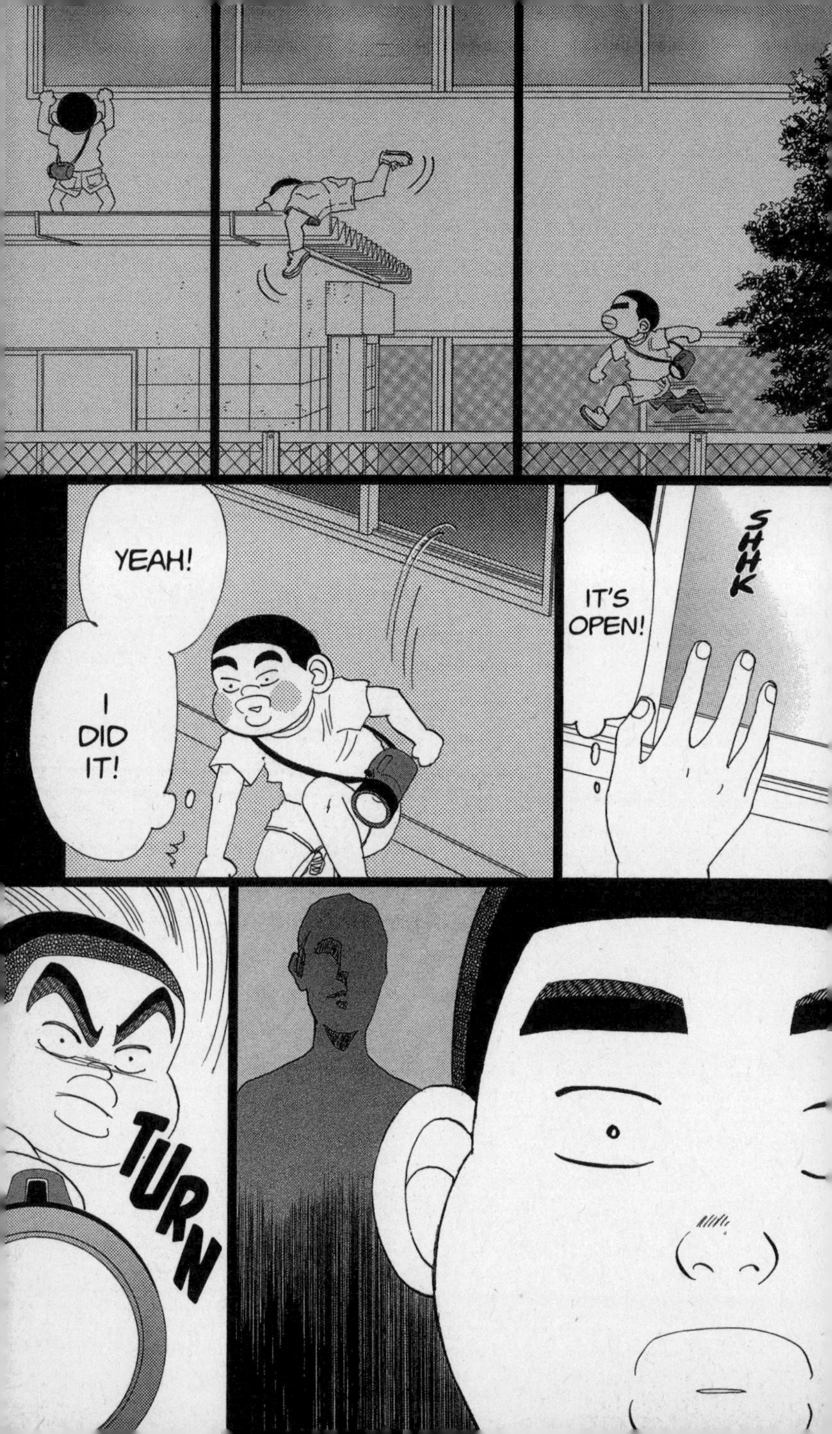
SHHK
IT'S OPEN!
YEAH!
I DID IT!
TURN

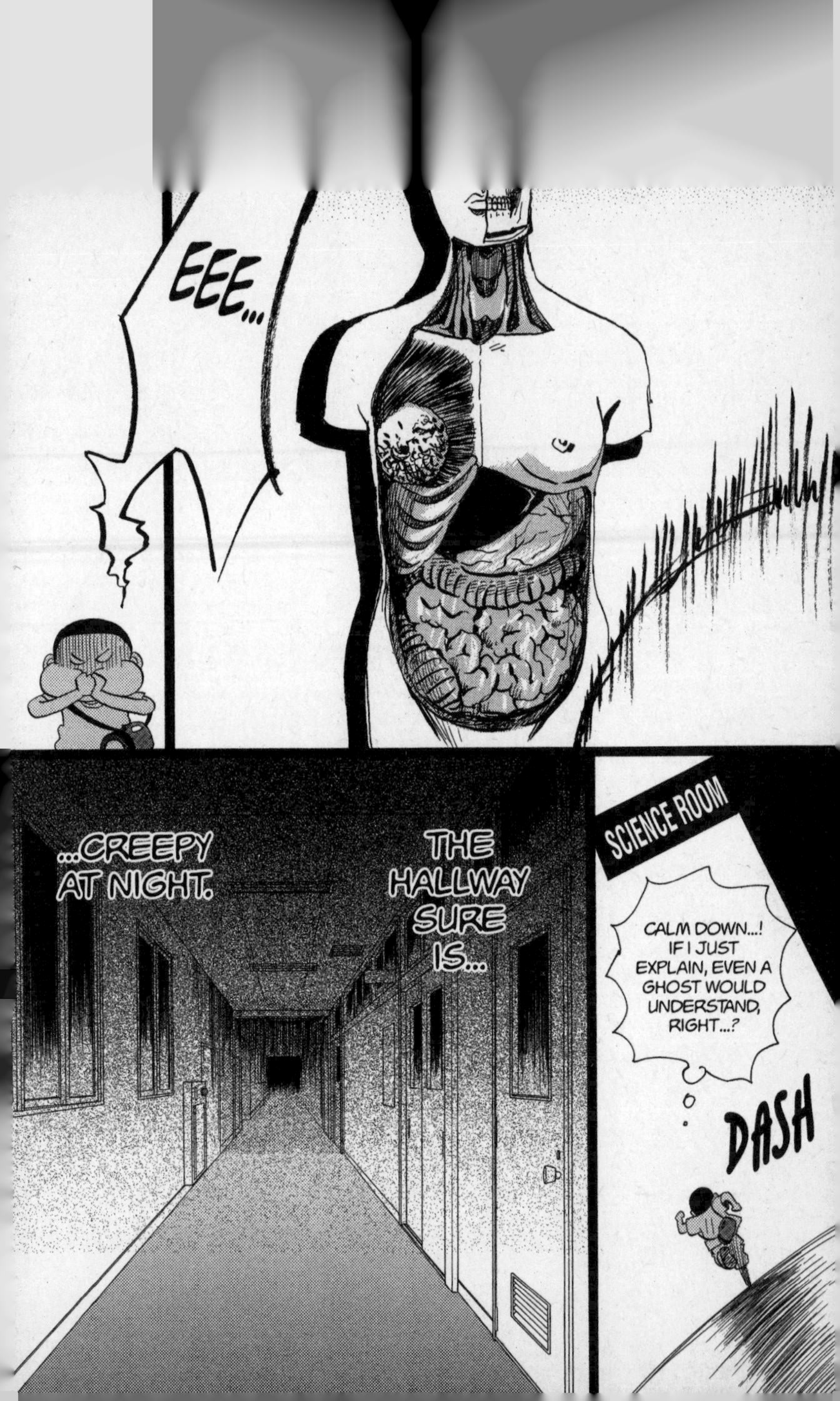
YEEE...
SCIENCE ROOM
CALM DOWN...! IF I JUST EXPLAIN, EVEN A GHOST WOULD UNDERSTAND, RIGHT...?
DASH
THE HALLWAY SURE IS...
...CREEPY AT NIGHT.

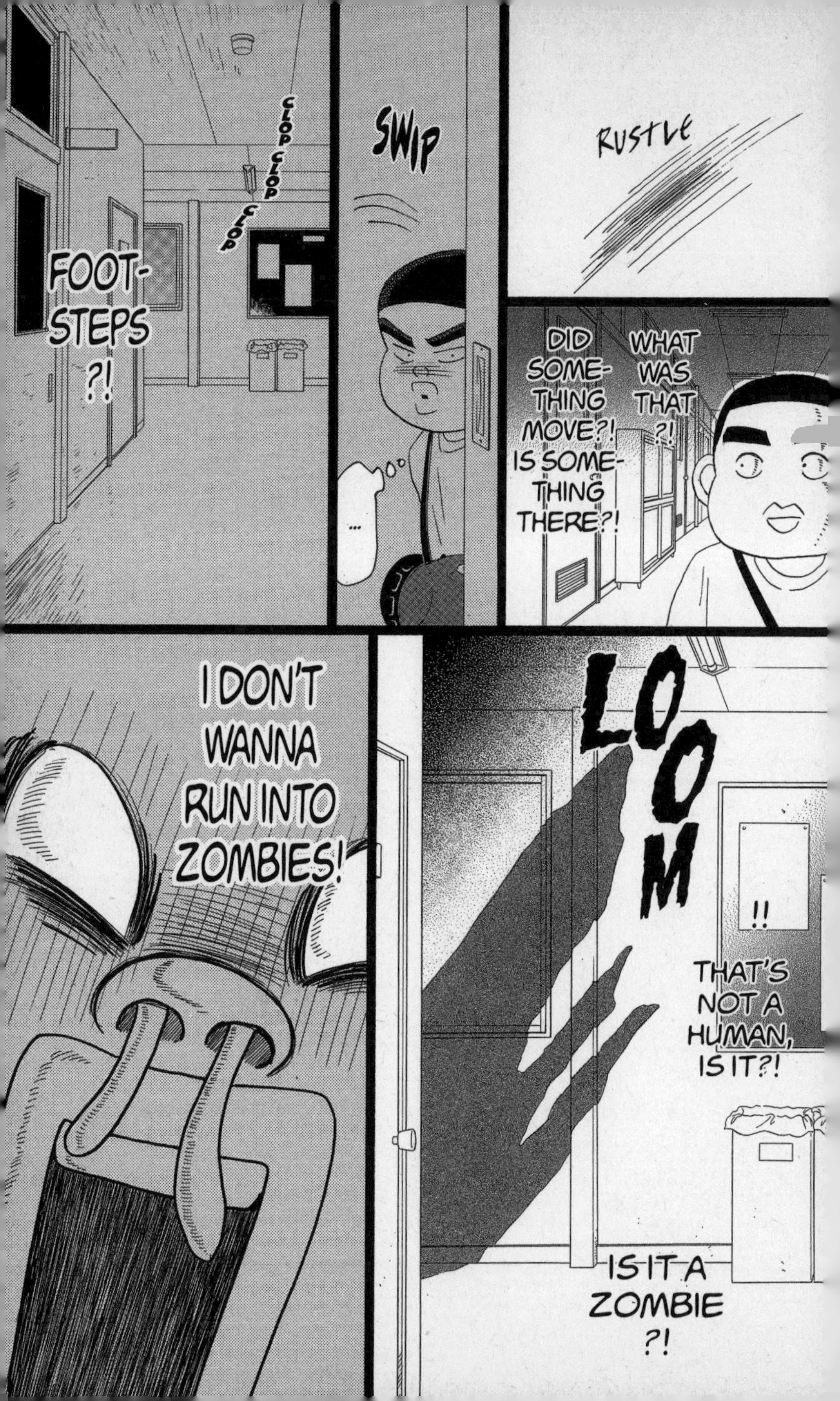
RUSTLE
WHAT WAS THAT?!
DID SOMETHING MOVE?! IS SOMETHING THERE?!
SWIP
...
CLOP CLOP CLOP
FOOTSTEPS?!
LOOM
!!
THAT'S NOT A HUMAN, IS IT?!
IS IT A ZOMBIE?!
I DON'T WANNA RUN INTO ZOMBIES!

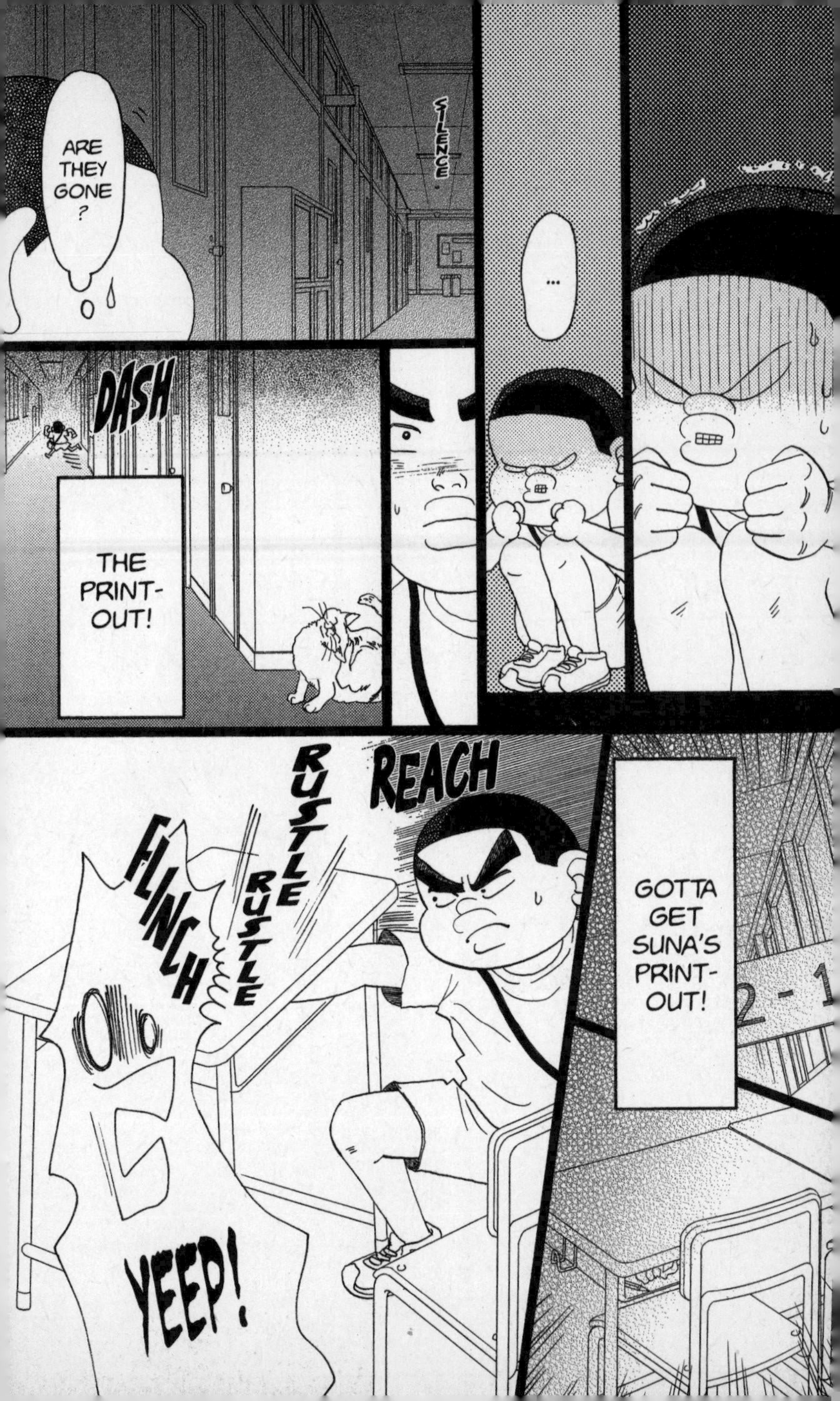
...
ARE THEY GONE?
SILENCE
DASH
THE PRINT-OUT!
GOTTA GET SUNA'S PRINT-OUT!
2-1
REACH
RUSTLE
RUSTLE
FLINCH
YEEP!

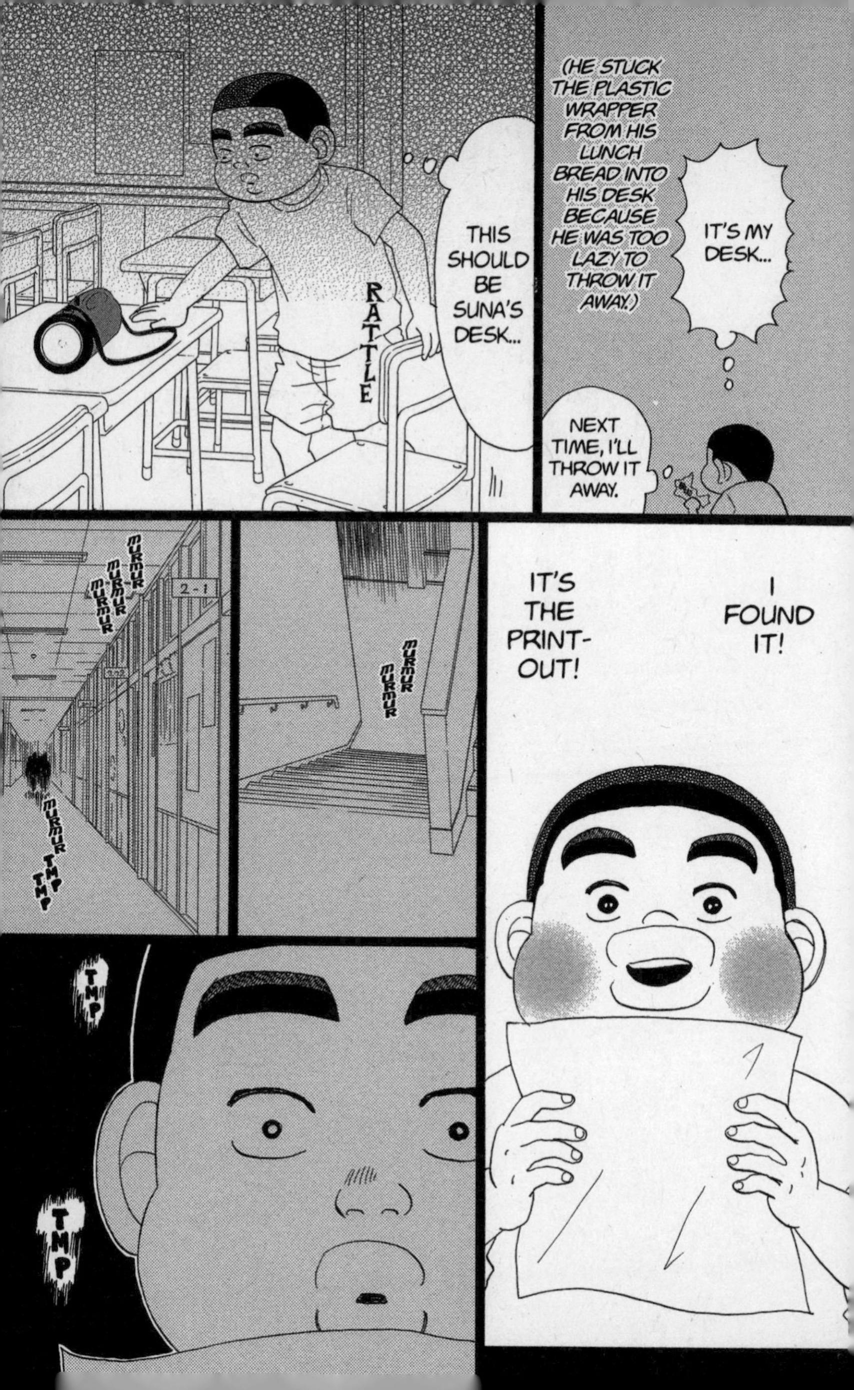
IT'S MY DESK...
(HE STUCK THE PLASTIC WRAPPER FROM HIS LUNCH BREAD INTO HIS DESK BECAUSE HE WAS TOO LAZY TO THROW IT AWAY.)
NEXT TIME, I'LL THROW IT AWAY.
THIS SHOULD BE SUNA'S DESK...
RATTLE
I FOUND IT!
IT'S THE PRINT-OUT!
MURMUR MURMUR
MURMUR MURMUR MURMUR
MURMUR
TMP TMP
TMP
TMP

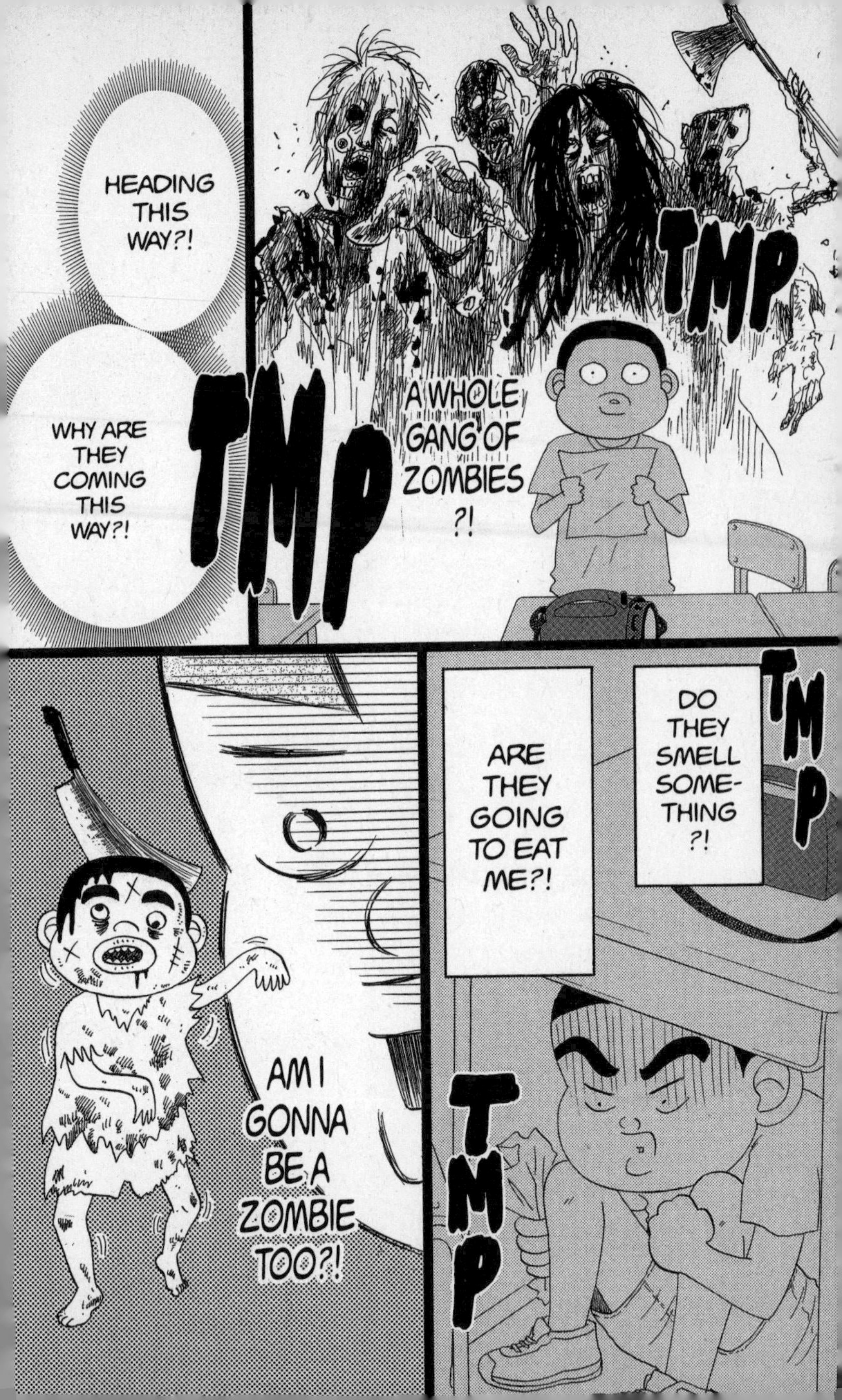
TMP
A WHOLE GANG OF ZOMBIES ?!
TMP
HEADING THIS WAY?!
WHY ARE THEY COMING THIS WAY?!
TMP
DO THEY SMELL SOME- THING ?!
ARE THEY GOING TO EAT ME?!
TMP
AM I GONNA BE A ZOMBIE TOO?!

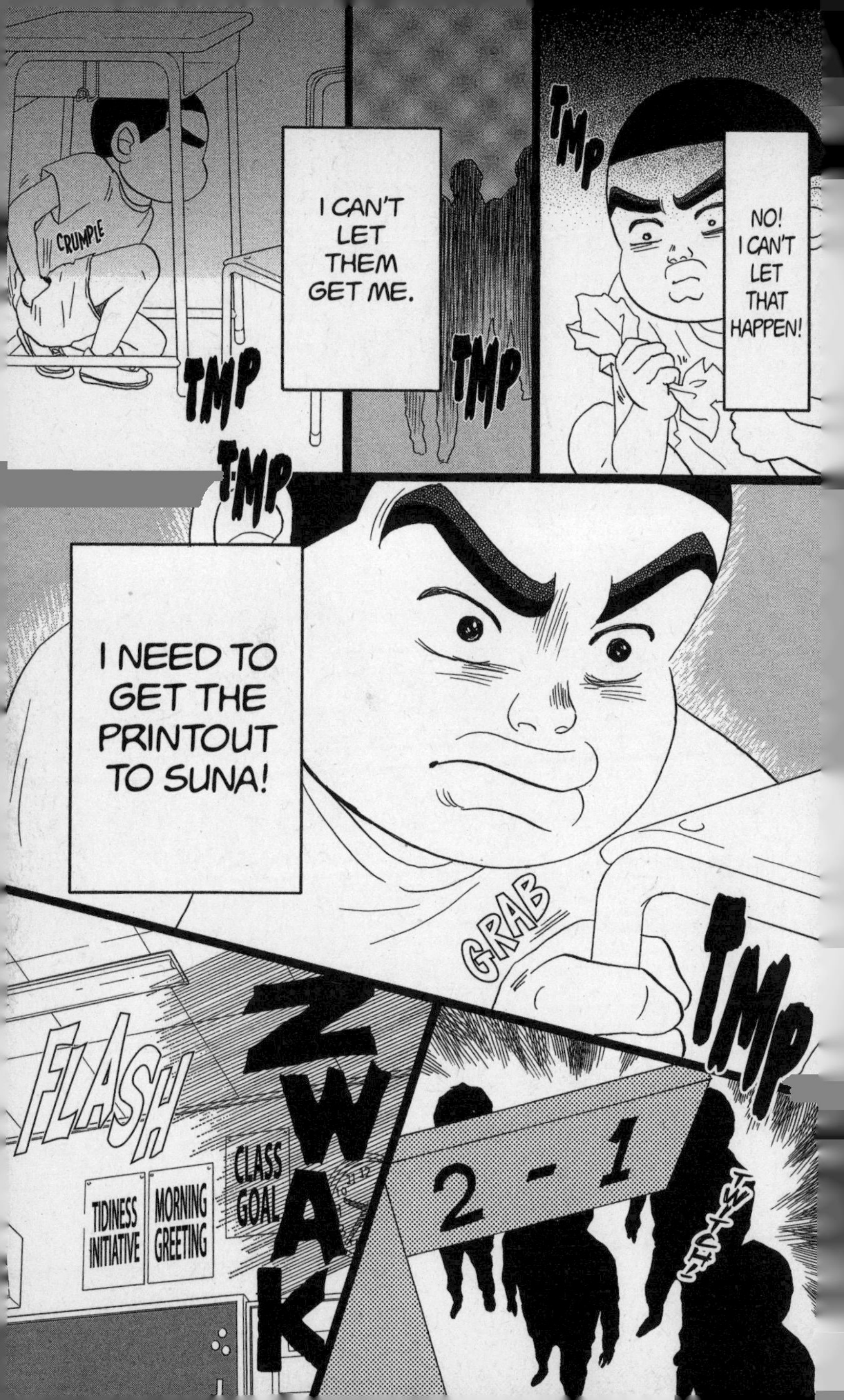
TMP
NO! I CAN'T LET THAT HAPPEN!
I CAN'T LET THEM GET ME.
TMP
CRUMPLE
TMP
TMP
I NEED TO GET THE PRINTOUT TO SUNA!
TMP
GRAB
2-1
TWITCH!
ZWAK
FLASH
CLASS GOAL
MORNING GREETING
TIDINESS INITIATIVE

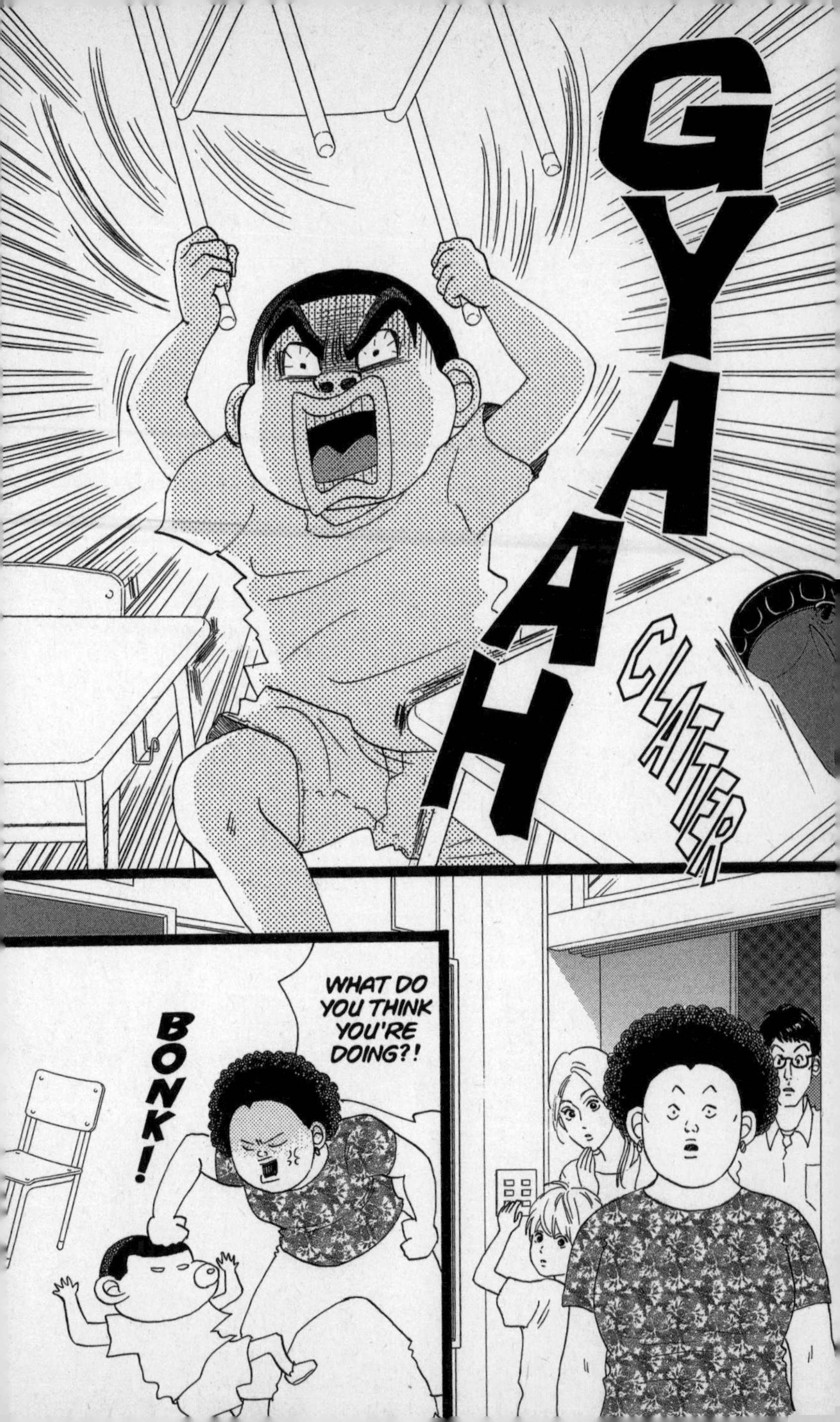
GYAAAHH
CLATTER
WHAT DO YOU THINK YOU'RE DOING?!
BONK!

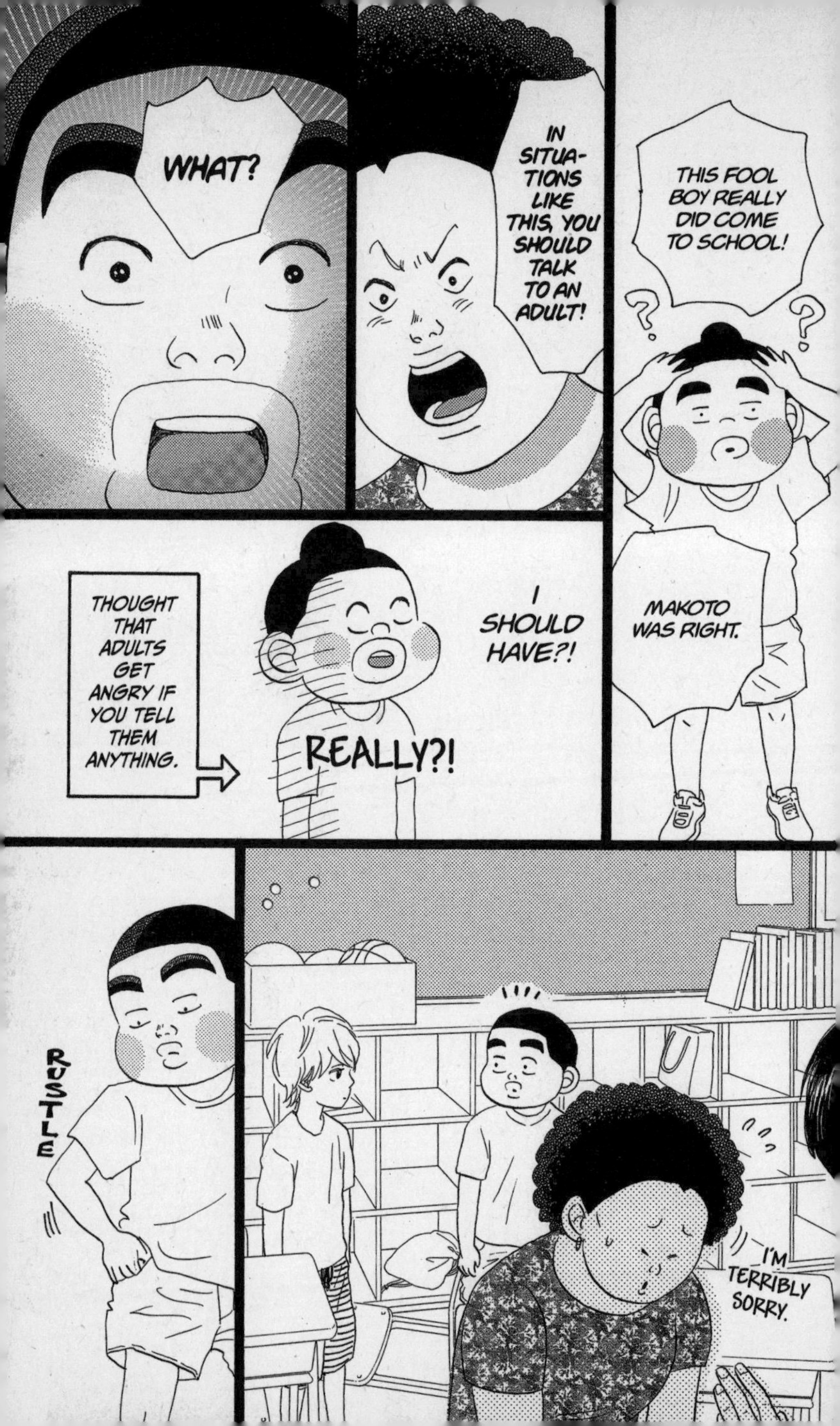
THIS FOOL BOY REALLY DID COME TO SCHOOL!
MAKOTO WAS RIGHT.
IN SITUATIONS LIKE THIS, YOU SHOULD TALK TO AN ADULT!
WHAT?
I SHOULD HAVE?!
REALLY?!
THOUGHT THAT ADULTS GET ANGRY IF YOU TELL THEM ANYTHING.
I'M TERRIBLY SORRY.
RUSTLE

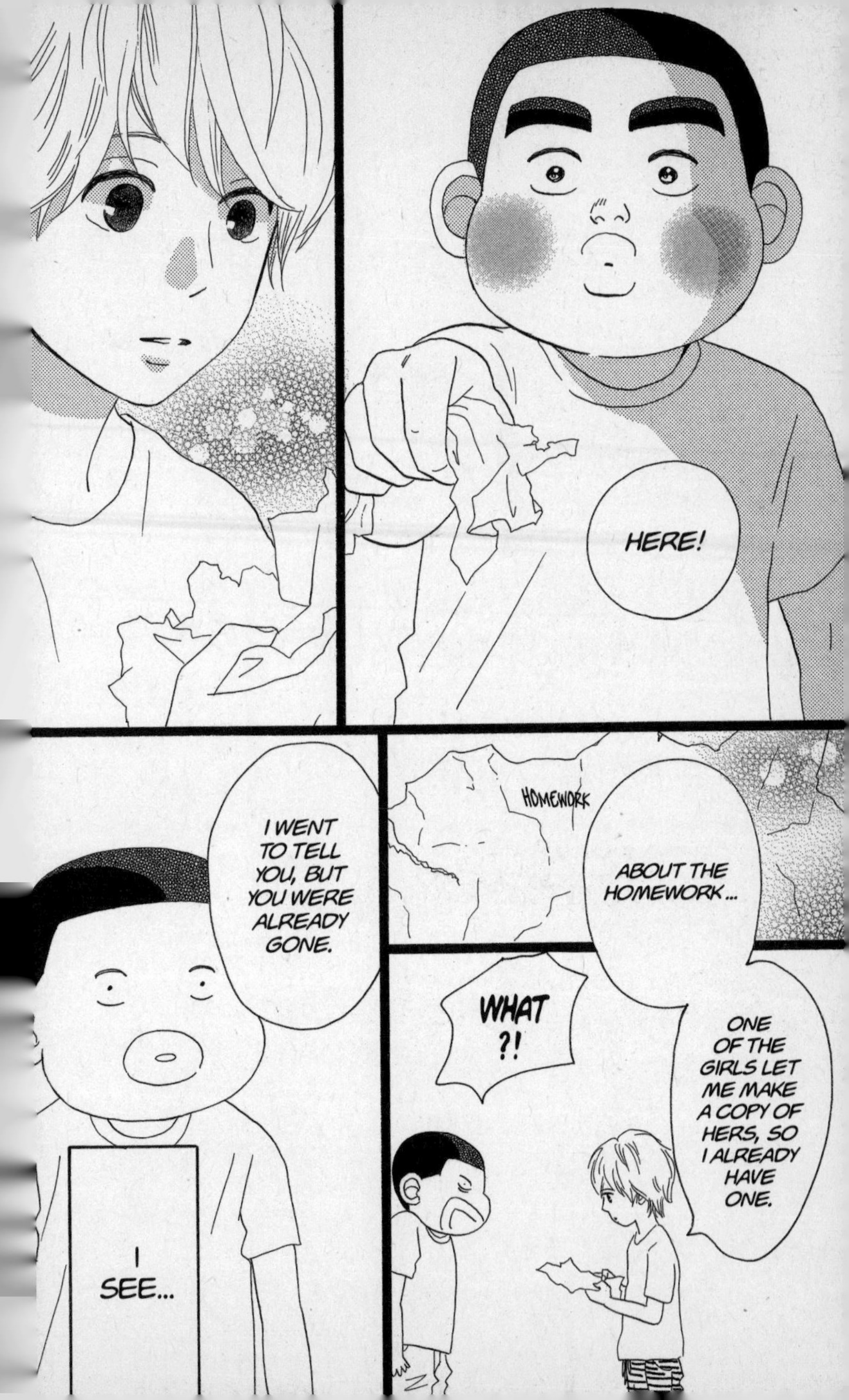
HERE!
HOMEWORK
ABOUT THE HOMEWORK...
ONE OF THE GIRLS LET ME MAKE A COPY OF HERS, SO I ALREADY HAVE ONE.
WHAT?!
I WENT TO TELL YOU, BUT YOU WERE ALREADY GONE.
I SEE...

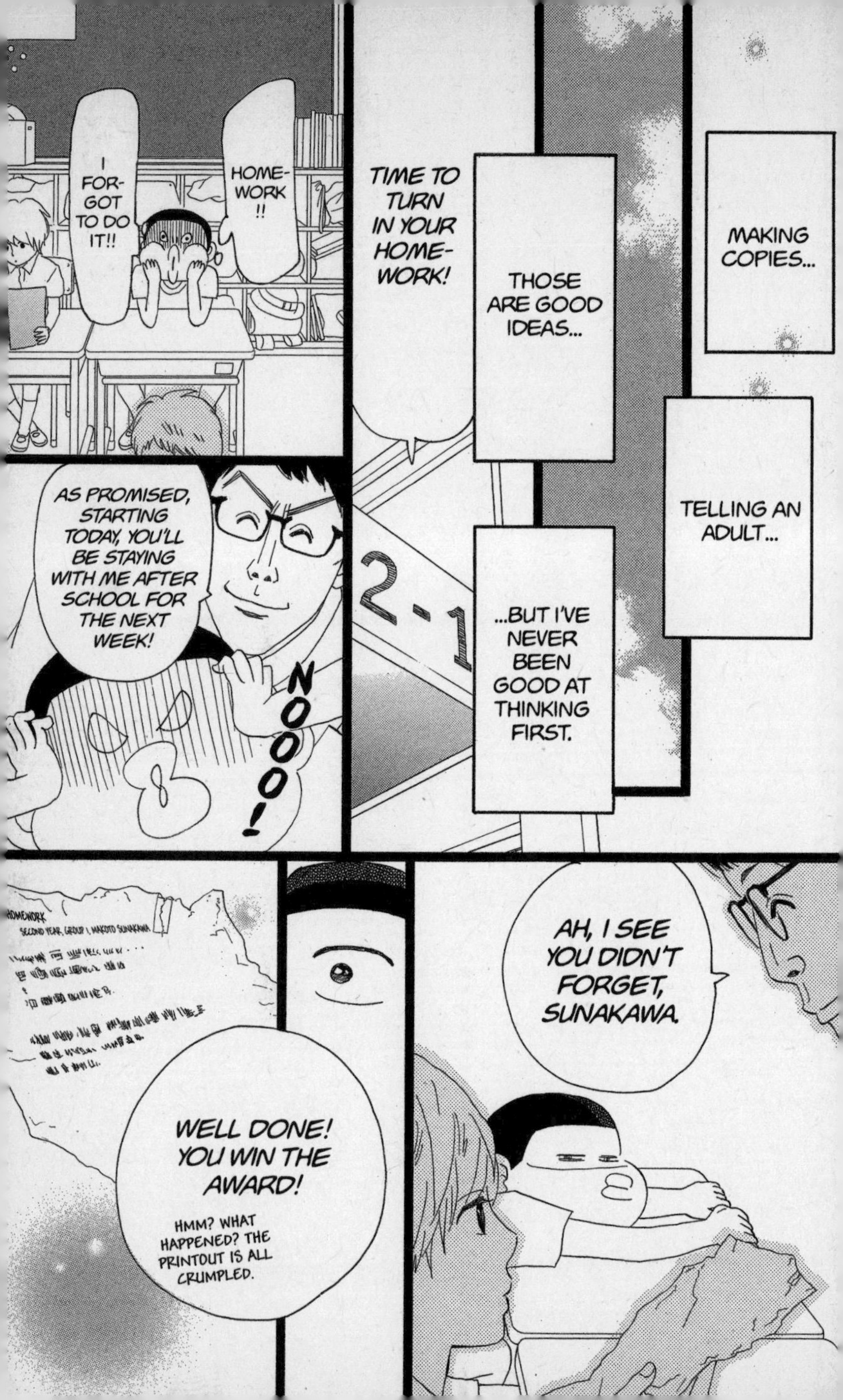
MAKING COPIES...
TELLING AN ADULT...
THOSE ARE GOOD IDEAS...
...BUT I'VE NEVER BEEN GOOD AT THINKING FIRST.
TIME TO TURN IN YOUR HOME-WORK!
2-1
HOME-WORK !!
I FOR-GOT TO DO IT!!
AS PROMISED, STARTING TODAY, YOU'LL BE STAYING WITH ME AFTER SCHOOL FOR THE NEXT WEEK!
NOOOO!
AH, I SEE YOU DIDN'T FORGET, SUNAKAWA.
WELL DONE! YOU WIN THE AWARD!
HMM? WHAT HAPPENED? THE PRINTOUT IS ALL CRUMPLED.
HOMEWORK
SECOND YEAR, GROUP 1, MAKOTO SUNAKAWA

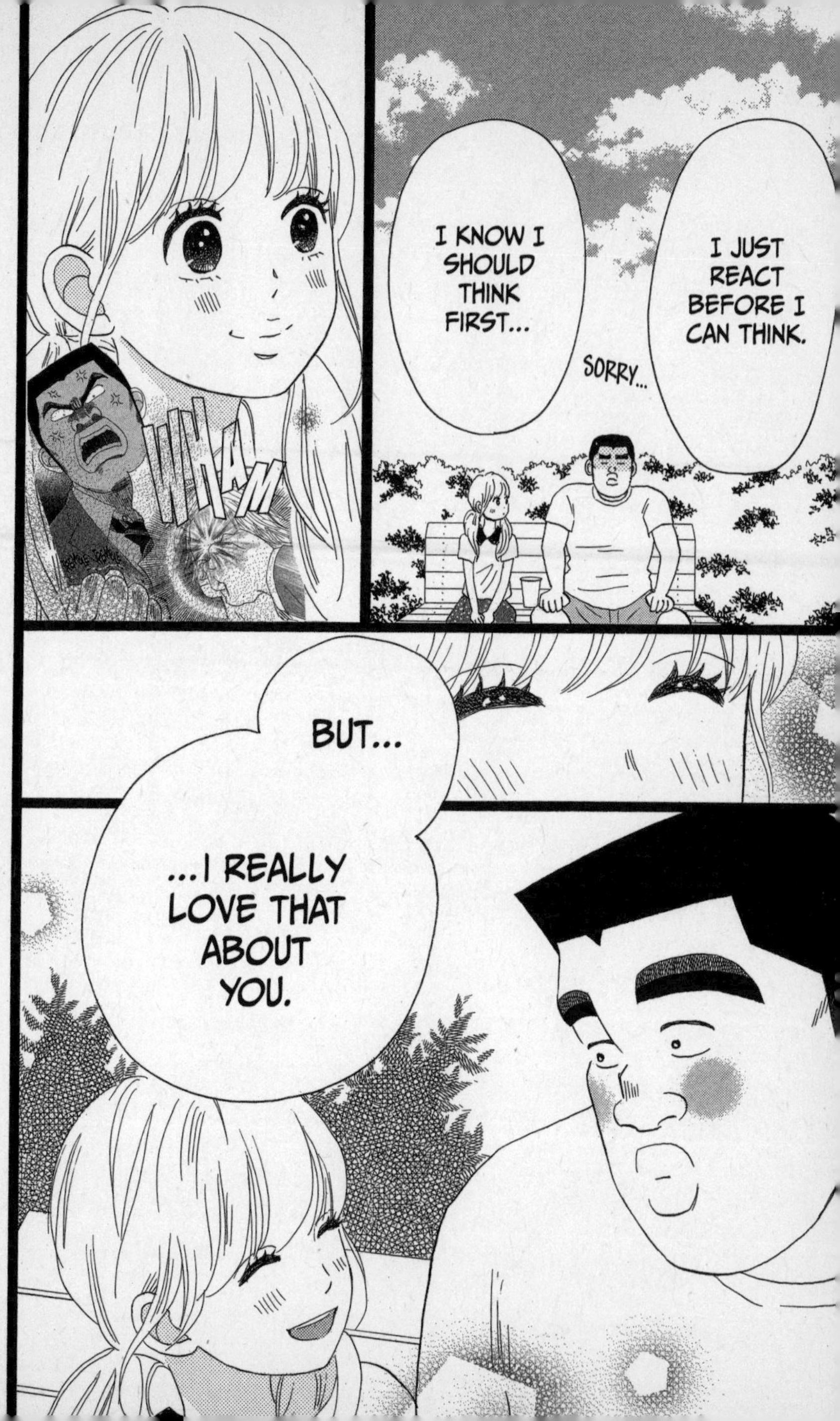
I JUST REACT BEFORE I CAN THINK.
I KNOW I SHOULD THINK FIRST...
SORRY...
WHAM
BUT...
...I REALLY LOVE THAT ABOUT YOU.

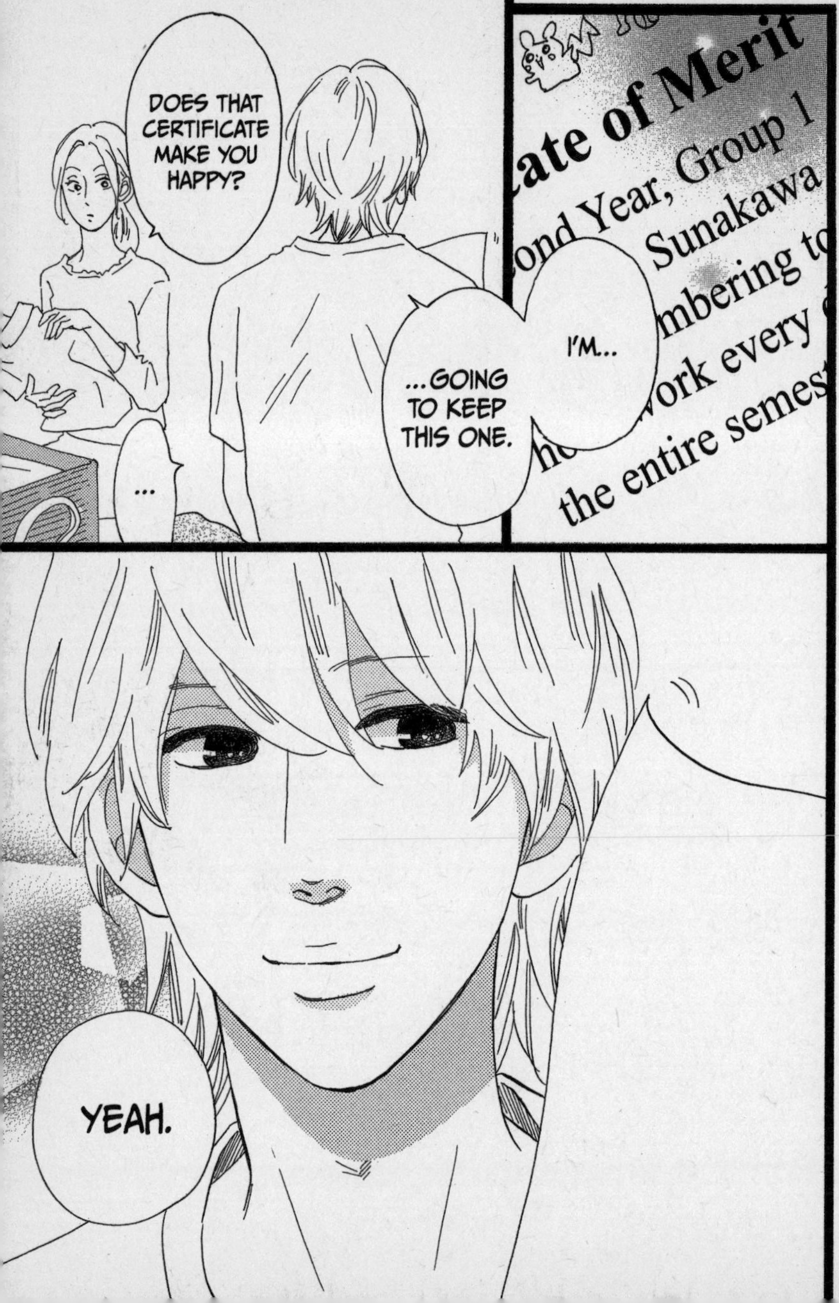
cate of Merit
ond Year, Group 1
Sunakawa
mbering to
work every
the entire semes
DOES THAT CERTIFICATE MAKE YOU HAPPY?
...
I'M...
...GOING TO KEEP THIS ONE.
YEAH.

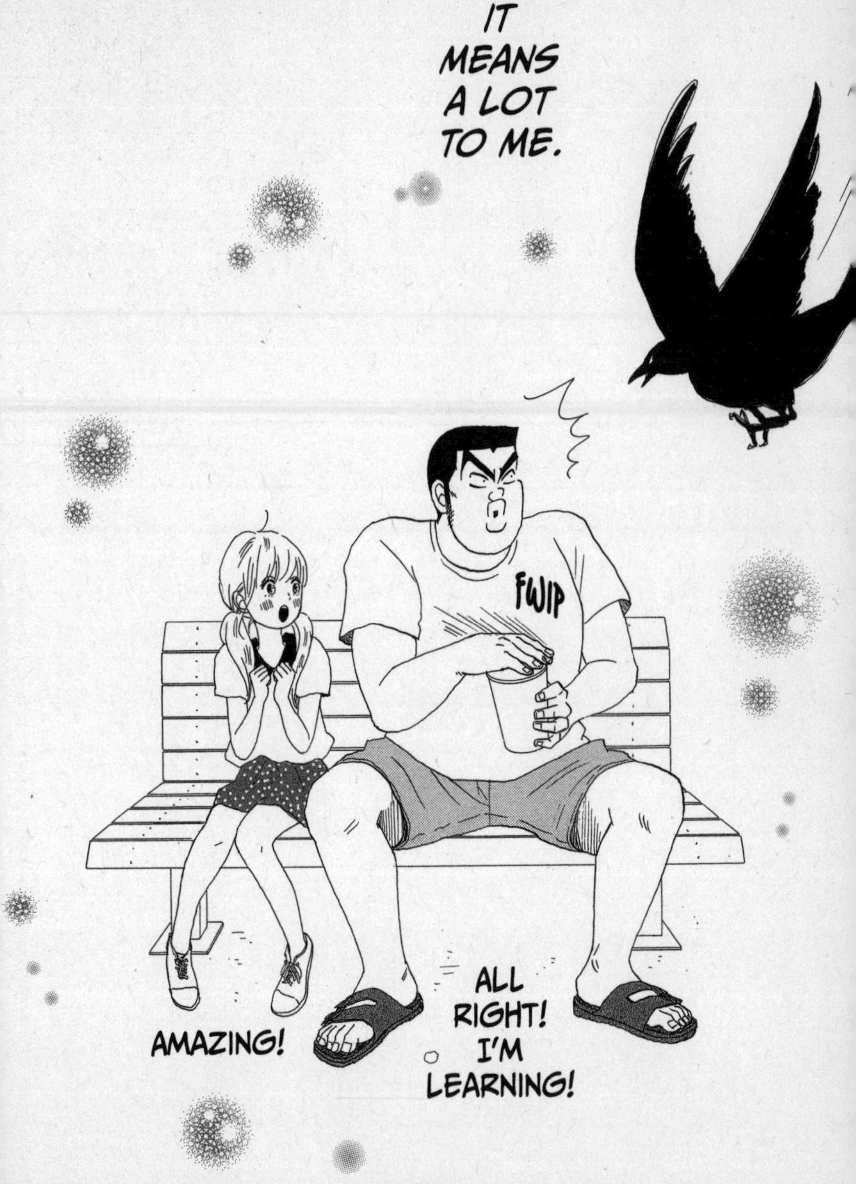
IT MEANS A LOT TO ME.
FWIP
ALL RIGHT! I'M LEARNING!
AMAZING!
THE END

Isn't it fun to discover something that you love? (o>ω<o) I hope that My Love Story!! becomes one of those things.
— Kazune Kawahara

Ⓚ

**ARUKO** is from Ishikawa Prefecture in Japan and was born on July 26 (a Leo!). She made her manga debut with *Ame Nochi Hare* (Clear After the Rain). Her other works include *Yasuko to Kenji*, and her hobbies include laughing and getting lost.

**KAZUNE KAWAHARA** is from Hokkaido Prefecture in Japan and was born on March 11 (a Pisces!). She made her manga debut at age 18 with *Kare no Ichiban Sukina Hito* (His Most Favorite Person). Her best-selling shojo manga series *High School Debut* is available in North America from VIZ Media. Her hobby is interior redecorating.

My Love Story!! is being made into a movie! I'm very glad that I can keep announcing good news in this section. Now about the cover for volume 9... I had Takeo dress up as a certain character. What'll happen in volume 10? I'm getting excited!
— Aruko

Ⓐ

# MY LOVE STORY!!

Volume 9
Shojo Beat Edition

## Story by **KAZUNE KAWAHARA**
## Art by **ARUKO**

————————//————————

English Adaptation ♡ **Ysabet Reinhardt MacFarlane**
Translation ♡ **JN Productions**
Touch-up Art & Lettering ♡ **Mark McMurray**
Design ♡ **Fawn Lau**
Editor ♡ **Amy Yu**

————————//————————

ORE MONOGATARI!!
© 2011 by Kazune Kawahara, Aruko
All rights reserved.
First published in Japan in 2011 by SHUEISHA Inc., Tokyo
English translation rights arranged by SHUEISHA Inc.

Printed in the U.S.A.

Published by VIZ Media, LLC
P.O. Box 77010
San Francisco, CA 94107

10 9 8 7 6 5 4 3 2 1
First printing, July 2016

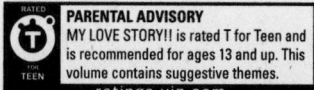

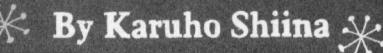

# You may be reading the **wrong way!!**

IT'S TRUE: In keeping with the original Japanese comic format, this book reads from right to left—so action, sound effects, and word balloons are completely reversed. This preserves the orientation of the original artwork—plus, it's fun! Check out the diagram shown here to get the hang of things, and then turn to the other side of the book to get started!

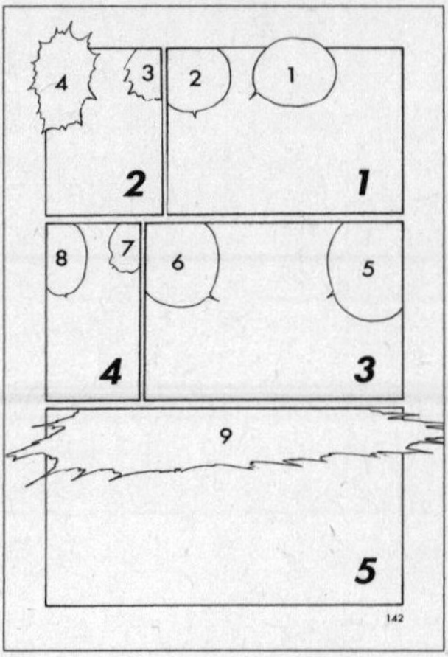
1
2
1
3
4
2
5
6
3
7
8
4
9
5
142

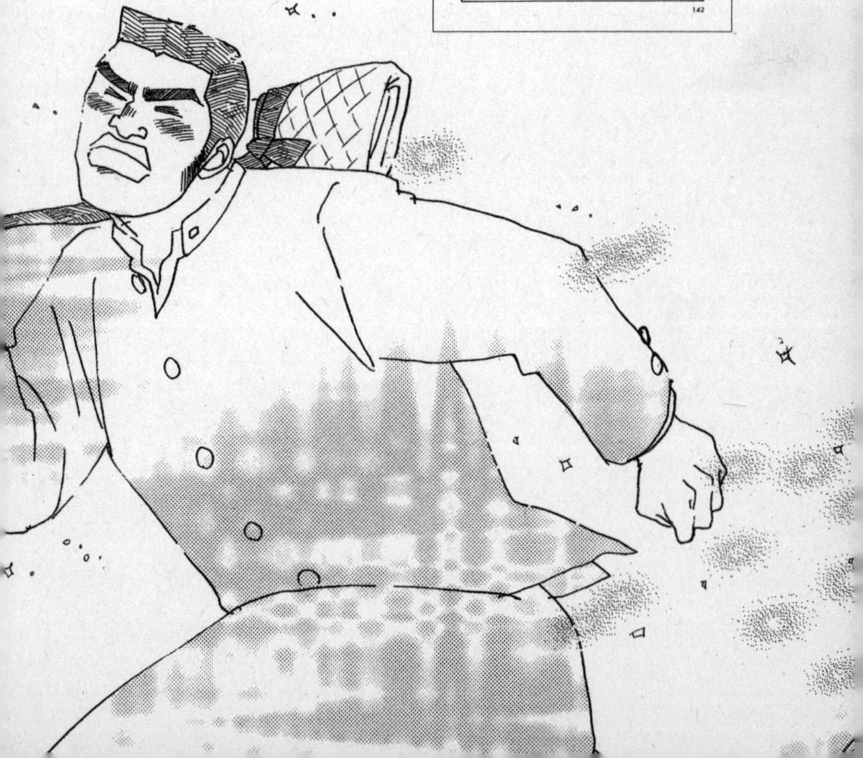